*Westerns in a
Changing America,
1955–2000*

ALSO BY R. PHILIP LOY

Westerns and American Culture, 1930–1955
(McFarland, 2001)

Westerns in a Changing America, 1955–2000

by R. PHILIP LOY

McFarland & Company, Inc., Publishers
Jefferson, North Carolina, and London

LIBRARY OF CONGRESS CATALOGUING-IN-PUBLICATION DATA

Loy, R. Philip, 1940–
    Westerns in a changing America, 1955–2000 / by R. Philip Loy.
      p.   cm.
    Includes bibliographical references and index.

    ISBN 0-7864-1871-0 (softcover : 50# alkaline paper)

    1. Western films— United States— History and criticism.
I. Title.
PN1995.9.W4L694 2004
791.43'6278 — dc22

                         2004009588

British Library cataloguing data are available

Cover photograph: Kevin Costner in Wyatt Earp *(1994)*

Manufactured in the United States of America

*McFarland & Company, Inc., Publishers
  Box 611, Jefferson, North Carolina 28640
  www.mcfarlandpub.com*

To Family

Janet Claire Donaldson Loy,
who has made 39 years of marriage a special time.

Lisa Christine Loy Belcher and Michael Alan Belcher,
a daughter and a son-in-law who always manage to find
Western film–related presents for those special times.

Bradley Michael Belcher and Lauren Claire Belcher,
grandchildren who have made life much richer
in the twenty-first century.

TABLE OF CONTENTS

Part II. Changing Images

PREFACE

From the time I was four years old until my years in graduate school during the early and mid–1960s, I was an avid Western movie fan. Westerns remained my preferred genre all throughout high school and college, even when my friends thought they had outgrown such things. But for a number of reasons, I stopped attending movies after the middle 1960s, and I generally ignored Westerns. About 1965, I saw *The Sons of Katie Elder* at a drive-in theater, but nine years would pass before I attended another Western, *High Plains Drifter*. And it would be eleven more years before my wife and I went to see *Silverado* in a Muncie, Indiana, theater. Even though I had rediscovered Westerns by the early 1980s and was doing research for my first book on them, another eighteen years would transpire before I saw *Open Range* in a theater.

Throughout the 1970s and beyond, I watched an occasional Western on one of the television movie channels, and when we acquired a small satellite dish, I purchased *Unforgiven* and *The Quick and the Dead*. In addition, I rented videotapes of films such as *Dances with Wolves*, *Tombstone* and *Wyatt Earp*. For the most part, however, my fondness for the Westerns of my childhood caused me to shy away from more modern expressions of the genre and to focus on B Westerns. However, after the publication of my first book, *Westerns and American Culture, 1930–1955* (McFarland, 2001), I knew I had to complete the project by examining the manner in which Westerns reflected the substantial social, economic and political changes that shaped American culture of the last forty-five years of the twentieth century.

1

The present volume is that effort. It has been a wonderful way to reconnect with the genre I still admire. I discovered excellent Westerns made after 1955 that I had never watched. From *Sergeant Rutledge* through *Chisum*, to *The Ballad of Little Jo* and *Geronimo: An American Legend*, I realized that Western films are still being made that are both entertaining and reflective of the era in which they were produced.

In that sense this book has been a wonderful journal of discovery and rediscovery. I invite readers along as we probe the manner in which Westerns changed after 1955, as American life experienced the traumas and challenges of the last half of the twentieth century. As with the first book, I have not viewed all of the Westerns produced after 1955, and neither European Westerns (the so-called Spaghetti Westerns) nor parodies, such as *Blazing Saddles*, are included. While both film types are worth serious examination, they lie beyond the scope of this book. And I know very little about television Westerns.

I invite readers to add the Westerns they have seen to the films I discuss, and I invite them to interact with the analysis. Have I got it right? Above all, I hope readers will recognize how Westerns, comprising that most American of all film genres, have been used and continue to be used as vehicles for commentary on current American problems and conditions.

The book is divided into two parts. Part I considers shifting themes as the genre reacted to changes unfolding in the broader social landscape of American culture. From the late–1950s films of Randolph Scott and Audie Murphy through Sam Peckinpah's work to the postmodern *Unforgiven*, Westerns reacted to the civil rights movement, the war in Vietnam and economic upheavals as post–World War II industrialism collapsed. John Wayne, however, offered viewers an understanding of those events that contrasted sharply from the Westerns of Clint Eastwood and Sam Peckinpah.

Part II examines the manner in which images of cowboys, outlaws, lawmen, Native Americans and women changed in Westerns over the last half of the twentieth century as the genre offered viewers new understandings of the frontier experience.

Parts of chapters 2, 4, 5, 6 and 8 were read as papers at annual meetings of the Popular Culture Association, and I thank Dr. Dwight Jessup, Vice President of Academic Affairs and Dean of the University of Taylor University, Upland, Indiana, for providing generous financial assistance so I could present papers at those conferences.

Darlene Jordan, my program assistant, provided invaluable service, and without her the manuscript would not yet be complete. I appreciate the quick response of Stephen Sally to my plea for help in locating photographs from some of the films. Raymond White, professor emeritus of history, and Gary Kramer of Ball State University patiently listened and reacted to arguments found throughout the volume as we drove to film festivals or talked at our favorite watering hole after monthly meetings of the East Central Indiana Western Film Club. Beulah Baker of the Taylor University English Department shared with me volumes from her personal library, and she reacted to the ideas found in chapters 2 and 7, as well as educating me on the English poet William Blake. However, I have a strong will and a stubborn personality: the errors are all mine.

PART I

Shifting Themes

Chapter 1

RANDOLPH SCOTT AND AUDIE MURPHY IN CHANGING TIMES

As Americans celebrated the opening of the new decade on January 1, 1950, the country neared the midpoint of the twentieth century. It had been a century in which novels, stage productions, wild west shows and movies celebrated the ever westward expanding American frontier of the nineteenth and early twentieth centuries; and those genres had been crucial, if not dominant, elements in American popular culture. There were few reasons to believe that Westerns would not continue to occupy a central place in American entertainment. While wild west shows and stage productions were in history's dust bin by 1950, newsstands still prominently displayed novels and magazines about the wild west, and approximately 130 Western movies were released in 1950, many of them series B Westerns starring well known cowboy actors such as Roy Rogers, Gene Autry or William Elliott (Adams and Rainey).

In 1950, the Republic Studio lot was busy filming Roy Rogers, Monte Hale, Allan "Rocky" Lane and Rex Allen. Monogram had active production units for Johnny Mack Brown and Whip Wilson. At Columbia, Gene Autry and Charles Starrett were still turning out five or six Westerns each year. Certainly, pre–World War II cowboy stars such as Hoot Gibson, Tim McCoy and Ken Maynard were no longer active, and the Eddie Dean and Jimmy Wakely production units had shut down. But Lash LaRue and

Sunset Carson had switched to smaller companies and were still making B Westerns. Youngsters just beginning to discover cowboy movies in 1950 had every reason to believe that they would be able to enjoy Saturday afternoons watching their favorite cowboy stars on the silver screen just as their parents had done before them. However, in five short years that expectation had faded. Motion picture companies shut down the production units of aging cowboy stars such as Johnny Mack Brown and Charles Starrett, and William Boyd, Roy Rogers and Gene Autry switched their focus to television. By 1955, increasing numbers of motion picture theaters had closed, most of them second and third run neighborhood houses and small-town theaters that had been primary outlets for B Westerns.

In 1951, Roy Rogers, impressed no doubt by the success of *The Gene Autry Show*, wanted to do television, and when Herbert Yates at Republic Pictures refused, Rogers did not renew his contract. Republic released its last Rogers film, *Pals of the Golden West*, on December 15, 1951 (Adams and Rainey, 408). The last Monte Hale Western, *The Missourians*, had been released on November 25, 1950 (Adams and Rainey, 396). Allan "Rocky" Lane's production unit issued its last film on September 8, 1953 (Adams and Raney, 439), and Rex Allen followed quickly when Republic released his last Western on February 10, 1954 (Adams and Rainey, 444). Monogram had shut down the Johnny Mack Brown and Whip Wilson production units in 1952. By 1955, Lash LaRue, Sunset Carson and William Elliott appeared on the silver screen only in re-releases.

For a few more years, cowboy stars continued to appear in studio re-releases of their films (for example, in Marion, Indiana, the Lyric Theaters showed a B Western with a cowboy hero twenty-three out of the fifty-two Saturdays in 1955, but that trailed off to only eleven Saturdays in 1956). Local television stations ran 53-minute edited versions of B Westerns as well as made-for-television programs with Roy Rogers, Gene Autry, Guy Madison and William Boyd.

Several elements account for the demise of the series B Western by 1955. Television made a major impact on American entertainment habits. Families stayed home to watch their favorite programs, and among them were half-hour shows starring B Western cowboy actors (Schatz, 440). In addition, many edited B Westerns were shown on early evening television programs such as *The Old Corral, Chuckwagon Theater,* or *Cowboy Roundup.* There was no need to go downtown to the show when one could see the same movies free in the comfort of one's living room. Unlike their parents, the early wave of baby boomers became fans of Westerns via the small-screen television tube, not large-screen movie theaters.

Viewer tastes shifted as the country continued to change demographically. Migration from rural areas to larger urban locations, which had been underway for much of the twentieth century, accelerated as younger folks left rural and small-town America during World War II for high-paying jobs in defense plants. Few returned to their previous homes once the war ended. In addition, sons and daughters, and grandsons and granddaughters, of late nineteenth and early twentieth century European immigrants, nearly all of whom had settled in large urban areas when they arrived in the United States, moved from the old neighborhoods to the rapidly expanding suburbs as they achieved middle class status.

Peter Stanfield, in his excellent *Horse Opera: The Strange History of the 1930s' Singing Cowboy*, observes that B Westerns, and particularly the singing cowboy B Westerns, appealed most directly to children and adults of rural America, and working class immigrants of the cities. He notes, "Their films [B Westerns] promote action and spectacle, not narrative coherence. The intended audience ... values the exhibition of performance" (Stanfield 2002, 41). Middle class viewers, especially urban middle class moviegoers, did not like Westerns for exactly that reason; they lacked "narrative coherence," contained elementary plots, and included distracting songs and comedy. By the middle 1950s, as rural America emptied and younger generations fled the old ethnic enclaves, B Westerns lost much of their audience!

Changes in the film industry itself were no less important. In 1948, the Supreme Court of the United States ruled that antitrust laws applied to motion pictures. No longer could one company control production, distribution and exhibition. The Screen Actors Guild and unions representing all facets of the production process were able to earn higher wages and benefits for their members. Not surprisingly, the cost of making a motion picture increased substantially. As costs increased, B Westerns took on a streamlined look, with more stock footage, fewer riders in the outlaw gang and posse, and less location shooting. With some exceptions (Tim Holt films at RKO and Roy Rogers Westerns at Republic), most B Westerns by 1950 looked like they had been shot on studio lots. In retrospect, it is clear that the days of the series B Westerns were numbered by 1950. However, the demise of small-budget series B Westerns did not doom the entire genre. In fact, throughout the 1950s the genre boomed with the production of a large number of middle level B Westerns and a handful of superwesterns, such as *The Searchers* (Warner Brothers, 1956) and Gary Cooper's *Man of the West* (United Artists, 1958).

Two Guns and a Badge (Allied Artists, 1954), starring Wayne Morris, is considered the last series B Western, but non-series B Westerns continued to appear in theaters throughout the 1950s. Smaller budget B Westerns with Bill Williams, Skip Homeier and Jim Davis, as well as bigger budget Westerns with Randolph Scott, Audie Murphy, Joel McCrea, Rod Cameron, George Montgomery, Rory Calhoun and Dale Robertson, provided weekend family entertainment (often shown at drive-in theaters) until the late 1950s.

Universal-International pictures tried to fashion Audie Murphy into a 1950s cowboy hero. Murphy efforts of the 1950s, such as *Destry* (1955), *Walk the Proud Land* (1956) and *The Guns of Fort Petticoat* (Columbia, 1957), are films in the tradition of 1930s and 1940s B Westerns. Warner Brothers even made a small effort to revive the cowboy hero with Clayton Moore as the Lone Ranger in *The Lone Ranger* (1956) and *The Lone Ranger and the Lost City of Gold* (1958). Allied Artist (the new name for Monogram) made some good traditional B Westerns with Joel McCrea, this author's favorite mid–1950s cowboy star. *Wichita* (1955), *The First Texan* (1956) and *The Tall Stranger* (1957) were entertaining Westerns.

Republic (king of the B Westerns from 1935 until the early 1950s) continued to churn out traditional B Westerns until the middle 1950s. *The Last Command* (1955) may have been Herbert Yates' revenge on John Wayne for leaving the studio. Wayne wanted to film the Alamo story, but Yates would not agree to spend the money that Wayne needed for the project. *The Last Command*, Republic's version of Wayne's dream, is little more than a B Western.

Republic also continued to appeal to religious sentiments of the Southern and Midwestern heartland by producing Westerns with overt Christian themes. *The Twinkle in God's Eye* (1955) stars Mickey Rooney as a young pastor winning over Lodestar, a tough mining town, and its chief agnostic, Hugh O'Brian, to Christianity. In *Stranger at My Door* (1956), screenwriter Barry Shipman and director William Witney team up to create an entertaining Western. MacDonald Carey plays a minister whose family opens its home to a young outlaw (Skip Homeier). Carey never gives up trying to convert the lad, and the film ends in an emotion-jerking scene with Carey standing over the body of the young outlaw who had been killed in the yet-to-be-finished church. Both *The Twinkle in God's Eye* and *Stranger at My Door* have much in common with 1930s and 1940s B Westerns such as *Stone of Silver Creek* (Universal, 1935), *Angel and the Badman* (Republic, 1947) and *Hellfire* (Republic, 1949).

All of these films shared a common trait; they represented continuity with the previous decades. For the most part, they are traditional Westerns highlighting the fact that much in the 1950s resembled the preceding twenty-five years. In all of these films, heroes, heroines and villains fit traditional Western images. Themes such as pursuing justice, standing up for the rights of the underdog, and acting with courage and integrity abound.

Other film efforts, such as *Run of the Arrow* (Universal-International, 1957), *Gunman's Walk* (Columbia, 1958) and *Last Train from Gun Hill* (Paramount, 1959), are less sure of those values, and are more inclined to offer multi-dimensional characters, more likely to depict raw sexuality, and less likely to have a happy ending. *Raw Edge* (Universal-International, 1956) is a good example of a "revisionist" 1950s Western. The hero (Rory Calhoun) travels to Oregon to help his brother run a ranch, only to discover that his brother has been murdered and his Indian wife taken as booty by Robert Wilkie, the first man to claim her. The horror on Mara Corday's (the Indian wife) face as she is surrounded by a circle of leering men all intent on claiming her as a sexual prize immediately sets this film apart from traditional Westerns.

Much of the film, however, remains traditional, as Calhoun goes after Herbert Rudley (whose character is the iron ruler of the local community, and on whose order Calhoun's brother had been murdered). On the other hand, the sexual tension that permeates *Raw Edge* is extraordinary for the 1950s. Yvonne de Carlo plays Rudley's wife, the man Calhoun intends to kill for murdering his brother. When Emile Meyer and Neville Brand, employees of Rudley, figure out that Rudley will not likely return to the ranch, they commence to wrangle over who gets de Carlo. Much like Corday, de Carlo has to confront the real possibility of being forced to marry and to sleep with the first man strong enough to claim her. That theme alone distinguishes *Raw Edge* from traditional Westerns that shied away from such emphasis on human sexuality.

Raw Edge suggests that there was something different about many 1950s Westerns. They began to shift foci, as the hero became more frequently a loner, an alienated individual more akin to the contemporary anti-hero than the cowboy hero of the 1930s and 1940s. Darker and more explicit sexuality began to appear. The heroine's blouse or dress often would rip as she tried to fend off the advances of the villain, who was less interested in marrying her and more inclined to sexual assault. Cowardice, greed, and intolerance often were projected as dominant community attributes.

By the mid–1950s, motion picture advertisements (such as lobby cards) often highlighted those elements in the films. For example, the title lobby card for *The Desperados Are in Town* (20th Century–Fox, 1956) depicts two men holding a woman as if they were preparing to assault her, while a smaller picture on the left of the card shows a woman whose dress is pulled up high on her legs. A lobby card for *Joe Dakota* (Universal-International, 1957) asks, "Why did this town without a conscience ... fear this man without a name? What [sic] did they try to hide from him?"

Westerns of the middle and late 1950s mirrored the decade in which they were made. Like the decade itself, films of the 1950s contained a great deal of the old, as well as hints of the new. The 1950s were marked by political, social and economic conservatism. President Dwight Eisenhower, the oldest sitting president at that time, and one who read Western paperback novels, pursued right-of-center economic and social policies while continuing to confront an aggressive Soviet Union. The Congress, controlled by a coalition of northern conservative Republicans and southern conservative Democrats, worked cooperatively with President Eisenhower. Mainline protestant churches represented and reinforced 1950s traditional social and religious values. And the United States still dominated the world's industry and commerce, ensuring full employment and high wages.

Journalist David Halberstam commented on these trends in his book *The Fifties*: "Social ferment ... was beginning just beneath this placid surface" (Halberstam, ix). He continued, "In the years following the traumatic experiences of the Depression and World War II, the American Dream was to exercise personal freedom not in social and political terms, but rather in economic terms" (Halberstam, x). Historian William Manchester agrees with Halberstam and writes about college students of the early 1950s: "For the majority, acts of social significance were replaced by the panty raid or something called 'stuffing' in which the largest possible number of undergraduates would squash themselves into some small space" (Manchester, 577). Manchester goes on to observe that college students of that time conformed to the dictates of society and in turn expected a share of the good life (Manchester, 580). He writes, "In the conflict between independence and the system, they came down hard on the side of the system. They sought not fame, but the approval of others" (Manchester, 578). In that, Manchester concludes, they were simply adopting the values of the older generation (Manchester, 577).

Surely there were difficult moments. Citizens continued to dispute passionately the civil liberty implications of McCarthyism; the economy in 1957 and 1958 experienced a nasty recession; and always looming on the horizon was a potential nuclear exchange should either the United States or the Soviet Union, the world's two superpowers, misjudge one another. As the decade ground to a close, Americans were caught up in the emerging civil rights movement. Confrontation at Central High School in Little Rock, Arkansas, was followed by the Montgomery bus boycott, and folks outside of Montgomery, Alabama, began to hear about the young African-American preacher, Dr. Martin Luther King.

On the whole, however, at least from the vantage point of a white male who went to high school during the heart of the decade (from 1954 to 1958), it was a good time to grow up. Few young people were wealthy, but most had access to enough money for movies, basketball games and dates. Most teenagers of the 1950s were nurtured in stable homes and experienced the care and concern of teachers who wanted them to become responsible adults. David Halberstam suggests that young people of the fifties "seemed, more than anything else, 'square' and largely accepting of the given social covenants" (Halberstam, x).

Guns, drugs and alcohol were not problems at most high schools. The rebels sneaked off of the school grounds to smoke cigarettes as a way of demonstrating their adulthood! Science produced the marvels of television, the polio vaccine and a plethora of wonder drugs, and that same science shook American confidence to the core when the Soviet Union launched Sputnik and beat the United States into space. Still, it was a good time to be alive and to grow up knowing that a prosperous economy meant that 1950s teens would live better than their parents had lived.

But social stability, political conservatism and faith in traditional values were only part of the story. Teenagers growing up in the 1950s (although they did not realize it at the time) were early participants in what would come to be called the "sexual revolution." Young males sneaked copies of *Playboy* into their rooms when it was only a struggling magazine. Soft-core pornographic novels that had been unavailable ten years earlier were often displayed at the local drugstore. By the mid–1950s, teenagers were celebrating the emergence of rock 'n' roll music as millions of them danced to Elvis Presley, Bill Haley, Little Richard and Chuck Berry.

Movies, too, projected a more permissive sexuality. Films such as *Baby Doll* (Warner Brothers, 1956), with Carroll Baker, and *And God Created Woman* (Iena/UCIL/Cocinor, 1956), starring Brigitte Bardot, the latest French sensation, appear tame when measured by early twenty-first century films; but in the 1950s they were thought of as scandalous, and moviegoers flocked to see the films for that reason. As the motion picture industry changed, the Lyric Theater in Marion, Indiana (one of the author's childhood haunts), resorted to foreign imports to attract patrons. In 1955 and 1956, Roy Rogers, Gene Autry, Rocky Lane and Lash LaRue would still gallop across the Lyric screen on Saturday, or Johnny Weissmuller (as Jungle Jim) would wrestle a lion. But on Sunday the Lyric screen would be filled with foreign imports, with the audience alert to the quick display of a bare breast.

Heroes became like James Dean, moody and rebellious, projecting adolescent uncertainty in the face of a changing world. Or they became tough cynics, trusting no one, feeling responsible for no one and concerned only about number one. Hollywood under the strictures of the production code had treated clergy and religion carefully and with respect, but as the 1950s ended, clergy often were portrayed as hypocrites or cowards, and religion frequently was depreciated.

Most people growing up in the 1950s were reared in stable homes, nurtured by supportive churches and schools, taught traditional moral codes and encouraged to be industrious, thrifty citizens. But they were also challenged to be free from those nurturing institutions, to assert their "rights," to measure success in materialistic terms and to re-examine traditional moral values. Without realizing it, 1950s teenagers were the scouts, the skirmish line and the early victims of the restlessness and permissiveness that gripped the United States in the 1960s and 1970s.

Between 1955 and 1960 Hollywood films reflected the paradox that was the 1950s. As the archetype American film, 1950s Westerns displayed both continuity with their rich heritage, and change driven by increasing education, suburbanization and affluence. Old values were no longer uncritically accepted. Westerns began to reflect the changing state of affairs, not the values of the years before World War II that many 1950s sophisticates discarded as dated and naïve.

Five actors dominated the Western film genre from 1955 to 1960: Randolph Scott (13 films), Audie Murphy (11), Joel McCrea (10), George Montgomery (12) and Rory Calhoun (11). With the decline of the series B Western, and in the midst of shifting values in the United States, if any actors could be regarded as heirs to the B Western cowboy stars of the 1930s and 1940s, it would be these five men. Among the quintet, Randolph Scott's and Audie Murphy's films provide good case studies of the manner in which Westerns reflected a 1950s changing American culture. Some of them were more like the traditional B Westerns of the 1930s and 1940s, but as the decade closed, Scott and Murphy's films increasingly projected a new view of the West, and in doing so reflected changes that were looming on the American horizon.

By the time Randolph Scott retired from making motion pictures in 1962, he was more closely identified with the Western film genre than any other actor. Scott had first made Westerns for Paramount in 1932, appearing in ten film adaptations of Zane Grey novels from 1932 through 1935. For the next ten years Scott continued to appear in Westerns, but that work made up less than one-third of his total film output. However, in

1946 Scott returned to Westerns as his primary focus. Out of the forty-one movies in which Scott appeared between 1946 and 1960, only two of them were not Westerns. By the time he retired after making *Ride the High Country* (MGM, 1962), Randolph Scott was the consummate westerner. His name was nearly synonymous with Western films.

In *Last of the Cowboy Heroes: The Westerns of Audie Murphy, Joel McCrea and Randolph Scott,* Robert Nott describes the "code of the west":

> A cowboy was honest, brave, and kind to his horse. He treated women with respect, looked out for the helpless homesteader and was someone the kids could look up to. He didn't go looking for trouble, but he sure wasn't going to ride around it if it came his way. He was good with a gun, knew the land, and was chockfull of common sense. It helped to have a sense of humor [Nott, 57].

That code describes Scott's film characters up to the 1950s, but then his characters began to change. In Nott's words, Scott becomes a "darker Western hero" (79). The Ranown (the Randolph Scott–Harry Joe Brown production company) films were important components in the transition to "adult" Westerns (Nott, 143). Nott describes the change:

> The Scott character — generally a loner — was edging closer to the sort of Western hero that would populate the genre within the next decade. He was bitter, defiant, vengeful, and somewhat selfish. There was still nobility to his quest ... but it seemed as though he would only help others if it happened to coincide with his own agenda [Nott, 143].

The four Scott films released in 1955 have much in common with most of the Westerns he made prior to that year. *Ten Wanted Men* (Columbia), *Rage at Dawn* (RKO), *Tall Man Riding* (Warner Brothers) and *A Lawless Street* (Columbia) are conventional Westerns for the most part, with *Rage at Dawn* and *A Lawless Street* the most conventional. In *Rage at Dawn,* Scott's character (James Barlow) is a detective sent to Indiana (the California filming location certainly did not look like southern Indiana) to infiltrate the notorious Reno Brothers gang (played by Forrest Tucker, J. Carrol Naish and Myron Healey, some of the best known character actors in Hollywood of that day). Scott establishes his credentials by beating the Renos to a railroad holdup. Once Scott is accepted into the gang, he is able to lure them into a trap in which the brothers are either captured or killed.

The love interest in the film is provided by Mala Powers (playing Laura Reno, sister of the outlaws). She hates her brothers' lawless ways and becomes distraught when she learns that Scott is an outlaw as well. But, true to its conventional Western characteristics, Scott and Powers are united as "The End" rolls across the screen.

There is more dialogue and less action than in other conventional Westerns, but by and large all of the film elements are predictable. Scott is a calm, in control, bigger than life hero. The Reno brothers are the mean-spirited bullying lot so characteristic of conventional Western villains, and Mala Powers is the feminine heroine who detests lawlessness and killing. The only thing that distinguishes *Rage at Dawn* from earlier Westerns is the ending. Scott arrives too late to save the Renos from a lynch mob, but the leader of the mob, played by Trevor Bardette, is taken into custody and told he will have to answer to a judge for his illegal behavior. Even in the lynchings there is no graphic violence, and justice does triumph in the end. All in all, *Rage at Dawn* has more in common with Scott's earlier Westerns than those he would make in the late 1950s.

The same may be said for *A Lawless Street*. Scott plays Calem Ware, an old-time marshal known for a fast draw (to face him meant almost certain death). However, Scott's gun hand is crippled by arthritis, a fact unknown to all except himself. Scott is able to maintain Medicine Bend as a decent place in which to live because no wandering gunman is brave enough to challenge the famous marshal, and because he is able to prevent Warner Anderson, who plays a saloonkeeper, from creating a wide-open town. Unfortunately for Scott, Michael Pate, playing the gunfighter Harley Baskam, rides into town knowing that Scott can barely hold a gun. In the shootout that follows, Pate seriously wounds Scott (Pate believes he has killed him), and Anderson uses Pate to force the other saloonkeepers to deed over their property to Anderson. Medicine Bend is now the wide-open town that Anderson wants. Wallace Ford, playing Dr. Amos Wynn, nurses Scott back to health, and in the final frames Scott manages to shoot and kill Pate. In Scott's words, the snarling beast (meaning the town) has been tamed.

Angela Lansbury, of television's *Murder She Wrote* fame, plays Scott's wife, an actress who left him because she could not stand the uncertainty of Scott's profession. She has been invited to Medicine Bend by Warner Anderson, who does not know of her marriage to Scott and who expects her to become his wife. In the end, however, Scott and Lansbury ride out of town together; the beast has been tamed and it is time for Scott to hang up his guns.

In neither film does Scott's characters fit Nott's description of the transition to "adult" Westerns. Scott is not a darker Western hero, a loner or one who is bitter or defiant. Quite the contrary, Scott's characters in

Rage at Dawn and *A Lawless Street* are committed to creating peaceful communities free from outlaws like the Renos, gunmen like Pate and evil saloonkeepers like Anderson. Furthermore, both films affirm traditional gender relationships that end in either the renewal of marriage or the hint of one to come.

Rage at Dawn and *A Lawless Street* have all of the trappings of conventional Westerns. They demonstrate the continuity with the past one finds in the 1950s. So do *Ten Wanted Men* and *Tall Man Riding*, for the most part, but both films also offer hints of the future. In *Ten Wanted Men* Scott plays a land and cattle baron, the acknowledged leader of the community in which he lives, and one who clearly relishes his exalted status. Richard Boone is the villain who both envies and opposes Scott. The film's title comes from the wanted men Boone hires to drive Scott off of his land. While traces of what is to come in Westerns can be seen throughout the film, one particular episode stands out. Boone and his outlaws sadistically and graphically murder Lester Matthews, playing Scott's brother and a lawyer, on the trail. Boone, in true Western fashion, gets his, however, when Leo Gordon, leader of the wanted men, turns on Boone and ransacks his safe before Scott dispatches them.

Scott's character is unlike the conventional hero in a couple of ways. Most prominent, he is a man used to getting his own way. So, at the film's end, Scott restores the sheriff to his office and resumes the control he always had over the affairs of the town. Surprisingly, the film offers very little in the way of love interest. In the end, Scott rides off with Jocelyn Brando, whom he has just married, but throughout *Ten Wanted Men* Scott appears as a man with only minimal romantic interest in her.

The ending of *Tall Man Riding* marks it as a conventional Western, but throughout the film, Larry Madden, Scott's character, is a bitter, revenge-oriented individual. He had been bullwhipped and chased off of his own ranch and out of town by Robert Barrat, playing Tuck Ordway, owner of the War Bonnet and the most powerful cattleman in the territory. Scott had been in love with Dorothy Malone, Barrat's daughter, but Scott would not marry her until he became successful and so could stand independent of Barrat. The latter misunderstood Scott's intentions and acted to protect his daughter's reputation. Now Scott is back with an attorney (John Dehner) who has discovered that Barratt never filed on his land, so it is open to settlement.

In an arranged gunfight with Barratt in a darkened room, Scott discovers that the latter is nearly blind. Scott disavows his vengeance and prepares to leave town. However, Dehner is unwilling to walk away from the money to be gained in a land rush, so he joins forces with John Baragrey,

In *The Tall T* (1957), Randolph Scott's character is more complex than traditional cowboy heroes.

playing Purlo, a saloonkeeper who also had been bullwhipped by Barratt and seeks revenge on the old man.

All ends well, however as Scott helps Barratt save his ranch house, reconciles with Barratt, and reunites with Malone. The film ends with Scott and Malone, arm in arm, walking toward the door of the ranch house, signifying that Scott is now a big enough man to live under Barratt's roof and take over managing the ranch, a typically happy ending familiar in Westerns.

Using Nott's analysis once again, Scott's character in *Ten Wanted Men* is somewhat selfish, a man used to getting his own way and one who does not tolerate any challenge to his authority. Scott may play the part in a friendly manner, but that does not detract from the underlying nature of his character. On the other hand, Larry Madden, Scott's character in *Tall Man Riding*, is a bitter, defiant and vengeful person right up to the film's end. He is on a quest: Scott intends to kill Barratt and take his land. But in the end, Scott gives up the quest — once he discovers Barratt is nearly blind — and not only kills a man who tried to kill Barratt but also helps the latter save his ranch house in the land rush that follows opening up the War Bonnet for homesteaders.

Tall Man Riding's ending seems a bit forced. The abrupt transformation in Scott is less than believable to contemporary viewers, but that was not the case with motion picture patrons in 1955. Scott was simply portraying the hero viewers had come to expect from him. Larry Madden had to change because, after all, Randolph Scott did not play bitter, defiant and vengeful characters. But things were about to change!

Over the next four years Scott appeared in four Westerns indicative of the changes occurring in the genre and overtaking American culture. The four films, some of Scott's best, are *The Tall T* (Columbia, 1957), *Decision at Sundown* (Columbia, 1957), *Ride Lonesome* (Columbia, 1959) and *Comanche Station* (Columbia, 1960). All four efforts highlight the changes taking place in Scott's characters, indicating that audiences wanted more complex and (dare one say) realistic characters, and suggesting that the time was ripe for more controversial themes.

The Tall T opens with Scott's character, Pat Brennan, a man who lives a lonely existence on a small ranch, trying to make a go of ranching by himself. However, in quick succession he loses his horse in a bet and stumbles upon a gang of three killers who had just murdered the stagecoach relay station master and his young son. At this point Scott hooks up with the characters that will shape the film. Richard Boone (Usher), Skip Homeier (Billy Jack) and Henry Silva (Chink) are the three outlaw killers. Maureen O'Sullivan, as Doretta Mims, is on her honeymoon with John Hubbard, who plays Willard Mims. Hubbard is a coward, quite willing to sacrifice the safety and life of his bride for his own well being, and viewers learn quickly that he only married O'Sullivan for her money; her father owned a rich copper mine. In order to save his own skin, Hubbard proposes that the three outlaws hold them for ransom rather than kill them.

Two elements in this film strikingly suggest changes in the Western genre. First, as with other Westerns of the 1950s, Homeier and Silva are modeled after 1950s juvenile delinquents. They are young toughs eager to kill and steal as a means of demonstrating their manhood. Specifically, Richard Boone, as the outlaw leader, has to continually restrain Henry Silva from an overly eager urge to kill. Homeier and Silva are merely western counterparts to the urban toughs of *The Blackboard Jungle* (MGM, 1955), young men who like to kill and destroy for the thrill it gives them. The sexual tension in *The Tall T* also distinguishes it from previous films as well. At one point, Homeier and Silva engage in a conversation in which Silva reminisces about the women with whom he has had sexual intercourse. Homeier is less experienced and clearly envies his more worldly compatriot.

Scott is able to use Homeier's sexual inexperience to advantage. After Hubbard brings back word that O'Sullivan's father will pay the ransom (and after Hubbard is murdered), the next day Boone rides to get the ransom money. Scott makes Silva wonder whether or not Boone will return or simply take the money and ride away. Silva goes after Boone to make sure that he returns with the ransom money. At that point, Scott tells O'Sullivan to unbutton her blouse, and then asks Homeier what he is waiting for, clearly intimating that both Boone and Silva had been with O'Sullivan the day Homeier had been away from camp. When Homeier goes to O'Sullivan, Scott is able to kill him. Hearing the shots, Silva returns to camp to be killed as well. Predictably, Scott kills Boone when he returns with the money, and O'Sullivan and Scott ride off together at the film's end.

The Tall T does not offer viewers an alienated hero. In fact, Scott is a traditional cowboy hero in nearly every way. He is calm in the face of death and cooperative in order to remain alive until he has the opportunity to act. On the other hand, the sexual tension and the images of Homeier and Silva as western equivalents of 1950s juvenile delinquents suggest that it is a Western of a different order, certainly different from the ones Scott made in the late 1940s and early 1950s.

The other three Scott programmers, *Decision at Sundown, Ride Lonesome* and *Comanche Station* are quest films. In each of the three, Scott's character is searching for something or somebody; In *Decision at Sundown* and *Ride Lonesome* the quest is for revenge, and in *Comanche Station* Scott engages in a ten-year search for his wife who has been kidnapped by Indians. *Decision at Sundown* is by far the bleakest and most troubling of the three films.

Scott (Bart Allison) and his partner Noah Berry Jr. (Sam) ride into Sundown to kill John Carroll (Tate Kimbrough), who Scott falsely believes is responsible for his wife's death while Scott was away fighting the Civil War. Carroll is clearly a slick-talking con artist. He has the people of Sundown afraid of him, and is about to marry Karen Steele (Lucy Summerton). Scott stops the wedding and makes clear to the folks gathered in the church that he has come to kill Carroll.

It is Scott's character, Bart Allison, that makes this film both interesting and unusual. Even though his wife, Mary, killed herself a week before Scott returned from the war because she could not face him knowing about her unfaithfulness, Scott won't acknowledge the truth about his wife. Berry Jr. sadly notes that you can't convince a man about something he does not want to know about. When Berry Jr. tells Scott that Mary was not the woman he thought she was, Scott throws Berry Jr. out of the liv-

This title card for *Decision at Sundown* (1957) emphasizes that it is a new kind of Western.

ery stable to which they had fled to escape Carroll's hired guns. Once outside, the Sheriff's gunman murders Berry Jr. Later that day Steele comes to the livery stable to find out about Mary and to discover why Scott had stopped her wedding. She challenges Scott to understand that one cannot take revenge for something that one has never had. Scott's response is to slap Steele on the rear and shove her out of the livery stable. Scott's Bart Allison is a hard man, a man with a one-track mind bent on revenge.

When Scott emerges from the livery stable to face Carroll's hired gunman/sheriff in a gunfight, Scott is hatless and has a wild look about him. He is a man consumed by hate: hate for the sheriff responsible for Berry Jr.'s murder, and hate for Carroll, who he believes stole his wife. But it is Scott's hate-filled, revenge-driven obsession to kill Carroll that rallies the townsfolk to reclaim their self-respect and stand up to Carroll. At the film's end Carroll rides out of town with Valerie French, who plays Ruby, his mistress, and the saloon is filled with townsfolk celebrating their free-

Randolph Scott as the classic loner in *Comanche Station* (1960).

dom from Carroll's oppressive yolk. But when they ask a drunken Scott
to drink with them, he refuses. Scott lectures them on how a man is supposed to act; he has no respect for the manner in which they permitted
Carroll to control them. Sadly, however, Scott can't act like a man is supposed to act either. He would not face the truth of his wife's infidelity. He
remains a man unchanged; Scott had given the town courage to stand up
to Carroll, but he was unable to control himself. The film ends with Scott
riding out of town — leading Berry Jr.'s horse — a lonely alienated figure.
Nott is surely right in his assessment that "Bart Allison is the most unsym-
pathetic hero Scott ever played" (Nott, 136).

In *Ride Lonesome*, Scott's character, Ben Brigade, is not alienated like
Bart Allison in *Decision at Sundown*, but he is no less revenge driven. Scott
captures James Best (Billy John), and viewers are led to believe that Scott
is a bounty hunter bent on taking Best back to Santa Cruz to stand trial
for murder. However, as the film unfolds, viewers learn that Scott is luring
Lee Van Cleef (playing Best's brother Frank) into a trap. Years before, Van
Cleef had kidnapped and hung Scott's wife in an act of revenge. Now Scott

is using Best as bait, promising to hang him on the same tree that Van Cleef hung Scott's wife. At the film's climax Scott kills Van Cleef, and the movie takes a surprising turn.

While returning Best to Santa Cruz, Scott had stumbled upon two men — Pernell Roberts and James Coburn — who were also looking for Best. The governor had promised amnesty to anyone bringing in Best, and Roberts and Coburn see in the amnesty promise a chance to start life over. Tension between Roberts and Scott builds throughout the film, and viewers assume that some sort of showdown between the two men is inevitable. However, right before the climactic gunfight viewers expect, Scott hands Best over to Roberts and Coburn. Scott has gotten from Best what he needed, so he gives the other two men a chance for amnesty as well as the promise that if they don't go straight he will come after them!

Karen Steele (Mrs. Lane) is also the heroine of this Scott programmer. She is key in establishing Scott's loneliness, even as he realizes his revenge. After Van Cleef is dead and Best has been turned over to Roberts and Coburn, Steele asks Scott if he is going on to Santa Cruz. When Scott tells her he won't be going on with them, Steele merely responds that she didn't think he would. The film ends as Scott stands watching the hanging tree burn. Van Cleef is dead and the tree on which the villain hung Scott's wife is burning to the ground, yet Scott remains a lonely, unfulfilled human being.

To a lesser extent, the same theme pervades *Comanche Station*. Scott's Jefferson Cody has spent ten years hunting for his wife, who was kidnapped by Indians, and at the beginning of the film he buys Nancy Gates (Mrs. Lowe) from a band of Indians and sets out to return her to her husband. Claude Akins, Skip Homeier and Richard Rust portray three gunmen who intend to take Gates away from Scott so they can return her for the reward money. Unlike *Ride Lonesome*, Scott kills Akins and the other two, but he does not claim the reward. When he returns Gates to her husband, Scott discovers that the man is blind, so he rides away. The closing frames of Scott leading his packhorse up and through the rocks of the Alabama Hills near Lone Pine, California, are of a lonely man on a quest whose success will never be realized.

Scott would make one more film after *Comanche Station* (*Ride the High Country*, discussed at length in Chapter Three), but his post–1955 Westerns are important films. Taken together, they suggest changes unfolding in the Western genre, and, more importantly, they capture a nation and a culture in transformation.

Audie Murphy was someone nearly all young males growing up in the years immediately following World War II knew something about. Born in 1924 to a poor Texas family, Murphy sharpened his hunting skills during the depression in order to feed his mother and younger siblings. Although small and baby-faced when he entered the United States Army in World War II, Murphy advanced from a private to first lieutenant (Nott, 42; Graham). He demonstrated both exceptional leadership ability and courage in combat, becoming the most decorated soldier of World War II.

Like thousands of other G.I.s, Murphy had to build a life when the war ended. However, unlike other returning veterans, Murphy did not use the G.I. Bill of Rights to further his education or begin a business; and, unlike most other veterans, Murphy was famous. His picture had appeared on the cover of *Life*, and he attracted attention wherever he went. Capitalizing on his newfound fame, Murphy accepted an offer from film star James Cagney, who brought him to Hollywood and placed him under a personal contract (Nott, 43). According to Nott, Murphy once remarked, "I did like the idea of making some money in movies" (Nott, 43). In 1950, Universal signed Murphy to a contract, hoping to make him their new cowboy star. From his first feature, *Kid from Texas* (Universal, 1950), through *Destry* (Universal-International, 1954), Murphy fashioned a persona as a somewhat shy, aloof and baby-faced but determined hero. Both *Destry* and *Ride Clear of Diablo* (Universal, 1954) are the best expressions of this pre–1955 Murphy persona, and they are among the best Westerns in which he would appear.

Walk the Proud Land (Universal, 1957) is a good little Western. Murphy plays John Clum, an easterner sent by the Interior Department, and acting under instructions from President Grant, to the San Carlos Apache Indian reservation. The film is remarkably pro–Indian, as Murphy's Clum defends the Apaches and forces the army to leave the reservation. Consistent with the image of the cowboy hero of the 1930s and 1940s, Murphy will not accept setbacks as he defends Indian rights with courage and determination. Charles Drake plays Tom Sweeny, the cavalry officer that Murphy forced off of San Carlos. Once Drake retires from the army, he joins Murphy on the reservation and helps train the Apache police force that patrols San Carlos. In a highly improbable conclusion, Murphy and Drake and their small police force capture Geronimo and his renegade Apaches. Certainly, *Walk the Proud Land* is a B Western that resembles *Broken Arrow* (20th Century-Fox, 1950) and Tim McCoy's excellent defense of the Indians in his 1932 *End of the Trail* (Columbia, 1932).

The Guns of Fort Petticoat (Columbia, 1957) has even more 1930s and 1940s B Western characteristics than did *Walk the Proud Land*. The film

Audie Murphy teaches the women how to shoot in *The Guns of Fort Petticoat* (1957).

opens with Colonel Chivington's raid on the Indian village at Sand Creek. When Murphy objects to the raid, noting that it will force all the tribes onto the warpath, he is placed under arrest. But knowing the attack on Sand Creek endangers defenseless Texas women whose men are away fighting the Civil War, Murphy (even though as a Texan he is fighting for the North) deserts his post and heads for Texas to warn his former neighbors.

Frustrated at first by women who consider him a traitor, Murphy uses the body of a dead woman killed when Indians attacked her homestead to convince them that they are in danger. Murphy is able to get the women to an old mission compound where he trains them to shoot and defend themselves. The women successfully beat back an Indian attack on the mission. But they are nearly out of ammunition and in danger of being overrun by the Indians when *The Guns of Fort Petticoat* draws from one of the classic strategies of a 1930s or 1940s B Western. Murphy tracks down and kills the medicine man, and hangs his body from the archway entrance to the mission. The Indians, of course, are afraid to fight without their

THE STRANGEST KILLER WHO EVER STALKED THE WEST!

Twenty-four "victims" had died
before his lightning draw...
until he came to the
quiet town that had
marked him for death!

AUDIE
MURPHY

JOAN
EVANS

CHARLES
DRAKE

AUDIE
...in the
most
unusual
role
of his
exciting
career!

CINEMASCOPE in Eastman COLOR

NO NAME ON THE BULLET

The title card from *No Name on the Bullet* (1959) stresses Murphy's role as a
killer.

medicine man, so they ride away, leaving a few of the women dead from
the fighting, but most of them unharmed.

Murphy then does what one would expect from a B Western hero; he
rides back to his military post to face charges of desertion. Chivington is
about to pronounce sentence on Murphy's actions when a general arrives,
followed immediately by the women from the mission. In an improbable
sequence of events (but ones easily understood by those who know B Westerns), Murphy is commended for helping to save the women, Chivington
is placed under arrest for the Sand Creek Massacre, and Murphy and
Kathryn Grant leave together with the promise of marriage in the air.

As with the Randolph Scott pictures, Audie Murphy's Westerns
tended to have a great deal in common with pre–1950s Westerns, right up
to the middle and later 1950s. However, after *The Guns of Fort Petticoat*
Murphy's films began to change, and no film better demonstrates that
change than *No Name on the Bullet* (Universal, 1959).

In his biography of Audie Murphy, Don Graham calls *No Name on the Bullet* the best Western that Murphy ever made (Graham, 272). Murphy, as John Gant, a hired killer and assassin, rides into Lordsburg and registers at the local hotel. Townsfolk clearly understand that Murphy is there to kill somebody, but the haunting question is who! Two elements make this film different from the more traditional Westerns in which Murphy had starred earlier in the 1950s.

First, there is nothing heroic about Murphy's character. As Graham notes, Alan Ladd's Shane (*Shane*, Paramount, 1953) and Gregory Peck's Johnny Ringo in *The Gunfighter* (20th Century–Fox, 1950) had been men trying to escape their past. Both longed to settle down, to be freed from the ever-present threat of sudden death at the hands of someone out to earn a reputation. There is none of that in Audie Murphy's John Gant. He is a man who enjoys his profession, he enjoys seeing people suffer and he enjoys killing. According to Graham, Murphy plays Gant as outlined in the script. Gant is calm, aloof, and expressionless, but a man whose eyes see all (Graham, 272). In fact, some fellow actors thought that Gant was like Murphy himself. Actress Linda Lawson spoke of his "quiet deadliness" (Nott, 111), and actor Morgan Woodward thought of Murphy's eyes as having a "deadly gleam, a deadly wild look" (Graham, 272).

Charles Drake plays Luke the physician, Murphy's opposite. He heals while Murphy kills, and in the dialogue between the two men, viewers hear Murphy's cynical justification for his actions. Murphy believes that people are basically hypocrites who are trying to hide or are running from something dreadful in their past. He observes to Drake, "Man's guilt is his own burden." And Murphy tells Drake that he is wasting his time trying to cure people — they are going to die anyway. While Murphy's Gant does not kill a single person in the entire film, he provokes three deaths and causes two or three other people to get shot by raising fear and anxiety in the entire town. Yet none of it seems to bother Murphy. It is not the immorality of his behavior that makes the film troubling; it is the amorality of Murphy's character. His matter-of-factness about death and his aloofness from the suffering he brings makes this a troubling, but very contemporary, Western. Yet, *No Name on the Bullet* is an excellent little film, and it is surprising that it has not received more critical acclaim (Nott, 112).

As the film reaches its climax, viewers learn that Murphy has come to Lordsburg to kill Edgar Stehli, playing Judge Benson. That judge and some former associates, now all high-placed public officials, had been involved in illegal activity, and the others are fearful that the judge will tell all he knows. When Joan Evans, playing Stehli's daughter, learns the truth about her father, she goes to Murphy's room to plead with him not to harm the old man because he has only a few weeks to live. Murphy won't be moved, and when Evans tries to kill him he takes the gun away from her. It is then that Murphy learns that Stehli will not resist; Murphy will have to murder him instead of making it appear as self-defense. If that happens, Stehli, as a former judge, knows Murphy will be tried and hanged for murder. But Murphy's Gant is too shrewd for that trick. He rips the front of Evans' dress, and when he goes to Stehli's house to kill him, Murphy makes the old man believe that he has raped Evans. The old man, in a fit of rage, gets his rifle and tries to shoot Murphy, but collapses and dies before Murphy can kill him. Graham is struck by the look on Murphy's face as he watches the old man collapse. He calls it "a terrible smile" (Graham, 273). That may be the most terrible moment in the entire film. The old man has just a few weeks to live, but Murphy was paid to kill him and he intends to do it. Not only does he intend to kill Stehli, Murphy's Gant appears to relish the task. Graham is right; one remembers that "terrible smile" after much of the film fades from memory.

Charles Drake and R.G. Armstrong (playing Drake's father) ride up in time to see that Stehli is dead, and Drake goes after Murphy with a blacksmith's hammer. Murphy shoots Drake in the shoulder, but Drake throws the heavy blacksmith hammer at Murphy and breaks his right — his gunhand — shoulder. It appears that Murphy will shoot Drake, but he simply climbs on his horse and rides away, observing that everything ends sometime. Murphy understands that his broken shoulder makes him vulnerable, and that he probably does not have long to live before someone guns him down. But that is all right because, in Gant's words, everyone has to die sometime. Even facing his own death, Murphy's Gant remains the aloof, detached human being that he had always been. Graham observes, "Audie's portrayal of a bored, cynical, world-weary gunfighter caught perfectly the flavor of his off-screen personality" (Graham, 274).

One can only speculate, but it is likely that World War II took a tremendous toll on Murphy's psyche. Certainly Audie Murphy was (and is) an American hero. It is also true that in the World War II campaigns in Italy and Southern France, Murphy was immersed in killing. Nearly all of his friends died. A lingering memory from the final frames of *To Hell and Back* (Universal-International, 1955), the film that celebrated Murphy's war exploits, is of the faces of his dead friends rolling across the screen at the Congressional Medal of Honor ceremony. The bored, cynical and detached nature of his off-screen personality was probably shaped during the war as a way of dealing with the deaths of so many friends.

Murphy's portrayal of John Gant, ostensibly the hero of *No Name on the Bullet*, is not the only notable thing about the film. Its view of humanity is also stark. Lordsburg is a town full of cowards, crooks and hypocrites. Warren Stevens plays a coward who ran off with another man's wife and is now sure Murphy came to kill him; but Stevens can't consummate a gunfight with Murphy that he provoked, so he leaves Lordsburg the coward that he really is. A banker commits suicide, convinced that Murphy has been hired by a local mine owner who knows that the banker is secretly trying to steal his mine. And so it goes. At one point in the film, Murphy observes to Drake that they are the only two honest men in Lordsburg.

No Name on the Bullet continues the trend toward cowardly, hypocritical townsfolk that first appeared in *High Noon*. That view stands in marked contrast to the image projected in nearly all pre–1955 B Westerns (Loy, 126). But the image of small-town westerners as cowards and hypocrites would continue to accelerate after 1955, reaching its apex in *High Plains Drifter* (Universal, 1973). It is not an image that has much historical truth. The decent, peaceful residents of Northfield, Minnesota, and Coffeyville, Kansas, demonstrated both courage and skill with firearms when the James/Younger and Dalton gangs tried to rob banks in their towns. Rather than rooted in nineteenth century history, the image of citizens as cowards and hypocrites reflects a 1950s country caught in the grips of McCarthy-like accusations and anti-communist hysteria. And it would continue into the troubled 1960s. Social change prompted by the civil rights movement, and political and social turmoil brought on by demonstrations for and against the war in Vietnam, seemed to underscore the notion that nobody was very honest.

That image continues in two other Murphy programmers, *Hell Bent for Leather* and *Posse from Hell*. The former opens as Jan Merlin, a cold-blooded killer, absconds with Murphy's horse. As Merlin rides away he drops his distinctively marked shotgun. Retrieving the gun, Murphy walks into a small settlement. The townsfolk are at a funeral for a couple that Merlin murdered, but when the stable keeper sees Murphy and the shotgun, he sends for help. The irate citizens, led by old-time cowboy star Allan Lane, are set to lynch Murphy when Stephen McNally, who one supposes is a United States Marshal, rides up and rescues Murphy. However, it turns out that McNally was only a deputy town marshal who had swept out the jail until he volunteered to track down Merlin. Now insane with the need to take someone back, he tries to kill Murphy and claim that he is Merlin.

Murphy escapes from McNally and kidnaps Felicia Farr, the daughter of a thief, and an outcast in her own right. Together they track down Merlin. The image that lingers from this film, however, is of a crazed marshal and a group of townsfolk so bent on revenge that they are unwilling

Audie Murphy and Felicia Farr escape in a buckboard in *Hell Bent for Leather* (1960).

to listen to reason, or to consider, until the very end of the film, that Murphy might be Clay Santell, as he claims and not Merlin's Travers.

If anything, the image of community is even starker in *Posse from Hell*. The film opens as four gunmen ride into a town, where they kill several citizens, leave the town marshal mortally wounded and take a girl, Zhora Lampert, with them when they ride away. Murphy, playing Banner Cole, a gunfighter, is a friend of the sheriff. As he dies, the sheriff challenges Murphy to do something right for once and go after the killers, "Not out of hate but out of likin'." He hands Murphy a badge and tells him that the town's citizens are good people who have been hurt. Murphy agrees to head up the posse, but he warns that it will not be easy to capture the four killers. Right away the character of the town begins to unfold, and it varies dramatically from the sheriff's words. Fewer men are willing to ride in the posse than one would suppose, and when Murphy makes it clear he will be in charge, several more of them back out.

Robert Keith, as Captain Brown, a Civil War veteran, typifies the community. Keith believes that his military experience ought to give him command, and he resents Murphy. At the posse's first encounter with what it thinks are the killers, Keith is afraid, goes crazy and starts to shoot wildly at innocent men. Clearly, Keith is not the Civil War hero he claims to be. He is an egotistical, cowardly hypocrite. Murphy sums it up when, as the men water their horses, he tells them, "None of you are worth a damn."

One by one, members of the posse drop off as the pursuit continues, until finally only Murphy and two others are left. The two others are John Saxon playing an easterner unskilled in weapons or horses who was shamed by his boss (a banker concerned only about the bank's money) into joining the posse, and Rudolph Acosta, appearing as an Indian who is constantly insulted and put down by Caucasian members of the posse. One of the posse members is a young would-be gunfighter who, at a shootout at a ranch house, dies because, while good at shooting at rocks, he can't kill a man face to face. Saxon, on the other hand, demonstrates remarkable courage, even if he is not a good shot. Both Saxon and Acosta, the town's two outcasts, so to speak, stick with Murphy to the end and help him kill the four outlaws. When Acosta is killed, Murphy remarks, "There were some good men here." The good men, however, were outsiders, men rejected or denigrated by the so-called respectable citizens.

The other striking element in the film is the treatment of Zhora Lampert. She runs into the saloon in which the four outlaws are holding hostages because her uncle is in there. The leering look on Henry Wills and Vic Morrow's faces suggest Lampert's fate. The four outlaws rape her, and the film, unlike Westerns prior to 1955, makes that very clear. When she is finally rescued, Lampert steals a gun and tries to kill herself. Murphy tells her that a gun is not the answer, and that she is just going to have to learn to live with it — "it" being not only the shame of the sexual assault but the attitude and the vicious gossip of the townsfolk.

After Acosta is murdered, Murphy and Saxon come upon the cabin in which Lampert and her uncle (Royal Dano) live. She is preparing to take a bath and invites Murphy to watch her undress and bathe; after all, she says, satisfying men is now the only thing she can do. Murphy scolds her for that attitude and tells her that as far as he is concerned she has never been touched.

The final shootout with the outlaws occurs around the cabin. Saxon breaks his leg when his horse is shot and falls on him. Murphy then kills Vic Morrow, who plays the leader of the outlaws. The wild look on Murphy's face as he pumps bullet after bullet into Morrow's body is reminiscent of the look on Randolph Scott's face as he kills the sheriff who murdered Berry Jr. in *Decision at Sundown*. Murphy then carries Saxon the three or so miles into town before he collapses.

When Murphy awakens more than a day later, Lampert is nursing him. When he asks her about the attitude of the townsfolk, she says it is worse than she expected, particularly from the women, underscoring a very negative and cynical image of human beings. When Murphy is offered the sheriff's position, two members of the town council (one of whom is the town banker) want to know what happened to the money, and they further question Murphy's reputation as a gunfighter. Murphy is prepared to turn down the offer and walk out when he remembers the words of his friend, the fallen sheriff: that there are a lot of good folks in the town. Murphy and Lampert walk to the cemetery together and as he gazes down at the grave of his friend, Murphy decides to take the job, remarking to Lampert, "There is always someone or something worthwhile. We just have to look hard enough." Unlike *No Name on the Bullet* or even *Hell Bent for Leather*, *Posse from Hell* ends on a positive note. The townsfolk have not changed (witness their attitude toward Lampert), but Murphy, as a result of the bravery of Acosta and Saxon, is no longer the cynical person he was when the pursuit commenced. He is now prepared to marry Lampert (herself a fallen woman in the eyes of society) and to become sheriff in a town in which he now sees something worthwhile.

Seven Ways from Sundown is even more like Murphy's pre–1955 films than *Posse from Hell*. Murphy's character, Seven Ways from Sundown Jones, pursues Barry Sullivan, who portrays the outlaw-killer Jim Flood. Sullivan plays the easygoing, likeable outlaw so recognizable in classic Western films. Murphy is the inexperienced Texas Ranger who comes to like Flood, but nevertheless brings him in.

Murphy's brother, Two Jones, had been a Texas Ranger and, unknown to Murphy, Sullivan was the one who had killed him. But Kenneth Tobey, playing Murphy's superior, had hid behind a rock rather than come to Two Jones' assistance. Tobey had sent the inexperienced Murphy with John McIntire to capture Sullivan. Tobey hoped that Sullivan would kill Murphy and thus spare Tobey the risk of being unmasked as a coward. Sullivan kills McIntire instead, and when Murphy brings Sullivan to the ranger station, Sullivan threatens to disclose Tobey's secret. Tobey lets Sullivan out of jail, with the hope that he will escape, but Sullivan kills Tobey before he escapes. Sullivan eludes the posse and returns to try to convince Murphy to go with him; Murphy refuses and, in the final shootout, kills Sullivan. Justice, in good B Western fashion, has been served. Tobey gets his for failing to protect a fellow ranger, and Sullivan, the outlaw and killer, dies as well.

Both *Seven Ways from Sundown* and *Posse from Hell* suggest the more optimistic outlook of the Kennedy years looming on the horizon in 1960 and 1961 (see Chapter Three). But both films also indicate the value confusion of the 1950s. Were people primarily cowards and hypocrites, such as the citizens of Lordsburg in *No Name on the Bullet* and the posse in *Posse from Hell*, or were they more like those living in Sundown? John Carroll had duped them, but Randolph Scott had awakened their guilt, and they responded by chasing Carroll out of town. In either case, neither set of townsfolk resembles citizens in pre–1955 B Westerns, who always rallied to help the cowboy hero round up the bad guys.

A changing view of the hero had emerged by the late 1950s as well. While the new hero was unlike John Gant in *No Name on the Bullet*, and not as alienated as Scott's character in *Decision at Sundown*, he was more of a loner, someone who had little faith in his fellow human beings. Randolph Scott's roles in *Ride Lonesome* and *Comanche Station*, and Audie Murphy's characters in *Hell Bent for Leather* and *Posse from Hell*, suggest that a new type of hero was emerging from the American cultural landscape. The new hero was something of a loner, a harder individual less easily moved by tragedy, more cynical, a man by and large incapable of being fully human.

The majority of Westerns produced prior to 1955 had projected positive images of community. Family was valued, and the inhabitants of the small-town West were presented as brave folk who cared about the community in which they lived. In turn, the hero was someone who lived in the community and helped its inhabitants overcome whatever evil befell them, or a person who rode into town and organized and energized local resistance to the bad guys. As an outsider, the hero might agree to become part of the community and marry the heroine, or, more often than not, he would ride away with a friendly wave to his new friends. Whatever the case, the films affirmed the importance of community, and the hero was seen as a central element in that relationship. Community as inhabited by brave, resolute people, people who were allies and friends of the hero, diminished considerably after 1955. The post–1955 films of Scott and Murphy discussed above are evidence of that trend.

The Randolph Scott and Audie Murphy Westerns of the late 1950s, 1960 and 1961 highlight changes occurring in American culture. John Kennedy, in his 1960 presidential campaign, promised to get the country moving again by breaking from the conservative qualities that dominated the 1950s. And in his 1961 inaugural address, Kennedy spoke of the torch of leadership being passed to a new generation of Americans. In 1960 and 1961 it was unclear what all of that meant. Standing in the first decade of the twenty-first century it is easy to see that the 1960s were crucial years, years in which the nation transitioned from values and perspectives that had dominated the country from the "roaring twenties" to values and perspectives that would dominate the country to the end of the millennium. As was the case throughout the twentieth century, Western films mirrored that change. Randolph Scott and Audie Murphy were late 1950s and early 1960s prophets. Their films, while retaining much of the old, pointed to the future of American culture.

Chapter 2

THE DESCENT OF THE HERO

Literary scholar Alfred Kazan wrote in the 1955 Postscript to his *On Native Grounds*, "The key word in our time is not rebellion but knowledge. Man's very nature is a predicament to him; and society is...but a collection of people whose own traditions are dead, and who are looking for convictions" (Kazan, 411). Westerns after 1955 began to underscore that predicament and searching, as they included more controversial themes such as racial prejudice, marital infidelity, rape, cowardly citizens, emotionally deranged characters and graphic violence. Those elements had never been entirely absent from Westerns prior to 1955, but after that year the implicit and the suggested became more explicit. Viewer imagination was relied upon less and less as the screen made obvious things only hinted at prior to 1955. As a consequence, images of the hero began to change, and Westerns after 1955 reflected more and more the descent of the hero.

In his 1976 book *The Filming of the West*, Jon Tuska labeled an important contemporary trend in the genre as "Westerns without heroes" (Tuska 1976, 559) and George N. Fenin and William K. Everson, commenting on Gregory Peck's role in *The Bravados* (TCR, 1958), describe Peck as a "tyrant hero" (Fenin and Everson, 337). While Tuska, and Fenin and Everson, recognize that depictions of the hero changed dramatically, the latter's description may be more apt than Tuska's. Westerns of the late 1950s and 1960s had heroes, but they were different from traditional western heroes. Northrop Frye in *The Anatomy of Criticism* offers a typology of the hero that is useful in exploring that difference. The typology formulated by Frye applied specifically to literature, and it concerned only the actions of the hero, but it can be adapted to Western films and the moral qualities of people as well (Frye, 33–34). Central to Frye's typology is the notion that, since the late nineteenth century, the hero has become increasingly complex and less heroic in United States and European literature.

According to Frye, a Type One hero is one who differs in *kind* (italics mine) from other people and the environment. The divine beings of Greek and Roman mythology, as well as leading personalities in the Christian Old and New Testaments, are examples of this kind of hero, but they hardly fit a discussion of Western films.

A Type Two hero is one who is superior in *degree* (italics mine) from other people and the environment because the hero is not "bound by ordinary laws of nature" (Frye, 34). The hero is one who can, for instance, talk to animals and who possesses prodigious amounts of strength and endurance. In addition, films portraying this type of hero often feature witches and sorcery (Frye, 34). Type Two film and literary heroes include Tarzan, Superman, Captain Marvel, Merlin the Magician in the King Arthur legends and figures in recent fantasy films such as *The Beastmaster* (MGM, 1983).

Type Three heroes differ in degree from other people but are like them in relation to the environment. The hero is a leader whose ability to persuade originates in charismatic qualities that attract other people to him, or in rational-legal authority that provides a basis for action or tradition, such as the male authority figure in a family (Loy, 103–104). Even though the hero is a leader, he or she is never free from criticism, and is one whose actions are always under close scrutiny. The traditional cowboy heroes of the 1930s and 1940s were Type Three heroes. Type Three heroes figure prominently in film and fiction of the romantic mood. Bigger-than-life heroes who always get the pretty girl, and upbeat endings mark films in which Type Three heroes appear.

A Type Four hero is one who is superior to neither other people nor his environment. He shares a common humanity with other players in the drama, subject to the same drives, temptations and behavior patterns as anyone else. Westerns featuring this type of hero became more common in the early 1950s. The central characters in Randolph Scott's *Comanche Station* (Columbia, 1960) and *The Tall T* (Columbia, 1957), Gregory Peck's *The Gunfighter* (20th Century–Fox, 1950), and James Stewart's *The Naked Spur* (MGM, 1953) are good examples of this type of hero. Realism in film and fiction is the hallmark of this type.

Finally, the Type Five hero is someone with *inferior* (italics mine) moral qualities; he is someone others look down on and hold in contempt or fear. Audie Murphy in *No Name on the Bullet* (Universal-International,

1959) and Randolph Scott in *Ride Lonesome* (Columbia, 1959) suggest how this type can be employed in a Western. Joel McCrea and Randolph Scott in *Ride the High Country* (MGM, 1962; a film discussed at length in Chapter 3) offer binary images of a Type Three hero (McCrea) and one who lacks the moral qualities characteristic of Types Four and Five (Scott). Naturalism is often the mood of film and fiction featuring Type Five characters. The world is presented as an amoral, messy place — one in which people are moved to act only for selfish reasons, a place of conflict in which human relationships frequently mirror the animal kingdom, and only the strongest survive.

While never totally absent before 1955, as one moves further from that year and closer to 2000, Type Four and Five heroes become much more prevalent in Westerns. The hero often was shaped by forces that affect the rest of humanity. Heredity, environment, blind chance and human drives are elements exploited by the films to explain the ostensible hero's motivations, actions and moral qualities (or lack thereof). In that manner, Western films after 1955 increasingly borrowed from American literature's realism and naturalism of the late nineteenth century onward. In a literal sense, the western hero descended from his lofty perch as one who possessed heroic leadership qualities to William Munny sliding around in the muck of his hog pen in *Unforgiven* (Warner Brothers, 1992; see Chapter 5). A number of the 1950s and 1960s Western films of James Stewart, Gregory Peck, Gary Cooper and Glenn Ford are good cases studies of the descent of the hero. However, in order to obtain a clearer notion of that descent, some attention to a few of their Westerns prior to 1955 is helpful.

The best of James Stewart's Westerns are the five he made for director Anthony Mann from 1950 to 1955. Douglas Pye, in "The Collapse of Fantasy: Masculinity in the Westerns of Anthony Mann," argues that the setting for the Mann films is one of social change. Quoting John Cawelti, Pye believes that Stewart's Mann Westerns are about the transformation of the Old West into modern society and "the hero's increasing complex and ambiguous relationship to that process" (Pye, 168). If the change Pye finds is understood as moral change, there is a great deal of truth in his comment. On the other hand, if Pye has in mind a time dimension, his comment is not an accurate description of the films. The movies themselves, with the exception of *The Far Country* (Universal-International, 1955), are set squarely in the Old West. *Winchester '73* (Universal-International, 1950) and *Bend of the River* (Universal-International, 1952) occur in the 1870s, and *The Naked Spur* has a post–Civil War 1868 setting. Surely *The Man from Laramie* (Columbia, 1955) is about the Old West, a place ruled by the power of the strong, and a father's fear that his son is too weak to hold what the father has built.

In fact, Stewart's Mann films are not about socially transforming events that force the Old West to give way to the modern era (unlike *The Man Who Shot Liberty Valence* [Paramount, 1962; discussed in Chapter 3]); rather, they are about the psychological reactions of the main characters as events and circumstances thrust them into situations mostly beyond their control. Above all, Stewart's Anthony Mann films are character studies; they grapple with a changing understanding of what it means to be a hero.

Douglas Pye offers two further observations about Stewart's characters in his Mann Westerns. For one, in all five of the films Stewart is a wandering man. Stewart's characters appear to be escaping from either the responsibilities of civilization or from the past. With the obvious exception of *Bend of the River*, Stewart is not a man concerned with bringing civilization to the frontier wilderness. Pye also notes that Stewart's characters possess the same qualities as do the villains. In Mann's Westerns, as in life, all of the characters are flawed in some manner and to some degree.

Jon Tuska, in *The American West in Film: Critical Approaches to the Western*, adds that Mann's Westerns are not about the natural order but about the moral order. With the exception of *Winchester '73*, the films were shot in color and on location. The natural beauty and, at times, the stark barrenness of the locations make the films aesthetically attractive. But, as Tuska observes, the films are not about the unity of the natural and moral orders; quite the contrary, the moral order is frequently at odds with the natural order. Stewart's heroes are ones who must overcome harsh natural impediments, such as high mountains, towering cliffs, narrow mountain trails and rushing rivers.

As Stewart's characters work to overcome the natural obstacles before them, Tuska argues that the characters are neurotic; they are obsessed and driven by self-doubt and "emotional eccentricity" (Tuska 1985, 88). They are also loners. With the exception of *Bend of the River*, Stewart is not part of any community and displays no desire to become one. But, Tuska also notes, unlike in other so-called "adult" Westerns, Stewart usually has a sidekick. Millard Mitchell served that role in *Winchester '73* and *The Naked Spur*, while J.C. Flippen and Wallace Ford were sidekick-like characters in *Bend of the River* and *The Man from Laramie* respectively. And, of course, Walter Brennan, giving his usual fine performance, played Stewart's sidekick in *The Far Country*. Even though Stewart's sidekicks are generally unlike 1930s and 1940s sidekicks (with the exception of Brennan and possibly Mitchell in *Winchester '73*), they do soften the neurotic qualities of Stewart's main characters.

William R. Meyer, in *The Making of the Great Westerns*, adds to Tuska's description of Stewart's characters as neurotic by observing that they were also laconic; like Clint Eastwood, Stewart's dialogue tends to be sparse. He is not given to long, philosophical speeches; rather, Stewart replies in short, direct sentences. Meyer goes on to fittingly describe Stewart as projecting a "tense, sometimes passionate screen persona" (Meyer, 253).

Historian William Manchester describes the United States by the mid–1950s as a "rootless" place. For example, he notes that a Montgomery Ward executive and his family had moved twenty-eight times in twenty-six years (Manchester, 781). But to compensate for that rootlessness, people became joiners. As political scientist Robert Putnam argues in *Bowling Alone: The Collapse and Revival of American Community*, mid–1950s rootless existence did not lead to social isolation because people joined all sorts of community organizations, from the Red Cross to the PTA. With social joining, however, came a need to conform. Suburban life was one of over-organized and regulated conformity.

In writing about the last four years of the Eisenhower Administration, Manchester titles the chapter "The Crusade Falters," and so it did. In many ways the films Jimmy Stewart made with Anthony Mann in the 1950s can be read as reactions to the joining, conforming and over-organized qualities of American life in the 1950s. Stewart's characters in all five films were rebelling against those trends. However, the Mann pictures are not neatly linear in progression. That is, Stewart's characters in the five movies do not regress consistently from Type Three heroes to Types Four and Five. But in all five films Stewart offers viewers a hero that differed from traditional images of the hero in Westerns up to 1950.

Winchester '73 is a story pitting brother against brother. The title of the film suggests that it is about a gun, and to some extent it is. But the Winchester rifle is mostly a gimmick, somewhat reminiscent of Saturday matinee serials that often included a search for some object or place. The rifle serves that purpose in *Winchester '73*. Shifting ownership provides continuity between diverse sections of the film. Even though Stephen McNally steals the Winchester from James Stewart, the film is about Stewart's relentless search for McNally, the man who killed their father. It traces the rifle as it changes hands, but always Stewart's search for Stephen McNally is the central focus of *Winchester '73*.

In *Winchester '73* Stephen McNally and James Stewart are brothers, but in the words of Millard Mitchell, Stewart's sidekick, McNally was "just plain bad." He had shot and killed his father when the old man refused to hide him from a posse after McNally robbed a bank. Later in the film, viewers understand the meanness in McNally when he humiliates Charles Drake in front of Shelley Winters by making Drake put on an apron and serve coffee; and McNally does the same to Dan Duryea when he forces the latter to give up the Winchester rifle.

Why McNally turned bad, whereas Stewart did not, is never explained in the film. Was it heredity? Is *Winchester '73* a parallel to John Steinbeck's widely acclaimed *East of Eden* in which genetic causation is the hinted explanation of the "bad" brother's behavior? Was it some facet of the social environment, or just plain chance? The questions remain unanswered; viewers must do with the fact that McNally is just plain bad.

Stewart, the good son, is on a mission to revenge his father's death by killing his brother. But the mission has become an obsession. When McNally and his two friends flee Dodge City after assaulting Stewart and stealing the Winchester rifle that Stewart had won in a shooting contest, Stewart and Mitchell give chase. Stewart is sure the three will head for Riker's store, but Stewart and Mitchell have been on the trail, riding hard. Mitchell wants to stop and rest, but Stewart insists that they push on. Once they arrive at Riker's store and discover that the three outlaws were heading for Tascosa, Stewart won't even permit Mitchell to eat; they start immediately for Tascosa. Mitchell underscores the Type Four nature of Stewart's character when he says about the hunt to find and kill McNally, "You're beginning to like it."

The climactic rifle battle between Stewart and NcNally also distinguishes *Winchester '73* from Westerns of the 1930s and 1940s. Not only is the fight itself well staged and entertaining, its conclusion is strikingly different. On occasion, B Westerns of the 1930s and 1940s used the brother against brother theme (*The Saga of Death Valley* [Republic, 1939] and *Fugitive from Sonora* [Republic, 1943] spring immediately to mind), but the small-budget programmers seldom, if ever, had one brother purposely kill the other brother; in fact, normally the two brothers reconciled before the "bad" brother died. Not so in *Winchester '73*; Stewart and McNally revel in the opportunity to kill one another. McNally taunts Stewart, temporarily trapped in an exposed position, reminding Stewart that their father had taught them not to let that happen. And in the final scene of the battle, Stewart takes careful aim and kills McNally when the latter rises up and exposes his location on top of a boulder.

Stewart had his revenge; McNally is dead. But now what for Stewart? Will he try to establish a relationship with Shelley Winters? Will he and

Millard Mitchell go back home and become ranchers? Or has the pursuit of McNally so consumed Stewart that he will never be able to live a normal life? Unlike the upbeat ending of most 1930s and 1940s Westerns, *Winchester '73* never answers any of those questions, but viewers are left with the haunting fear that it is the latter. McNally is physically dead, but maybe Stewart, having finished the task of killing McNally, a task that burned deep in his psyche, is emotionally dead. In large part, it is that uncertainty that makes Stewart's character in *Winchester '73* a Type Four hero.

However, in *Bend of the River* Stewart's Glenn McLyntock is a Type Three hero, but one with a more complex nature than the traditional 1930s and 1940s Western heroes. Stewart is a man running from his past. He had been a raider along the Kansas-Missouri border, and at one point nearly had been lynched by a group of irate citizens (his life was spared only because the rope broke). *Bend of the River* opens as Stewart leads a group of homesteaders to the Oregon Territory. He hopes to settle with them, bury his outlaw past and start a new life.

Early in the action, Stewart saves Arthur Kennedy from a lynch party, but Kennedy, who also had been a border raider, recognizes Stewart. The two men strike up a friendship and fight Indians together, but Kennedy understands that Stewart is trying to run from his past. At one point Kennedy asks Stewart what he is running from. Stewart replies that he is running from Glenn McLyntock, prompting Kennedy to ask the inevitable question: "What happens when he catches up with you?" On the ultimate level *Bend of the River* is about that question: can a man really change or does his past always catch up with him? J.C. Flippen adds his opinion to the mix while he and Stewart sort apples. Flippen, who does not like Kennedy because he recognizes him as a border raider, observes that people are a lot like apples— one rotten apple can spoil the whole barrel. You have to throw out the rotten one in order to save the rest of the barrel. Stewart can only respond that people are not the same as apples. But are they?

Kennedy, it turns out, is indeed like Flippen's rotten apple. When the promised supplies do not arrive from Portland, Stewart and Flippen go after them. Once in Portland, they learn that gold fever has swept the area. But they get the supplies and start over the mountains to the settlement. Stewart drives the men obsessively hard because they need to get the provisions to the settlement before the snows come and the food runs out. However, Kennedy threatens to disclose Stewart's real identity unless he agrees to take the supplies to the gold camp, where they can make far more money, instead of the settlement. Stewart won't do it, even with the threat of disclosure hanging over his head.

Kennedy and the rest of the crew, driven by greed, hijack the wagons, leave Stewart stranded and head for the mining camps. As they pull away, with Flippen and Julia Adams (who plays his daughter) prisoners aboard one of the wagons, Stewart tells Kennedy, "You will be seeing me." Flippen and Adams free a horse for Stewart, who is following the wagons on foot, and Stewart gets a gun. In a brutal climactic fight, Stewart kills Kennedy and delivers the wagons to the settlement before the winter snow, saving the people from starvation.

In thanking Stewart, Flippen acknowledges, "I was wrong, there is a difference between apples and men." Stewart, the former border raider, has a new life. As the film ends, he is set to marry Julia Adams and begin afresh in the Oregon Territory. Even though Stewart's character is more complex — more adult-like — his resolve to start a new life is realized. In that sense, *Bend of the River* is much more like traditional Westerns than the other four Stewart made with Anthony Mann.

Stewart's Type Three hero in *Bend of the River* gives way to a mean-spirited, amoral Type Five character in *The Naked Spur*. Stewart, a bounty hunter of sorts, is chasing Robert Ryan for the reward money. But he wants the money for a specific reason. As the Civil War began, Stewart thought a woman (Mary) was in love with him and would marry him after the war was over. So he deeded over his ranch to her, but she sold the ranch and ran off with another man. Now the ranch is for sale again, and Stewart intends to use the reward money to buy it back.

The cast includes Janet Leigh (Ryan's girlfriend, who ran away with him), Millard Mitchell (a prospector haunted by the desire to find a big strike) and Ralph Meeker (an Army deserter fleeing from Indians after raping an Indian woman). As Stewart, Mitchell and Meeker escort Ryan (and Leigh) back for the reward, they have to overcome the natural environment (mountain ranges, raging rivers and Indians), their distrust of each other fueled by Ryan's caustic, barbed comments, and Stewart's maniacal drive to get the reward money so he can buy back his ranch.

For Stewart, Ryan is no longer a human being; he is just a sack of money. There is no concern to take Ryan back to stand trial for his crimes. Greed, not justice, motivates Stewart, Mitchell and Meeker. Stewart wants land, Mitchell a new grubstake so he can continue his search for the bonanza that he knows awaits him, and Meeker just wants to escape the Army's clutches. None of the three (including Stewart, the star and ostensible hero of *The Naked Spur*) possess moral qualities that distinguish them very much from Ryan, the villain of the film.

Ryan plays on Mitchell's fantasy about a rich gold mine by convincing the old man that he — Ryan — knows where it is. Mitchell frees Ryan and, together with Leigh, they escape Stewart and Meeker. But Ryan kills Mitchell and waits on top of a mesa for Meeker and Stewart, who Ryan knows will come after him. Leigh begins to see Ryan for the killer that he is, and when she tries to stop him from shooting Stewart and Meeker, Ryan hits her, knocking her unconscious. Stewart kills Ryan, but his body drops into a raging, fast flowing river below the mesa. Meeker goes after the body — after all, the reward was for dead or alive — but is swept away and killed trying to retrieve Ryan from the raging current. Stewart, however, is able to get Ryan's body on a boulder beside the river and is prepared to return him for the reward money.

When Janet Leigh pleads with Stewart to give it up, to let the river have Ryan's dead body and go to California with her, Stewart, with a wild look in his eyes, refuses. "I am taking him back, he is going to pay for my land." "All I care about is the money, that is the way I am," Stewart tells Leigh. But even with Stewart's obsessive drive to reclaim his land, there is some humanity left in him. Stewart begins to cry, "I am going to sell him for money." Stewart can't believe that someone could still love him, and that Janet Leigh was willing to go to California with him. At the conclusion of *The Naked Spur* a chastened James Stewart and Janet Leigh leave Robert Ryan's body to the river and ride toward California together. The Type Five character that Stewart has played throughout *The Naked Spur* has become a Type Four hero. Still possessing few of the Type Three moral qualities of a hero, Stewart has nonetheless recovered a bit of his humanity. The promise of redemption hangs in the air. But then, it is a long way to California...

The Far Country opens as James Stewart (Jeff) drives a herd of cattle destined for the Alaska gold fields to Seattle. Along the way, two of the drovers he hired tried to rustle the cattle, and Stewart had killed them. After the cattle are loaded onto a steamer, and Stewart and his sidekick, Walter Brennan, are aboard, the sheriff comes to arrest Stewart for murder. Ruth Roman hides Stewart in her cabin, and in an exchange between the two one gets a sense of Stewart's character. He asks Roman why she hid him, adding, "Nobody ever did anything for nothing." Roman replies that she might need a favor some day, and when Stewart asks her what she wants, Roman tells him to just say thanks. Stewart's response — saying that is a term he seldom uses— marks him as a Type Five character.

His approach to life is "I take care of me." As he and Roman ride along the trail to the gold fields together, they hear a lone wolf. Stewart tells her that he never trusts anybody and he never asks for anything, just like the lone wolf. When Roman and her party head out over a glacier, they get caught in a snow slide. Stewart, who had chosen to go the long way around to the gold fields in order to avoid the glacier, refuses to go back to help the victims of the snow slide. At this point in *The Far Country*, Walter Brennan emerges as Stewart's conscience. When, at first, Stewart refuses to go back to help, Brennan tells him, "You are wrong, Jeff. You gotta help them." Here Brennan reprises a role he first played in *Red River* (United Artists, 1948). Just as his response to John Wayne in that film was frequently, "You are wrong, Mr. Dunson," so Brennan frequently reminds Stewart of his moral shortcomings in *The Far Country*. Even though Stewart goes back to help the victims, his expressed Type Five philosophy remained "I don't need other people, I don't need help. I can take care of myself."

That philosophy plays out at several points throughout *The Far Country*. On arriving at Dawson, Stewart sells his cattle to Roman, who outbid Connie Gilchrist (Hominy) and Kathleen Freeman (Grits). It is clear to Stewart that Roman is a corrupt woman who operates a saloon/gambling house and murders and steals from the prospectors, but that makes no difference — she offered him more money for the cattle. When the Northwest Mounted Police ask the people to appoint a sheriff until they can establish a post, the residents of Dawson ask Stewart to take the job. His selfish reply is, "I'm not interested." And he stands by when Robert C. Wilkie kills Chubby Johnson and forces J.C. Flippen, the sheriff, to back down in disgrace. The people of Dawson talk about staying through the winter and starting a real town, but Stewart remains aloof from those sentiments. As he and Brennan pack up their gold to leave by a river passage Stewart has discovered, he tells Brennan, "We got ours and I am getting out."

However, Brennan had talked too much in Roman's saloon. John McIntire's gang of outlaws waylay Stewart and Brennan as they are about to board a raft that Stewart had built for the trip down river. Brennan is killed and Stewart left for dead. McIntire, Roman and their gang now control Dawson and move the miners off of their claims. Stewart slowly recovers from his wounds and heads to Roman's saloon for a showdown. But the victims of McIntire and Roman's treachery are not impressed. They throw Stewart's words back at him; however, he is able to convince them to fight for what rightfully belongs to them.

In a final climactic gunfight, Stewart kills Wilkie, Jack Elam and McIntire. When Roman tries to warn Stewart that McIntire is coming out a side door, McIntire shoots her. Stewart asks the dying woman, "Crazy fool, why didn't you take care of yourself?" The rest of the good folks round up the gang at Roman's saloon, and the film ends with a promise that law and order has come to Dawson. It may even be that Stewart is going to marry Corinne Calvert and become part of the community, but that remains unclear. Just as in *The Naked Spur*, Stewart's character has changed somewhat, but unlike *Bend of the River* (where it was clear that Stewart has relegated his past to the past and had become a new man), *The Far Country* ends on an ambivalent note. In fact, Stewart's comment to a dying Ruth Roman suggests that he had not changed much at all.

Unlike *The Naked Spur* and *The Far Country*, films that featured Stewart as a Type Five (or, at best, a Type Four) character, *The Man from Laramie* finds Stewart a mixture of Type Three and Type Four characteristics. Stewart's Will Lockhart is a man with many admirable traits. On leave from the army, Stewart is trying to find the man who, indirectly at least, was responsible for his brother's death by selling guns to the Apaches. Throughout *The Man from Laramie* Stewart plays an easygoing, friendly person. At first, he likes Arthur Kennedy (portraying the foreman of the Barb, the biggest ranch in the area), and he gets along with Donald Crisp (owner of the Barb), who pays him for the wagons and mules Crisp's son, Alex Nicol, killed and burned.

But there is a darker side to Stewart's character in *The Man from Laramie* as well, one that appeared frequently in Stewart's previous four Anthony Mann films. For example, when Stewart finds the man who sold guns to the Apaches, he intends to kill him, not turn him over to the authorities for due process. Initially, he refused Aline MacMahon's offer to become foreman of the Half-Moon, the only ranch not controlled by the Barb. Being foreman would detract from his mission to find and kill the man who sold guns to the Apaches. When Donald Crisp tells Stewart of his dream that a tall man is coming to kill Alex Nicol, his son, Stewart only replies, "I have grief enough of mine without taking on yours." In short, Stewart's Will Lockhart is a man obsessed with a mission (find and kill the man responsible for his brother's death), and one unable to sympathize very much with other people's troubles. The self-centeredness one finds in Stewart's characters in *Winchester '73*, *The Naked Spur* and *The Far Country*, though somewhat muted, carries over to *The Man from Laramie*.

As the film unfolds, Stewart senses that the whole area is about to explode. Donald Crisp is going blind, but Alex Nicol is not man enough to take over for his father. Crisp understands that, and he tells Nicol so. Arthur Kennedy warns, "When the wolves learn that the old man is blind, people will move in and tear the place apart." But Nicol is a spoiled son, uninterested in the hard work of running a ranch and jealous of Kennedy. Nicol also has a sadistic streak. Not only did he enjoy burning Stewart's wagons and killing his mules at the beginning of *The Man from Laramie*,

James Stewart plays a Type Four hero in *The Man from Laramie* (1955).

when he catches Stewart alone, Nicol takes revenge for a beating Stewart gave him by shooting Stewart in his gun hand. Stewart's cry in agony, "You scum," accurately describes Nicol's character throughout the film. Cathy O'Donnell is in love with Kennedy, but she is beginning to have doubts about him. When she suggests to Stewart that the trouble all began when he showed up, Stewart's reply is, "My coming had nothing to do with the trouble here."

The final confrontations are set: Kennedy and Nicol (who are running guns to the Indians), Kennedy and Crisp, and Stewart and Kennedy. Kennedy kills Nicol when he can't dissuade Nicol from selling a great many more guns to the Apaches. Nicol does not care that they will kill women and children. Kennedy then blames Stewart for killing Nicol, but he can't make the charge stick. Crisp discovers a bill for wire fence and begins to surmise that his son was selling guns to the Apaches, so he forces Kennedy to go with him in search of the guns. Kennedy, fearful that the old man will find them, pushes him off a cliff. Stewart finds the now completely blind Crisp and returns him to the Half-Moon so Aline MacMahon can nurse him back to health. Stewart then goes hunting for Kennedy.

Stewart tracks down Kennedy, who has had a change of heart and is trying to signal the Apaches to come and get the guns. Stewart forces Kennedy to help him push the wagon over the cliff. The Indians coming for the guns see the wagon go over the cliff and believe that Kennedy has betrayed them. Stewart prepares to kill Kennedy, but Kennedy pleads with Stewart to tell him what he has done to Stewart; Kennedy reckons a man has a right to know what he is about to die for. Stewart, however, can't kill him; he can only utter, "Get away from me." So Kennedy rides away to be killed by the Apaches. Stewart, his mission accomplished, rides away, back to his post at Laramie. But as he goes he reminds Cathy O'Donnell that he will be at Fort Laramie should she take a notion to ride that way.

The descent of the hero is not clearly linear in the five Westerns Anthony Mann directed, but it is a descent nevertheless. In two of the films, *The Naked Spur* and *The Far Country*, Stewart portrays a Type Five character. He is a self-centered, egocentric, amoral individual, one who is morally inferior to most of the other characters. In both films, it is impossible to make a clear distinction between Stewart's character traits and those of the villains. *Winchester '73* and *The Man from Laramie* offer a Type Four hero; Stewart's characters have much in common with others in the drama. He is a vulnerable hero who can be harmed by the villains, and he experiences the same temptations and emotions as other people. Rather than a bigger-than-life cowboy hero, Stewart's characters in these two films are human beings confronted with difficult assignments and the need to overcome substantial obstacles. They react to the human and environmental forces confounding them much as any other person would. It is Stewart's characters' humanity that sets them off as Type Four heroes in both *Winchester '73* and *The Man from Laramie*. Only in *Bend of the River* does Stewart's Glen McLyntock exhibit those traits one normally associates with cowboy heroes of the 1930s and 1940s.

After the five films James Stewart made under the direction of Anthony Mann, he starred in several other Westerns. Three of them are of interest in understanding the descent of the hero in 1950s and 1960s Westerns: *Night Passage* (Universal-International, 1957), *Two Rode Together* (Columbia, 1961) and *Fire Creek* (Warner Brothers, 1968). All three pictures demonstrate that the descent of the hero in Stewart's films was not confined to Anthony Mann's Westerns.

Viewers meet James Stewart in *Night Passage* as he rides into a construction camp at the end of the rails. Stewart was once a troubleshooter for the railroad and set to marry a handsome woman; but he lost his job when he permitted his brother, Audie Murphy (playing the Utica Kid), to escape after stealing money from the railroad, and he lost his woman to J.C. Flippen, owner of the line. Now Stewart is forced to play his accordion and live on the nickels and dimes people drop into his hat. One senses Stewart's desperate straits when he remarks, "A lot of things used to belong to me, somehow I lost them." Far from a bigger-than-life hero, Stewart is an impoverished man searching for self-respect and trying to reclaim his good name and his job.

Dan Duryea's gang has held up three straight payrolls. The workers are threatening to quit unless they are paid, and Flippen is desperate to prevent further holdups; so he offers to Stewart the job of getting the payroll through to the end of the line. Stewart, who sees a chance to get his old job back, agrees. However, unknown to anyone, a clerk working out of Flippen's private car is in cahoots with the outlaws; when he tries to warn them that Stewart will be carrying the $10,000, he is unable to connect with Robert C. Wilkie, a member of the gang, who is supposed to get the information to Duryea.

When Duryea's gang stops the train, they can't find the money. Stewart hid it in a box young Brandon de Wilde carries. Earlier in *Night Passage*, Stewart had stopped Wilkie from roping de Wilde on the trail, and the young boy had sort of adopted Stewart, who promises him a job as waterboy at the end of the line. Foiled in his effort to get the payroll, Duryea takes Flippen's wife, Elaine Stewart, and holds her for $10,000 ransom.

Stewart trails the gang to an old abandoned mining town and, because everyone he knew had been fired from the railroad, pretends to join up with the gang. But in a private conversation with Audie Murphy, Stewart tells his brother that he still works for the railroad and that he has come to get the payroll (Duryea and his gang had taken de Wilde, along with Elaine Stewart). Stewart tries to convince Murphy to quit the gang, but Murphy scoffs at the good-versus-evil lecture. Murphy, in a speech reminiscent of his character in *No Name on the Bullet* (Universal-International, 1959), tells Stewart, "I like to steal. I like to see what happens when I take it away from them." But as Stewart plays his accordion, he sings the bullfrog railroad song that was a favorite of their father's.

As Stewart plays his accordion, the railroad clerk comes to the hideout to get his share of the payroll and discloses to the gang that Stewart was carrying it. In the shootout that follows, the saloon burns, and with it Stewart's accordion. The burning accordion suggests that that part of Stewart's life is past, that he is about to reclaim his self-respect and his job. At the conclusion of *Night Passage* the outlaw gang is killed, Duryea shoots Murphy and Stewart kills Duryea. As Murphy dies in Stewart's arms, he admits that the bullfrog railroad song had won him over. After all, it was their father's favorite tune.

At the conclusion of *Night Passage* Stewart has regained his good name and the workers are paid. Elaine Stewart returns to her husband, and Brandon de Wilde is set to become a waterboy. Happy endings abound; but throughout the film Stewart's character is very human, motivated by resentment and anger. In short, he is a Type Four hero.

According to Ronald Davis, John Ford regarded *Two Rode Together* (Columbia, 1961) as "the worst piece of crap I've done in twenty years" (Davis 1995, 302). And, Davis adds, "The film is by far the most cynical Western the director had made" (Davis 1995, 306). Whether or not those judgments are too harsh, one thing is certain: *Two Rode Together* is not an enjoyable or well-made film.

The antics of the Kleg brothers, played by Harry Carey Jr. and Ken Curtis, who repeats the character he played in *The Searchers* (Warner Brothers, 1956; a role he would make famous as Festus on television's *Gunsmoke*), are distracting. The uncouth, ill-mannered conduct of the two in provoking a brawl with Richard Widmark adds nothing to the film, not even humor. Ford, who had used Woody Strode so effectively in *Sergeant Rutledge* (Warner Brothers, 1960), wastes his talent as the unbelievable Stone Calf in *Two Rode Together*. The manner in which Strode, who believes that the buffalo shield has made him immune to white men's bullets, rushes into Stewart's camp — only to be gunned down with ease by Stewart — is a farcical moment in the film.

The story line of *Two Rode Together* is quite simple. A group of white folks who have had children, spouses or kin kidnapped by Comanches are at Fort Grant seeking assistance in finding their lost relations. John McIntire, commander of the post, sends Richard Widmark and a cavalry escort to Tascosa to secure the services of James Stewart, who knows Quanah Parker and has traded with the Comanches.

But the settlers themselves are a troubling lot. Davis notes about *Two Rode Together*, "Community is no longer viewed as a potential vehicle for good, but rather as the cause of evil and pain" (Davis 1995, 306). The pain is evident in the emotionally disturbed woman who sees every 16- or 17-year-old Indian as her kidnapped son; in John Qualen as Ole Knudsen, who continues searching for his young daughter Frieda 10 or more years after the Comanches took her; and in Shirley Jones, who can't live with the guilt that she hid while the Comanches kidnapped her younger brother.

The evil unfolds in the lynching of a young Indian man. Stewart and Widmark had returned him to Fort Grant, and, in order to satisfy his emotionally disturbed wife, Cliff Lyons (as William McCandless) agreed to take the boy, even though no one knew his real identity. The young man, however, is thoroughly Comanche, and, once the deluded woman unties him, he kills Mrs. McCandless. The settlers put together a kangaroo court, then try, convict and hang the boy. Tragically, as he is about to be hung, the boy hears a music box belonging to Shirley Jones, one her little brother had liked. He grabs it and cries out. It is then that Jones realizes that the condemned boy is her brother and that her search has been for naught. Evil also characterizes Jones' stepfather, Paul Birch, who agrees to give Stewart one thousand dollars if he will bring a 16- or 17-year-old white captive back, any captive that Birch can pass off as the kidnapped son. In their effort to get back their children and kin, the settlers are blind to the manner in which living as Comanches would have changed their loved ones. Their blindness, the result of frozen memories, led to the pain and evil with which they must live for the rest of their lives.

James Stewart's Guthrie McCabe is a Type Five character. Viewers first meet him dozing on the front porch of Annelle Hayes' Tascosa bordello. It quickly becomes apparent that Stewart, marshal of the settlement, likes being waited on and enjoys the good life. When Widmark learns that Stewart skims off ten percent of everything in town, his incredulity is met with Stewart's remark that he (Widmark) is a man of simple means, and "I am not." Although he does not know why McIntire sent for him, Stewart agrees to return to the fort with Widmark, in part to escape Hayes, who has been hinting at marriage, a thought that Stewart finds singularly unattractive.

As they ride through the wagon train on their way to the fort, the settlers cheer Stewart, but he does not know why. One of the settlers remarks, "I can see a light shining above his head, just like a halo." Stewart is their great hope; the one they believe will return their lost folks to them. In that they have severely misjudged Stewart's Guthrie McCabe. Stewart refuses to help McIntire, and the fact that he will disappoint a lot of people bothers him not at all. His response is: I know Quanah Parker, they don't.

When McIntire asks if money will help, Stewart's reply — "Yeah, it might" — demonstrates, once again, his Type Five character. When McIntire offers the pay of a first-class scout, $80 per month, Stewart peels off $400 and tells McIntire to go hire all the scouts he needs. But then Stewart begins to understand that he might get the people to pay for each captive that he brings back. When asked what a human life is worth, Stewart's cynical reply is "Whatever the market will bear." When he suggests $500 per captive, McIntire reminds him that there isn't $500 in the entire camp. Stewart won't be deterred. "If there is any hard cash around, I will smell it out," he tells McIntire. So McIntire appears to agree to let Stewart extort money out of the settlers. McIntire scoffs at Stewart, "They are expecting a messiah who will deliver their children from bondage, and I have to send them you." McIntire then orders Widmark to accompany Stewart to Quanah Parker's village. He tells Widmark, "The man [Stewart] is a scoundrel. I will use him and kick him out."

As Stewart smells out and collects the money, he tries to be frank with each person. But Stewart's frankness goes beyond truthfulness. He is brutal, cynical, even hostile with the truth. Rather than simply trying to get the people to understand what they are likely to find, Stewart appears to enjoy the pain his words cause. He tells John Qualen about the fate of his young daughter Frieda, a girl with yellow hair who is now in her mid-teens. Comanches, Stewart tells Qualen, mate young, so it is likely that the girl is now married, with one or two half-breed children. Qualen, however, won't be deterred, so Stewart agrees to bring the girl back, if they find her, for $250. When Shirley Jones shows him a picture of her brother taken when he was six or seven years old, Stewart scoffs. He tells Jones that the boy now has hair smeared with bear grease down to his shoulders. He has scars on each shoulder from when he was suspended by rawhide cords in the ritual of becoming a man. And Stewart tells Jones that if the now thoroughly Comanche young man caught her, he would rape her, then turn her over to others to be raped and sold in Mexico.

When they arrive at Quanah Parker's camp, Widmark learns that Stewart has done the unthinkable and the illegal: he brought rifles, pistols and knives to exchange for any white captives in the village. As the two men settle in a teepee to wait as events unfold, they meet the long-missing Mae Marsh (Hanna Kleg). They assure her that her husband is well and that her two sons (Carey Jr. and Curtis) have grown up to be fine young men. Of course, that is a lie of sorts because the two are uncouth, ill-mannered idiots. But Stewart and Widmark also agree to lie for her. She is unwilling to return, so they assure her that they will tell her husband and sons that she is dead. Her only reply is, "I am dead." She assures Widmark and Stewart that there are only two or three other white captives in the village. All the rest are dead or had been sold in Mexico.

When Quanah Parker agrees to exchange the white captives for the weapons, he produces the boy and a young blonde, who is likely Frieda Knudsen. But when the girl (who obviously has at least one child), for

James Stewart and Richard Widmark bargain with Henry Brandon as Woody Strode looks on.

whatever reason — shame, fear, love — runs back to her teepee, Widmark refuses to let Stewart take her back. Stewart intends to turn the boy over to Birch for $1,000. Linda Cristal, Stone Calf's woman, is Mexican, but Stewart tells her she can go or stay, so she starts back to the fort with them.

Once back at Fort Grant, Stewart is no longer treated as a savior; unable to bring back more than one captive, Stewart's halo is tarnished and the people will no longer speak to him. In addition, Birch does not want anything to do with the dangerous young Comanche Stewart brought back, and McIntire agrees to give the young man to the McCandless family. When Stewart protests that he returned him for Birch and that he has $1,000 coming, McIntire throws him in the guardhouse.

Both Stewart and Linda Cristal are social outcasts. McIntire and other officers treat Stewart with the contempt he has so richly earned, and the women turn up their noses at Cristal. After all, she had lived as Stone Calf's woman. As Stewart defends Cristal, one senses he is softening; one discovers a less cynical side to his character. Upon returning to Tascosa, Stewart makes an additional disheartening discovery. He has been voted out of office; Tascosa now has a new marshal who has taken Stewart's place and his ten per cent of everything. Annelle Hayes even offers to make Linda Cristal one of her girls. Humiliated by Hayes, Cristal runs out of the bordello and boards the stage headed for California. Stewart joins her, and the film ends with a promise of redemption for both. Cristal can start a new life, and maybe, just maybe, Stewart, in Richard Widmark's words, has discovered something that he wants more than ten per cent of. But one can't be sure...

In *Firecreek*, Stewart is a Type Four hero. The town of Firecreek consists of a handful of unpainted, dilapidated buildings populated by, in Dean Jagger's words, a bunch of losers. Jagger claims that J. Robert Power, who plays Arthur, a somewhat retarded helper at the livery stable, settled in the town because he wasn't that much different from anybody else. James Stewart portrays Johnny Cobb, a farmer who lives three or four miles from town. Although he is regarded as a leader, in Stewart's words, he is sort of an "honorary sheriff," a job for which he gets two dollars a month (and that is sometimes slow in coming). Beyond that, Stewart does not seem much different from anybody else in Firecreek.

Life in the peaceful community is disrupted when Henry Fonda and his gang of gunfighters (Gary Lockwood, Jack Elam, James Best and Morgan Woodward) ride into town. At that point, *Fire Creek* unfolds in two parts. One part, focusing on the Henry Fonda/Inger Stevens relationship, is of little interest here. The other involves the behavior of the four members of Fonda's gang. Early on, Stewart stops Lockwood from nearly drowning Best in the town's horse trough. That is when the gang learns that Firecreek has a sheriff of sorts and a jail. The gang cavorts about the town, breaking windows, frightening the residents and generally disturbing the peace. The climax begins to build after Power shoots Best in the back with Best's gun as Power tries to stop Best from raping Barbara Luna, who runs the town eatery.

Stewart puts Power in jail to await the judge, and, temporarily at least, is able to keep the other three from hanging Power. But Stewart, whose wife is pregnant, is called back to the farm that evening to be with his wife. The next morning, after his wife's health crisis has passed, Stewart returns to town to discover that the outlaws have hung Power and are preparing to leave town. When Stewart tells them he will follow them (how a man with an ill wife, two sons and a farm is going to do that remains unsaid) and turn them in to the nearest sheriff, Fonda shoots Stewart in the leg in order to prevent him from following the gang.

However, Stewart demonstrates that a common man, a man much like the rest of his neighbors, and one who is not particularly brave, can respond with courage in a crisis. Stewart gets a gun and prepares to stop Fonda and his gang. He kills Morgan Woodward, and in a fight with Jack Elam shoves a pitchfork into Elam's stomach. Stewart also kills Lockwood and then goes searching for Fonda. But Stewart's gun is empty, and Fonda shoots him in the shoulder. Preparing to kill Stewart, Fonda dies when Inger Stevens shoots him from a window.

James Stewart's Johnny Cobb is a remarkable man and a new kind of hero, really just a common man with no pretensions of being brave or any desire to become important. Stewart's Cobb is far from the bigger-than-life Type Three heroes. Stewart's Type Four character suggests that heroes need not be superior to other folks, that they can share a common humanity. Type Four heroes also offer the hope that ordinary people can do extraordinary things if circumstances require it. That is a lesson that very ordinary young men learned during World War II, and in Korea and Vietnam. It is surely a lesson reflected in most of James Stewart's Westerns.

Unlike James Stewart, Gregory Peck appeared in only a handful of Westerns, but, like with Stewart, several of his films offered viewers Types Four and Five heroes. Four of Peck's Westerns— *The Gunfighter* (20th Century-Fox, 1950), *The Bravados* (TCR, 1958), *The Stalking Moon* (National General, 1969), and *MacKenna's Gold* (Columbia, 1969)— are particularly relevant for understanding changes taking place in the Western genre throughout the 1950s and 1960s.

In *The Gunfighter*, Peck plays Johnny Ringo, an aging gunfighter who longs to escape his past and settle down with his wife and young son. Peck is a man who has ridden with outlaws and has killed — hardly qualifications for a hero. Not surprisingly, a man like Johnny Ringo cannot escape his past. The future, in fact, is certain; someone younger and faster with a gun will kill him. Peck, like most people living with a tarnished past, understands that likelihood on a cerebral level; however, factual reality in most people is constantly tempered by aspiration and hope. As Paul Seydor has written reality and aspiration continually confront one another in an ongoing dialectic in many Westerns (Seydor, 216). Maybe it won't happen, maybe Peck will not be killed, maybe he will be an exception. With that hope, Peck rides into Cayenne to see his wife and young son.

Millard Mitchell, who had ridden with Peck in the old days, is now marshal, and he tries to dissuade Peck from seeing his wife. Mitchell has shielded her true identity from the townsfolk, and the boy does not know that Johnny Ringo is his father. Peck can't remain in Cayenne long — Mitchell won't permit it, and three men are riding fast after Peck to avenge their brother (whom Peck had killed in an honest gunfight). After seeing his wife and son, Peck prepares to leave Cayenne as the three brothers arrive.

Early in the film, Peck had forced the town bully, Skip Homeier (Hunt Bromley), to back down in a saloon confrontation. Homeier, a wannabe gunfighter, waits for Peck in the stable and shoots him as Peck prepares to mount his horse. As he lies dying, Peck's Johnny Ringo gives viewers a glimpse of the Type Five character that he really is. He assures Mitchell that Homeier had shot him in a fair fight. But Peck's motives are far from pure. He wants Homeier to live with the reputation as the man who killed Johnny Ringo. Peck wants Homeier to live as he had lived, always on the run, unable to eat dinner in peace, to sleep with a gun at hand and forced to deal with all the other little Homeiers of the world who want to make reputations for themselves. What is often overlooked and under-appreciated in *The Gunfighter* is that Peck did not reform. Skip Homeier was simply the last man he killed!

The Bravados opens as Gregory Peck (Jim Douglas) rides into a town preparing to hang four men. He has trailed the quartet for six months, intent on avenging the rape and murder of his wife; but now he will watch as the law does what he intended to do. In town he meets Joan Collins (who seems terribly miscast in a Western). Collins is an old flame, a woman who once turned down his marriage proposal. Unmarried, she is now a wealthy rancher and community leader.

That evening Peck accepts the sheriff's invitation to see the four condemned men. Peck says nothing, he does not even want to know their names; he just stares at them. One of the four helps to establish Peck's hatred when he remarks, "He has got the face of a hunter." Collins comes to his hotel room after Peck has seen the four men and invites him to go to church with her that evening. Peck's response surprises her, "I don't go to church anymore." When Collins says she doesn't understand, Peck's curt response — "It's very simple, I just don't go" — helps viewers to recognize that Peck has been deeply hurt. He walks Collins to the church and, after turning away, ultimately decides to go inside. All during the service, Peck remembers — remembers his dead wife and the manner of her death. The priest reminds his charges that Caesars' law has sentenced the four men, but that they are yet creatures eligible for God's forgiveness. All of you, he tells the congregation, will rise at daybreak, the dawning of a new day, but for the four condemned prisoners it will be the midnight of their lives.

As the film cuts between the church service and the jail, the four men (with the help of a man posing as the hangman) break jail and take Kathleen Gallant (Emma) with them when they ride out of town. A badly wounded sheriff stumbles into the church and sounds the alarm. The town organizes a posse and prepares to give chase. Collins is surprised that Peck is going to sleep instead of riding with the posse. When she protests, he tells her it is too dark to trail the four escapees, and that he is going to get some sleep and then, "I am going to find them if it is the last thing I do."

The next morning Peck catches up with the posse that one of the gunman has pinned down in a narrow pass, and quickly takes charge. When Gallant's father asks why he is helping them, Peck replies, "I am not doing it for you, Mr. Steinmetz." The posse resumes the pursuit, and they overtake Lee Van Cleef, one of the four. Peck shows him a picture of his wife that he carries in his watch, and when Van Cleef protests that he has never seen her in his life, Peck hits him and then kills him in cold blood. He becomes judge, jury and executioner. Peck runs down the next of the four and hangs him by his feet to die.

The two surviving escapees stumble across Gene Evans' miner's shack located near Peck's ranch. They kill Evans, and Henry Silva discovers that Evans was carrying a sack of gold, which Silva stuffs in his shirt. In the meantime, Stephen Boyd, who professes a weakness for women, rapes Emma in the miner's shack. But he is interrupted as Collins and Peck's neighbor ride up. Mistaking them for the posse, Boyd and Silva ride to Peck's ranch to steal fresh horses and some food before they head for the border.

Peck and the posse follow the two survivors to the Rio Grande River, and when the posse turns back, Peck rides across the river. An international border can't and won't stop him. He finds Stephen Boyd in the cantina of a small Mexican town enjoying the company of a woman. Peck shows him the picture of his wife, and when Boyd protests that he never saw her before, Peck kills him. Silva escapes from the cantina, with Peck in pursuit.

Peck trails Silva to his house, where viewers discover that Silva has a wife and a very sick young son. Peck is about to capture Silva when the latter's wife knocks him unconscious with a flowerpot. When Peck regains consciousness, he is the prisoner. Silva is puzzled as to why Peck had been so persistent. What had he (Silva) ever done to Peck? When Silva, too, denies having ever seen Peck's wife, Peck asks him where he got the sack of gold; it had been stolen from Peck's house. Evans had told him that four men had raped and murdered Peck's wife, but when Silva replies that he got it from a dead miner, the truth suddenly hits Peck. Evans had raped

In *The Bravados* (1958), Gregory Peck plays a man who kills three men whom he wrongly believed killed his wife. Here he holds his daughter as he talks with Joan Collins.

and murdered his wife and stolen the gold, then he had blamed the four men he had seen ride by. Though they had tried to rob the bank and actually killed a man in the town about to hang them, the four had not raped and murdered Peck's wife. He had killed three men for the wrong reason. They were not innocent men, but they had not committed the crime for which three of them had died. Peck, in despair, cries out, "Oh God! Oh God!"

Peck rides back to the town and enters the church. The priest, who had known him in the past, hears Peck's confession that he had not killed for the sake of justice; he had killed for revenge, for something the men didn't do. He had set himself up as judge, jury and executioner. The priest assures Peck that there is forgiveness in confession, but all Peck can do is mutter, "I was wrong, I was wrong."

The townsfolk, however, do not understand. They regard Peck as a hero, as a man who led the posse and as a man who gunned down three very mean men. As Peck leaves the church, the townsfolk applaud and congratulate him. The priest admonishes them to pray for the souls of the dead men, and Peck asks them to pray for him as well, for he is now a man with a terrible burden to bear.

Fenin and Everson focus too much attention on the fact that Peck acted in good faith; he believed the four were guilty of raping and murdering his wife. They conclude that Peck's good faith "seemed to make everything, if not quite right ethically, at least morally tolerable and legally acceptable" (Fenin and Everson, 335). That comment misses Peck's anguish. The townsfolk might regard his actions as "morally tolerable and legally acceptable," but Peck does not.

In the eyes of the townsfolk, Peck is a Type Three hero, a natural leader who brought justice of a sort to the four men who had tried to rob their bank and had killed one of their friends. Peck knows differently; he knows he is no Type Three hero. In fact, in his eyes, he is morally inferior to everyone in the town. He has killed — murdered, in fact — the right men for the wrong reason. His desire for revenge morally tainted the acts for which the town lauded him. Rather than occupying the lofty heights of a Type Three hero, Peck descended to the depths of a Type Five human being. He might ride off into the sunset with Joan Collins, the promise of a new life hanging in the air, but Peck will always have to live with the fact that his drive for revenge destroyed him almost as thoroughly as the three men he killed!

Peck's MacKenna, of *MacKenna's Gold*, is also a different type of hero. Like Gary Cooper in *Man of the West* (United Artists, 1958) and Glenn Ford in several Westerns discussed later, Peck in *MacKenna's Gold* offers a variant of the Type Four hero: the hero as victim. *MacKenna's Gold* unfolds around the legend of Canyon del Oro, a canyon rich in gold supposedly protected by the spirits of Apache gods. At the beginning of the film, Peck (playing Sheriff MacKenna) is forced to kill an old Apache, Prairie Dog, who tries to ambush him. Prairie Dog has a map to the canyon and is trying to escape Omar Sharif's gang of cutthroats, who want the map. When Prairie Dog mistakes Peck for one of Sharif's gang, Peck kills him. But Peck does not believe in the legend of the Canyon del Oro, so he burns the map. Peck is burying Prairie Dog when Sharif and his gang ride up and take Peck prisoner. Sharif (playing Colorado) and Peck are old antagonists; Peck had run him out of the territory. Camilla Sparv is the gang's hostage. The gang had killed her father, a friend of Peck's, and had taken her captive. Her fate is uncertain, but in all likelihood she will be given to one of the Apaches who ride with Sharif or sold in Mexico. Julie

Newmar (as Heshke), an Apache woman who had once been in love with MacKenna but turned against him when he went after her outlaw brother, is also a member of the gang.

Sharif does not kill Peck because he remembers that Peck possesses a good memory; having seen Prairie Dog's map before he burned it, Peck can lead them to the canyon. Peck has no choice, so, even though he believes the canyon to be a myth, he agrees to take Sharif and his gang there. Before the outlaws start for the canyon, however, they are forced to accept a group of townsfolk who have heard about the map. Led by Eli Wallach, and including Edward G. Robinson as old Adams (supposedly the only white man to have been to the canyon, but whom the Indians had blinded), the townsfolk are gold crazed. For the most part, they are ordinary people given over to greed and an obsessive determination to find the canyon. A unit of cavalry pursuing Sharif and his gang trail the group (Peck, Sprav, Sharif's gang and the townsfolk).

Even though Peck does not believe in the legend, he knows that the only hope he and Sparv have of remaining alive is to stall for time, so he leads them on their fateful journey to the canyon. At one point the cavalry patrol ambushes the party and kills nearly all of the townsfolk and several of Sharif's men. The remaining members push on, followed closely by the soldiers. But they are soon joined by Telly Savalas, one of the soldiers, who had killed the men in his patrol and now wants to join the group to obtain a share of the gold. As they draw near the canyon, Sparv becomes gold crazy like the rest of them. Peck is running the bluff of his life, and he tells Sparv to forget finding any gold, just think about how to escape alive. However, it turns out that Peck is wrong. The canyon and its gold are real. Once in the canyon, Sharif kills Savalas and the remaining Apache from his gang, and then climbs up to a cliff dwelling to kill Peck and Sparv.

Sharif, Sparv and Peck engage in a brawl in the cliff dwelling, but the conflict is interrupted when a band of Apaches ride into the canyon. At this point the film enters the realm of fantasy. The ground begins to crack and the canyon walls commence to shake. The Apaches flee the canyon, and the three survivors barely make it to horses and safety before the entire canyon collapses on itself, burying forever the gold of the canyon. The face of Prairie Dog is superimposed over the destruction; the Apache Gods have protected their gold.

Throughout *MacKenna's Gold*, Gregory Peck is a vulnerable, restricted hero. Not only is he captured by the outlaws and forced to lead them to the canyon, he is without a gun for the rest of the film. And he is closely guarded, his every move observed. Twice he tries unsuccessfully to escape;

and at the conclusion of one attempt, Peck is roped and dragged along the ground by one of the Indians in Sharif's gang. Peck reminds one of Randolph Scott's character in *The Tall T* (Columbia, 1957). Both men lived at the mercy and whim of their captors, and both had to use all of their wits to stay alive. Unlike Scott, however, Peck does not kill Sharif. After Peck, Sharif and Sparv have escaped the canyon, Sharif rides away, with Peck's threat to track him down hanging in the air.

Since Peck does not believe in the legend of Canyon del Oro, and tells his captors that Robinson's stories of the canyon are just tales designed to get people to buy him drinks, it is not surprising that Peck is the only member of the group who remains unaffected by gold fever. What *is* rather surprising, however, is that Peck does not succumb to it even after he discovers that there really is a Canyon del Oro. Peck knows that Sharif will kill all of them and keep the gold for himself. So instead of rushing around picking up gold nuggets (as do Savalas, Sharif and Sparv), he searches for a way out of the canyon.

While there is always the hint of a Type Three hero in MacKenna, for most of the film he shares a common humanity with the rest of the characters in the drama. Unable to overcome his environment or to convince the others of the senselessness of their quest, Peck must share their fate. Like James Stewart in *The Far Country*, Peck's MacKenna offers viewers a hero as victim.

The irony of *MacKenna's Gold* is that Peck, who didn't believe there was any gold, is the one who jumps on Telly Savalas' horse as the three make their escape from the rapidly crumbling canyon. Savalas, before Sharif killed him, had stuffed his saddle bags full of gold nuggets. Peck is the only one to ride away with any gold at all!

Before turning to *Man of the West*, a few comments about Peck's *The Stalking Moon* suggest the often subtle manner in which Westerns reflected the changing American culture of the late 1960s. Peck's character (Sam Varner) is a wise and respected army scout, a Type Three hero. The commander of the post and Robert Forster, a mixed race scout whom Peck has mentored, try to talk him out of retirement. However, Peck is determined to retire to his ranch in New Mexico Territory. But Peck is clearly a leader, a man respected by other men.

On the day before Peck's retirement, the army patrol for whom he was scouting capture a band of Apaches, including a white woman (Eva Marie Saint) and her mixed-race son. *The Stalking Moon* becomes a suspense-filled Western as Peck takes Eva Marie Saint and the little boy to his ranch and then has to fight off and kill the little boy's father, who has tracked them there.

NATIONAL GENERAL PICTURES Presents

GREGORY PECK · EVA MARIE SAINT

in a Pakula-Mulligan Production of

THE STALKING MOON

co-starring

ROBERT FORSTER

with NOLAND CLAY · produced by ALAN J. PAKULA · directed by ROBERT MULLIGAN · screenplay by ALVIN SARGENT · adaptation by WENDELL MAYES
from the novel THE STALKING MOON by THEODORE V. OLSEN · TECHNICOLOR · PANAVISION® a New Excitement in Entertainment

After freeing her from her Apache captors, Gregory Peck escorts Eva Marie Saint and Noland Clay to the military outpost in *The Stalking Moon* (1969).

For our purpose, the most interesting element in *The Stalking Moon* is the difficulty Eva Marie Saint has in adjusting to life in the white community after ten years of being an Apache woman. At first she has difficulty conversing in English, a language she has not used for years. When Peck gets her to Silverton to catch the train East, it is clear that she does not know what to do. She is not sure that she has any living relatives in Columbus or anyplace else. When Peck discovers that his Army voucher won't get her any further than Topeka, he settles for that. The stationmaster gives him a long ticket and explains the confusing stops and train changes necessary to get from Silverton to Topeka. Peck hands the tickets to Saint, and as he walks away, the camera gives viewers a long shot of Saint and the boy sitting forlornly on the platform. Clearly, both are bewildered by this new world into which they have been thrust. As Peck looks over at Saint and the little boy, he realizes that they are helpless; they really have no place to go. Peck's conscience will not permit him to abandon them, so he offers to take them to his ranch. Even at the ranch Saint finds adjustment to her new life hard at first. For example, Peck has difficulty getting her to sit with him or converse and eat at the same table. Apache women do not do that.

Eva Marie Saint's difficult adjustment to her new life in *The Stalking Moon* can be read as an analogy for the bewilderment many older Americans were feeling in the late 1960s. The apparent rejection by the college-aged generation of their parents' conservative values toward sex, work, country and a host of other things, along with a war that increasingly made little sense, and escalating crime that turned urban streets into robbing and killing fields, all combined to create a country and a culture that older Americans did not understand. Older Americans felt like aliens in their own families and neighborhoods! They understood neither the language nor behavior of their children and grandchildren. At the time *The Stalking Moon* was released, in January 1969, the older Americans must have felt like Eva Marie Saint as she struggled to remember a language she had partially forgotten, and to live in a white world that had become foreign to her.

Like Gregory Peck in *MacKenna's Gold*, Gary Cooper is an example of hero as victim in *Man of the West*. With no family of his own, Cooper's Link Jones had been raised and victimized by Lee J. Cobb (Doc Tobin), who taught him to steal and murder, and Cooper had ridden as a valued member of Tobin's gang of cutthroats. But as Cooper tells Julie London, he just up and left the gang one day. Cooper understood he had a choice to grow up and become a human being or to remain and rot like Tobin's bunch. Cooper escaped Cobb's clutches, married, raised children and became a respected member of a small frontier community, Good Hope.

When the train Cooper is riding on stops for wood, all the men climb out to assist. It is then that members of Tobin's gang try to rob the train. But the train pulls away before they can get the gold; they do, however, steal the money Cooper was going to use to hire a schoolteacher in Ft. Worth. Stranded when the trains pulls out without them, Cooper, Julie London and Arthur O'Connell stumble onto the shack in which Cobb and the gang are holed up. Cooper becomes a victim again.

Cooper has to employ all the deceit at his command to keep the three alive; so he lets Cobb think he has come back to join them. As the suspicion of him and the abuse of London mounts, Cooper has to remain passive and cooperative. He makes Cobb believe that London is his woman, and encourages Cobb's dream of robbing a bank in the mining town of Lassoo. Lassoo in *Man of the West* (also directed by Anthony Mann) is much like Millard Mitchell's dream of the big gold strike in *The Naked Spur.* The gang, with Cooper, London and O'Connell in tow, head for Lassoo. Cooper feels the hate coming back. He tells London that he feels like killing, a sickness that makes him just like them. Cooper hates them and himself for the feeling. But he has no choice; either he kills Cobb and his gang or they will kill the three of them.

Lassoo turns out to be a deserted mining town with an empty bank. But in the shootout that follows, Cooper kills the three members of the gang and returns to kill Cobb. He yells to Cobb, "You have outlived your kind and you have outlived your time and I am coming to get you." Cooper then kills Cobb, and with Cobb's death wipes out any vestige of his [Cooper's] past.

One other element in *Man of the West* identifies the film as a post–1955 Western: sexual tension permeates the film. Julie London plays Billie Ellis, "the girl with a golden voice." Viewers first meet her in Crosscut (the town into which Cooper rides to catch the train to Ft. Worth) as she leaves her job at the Longhorn Palace. The cause is pointedly sexual — the boss won't keep his hands off of her. Later, as the three are walking down the railroad track (after being left by the train), London hikes up her long skirt; when Cooper stares, she indignantly asks what he is looking at. When Cooper replies her shoes, London responds that no man has looked at that part of her since she was fourteen years old.

Once they are captives of Cobb's gang, and while Cooper is outside digging a grave for one of the gang who had been shot while trying to rob the train, London screams. When Cooper runs inside he discovers that the gang is going to make London undress for them. Cooper tries to stop it, but Jack Lord holds a knife at Cooper's throat while London is forced to strip. The only thing that prevents her from being forced to undress completely is Cobb's preoccupation with Lassoo. That breaks the tension, and Cooper and London go to sleep in the barn. While the gang is at Lassoo, Cobb rapes London. Now she too is a real victim — not just of suggestive comments and unwanted probing hands, but of actual sexual assault. She is also a victim in another, probably far deeper, sense. She has fallen in love with Cooper, but he is a happily married man with a family. A relationship between the two is out of the question. So she will return to being a saloon singer who has to ward off continued unwelcome male advances!

Leonard Matthews, in his *History of Western Movies*, describes Glenn Ford's characters as "always casual, friendly, softly-spoken, the gentle demeanor hiding the danger that lurks within" (Matthews, 137). Matthews is perceptive; one has the impression that Ford's character is always about to explode. He reminds one of a caged animal longing for the freedom of the chase and kill. Usually Ford's heroes (or characters) were soft-spoken, smiling individuals—but individuals easily provoked and, if aroused, who could become a deadly enemy. Ford is also more transparent than either Stewart or Peck. Where James Stewart and Gregory Peck seldom engaged in extended soliloquies, Ford talks. Viewers know the motivating forces driving Ford's behavior. And Ford's character is often a victim of either circumstance or the past.

Jubal (Columbia, 1956) provides an excellent example of the sort of person Ford so frequently portrayed, and offers a good case study of the hero as victim. Ernest Borgnine rescues a half-frozen Ford at the beginning of the film. In spite of Rod Steiger's (playing Pinky) insults, Ford remains on Borgnine's ranch, first as one of Borgnine's cowboys, then as his foreman. Viewers begin to understand Ford better when he explains his background to Felicia Farr. This scene in *Jubal* is an excellent example of how Ford used dialogue to assist viewers in understanding his character. He tells Farr that he was born on a barge in the Ohio River to a mother who didn't want him. When he was seven years old Ford fell into the river, but his mother made no effort to rescue him. She wanted him to drown. When his father jumped in the river to save the boy, he was cut to pieces by the propeller blades of another barge coming down the river. His mother's response to Ford was that she wished it had been him. Ford tells Farr that that is when he started to run, and he has not stopped running since. Ford believes himself to be the source of the bad luck that follows him wherever he goes. His response to that bad luck is to run from it. Ford is foremost a victim of his own unwanted childhood.

He is also victimized by Valerie French, playing Borgnine's wife Mae. French hates her husband, and she has had an affair with Steiger. She immediately makes a play for Ford. About Borgnine, French tells Ford: "I don't have a conscience about him. He is an animal." French had been beautiful but poor. She is proud that twenty-three men had proposed to her, but she had rejected them all. She had married Borgnine because she thought he was a wealthy cattle baron who would buy her nice clothes and take her to places she had always heard about. But none of that happened; she is stuck on a ranch in the middle of nowhere, and she hates. She hates it — both the ranch and Borgnine.

Unlike Steiger, Ford rebuffs French's advances because he is loyal to

Borgnine. Borgnine is the only man who ever went out of his way to help Ford. Ford has found the home and friend he always longed for. But Steiger remains viciously jealous of Ford, even more so after Borgnine makes him foremen; and when Borgnine insists that Ford accompany French back to the ranch from a cattle drive, Steiger uses the occasion to accuse them of adultery. Borgnine won't believe it; he is naïve and has no sense of the depth of French's hatred of him. But he rides back to the ranch to learn if Steiger's accusations are true.

Ford, of course, did not remain with French, but rode into town to a saloon. When Borgnine confronts French, she tells him she never loved him and that she hates everything about him. Then she lies about Ford. Yes, they have been lovers, French tells Borgnine. Borgnine grabs his rifle and heads for town and the saloon. Ford is unarmed, but Charles Bronson throws Ford a gun and he kills Borgnine. Jack Elam lies about what he saw, and Steiger arouses the townsfolk, who now believe that Ford killed Borgnine because he and French were lovers.

Steiger then goes to the ranch and sits at Borgnine's chair. He informs French that everything, including her, now belongs to him. When French rejects Steiger and runs to the barn, he follows and beats her, but French does not die before clearing Ford of any wrongdoing.

Throughout the film, Ford is a Type Four hero. He is the quintessential victim. Victimized by his mother's rejection, Steiger's hate and French's infidelity, Ford has to kill the only true friend he ever had, and loses the only real home he has ever known. Ford, Charles Bronson and Felicia Farr ride away from the ranch as "The End" rolls across the screen. Ford has been vindicated and is about to start a new life with Farr, but throughout the film he is a troubled man endeavoring to grapple with forces beyond his control, forces that are trying to destroy him.

Glenn Ford is a victim of sorts as well in *The Fastest Gun Alive* (MGM, 1956). He runs a store in Cross Creek, but Ford is haunted by a memory. His father had been a famous marshal with six notches on his gun. The old man had taught the young Ford how to be a fast draw and an expert shot. But the boy was afraid of guns. People get killed using them, and he was afraid of dying. Ford was so afraid that he could not avenge his own father's death when the old man was murdered.

After running from several towns (trying to escape the memory of his own cowardice), Ford and his wife, now pregnant, opened up a dry goods store in Cross Creek. He has given up drinking, and Jeanne Crain (his wife) believes that he threw his father's gun into a pond. But Ford had lied to her; he still has the gun. For four years life has been good. Ford is a valued member of the community, but he is also growing restless. Ford

A contrite Glenn Ford turns over his trouble-making guns to the minister of the local church

Glenn Ford hands his gun to Joseph Sweeney as the congregation looks on in
The Fastest Gun Alive (1956).

finds the dry goods store constraining, and he feels scorned by the rest of
the men in the town because he does not carry a gun or drink. At a dance
he sits alone in the corner while his wife dances, and he suffers implied
male taunts because he will not drink the spiked punch.

The next morning, when Virginia Gregg returns a dress to the store
because it was brown instead of blue, Ford explodes. He goes to the saloon
and begins to drink, and as the men talk about Broderick Crawford (playing Vinnie Harold) being the fastest gun alive, Ford tells them they don't
know anything about shooting or fast guns. When they dismiss his talk as
a result of too much whiskey, Ford storms out of the saloon to get his gun.
In the shooting exhibition that follows, he shoots two silver dollars out of
the air and breaks a dropped beer mug before it hits the ground. When
the men see the six notches on the gun, they assume Ford had killed six
men. But Ford is afraid that the truth will come out, so he prepares to run

again. This time Jeanne Crain refuses to go with him. She likes Cross Creek and intends to make it a home for herself and her baby. Ford knows that word will get out and gunfighters will come to Cross Creek to challenge him; he is afraid to face them, so he prepares to leave Cross Creek, even without his wife. One can't be sure whether Ford decides to leave out of concern for the town or from his own fear.

On Sunday, when the entire town is at church, Crawford and his henchmen ride into Cross Creek to obtain food and fresh horses. They had robbed a bank, and a posse is only two hours behind them. But when Crawford learns about Ford's fast gun from young Christopher Owen, he has to find out whether or not Ford is faster than himself. In the meantime, Ford has laid his gun on the altar and prepared to leave town, and Crain agrees to go with him. But the townsfolk, at the insistence of Leif Erickson, take a pledge never to tell what they saw the day before; therefore no one will ever learn about Ford's fast gun. They convince Ford and Crain to remain in Cross Creek.

But when Crawford threatens to burn down the town unless Ford comes out of the church to meet him, the townsfolk turn on Ford. Just as Noah Berry Jr. (one of Crawford's gang) lights the torch, Leif Erickson yells for them not to burn down the town — he is coming out. Ford stops Erickson before he can put on the gun. By now the town knows that Ford had never killed anyone, that it was his father's gun and that he is afraid. Ford tells Erickson, "I am so afraid, I am sick to my stomach." As he walks out of the church, Ford kisses Crain and reminds her that they always knew this day would come.

Ford kills Crawford, proving that he is the fastest gun alive. But as the posse rides into Cross Creek with the dead bodies of Crawford's henchmen draped over their saddles, they discover that the town has dug two graves. One is for Crawford, but the other has a marker labeled George Templeton (Ford's character). In that grave is a casket full of rocks and the gun. In killing Crawford, Ford had exorcised the demon of memory, the memory of his own cowardice when his father was killed. Ford and Crain will run no more; now they can live like the rest of the folks in Cross Creek.

Glenn Ford is also haunted by memories of the past in *Santee* (Crown International, 1973). The film opens in a small village as Michael Burns (as Jody) waits for his father. His mother had raised Burns after she left his father, but now she is dead and Burns has come to live with the man he never really knew very well. That man, Robert Wilkie, it turns out, is an outlaw with a price on his head. He and three others are on the run, trying to escape Santee (Glenn Ford), the best bounty hunter in the area.

Ford catches and kills all four of them. Burns tags along as Ford takes the bodies back to claim the reward. He has vowed to kill Ford for shooting his father. But as the journey progresses, a tense friendship develops between the two, and Ford invites Burns to come out to his ranch, the Three Arrows. Burns accepts the invitation, and throughout the middle part of the film he becomes much like a son to Ford and Dana Wynter (playing Ford's wife).

Jay Silverheels plays John Crow, foreman of the Three Arrows, a ranch that has one of the finest herds of quarter horses in the territory. At the ranch, Ford is a friendly, easygoing, laughing person, loved intensely by Wynter and respected by Silverheels. No one speaks of what Ford does when he leaves for extended periods. The contrast between Ford at the ranch and Ford on the trail as bounty hunter is substantial. It is almost as if he were two different persons. Burns becomes quite attached to Ford at the ranch, just as Ford and Wynter have grown fond of him. They ask Burns to consider the Three Arrows his home, and the young man agrees.

One night Burns asks Silverheels why it is called the Three Arrows when the branding irons and sign at the ranch gate have only two arrows. It is then that Burns learns the truth about Ford. He had been a highly respected sheriff in a nearby town, with a son whom he adored. The ranch was named the Three Arrows for Ford, Wynter and their son, and Silverheels was given the charge to develop it so the three would have a home when Ford relinquished the sheriff's job. When the Banner gang drifted into town, Ford had permitted them to stay, even though he understood they might start trouble. One night the gang called Ford out of his office and shot him five times, and then they killed his son.

When Ford recovered from his wounds and the heartbreak of his dead son, he gave up his badge and became a bounty hunter. Ford, then, is a victim of his past, just as he had been in *Jubal*. He has never really gotten over the murder of his son. However, Burns has helped to heal the lingering hurt; he has become like a son, and Ford teaches him how to rope and brand calves, and to break wild horses. He also teaches him how to draw and shoot a gun. Burns has decided that he too will become a bounty hunter, and he intends to ride out with Ford the next time. Ford, however, has promised Wynter there won't be a next time; Burns has helped to erase the pain for both Ford and Wynter. It is time to let go of the past.

Ford's promise to Wynter is tested when the sheriff (an old friend) brings news that the Banner gang is back in the area. But Ford remains true to his word. Even when the Banner gang kills their friend the sheriff and robs the bank, Ford won't go after them. Burns will, however; and he starts out alone on their trail. Wynter, afraid for Burns' life, gives Ford his gun, and he goes after the young man. They catch the Banner gang at a bordello near the border, and, in the shootout that follows, the entire Banner gang is killed — but so is Burns. The film ends with Wynter and Silverheels in tears as Ford slowly drives a buckboard carrying Burns' coffin into the ranch to be buried next to their other son. For Ford and Wynter it seems that the heartbreak and the haunting memories will never end.

In many ways *Santee* symbolizes the state of American culture in 1973. The American people were haunted by memories of the 1950s and of the Kennedy years — which looked all the better from the retrospective perch of 1973. Recent events like Watergate, Vietnam and the social turmoil they provoked, as well as the realities of increasing crime and drug usage, unsettled American self-confidence. By the time *Santee* saw release in September 1973, the Watergate political crisis filled the front page of newspapers across the land. If Vietnam had caused people to doubt the honesty of political leaders, Watergate validated the assumption, increasingly held by a large majority of Americans, that few in public life were trustworthy.

No longer would Americans turn presidents into heroes, and with greater frequency journalists and scholars began to focus on the weaknesses and misbehavior of public personalities. Members of Congress resigned in public disgrace over behavior that would have gone unnoticed in earlier years. The Kennedy infidelities, Franklin Roosevelt's affair with Lucy Rutherford, and Thomas Jefferson's dalliance with Sally Hemmings — the list could go on for a page or more — were all mined for the slightest new insight and milked for all the shock value they were worth. By the mid–1970s, no public figure, no matter how revered, was free from public scrutiny. No person was thought to be a worthy Type Three hero; all had feet of clay. All leaders were merely human, no better and probably a lot worse than the people they sought to serve. By the mid–1970s the hero had truly descended from his lofty perch.

Jon Tuska ends his 1976 book *The Filming of the West* with the observation that he could not tell whether or not Westerns could survive with heroes (Tuska 1976, 584). Looking back from the first decade of the twenty-first century, it is apparent that the genre has not survived very well without them. And it is equally clear that American culture itself is hero-starved. Americans don't seem satisfied until every moral weakness of those who would be heroes has been identified and broadcast across the land. Contemporary Americans are a people with few heroes, and we are the worse off for it.

Chapter 3

WESTERNS OF THE NEW FRONTIER

An astute observer of the United States on January 1, 1960, might well have described public opinion as a mixture of concern and complacency. In many respects, the American people were a complacent lot. The economy had recovered from the 1957–58 recession, and the "greatest generation," yet basking in the glow of having destroyed two of the most monstrous political systems in the history of the world during World War II, was busily raising families, managing successful businesses and earning good wages in the factories of America. The political divisiveness of McCarthyism had abated, and the American people now expressed a great deal of confidence in their clergy, teachers and political leaders. Surely most Americans thought that the new, exciting decade of the 1960s would continue the good times Americans had experienced since the end of World War II.

Beneath that complacent optimism, however, stirred uneasiness about the future. The Soviet Union had clearly won the race into space, and the fear of a "missile gap" — which would make the country vulnerable to a Soviet attack — was openly debated. Fidel Castro's successful Cuban revolution embraced communism, and all Americans were mindful of the potential threat that Cuba posed to American national security. Berlin, Southeast Asia and the Congo stood as haunting reminders to Americans that they lived in a dangerous world, one more than capable of drawing the United States into a nuclear confrontation with the Soviet Union.

At home, change too was in the air. The civil rights movement was gaining momentum in the courtrooms and streets of the South. While no one could divine the future with certainty, it was clear to most perceptive Americans that the country stood on the edge of great racial change. It was equally clear that American political leadership was evolving. Dwight Eisenhower, the oldest sitting president in American history up to that time, was about to leave office. A much younger man, one born in the twentieth century, would replace him. While the conservative coalition of southern Democrats and northern Republicans remained a strong congressional force, liberal Democrats had swept the off-year congressional elections of 1958, and congressional liberals energetically advanced their policy and institutional agendas. New faces—men such as John Kennedy, Barry Goldwater, Richard Nixon, Lyndon Johnson, Hubert Humphrey and Jacob Javits—were emerging on the political landscape. As hard as it was for the complacent side of the American psyche to understand, the 1960s would not be like the 1950s. Americans were about to enter a decade that would shape and change the country for the rest of the twentieth century.

The presidential election of 1960 between Vice President Richard Nixon and Senator John Kennedy reflected the confused state of American public opinion. It was not a campaign in which specific issue differences marked the two candidates. On the other hand, it *was* a campaign about the future direction of the country. Kennedy, pledging to get the "country moving again," articulated a fear of the so-called missile gap and advocated governmental action against poverty and unemployment. Fearful of alienating white southern political support, Kennedy nuanced the evolving civil rights movement; but at the same time, African Americans rallied to him and provided critical votes in key northern urban areas. Vice President Nixon spoke for the foreign policy successes of the Eisenhower years and promised to carry on that tradition. Nixon appealed to those who believed that Kennedy was not tough enough to stand up to the Russians, and to those fearful of the unfolding civil rights movement. The vote outcome demonstrated how closely divided the American people were. Kennedy won a narrow and highly disputed victory.

Most people old enough to remember that tragic November 1963 day can recall with uncanny exactness where they were and what they were doing when they first learned that President John F. Kennedy had been assassinated in Dallas, Texas. Far fewer can remember with much precision January 20, 1961, the day John Kennedy was inaugurated President of the United States. Those fatal shots fired on a Dallas street encased the man and his administration in a shroud of myth that distorts memory. In truth, John Kennedy was not all that popular in the American heartland of 1960. At best, opinion toward him was mixed. The Midwestern and Southern states Kennedy carried in 1960 were closely contested. He lost the rest by lopsided margins. There are a number of reasons for that.

For one thing, people in the heartland of America did not trust John Kennedy's father, Joseph P. Kennedy. Joseph Kennedy was a wealthy power broker who appeared to relish power for its own sake, not a trait popular with the American people of that time. Years had passed since Joe Kennedy, then owner of Federal Booking Office, had sent his two silent screen cowboy stars, Fred Thomson and Tom Mix, riding into movie houses of the American heartland. Former President Harry Truman echoed middle America's concern as he expressed early reservations about the Kennedy candidacy by saying he was more afraid of "the pop than the pope."

Unlike Truman, many protestants of middle America were afraid of the pope; they did not trust Kennedy's religion! Anti-Catholic sentiment was particularly strong in the Midwest and South. In addition, naturally conservative folks in the American heartland did not like what they perceived to be Kennedy's urbane eastern liberalism. They were not sure he was tough enough to stand up to the Russians. And, as his administration wore on, they were increasingly dismayed by, and even hostile toward, his efforts to end racial segregation in the United States.

Life is full of ironies, and maybe one of the biggest ironies of all is that John Kennedy, a man who had so little in common with middle America, and who was regarded by it with suspicion, would be the last man in two decades to articulately express the ideology and values of the heartland. Michael Coyne catches part of that irony when he observed that Kennedy did not care for Westerns. Unlike President Eisenhower, who read paperback Western novels, Kennedy preferred the slick image of James Bond. Furthermore, Kennedy's focus on the future seemed to leave little room for the mythic past of the American West (Coyne, 105). Ironically, however, Kennedy drew richly from the American past.

Soon after his inauguration, the entire country was caught up in the Kennedy mystique. Those years are often referred to as Camelot, a then-popular Broadway musical based on the legends of King Arthur. Camelot conjures up images of high culture, grace, dignity and style, elements closely associated with the Kennedy legacy. But the Kennedy years were more than Camelot. They were years of determined toughness that embraced values of the American frontier. John Kennedy called his program the New Frontier.

Kennedy anchored his challenges to Americans of the early 1960s in a metaphor that recalled old challenges. To a generation whose parents and grandparents had settled the American frontier, Kennedy directed the call to explore outer space. He set a goal of putting a man on the moon by the end of the decade. Americans of that time responded to his challenge with a determination reminiscent of earlier generations who had settled the Great Plains and beyond. Early foreign policy failures at the Bay of Pigs and in Berlin were erased as President Kennedy faced the missiles of October in that fateful 1962 autumn. And the Russians backed down! Surely one of the memorable images remaining from the Kennedy years is President Kennedy standing before his desk, evening descending on Washington, D.C., as the Cuban missile crisis unfolded. Even confrontations over racial integration at the University of Alabama and the University of Mississippi, neither of which were received well in the American heartland, made clear that this President was tough. He was not afraid of a showdown, be it with the Russians, the Governor of Alabama or Jimmy Hoffa.

In retrospect, it is easy to see that the Kennedy mystique looms larger than his accomplishments. He was generally ineffective at persuading Congress to adopt New Frontier social legislation. And his foreign policy results were at best checkered. Kennedy, after all, continued the United States on the course that led to Vietnam. The point is not to glorify Kennedy; rather, it is to remind readers that the Kennedy years were more than Camelot. They were also years of the New Frontier.

It was a time of physical fitness campaigns, confrontations at home and abroad, and a challenge to go beyond the horizon into the deep reaches of space. The New Frontier was a reaffirmation of the values and beliefs to which so many Americans yet subscribed, values and beliefs that had been central to pre–1955 Westerns. In fact, as Kennedy articulated those values and beliefs, he painted them on a bigger canvas than any President before him had dared to try. Others had challenged Americans to fulfill their God-ordained obligation to settle the North American continent. Others had confidently assured Americans that they were bearers of a truly superior civilization destined for success. But Kennedy went beyond them.

His widely quoted inaugural address eloquently reflects self-confident optimism. That optimism, combined with Kennedy's unflinching belief in human progress, opened up the entire globe, even the entire universe, to Americans. God, so it seemed, was calling Americans to share their talents and treasures with all of humankind, and to spread the democratic form of government around the world. With that optimistic confidence, Americans sent Peace Corp volunteers to share Yankee know-how with less developed countries, and Americans launched an Alliance for Progress to turn dictatorial Latin American regimes into working democracies. Unlike the difficult years that followed, it was a good time to be an American!

Not surprisingly, it was a time that produced some good Westerns. It ought to be no great surprise that as a young President used the metaphor of a new frontier to symbolize his efforts, Hollywood responded with a few films about the old frontier. John Wayne's long awaited *The Alamo* (United Artists, 1960), *The Magnificent Seven* (United Artists, 1960) and John Ford's *Sergeant Rutledge* (Warner Brothers, 1960) all appeared on the big screen in 1960. Three years later, *How the West Was Won* (MGM, 1963) was released. They stand as book ends supporting two outstanding Westerns of 1962: *The Man Who Shot Liberty Valence* (Paramount, 1962) appeared in April, and was followed by *Ride the High Country* (MGM, 1962). In August 1963, Allied Artists released *The Gun Hawk*.

Sergeant Rutledge was released in the spring of 1960, and while the critics did not like it, in many ways it is a remarkable film for that time (Ronald Davis 1995, 298–299). As Ford biographer Ronald L. Davis notes, "The picture was consistent with the contemporary civil rights movement" (Davis 1995, 296). It was more than consistent; it expanded the boundaries of the civil rights movement as they existed in 1960 and suggested themes that would dominate the movement for the rest of the decade. Surely, the concluding courtroom scenes are disappointing. Fred Libby's (playing Chandler Hubble) histrionic confession on the witness stand that he murdered and raped Lucy (Toby Richards) is a bit contrived, but throughout the remainder of the film, Ford confronts white racial attitudes and fears as they existed in the early 1960s.

Woody Strode plays Sergeant Rutledge, a black man who is a soldier's soldier. The dignified Rutledge believes in the Ninth Cavalry. He is called "top soldier" by his black comrades (the film was initially released as *Captain Buffalo*). The theme song "Captain Buffalo" speaks of a man bigger than Lookout Mountain and taller than the Redwoods, a man mightier than John Henry. That is a remarkable tribute to a black soldier in 1960. And as the film unfolds in flashbacks during the court martial trial, the black soldiers (buffalo soldiers) under the command of Jeffrey Hunter (Lieutenant Tom Cantrall) demonstrate military discipline and bravery as they drive a renegade band of Apaches back to the reservation.

The plot unfolds as Strode discovers the naked body of Lucy Dabney when he rushes to Major Dabney's house to inform him that an Apache raiding party has left the reservation. Rutledge stoops to cover the naked body of the young woman who had been his friend, when the major comes into the room and assumes that Strode has raped and killed his daughter.

Shots are exchanged, Dabney is killed, and Strode, wounded, flees. Hunter is assigned the task of returning Rutledge to the post for court martial proceedings, as well as chasing the Indians back to the reservation.

In the meantime, Constance Towers (playing Marcy Beecher) had debarked at a deserted railroad station to await her father. There she discovers that Apaches have murdered the stationmaster. Strode arrives at the station in time to kill two Apaches (Towers kills a third) and to protect Towers from further harm. The wounded Strode insists that Towers stay in the other room while he sleeps. He did not want to be caught sleeping in the same room with a white woman! Hunter and his squad of buffalo soldiers arrive at the station, arrest Strode and prepare to escort Towers to her father's ranch. Hunter can't believe that Strode killed and raped Lucy, but he is determined to take the accused back to the post.

Before the squad can get to the Towers ranch, Apaches raid it and kill Constance Towers' father. Apaches then attack the patrol, and Strode goes after a wounded soldier whose horse runs away with him. When the soldier dies, Strode escapes toward freedom. Later, however, he discovers that the Apaches are about to ambush the column, so he rides back across the river to warn them of their impending fate. After a fight, the Apaches are beaten off and head back to the reservation, but Hunter remains determined to take Strode back to the post to stand trial — even though Strode has saved the entire squad. Towers is incensed. Strode has proven he was a "top soldier" by warning the column and saving them all from certain death. In the eyes of both Towers and Strode's fellow buffalo soldiers, he is a hero. The consensus is that Strode will be awarded the Congressional Medal of Honor for his action.

Several elements in the film make it an excellent commentary on the civil rights movement of the early 1960s. The first of these, already noted, is the theme song, "Captain Buffalo," in which a contemporary black man is presented as a mighty man, a man greater than the legendary John Henry. The second element is the opposite of the first. The ladies of the fort, particularly Billie Burke (playing Mrs. Cordelia Fosgate, wife of Colonel Otis Fosgate, the head of the court martial tribunal), have already decided that Strode is guilty as charged, if for no other reason than he is a black man. In a flashback, viewers learn that Burke had known Lucy Dabney at a previous posting and was alarmed at the friendship between Strode and Lucy. It was not proper, in Burke's eyes, for a young white woman to befriend a black male. Surely the vast majority of white Americans of 1960 would have agreed with that assessment!

Burke's racist outlook is reinforced by Carleton Young, who plays the

In *Sergeant Rutledge* (1960), Woody Strode (center), as First Sergeant Braxton Rutledge, is on trial for murder. He is defended by Jeffrey Hunter (left) against Carlton Young's racist prosecution.

prosecutor. Near the end of the trial, Hunter suggests that the son of the Sutler store owner, a young man who had been killed by the Apaches, and who had been sweet on Lucy, had committed the crime. That is too much for Young, who bitterly denounces Hunter's efforts to besmirch the reputation of a dead white boy to save the life of a Negro. In Young's racism, one is reminded of *To Kill a Mockingbird* (Universal, 1962). In that film Gregory Peck proves that a black man accused of raping a white woman was incapable physically of committing the crime; nonetheless, an all-white jury returned a guilty verdict. In the climate of the early 1960s, it was unlikely that a black male accused of murder and rape could get a fair trial in most southern and border states. *Sergeant Rutledge* makes a similar point. In that social context, one can understand why Strode ran away.

One other element makes *Sergeant Rutledge* a striking film for 1960. Constance Towers is shown administering first aid to the wounded black soldiers, and at one point she cradles the head of a black soldier in her lap. The social distance and lack of physical contact between black males and white women in Hollywood productions during the 1930s and 1940s is challenged in *Sergeant Rutledge*. The film is clearly a harbinger of the Civil Rights movement that was about to descend on the country with full force.

Woody Strode understood that point. Phil Hardy, in *The Western*, quotes Strode as saying, "You never seen [sic] a negro come off a mountain like John Wayne before. I had the greatest Glory Hallelujah ride across the Pecos River.... I carried the whole black race across that river" (Hardy, 277). An African American wrote Ford about *Sergeant Rutledge*, claiming that it was "the most significant Negro-theme movie that I have ever seen. If it were up to me, I would have it shown in every classroom in America" (Davis 1995, 299).

The Alamo and *The Magnificent Seven* were both released in October 1960 at the height of the presidential campaign. *The Alamo* had been Wayne's dream since at least 1948, and he had been actively working on the project since 1956. The furthest thing from Wayne's mind was to make a film celebrating the Kennedys, who Wayne regarded as "self-serving snobs lusting after power and lacking any moral vision" (Roberts and Olson, 472–73). Furthermore, Wayne believed that *Profiles in Courage*, a book for which John F. Kennedy won a Pulitzer Prize, had been ghost written (Roberts and Olson, 473). To Wayne, the message in *The Alamo* was that, "Americans needed to be ready once again to take a firm stand against aggression and dictatorship" (Roberts and Olson, 460). Wayne told Louella Parsons that, "The eyes of the world are on us. We must sell America to countries threatened with Communist domination" (Roberts and Olson, 472).

Even though John Wayne disliked John Kennedy and campaigned energetically for Vice President Richard Nixon in 1960, Wayne's political goal in making *The Alamo* was echoed by President John Kennedy in numerous speeches, and in his actions throughout his presidency. Certainly one of the underlying objectives of the Peace Corps was to sell America to the rest of the world. Continued American presences in Laos and South Vietnam, as well as the Cuban Missile Crisis, were indications that Kennedy believed that Americans needed to take a firm stand against Communist aggression and dictatorship. Whatever Wayne's intentions, it is clear that *The Alamo* fits well the Cold War warrior outlook of not only

President John Kennedy, but Secretary of State Dean Rusk and Secretary
of Defense Robert McNamara as well.

If *The Alamo* reflected Kennedy's (as well as Wayne's) underlying foreign policy orientation, *The Magnificent Seven* portrayed the activism that
was the hallmark of American foreign policy throughout the 1960s. In fact,
the opening thirty minutes of the film anticipate issues that shaped policy debates throughout the decade. *The Magnificent Seven* opens as a gang
of Mexican bandits, led by Eli Wallach, ride into a poor village, stealing
from and frightening the peasants who live there. After the bandits ride
away, men of the village decide to go across the border to buy guns with
which to defend themselves. The setting then switches to a border town
in which town bullies will not permit an Indian to be buried on boot hill
among white men. Yul Brynner and Steve McQueen, a couple of drifting
gunfighters, volunteer to drive the hearse to boot hill, and they force the
town bullies to back down. A delegation from the Mexican village had ridden into town and observed Brynner and McQueen in action, so they visit
with Brynner and plead with him to help them defeat Wallach.

Wallach is a bandit terrorizing his own people — and in Southeast
Asia, Latin America and Africa of 1960 the American people saw more
than a few twentieth century Wallachs. The only answer, if democracy was
to be preserved and extended, was for American forces to engage in
counter-insurgency. The seven gunfighters are 1960s United States
counter-insurgent fighters dressed in western garb. And, clearly, the
unwillingness of the border town bullies to permit an Indian to be buried
on boot hill reflected the racial segregation being challenged throughout
the South by local African Americans, as well as northern activists— outsiders to the South, just as Brynner and McQueen had been in the border
town.

Richard Slotkin calls *The Magnificent Seven* "a 'liberal' Western whose
heroes will rescue a hapless Mexican village from bandits and who will
themselves be redeemed by the experience" (Slotkin, 474). This, Slotkin
believes, anticipates "the New Frontier's call for citizens to ask not what
their country can do for them, but what they can do for their country"
(Slotkin, 475). To a great extent the seven gunfighters capture the tough-
minded spirit that President Kennedy sought to inspire, for, as Slotkin
notes, the seven were "men 'without illusions' who nonetheless fulfill the
most idealistic explanations" (Slotkin, 475). Slotkin summarizes his point
by observing:

> The good work of saving Mexico is not to be undertaken in the sentimental or idealistic spirit of romantic missionaries; it is to be firmly based in "realism," the implications being that pure idealism is too rare and perishable a quality to sustain a long, dirty, twilight struggle [Slotkin, 476].

The tension that has always existed in American foreign policy between gritty realism and utopian-leaning idealism is played out near the end of the film. Wallach and his bandits, after being beaten off in an initial raid, sneak back into the village while the seven are out on a scouting mission. Outnumbered and surrounded, the seven are forced to give up their guns, but Wallach decides not to kill them because he does not want other gunfighters coming to avenge their deaths. Wallach permits them to leave the village unharmed, and even gives them back their guns when they are well away from it. As they pack to leave, Brynner and McQueen acknowledge that the mission has become more than a job; they really care for these poor peasants and want to help them make their lives better.

Once they have their guns back, the seven stage a commando style raid on the village and kill Wallach and most of his men; but four of the seven also die in the fight. Wallach finds their motives bewildering and, as he lay dying, asks Brynner "why"— why would seven gringos fight and die for a small, poor Mexican village. The answer seemed clear to most Americans in 1960: if democracy was to be preserved, and if dictators who denied their people peace and prosperity were to be stamped out, the American people must act. The need for counter-insurgency to destroy the Wallachs of the world was nearly an article of faith in both the Kennedy Administration and the country as a whole. By the end of the decade, that notion would divide the American people as they had not been divided since the Civil War, but 1960 was another matter altogether.

Not only did the Kennedy Administration affirm a foreign policy that ended with the debacle in Vietnam, it served as a bridge between the old values (still a force in American life in 1961) and the new values looming on the horizon. *The Man Who Shot Liberty Valence* and *Ride the High Country* have more in common with older America than they have with a country shaped by a new morality and a post–Vietnam outlook.

The Man Who Shot Liberty Valence opens in a transformed West. The railroad has brought the benefits of progress and peace to the once-violent town of Shinbone. In the midst of that, James Stewart, playing

John Wayne is the man who shot Liberty Valance.

Senator Rance Stoddard, and his wife Hallie, played by Vera Miles, return to pay their last respects to Tom Doniphan, John Wayne's character in the film. No one in the town except a few old-timers even know who Wayne was. The local newspaper was totally unaware of his death. After all, he was nobody important! The editor, surprised that a United States Senator would be concerned about such a nobody, demands to know who Wayne was, and why Stewart has come so far to pay to his respects to a dead man. Stewart placates the editor by telling the story of the man who short Liberty Valance. By that time, Stewart had become a prominent politician, in part because the public believed that he had killed Valance. Now Stewart would set the record straight, and give credit to John Wayne, the real hero.

As Stewart tells his story, one sees images and themes familiar to those who grew up with cowboy movies. Stewart goes west as a young attorney determined to replace the gun with law books. Wayne scoffs at the idea; he tells Stewart that law books may mean a great deal to him, but out here a man settles his own problems. Violence, not law, is Wayne's method, and ultimately Stewart uses a gun against Liberty Valance — not because he wants to, but because he has to. However, viewers learn early in the film that Stewart's way, the law's way, had triumphed.

Stewart sees that the undertaker failed to put boots on the corpse. Angrily, he orders the undertaker to replace Wayne's boots and spurs, and his gun belt as well. Andy Devine, playing Link Appleyard, the man who had informed Stewart of Wayne's death, intervenes. According to Devine, Wayne "didn't carry no handgun, not for years." Law books had replaced the gun. Stewart's way had won the day.

The Man Who Shot Liberty Valance also includes two other themes prominent in pre–1955 Westerns: homesteaders versus cattlemen, and organized versus unorganized territory. The cattlemen, committed to an open range, oppose both homesteaders south of the Picket Wire River and efforts to organize the territory. Homesteaders, on the other hand, recognize that territorial status is the only way to protect their claims.

Lee Marvin plays the evil gunman Liberty Valance, whose gang intends to keep the territory wide open. Marvin tries to ramrod his election as one of the delegates from Shinbone to the territorial convention. But the homesteaders and residents of Shinbone won't be cowed. They elect Stewart and Edmond O'Brien, playing the local newspaper editor, as delegates. Both men support the territorial cause. Marvin then orders Stewart out of town, and tells him that if he is around that night, Marvin will kill him. Thus the fatal confrontation is established.

All of these — law books versus guns, homesteaders versus cattlemen, and organized territory versus unorganized territory ruled by force — are distinctive attributes of traditional Westerns. Good Triumphs over evil, law replaces violence, and the homesteaders (as carriers of progress) defeat the cattlemen.

Stewart ties all of these elements together with his school. Soon after arriving in Shinbone, he opens up a school for the many residents who cannot read or write. Stewart helps his pupils learn by studying the country and how it is governed. In a nice bit of irony, director John Ford even has black actor Woody Strode recite from the Declaration of Independence. And Stewart draws his class's attention to an article O'Brien wrote for the local newspaper in which he defends territorial status. Stewart stands for law, and he teaches about the government. He believes American values are worth learning about and defending.

Yet one thing is certain; without John Wayne, the cowboy hero, Stewart's efforts would have failed. Marvin would have killed Stewart had Wayne not shot Marvin from a side street. In *Angel and the Badman* (Republic, 1947) Harry Carey was the man of violence who pulled the trigger and thus protected John Wayne (Loy, 65). Now Wayne is the man of violence who saves Stewart's life.

However, unlike in other John Wayne Westerns, Stewart wins the praise as the man who killed Liberty Valance, and he gets the girl. Wayne had always believed Vera Miles would marry him, and he had been building a house for her. Now he realizes that he has lost Miles to Stewart. Embittered, Wayne gets drunk and burns down the house. But Wayne does not let bitterness consume him.

Stewart is on the verge of being nominated territorial representative to Congress, but he can't stand the thought that an act of violence — the shooting of Liberty Valance — had earned him acclaim. When he is about to refuse the nomination, Wayne pulls him aside and tells Stewart who *really* shot Liberty Valance. Wayne challenges Stewart to go back and accept the nomination for Miles' sake, and to finish what he had begun. Wayne, the man of violence, is the real hero. He steps aside as the forces of law and order and civilization replace him. He even loses the girl to the man who represents those forces. Nevertheless, Wayne remains the hero!

So Stewart tells his story to the editor, and he tells it at some cost. He was regarded by many as a potential candidate for the vice-presidential nomination, a cap to an illustrious political career. Of course, that would be jeopardized once it became known that Wayne, not Stewart, shot Liberty Valance. The editor of the local newspaper, however, throws his notes into the stove. When Stewart expresses surprise, the editor replies, "This is the West, sir. When the legend becomes fact, print the legend."

The editor's comment, long debated by film scholars, has several possible meanings. It could mean that at some point legend and fact become so intermingled they are indistinguishable. The lives and legends of western personalities such as Jesse James, Wyatt Earp and Billy the Kid fit that interpretation. It could also mean that after a time it is better to perpetuate the legend, even at the cost of truth.

It could mean either of these things, but it could also mean something else. It could mean that Stewart, in his years of public service, in his willingness to face Liberty Valance, and in his truthfulness, proved that he was indeed a man of courage and integrity. In Stewart, the legend had become a fact, so print the fact!

As the train pulls away from Shinbone after the funeral, Stewart and Miles compare the fruitful plains with the earlier West they had known. Then Stewart surprises Miles by saying he is thinking about retiring from politics. He has a hankerin' to come back to Shinbone and live, maybe practice a little law. Miles is pleased. My roots are here, she says, and I guess my heart is here.

So as Stewart and Miles reflect on the life of Tom Doniphan, the man who really shot Liberty Valance, they rediscover their roots. In the midst of the new West, a new era of life, in fact, the life of the John Wayne, the cowboy hero, reminds them that old values are still important, even necessary, in a rapidly changing time.

At first glance, *The Man Who Shot Liberty Valance* and *Ride the High Country* appear to have little in common. The former received widespread play in this country, while *Ride the High Country* was released by MGM as the second feature of a double bill. Lightly regarded by Americans, the film won prizes at several European film festivals and made MGM a great deal of money in the European market (Tuska 1976, 512). Furthermore, *Ride the High Country* lacks the majestic reach of *The Man Who Shot Liberty Valance.* One does not find in the former film concern for the triumph of law and civilization. Conflicts in *The Man Who Shot Liberty Valance* touch on socially transforming events. They are about the expansion of the country itself. If Tom Doniphan had not shot Liberty Valance, one senses that somehow the West would have been different. Not so in *Ride the High Country.* If Randolph Scott, Joel McCrea and Ronald Starr had split the $11,000 in gold dust and ridden off in different directions, it would have made little difference.

Ride the High Country, however, is about values central to traditional Westerns and to American culture of the 1930s and 1940s. The film is about

Mariette Hartley, Ronald Starr, Joel McCrea and Randolph Scott head for the mining camp in *Ride the High Country* (1962).

integrity and courage, and above all a determination to uphold one's integrity even at the expense of material success. *Ride the High Country* is about personal honor, a characteristic important to the cowboy hero and to the American people in the early 1960s. That is why *Ride the High Country* merits consideration.

From the opening scenes, one realizes that the West, while not yet completely transformed, has changed. Joel McCrea rides into town, and is nearly caught up in a race between a horse and a camel. A modern-looking policeman helps us to realize the change when he yells at McCrea, "Get out of the street, old man. Can't you see you're in the way?"

McCrea then discovers his old partner, Randolph Scott, running a carnival game. Wearing a red wig, Scott challenges customers to out-shoot the former lawman who had cleaned up notorious outlaw gangs. He embellishes the past in order to make a few cents in the present. Scott is too old, and his skills as a gunman are no longer needed, so he earns a living fleecing dudes.

When McCrea goes to the bank to make arrangements to escort gold from mines in the high Sierras to the bank in the valley, he discovers that he won't be responsible for $250,000, just $20,000. The banker reminds McCrea that the big strikes are over. The days of the forty-niners have passed. The banker assures McCrea, "The day of the steady businessman has arrived." If McCrea is disappointed in the amount of money, the banker is disappointed in McCrea. He had expected a younger man. Alas, even cowboy heroes age! But they strike a mutual agreement in spite of their disappointments. Joel McCrea, Randolph Scott and Ronald Starr set out for the mining camps.

At this point the conflict begins. Scott and Starr intend to keep the money. Scott believes he can talk McCrea into cooperating, but he will take it by force if necessary. Scott keeps reminding McCrea of how they served the public, brought law and order to the West, and received so little in return. However, McCrea remains firmly committed to his code. At one point McCrea reminisces about an old sheriff who arrested him as a young man for unruly, drunken behavior, and took him behind the jail and beat the daylights out of him. McCrea chuckled, "He was right, I was wrong. That makes all the difference." Scott won't stand for it. He wants to know what McCrea expects from life. To that, McCrea replies, "All I want is to enter my house justified." Clearly, Scott intends to steal the money. McCrea's honor and integrity require him to complete the job for which he is being paid $20 a day; he intends to take the money to the bank.

As *Ride the High Country* unfolds, the three men rescue Mariette Hartley from the Hammond brothers, even though Hartley is legally married to James Drury (as Billy Hammond). Ronald Starr, sweet on Hartley, develops serious reservations about stealing the money, but Scott insists. One evening Scott and Starr steal the money and sneak away, but McCrea catches them. When the Hammonds come after Hartley, McCrea gives Starr his gun on the promise he will return it after the fight. He keeps Scott tied up.

That evening, after they have beaten off the Hammonds in a running gunfight, McCrea permits Scott to sleep with his hands untied. McCrea tries to assure Hartley that Starr will receive a light sentence; McCrea will testify for him. Hartley asks about Scott. McCrea replies that he will not testify in support of Scott, concluding, "He was my friend." Scott, however, escapes and goes back to get the horse and gun belonging to one of the dead Hammonds. McCrea, Starr and Hartley push on for her father's farm.

The Hammond brothers get there first. They kill Hartley's bible-spouting father (R.G. Armstrong) and lie in ambush, waiting for McCrea. The Hammonds have McCrea, Starr and Hartley pinned down in a ditch when Scott rides in, gun blazing. At that point, Scott and McCrea call out the Hammonds, and in a stand-up gunfight they kill all three Hammonds; however, McCrea is mortally wounded.

Scott assures his friend that he will take the money to the bank. "Hell," McCrea says, "I always knew you would. You just forgot for a little while." Then telling Scott to get Starr and Hartley away, he says to Scott, "I'll go it alone." Looking up at Scott, McCrea says simply, "So long partner." Scott's reply is equally simple: "I'll see you later." With that, the film ends. There is really nothing more to say; McCrea had kept his sense of personal honor, and Scott had recovered his. As in *The Man Who Shot Liberty Valance*, old values win in the end. Honor and friendship triumph over greed.

Paul Seydor makes this point when he writes, "The journey into the past is thus triumphantly completed, and with it Gil's [Randolph Scott] redemption...has left him fortified against temptation and fit at last to deliver the gold when Steve is no longer able" (Seydor, 59). The same thing applies to the Hammond brothers. When McCrea and Scott called them out, one of the brothers suggested that they kill the two men as soon as they raised up, but the oldest Hammond calls on family honor and they go out to meet McCrea and Scott as honorable men would do. Seydor concludes, "Even these limited, gross people are seen to be capable of modeling themselves for one brief moment after the superior example set by the two men, becoming in the process worthy foes" (Seydor, 59).

The two films reflect important elements of the Kennedy ethos. In his 1961 Inaugural Address, President Kennedy spoke of our "ancient heritage" while reminding listeners that the torch of leadership had passed to a new generation of Americans. An often overlooked aspect of the Kennedy legacy was his insistence on the pertinence of old values — our ancient heritage — while refashioning them to fit the new political, social, economic and cultural realities of the 1960s. James Stewart in *The Man Who Shot Liberty Valance*, and Joel McCrea in *Ride the High Country*, have the same objective. Old values must prevail in changing times. Contexts may alter, but values such as honesty, truthfulness and civility are important attributes of our ancient heritage. Americans must hold to them steadfastly! That is the lesson of the two films, a lesson that reflects the ethos of the Kennedy years.

During the early 1960s a large majority of the American people developed a fascination with the Kennedy family. Not only was John Kennedy President of the United States, his brother Robert was Attorney General, and in 1962 younger brother Edward (Ted) was elected to the Unites States Senate from Massachusetts. Newspapers and magazines featured stories about the parents, the Kennedy girls and their husbands; the rugged touch football games; the family's love of the sea; and John Kennedy's wife, Jacqueline, with her foreign language skill and her beauty and grace. The Kennedys established themselves alongside of the two other well-known American families of American politics, the Roosevelts and the Tafts. In February 1963, *How the West Was Won*, a film that celebrated the importance of family in westward expansion, was released. The film traces the role of one extended family as it settled and conquered the West of the nineteenth century.

How the West Was Won opens as Carroll Baker (as Eve Prescott) and Debbie Reynolds (Lilith Prescott) leave New York with their parents to go west. Tragedy follows them and both parents are killed running rapids after they take a wrong fork of the Ohio River. Both parents are buried on a bluff overlooking the river, and Carroll Baker remains there to marry James Stewart (Linus Rawlings). They begin a farm and raise two sons. In the meantime, Debbie Reynolds works as a singer until she marries Gregory Peck (Cleve Van Valen), a gambler and con artist. Together, Reynolds and Peck participate in the railroad boom in California before and after the Civil War.

George Peppard (Zeb Rawlings), Carroll Baker's oldest son, fights in the Civil War (a war in which his father is killed), and when he discovers his mother has died during the war, goes west to help build the transcontinental railroad and to become a frontier marshal. The film ends with Peppard, now married and a father, and Reynolds (his Aunt Lilith) reunited in Arizona. The greater Prescott family has been instrumental in taming the West.

Narrator Spencer Tracy provides the glue that holds the film together. The last few frames, scenes of the West of the 1960s, remind viewers of the sacrifice, courage and values of the pioneering families that made the new West possible, the West of the New Frontier. The challenge seems straightforward; the generation of the 1960s must emulate the courage and sacrifice of the pioneers while refashioning the values of their ancient heritage to fit the West of the New Frontier.

Contemporary viewers probably find *How the West Was Won* excessively sentimental, maybe even maudlin, and boorish. Viewers of the 1960s saw the film differently. With its focus on family, its majestic scenery and its celebration of those who built a country out of wilderness, *How the West Was Won* captured the spirit of the American people of that day, a people enraptured by the Kennedy family and the Kennedy ethos.

In *Ride the High Country*, Joel McCrea reminisces about an old sheriff who reformed a young and wild McCrea from his drunken, unruly ways. Rod Cameron, as the aging sheriff Ben Corey, plays such a role in *The Gun Hawk*. Cameron had tried to convince Rory Calhoun (playing Blaine Madden) to become his deputy, but Calhoun refused; he was more interested in the wild side of life. And when the young saddle tramp and would-be gunfighter Rod Lauren (as Reb) rides into town, Cameron tries unsuccessfully to befriend him as well. Cameron plays a traditional kind of Western lawman; he is wise, strong and determined, yet patient. Cameron enforces the law with a minimum amount of violence and a large dose of justice. He keeps warning his young deputy, Morgan Woodward, that a badge is not a license to settle personal scores or wreak vengeance on those who have wronged him. In short, Cameron's character in *The Gun Hawk* models the values of which Kennedy spoke when he referenced our "ancient heritage."

When Calhoun rides back into town after a three-year absence, Cameron warns him not to start any trouble. An older and wearier Calhoun replies, "I don't even have to start trouble anymore." Calhoun rescues Lauren from a fight begun when two men catch the kid cheating at cards, and even though Calhoun tries to ignore the kid, Lauren follows him around much like a little boy hero-worshipping an older man.

That evening in the town saloon, the Sully brothers (Lane Bradford and Glen Stensel) refuse to buy an old drunk a glass of whiskey and shove him away onto a table. Calhoun intervenes and forces the Sully brothers to buy the old-timer a drink. Resentful of having to back down from Calhoun, the brothers entice him into an alley. During the ensuing gunfight, the old man (who turns out to be Calhoun's father, a man of whom he was ashamed) is killed. Cameron warns Calhoun that he will go after the killers; it is a job for the law. Calhoun won't buy that; he replies, "It is my debt, can't let somebody else pay it for me." Calhoun tracks down and kills the Sully brothers.

Cameron goes after Calhoun in order to arrest him for murder, and shoots him in the right arm when Calhoun, betting that Cameron will not shoot him in the back, tries to ride away. As Cameron bends over Calhoun's body, Lauren, who has followed both of them from town, knocks out Cameron and rescues Calhoun. Lauren takes out the bullet, but Calhoun's right arm hangs useless at his side. Together the two men ride to Sanctuary, a haven for outlaws. A man known as the Gun Hawk runs the town. The Gun Hawk enforces town rules: no cheating at cards, no killing and no stealing. Much to his surprise, Lauren learns that Calhoun is the Gun Hawk.

Rod Lauren (left) is the wannabe gunfighter that both Rod Cameron and Rory Calhoun try to reform in *The Gun Hawk* (1963).

Poison (gangrene?) infects the wound, and Calhoun knows that he is dying. In the meantime, Cameron, taking up the pursuit, rides into Sanctuary and tries to arrest Calhoun, but is forced by the townsfolk to leave. The ever-patient lawman that he is, Cameron realizes that Calhoun can't use his arm and may be dying, so he observes Sanctuary from a mountaintop overlooking the town.

Near the end of *The Gun Hawk* Calhoun tells Lauren, "I look at you and it's me ten years ago." But Calhoun does not want that sort of a life for Lauren, so he forces the young man to face him in a shootout, with the whole town looking on. Of course, Lauren kills Calhoun, who can't use his right arm, permitting the older gunfighter to die with dignity. But Lauren, who has now killed, must leave Sanctuary, just as Calhoun knew he would have to do. Cameron and Lauren ride away together. Calhoun had helped the younger man to go straight, and the older sheriff is there to help the process along. The film ends with the promise that what Cameron had failed to do for Calhoun he can now do for Lauren.

The Gun Hawk is little more than a ninety-minute B Western. It lacks the majestic scenery of *Ride the High Country* or the socially transforming qualities of *The Man Who Shot Liberty Valence*. Yet through Cameron's willingness to mentor younger men, and Calhoun's realization of his mistakes, Lauren is spared from a certain life of crime. Through the life of one cowboy hero (Cameron) and the death of another (Calhoun), the old values triumph. Within three months from the day *The Gun Hawk* hit theaters, John Kennedy was dead, and the United States began to experience the social and political turmoil that would mark the rest of the decade, a decade that demonstrated that the old values would not easily fit the changing times. *Lonely Are the Brave* (Universal-International, 1962) anticipated that difficulty.

Released in June 1962, *Lonely Are the Brave* is set in the contemporary West. The film opens with Kirk Douglas (playing Jack Burns) resting beside a campfire in the wide-open spaces while his horse grazes nearby. However, viewers quickly learn that this is not the Old West when the quiet is broken by the scream of jet airplanes overhead. Douglas stamps out the campfire, saddles his horse and rides away. At one point he must cut a wire fence that impedes his freedom of movement. The wide-open range of the Old West has given way to the modern West of fences. And if that is not enough, Douglas' horse, Whiskey, spooks as they cross a modern highway, with automobiles and trucks whizzing by. The images are stark. Douglas is a cowboy trying to live an outmoded lifestyle. He and his horse are out of place in a world of fences, highways and automobiles.

Douglas is on his way to visit Gena Rowlands (as Jerri Bondi) whose husband, Michael Kane, playing Paul Bondi, is in jail. Living out the values expected of a cowboy, Douglas has come to help (Loy, 135). Viewers learn that Kane is in jail because he gave aid and advice to illegal immigrants. Now he faces a two-year prison term. Douglas is not surprised. He tells Rowlands that both he and Kane hate fences; westerners like the wide-open country. The fences in this case are modern laws, rules and regulations by which people are expected to live.

Douglas speaks of the wide-eyed mountain girl to whom he and Paul are attracted. When Rowlands looks surprised, Douglas tells her that the wide-eyed mountain girl is really an attitude: "Do what you want to do and hell with everybody else." Rowlands' response places the film in

Kirk Douglas won't adjust to the modern world in *Lonely Are the Brave* (1962). He talks with Gena Rowlands as both stand beside his horse Whiskey.

context. The problem, she claims, is that, "You and Paul live in a world that doesn't exist. Either live by the rules or suffer the consequences."

Still determined to help Kane, Douglas gets himself arrested. When he breaks out of jail, Kane will not go with him. Kane tells Douglas, "I don't want Seth [his son] to grow up to be like we were." Douglas' response, "You grew up on me — you changed," highlights the theme of the film: times have changed, and Douglas, the old cowboy, either can't or won't alter his behavior. Modern cities, highways and fences, including all the rules and regulations of the modern state, have replaced the wide-open spaces. The values, the old values, by which Douglas has lived don't fit anymore. Kane and Rowlands understand that and are prepared to adapt. Douglas is an atavistic symbol of an aging past, one that will never be recovered.

Douglas, however, is not prepared to accept the new world. After he escapes from jail, Douglas returns to Rowlands' house to retrieve Whiskey and make his escape. When Rowlands asks, "Will I ever see you again," Douglas responds, "Oh sure, these things always blow over." It is as if Douglas naively thinks that the contemporary West — the West of cities, highways and rules — will somehow recede, and the Old West — the West of Douglas' atavistic longings — will return. Douglas turns Whiskey toward the mountains; once over them he can get to Mexico and wait for the Old West he so fervently desires to reassert itself.

The pursuit begins. The sheriff (played by Walter Matthau) uses jeeps and helicopters to track down Douglas as he climbs up the mountain with Whiskey. But Douglas, ever the resourceful cowboy, eludes their efforts and makes it over the mountain. Freedom seems imminent. In a driving rain, Douglas and Whiskey come to a modern highway. Once he gets across it, Mexico and freedom will be within reach. But Whiskey spooks, just as she did at the beginning of the film, and a truck hauling toilets — a vivid symbol of the modern world Douglas rejects — strikes down rider and horse. Whiskey has to be destroyed and Douglas is hauled away in an ambulance. Viewers can't be sure whether or not he will live, but one thing is certain: the world that Douglas valued has died. The death of Whiskey, the cowboy's horse, symbolizes the death of the Old West and its values of freedom — no fences, no rules — that Douglas personified.

Lonely Are the Brave suggests that Kennedy's efforts to reaffirm the values of our ancient heritage and to shape them so they would fit the 1960s and beyond were doomed to failure. In fact, in retrospect it is easy to see that the opposite happened. Douglas' Jack Burns seems to speak for the generation of college-bound baby boomers who liked that wide-eyed mountain girl ("do what you want to do and hell with everybody else"). To 1960s baby boomers, Jack Burns' "Do what you want to do and hell with everybody else" becomes the sexual license, anti-materialism, anti-organization and political radicalism that infected every facet of American life for nearly a decade.

Ironically for contemporary viewers of *Lonely Are the Brave*, Carroll O'Connor plays the toilet-hauling truck driver who hits Douglas and Whiskey. O'Connor, of course, went on to play Archie Bunker in the smash television hit *All in the Family*. As Archie Bunker, O'Connor is the bigoted, opinionated symbol of all that opposes Douglas' wide-eyed mountain girl.

Films such as *The Man Who Shot Liberty Valence*, *Ride the High Country* and even *The Gun Hawk* speak to American desires to maintain the relevance of old values in an increasingly urban, fast-paced, technological society. One suspects, however, that it is not possible. The old values are as hard to maintain in the contemporary world as it was for Kirk Douglas' Jack Burns to exist in 1962 as a carefree cowboy who lived by his own rules. With the exception of the films of John Wayne, post–1965 Westerns (particularly those made by such icons as Sam Peckinpah and Clint Eastwood) began to challenge the value structure that had dominated the genre since 1930. Increasingly, Westerns of the mid–1960s and beyond began to change dramatically. Just as John F. Kennedy was in the process of becoming a near-mythic figure, Westerns commenced to reflect the values and attitudes of the post–Kennedy era. While less than a decade separates *Ride the High Country* from Sam Peckinpah's *The Wild Bunch* (Warner Brothers, 1969) and Clint Eastwood's *Hang 'em High* (United Artists, 1968), the latter two films have so little in common with the former that it is as if they sprung from different eras.

Chapter 4

SAM PECKINPAH
IN THE 1960S

By the middle quarter of the twentieth century, prominent figures in the westward expansion of the United States had become towering personalities in American popular culture. Pre–Civil War Americans had thrilled at the legendary exploits of Daniel Boone, Davy Crockett, and mountain men, fur trappers and explorers such as Jim Bridger, John C. Frémont and Kit Carson. The trans–Mississippi West, with its Indians, cowboys, sheriffs, gunfighters, outlaws and notable women offered post–Civil War Americans a new source of popular culture heroes and legends, and both native-born citizens and the masses of recently arrived immigrants took to them like ducks to water. For one hundred years after the beginning of the Civil War, dime novels, pulp fiction, stage plays, wild west shows, radio, television and motion pictures offered audiences a substantial diet of Westerns. Recently, the popularity of Westerns in all genre expressions from the end of the Civil War to the middle of the twentieth century has generated a great deal of renewed interest — and no small amount of controversy.

In *West of Everything: The Inner Life of Westerns*, Jane Tompkins assigns the emerging popularity of Westerns in the early twentieth century to male reactions to the women's novels of the middle and late nineteenth century. The latter focused on home and domesticated Christian husbands who made marriage and religious faith dominant elements in their lives. Tompkins offers *In His Steps*, the widely read novel by Charles

Sheldon, as a prime example of the literature and worldview against which such writers as Owen Wister and Zane Grey rebelled. The latter offered readers, especially males, adventure stories and a naturalistic environment in which only the strong and the skilled survived. In Tompkins' view, Westerns became popular as males reacted to the feminized, Christianized understanding of social relationships and moral attitudes of the late Victorian era.

Richard Slotkin, in *Gunfighter Nation: The Myth of the Frontier in Twentieth-Century America*, and, more recently, Will Wright, in *The Wild West: The Mythical Cowboy & Social Theory*, offer a different understanding of the Western's increasing popularity in post–Civil War America. The Jeffersonian/Jacksonian dream of a country in which each citizen (specifically white male citizens) would be a land owner fully capable of supporting his family and free from the economic exploitation of others had ended by the beginning of the twentieth century. The shrinking of cheap western land led the Census Bureau to proclaim the end of the frontier in 1890, and Frederick Jackson Turner made the closing of the frontier the theoretical lynchpin that would dominate academic history of the West for nearly fifty years.

As the western frontier shrank and ultimately bumped against the placid waters of the Pacific Ocean, the industrial East rose to prominence. The Jeffersonian/Jacksonian dream of self-supporting, equal citizens drawing on the abundance of cheap land was undercut in the industrial East by the new social reality of a few wealthy citizens who owned the means of production and transportation, and the masses who were dependent on them for their livelihood. Furthermore, luminaries such as Theodore Roosevelt worried about the Teutonic/Anglo Saxon gene pool being debased by the masses of Eastern European immigrants flooding American cities. And that concern was joined to a support for segregation of the races and eradication of the western Indians.

For Slotkin and Wright, the westerner of popular culture reflected a longing for the rapidly disappearing Jeffersonian/Jacksonian social and economic expressions of the American experience. The cowboy of popular culture, nearly always of Teutonic/Anglo Saxon origin, was a model of self-sufficiency, a living rejection of the new industrial order, with its social classes and poverty. The cowboy sided with the small rancher and the homesteader against those who sought to bring Eastern values of social class and social control to the frontier. The cowboy was the embodiment of the Jeffersonian/Jacksonian dream in a society increasingly dominated and controlled by industrial and financial giants such as Rockefeller, Carnegie and Mellon. Slotkin and Wright place the Western's popularity squarely in this changing economic order. The Western reflected a long-ing for the economic and social values of the Jeffersonian/Jacksonian era, and a rejection of the social classes and mass poverty of the new indus-trial age.

Tompkins' argument is persuasive up to a point. The Western nov-els of Wister and Grey do display, at least, ambivalence to organized reli-gion, and their heroes are men caught up in a Darwinian struggle of the fittest. Surely, Wister and Grey's heroes are men proficient in the use of violence, hardly a Christian virtue. On the other hand, Tompkins' analy-sis does not fit most Western motion pictures. William S. Hart's silent Westerns draw heavily from an *In His Steps*–like morality. And Westerns produced from 1930 until the middle 1950s under the strictures of the Motion Pictures Producers and Distributor's Code continued to reflect the values, norms and attitudes of an Americanized version of Christianity. On the whole, it would seem that Slotkin and Wright offer better expla-nations of the Western's prominence from the late nineteenth century through the first sixty years of the twentieth century. Their argument that popular culture's cowboy of the post–Civil War nineteenth century was a symbolic expression of an America trying to fit its Jeffersonian/Jackson-ian roots into the realities of the industrial age is more intellectually sat-isfying than is Tompkins' view that the Western was an expression of popular culture's rejection of Christianity.

If Slotkin and Wright's accounts of the Western's emergent popu-larity in the late nineteenth century through the first sixty years of the twentieth century have merit (as I think they do), then Westerns produced from the middle 1960s to the end of the twentieth century ought to re-flect a culture coming to grips with a rapidly changing industrial order. Just as the United States began to shift from a predominantly agrarian society in the late nineteenth century (as cheap land disappeared) to an industrial society dominated by large urban areas, so too did that indus-trial society undergo substantial change in the last forty years of the twen-tieth century.

Changes in the American economy, and in its industrial sector in par-ticular, came in several dramatic waves after 1965. In the first wave of change, several large industries, most notably steel, collapsed. Rusting buildings along the southern shore of Lake Michigan and throughout the Beaver Valley of western Pennsylvania were vivid reminders of that col-lapse. The Gary, Indiana, works of U.S. Steel reduced its employees by the thousands, and other producers (such as Jones and Laughlin Steel Corpo-ration, and Youngstown Sheet and Tube) ceased production entirely. Thou-sands of steel workers faced early retirement and/or unemployment, and major cities such as Gary, Indiana, and Pittsburgh, Pennsylvania, long dependent on the steel industry, lost population and faced economic hard times.

The second wave of industrial change centered on the automobile industry. Increasing competition from Japanese companies in the 1970s shrank the demand for American manufactured cars. In response, domestic corporations such as Ford and General Motors, relied more on technology (e.g. robotics) and less on human labor. As a result, the auto industry employed far fewer people at the end of the 1970s than it had at the beginning of the decade. That downsizing was followed in the 1980s by out-sourcing as automobile components were frequently manufactured in other parts of the world and shipped back to the United States for assembly. As a result, previously large employers such as Delco-Remy restructured and downsized.

In a third wave of economic change, new types of corporations, such as dot.com companies and businesses like Enron, rose to prominence in the 1990s. High paying jobs in these emergent economic sectors went to the educated, while large segments of the less educated population were consigned to minimum wage jobs and were bypassed in the heady days of the 1990s booming economy. By the end of the twentieth century, the American economy had shifted from one of industrial dominance to a more diverse economy driven by service and new technologies.

As a new economy emerged in the last forty years of the twentieth century, the broader culture changed as well. Americans became more mobile and individualistic, and interpersonal relationships reflected an increasingly younger population less inclined to value traditional institutions such as marriage. The trends discussed in chapters 1 and 3 that began to appear in the 1950s emerged full bloom in the 1960s.

By the mid–1960s, Westerns commenced to reflect American fears, anxieties and disappointments over changing economic and cultural patterns. In turn, three men dominated the genre from 1965 through the 1970s. John Wayne, true to his political, economic and culturally conservative views, produced and starred in Westerns that challenged most of the assumptions of the new order. Clint Eastwood's Westerns, on the other hand, unlike John Wayne's films, reflected the descent of the hero; but they also resonated with people frustrated by the direction in which the country was drifting. Sam Peckinpah, far more than either Wayne or Eastwood, underscored the economic, cultural and moral confusion that highlighted the 1960s and early 1970s. In ways probably not fully appreciated nor understood, Sam Peckinpah changed Western films.

Jon Tuska, in his influential *The Filming of the West*, describes Sam Peckinpah as "the most important director of Westerns to have emerged since World War II" (Tuska 1976, 567). Tuska believes that Peckinpah possessed an awesome ability to "draw consistent character on the screen" and a profound understanding of human personality. He was, Tuska concludes, "one of the best Western filmmakers in the history of the genre" (Tuska 1976, 567). Michael Sragow is no less effusive when he describes Peckinpah as "the most perfect filmmaker of his generation" (Sragow, 1).

On the other hand, actress Maureen O'Hara told Boyd Magers and Michael Fitzgerald that she didn't think much of Sam Peckinpah, for whom she worked in *Deadly Companions* (Pathé-American, 1961). O'Hara said:

> I didn't enjoy Sam at all. I have to be honest. I didn't think he was a very good director. I think he was lucky that whatever happened in his career happened. I think it was luck, not talent. You have to forgive me. He was not a good director and if his films turned out successful that was luck — and people protecting him, like the cameramen and the producers. Different people protecting him made him look good [Magers and Fitzgerald 1999, 172–173].

From those three comments it appears that Sam Peckinpah's directorial legacy is like the man himself, a matter of some controversy. The controversies over Peckinpah's directorial talents lie beyond the scope of this work and need not detain us. However, in assessing Sam Peckinpah's role in refashioning Westerns of the 1960s and early 1970s, two things seem beyond dispute. First, Peckinpah's *The Wild Bunch* (Warner Brothers, 1969) is one of the most influential, if not *the* most influential, Western produced in the 1960s. And, second, Sam Peckinpah the man was in many ways a microcosm of the turbulent decade in which he gained national prominence.

Sam Peckinpah was born in 1925 into a solid California middle class family that experienced little of the devastating social and economic dislocation brought on by the Great Depression (Seydor, 336). On the other hand, the last vestiges of the cowboy way of life disappeared from the California landscape during Peckinpah's youth. Paul Seydor, in *Peckinpah, the Western Films: A Reconsideration*, observed that Peckinpah grew up just in time to see the Old West disappear (Seydor, 357). That left a lasting impression on young Peckinpah because, as he told Seydor, he felt rootless (Seydor, 361). Seydor contends that Peckinpah's Westerns lament the passing of the old values and virtues, such as courage, loyalty and friendship —

ones Peckinpah associated with the vanishing West of his childhood — and the emergence of the vices and materialism of corporate businessmen and politicians (Seydor, 361).

Although twenty years older than the oldest of the baby boomers, Peckinpah's life underscores many of the attitudes and much of the behavior associated with that now-famous post–World War II generation. Like many of them, Sam Peckinpah grew up in an economically comfortable home. His father had been an attorney who switched to ranching and wound up owning several thousand acres of California ranch land. Yet, according to Seydor, Sam was the most rebellious of the four Peckinpah children (Seydor, 336). And central to his rebellion was a rejection of the family's strong religious faith. His father believed in absolute moral truths that left Peckinpah "feeling constrained, dissatisfied, and disaffected" (Seydor, 347). But, as Seydor writes in a fascinating footnote, Peckinpah often carried a well-marked bible around with him (Seydor, 337). Even though he rejected the doctrines of organized religion, Peckinpah was (as described by Seydor) a man who believed in "something beyond the solitary and isolate individual, from which the individual takes his meaning and to which he is answerable" (Seydor, 338). As one who became a college teacher in 1965 and experienced the full impact on campus of the baby boomers, I recognize Seydor's description of Peckinpah's religious orientation as that of many of the baby boomers I knew well. They rejected many of their parents' moral absolutes, but at the same time they were searching for a new source of authority to put in the place of their de-emphasized religious faith.

Like the baby boomers, Peckinpah also used and abused alcohol and drugs, particularly cocaine. When Peckinpah was filming *Pat Garrett and Billy the Kid* (MGM, 1973) in Mexico, nearly everyone associated with the film became ill, and drinking made Peckinpah even sicker. James Coburn (who played Pat Garrett) described Peckinpah as a "genius for about four hours" (Seydor, 259). And as his drinking spun out of control, Peckinpah increasingly saw people as either for him or against him, an attitude that created even greater friction between him and other studio personnel. Alcohol and cocaine became means to deaden the disappointment over what the studios did to his films, but they also further alienated Peckinpah from the people he needed most if he was to remain a successful filmmaker. Caught in that downward spiral of alcohol and drug abuse, Peckinpah died at the early age of 59.

Probably the element that makes Peckinpah most like many of the baby boomers (particularly those in college) of the 1960s was his rejection of authority and his nearly endless fights with producers and studio executives. Peckinpah always saw himself as victimized by men who betrayed his work. Sam Peckinpah regarded himself as an artist, surely one who wanted people to view and enjoy his work, but an artist nonetheless. And therein lies the tension, because films are also commercial ventures. Studio executives must be concerned with the bottom line, including the commercial appeal of the product. Studios must recoup costs and, hopefully, make a profit.

Peckinpah found that commercial reality hard to accept, so he fought with Joseph Vogel of MGM over marketing strategy for *Ride the High Country* (MGM, 1962). MGM decided to release it as the bottom half of a double bill (Seydor, 64), and even though time has vindicated Peckinpah, he was still barred from the MGM lot. Peckinpah fought with Producer Jimmy Bresler on *Major Dundee* (Columbia, 1965) as Peckinpah tried to counter budget cuts and editing that he believed killed the film. Tensions flared on the set as well, and at one point Charlton Heston (playing Major Dundee) charged Peckinpah and tried to run him through with a saber (Seydor, 70). Filming *The Wild Bunch* provoked ongoing fights with Producer Phil Feldman, particularly conflicts over editing and marketing. Producer Gordon Carroll described the filming of *Pat Garrett and Billy the Kid* as "a battleground" (Seydor, 257). Much blame for that is due to MGM president James Aubrey, a man with little understanding of the motion picture business. While Peckinpah was victimized by studio mismanagement, Peckinpah's drinking and reputation for being difficult surely exacerbated an already difficult situation.

Like 1960s college baby boomers, Sam Peckinpah rebelled against and fought with corporate America. As a solitary screenwriter or director, Peckinpah was powerless to do much more than rant against studio insistence to shorten shooting times, reduce budgets or edit the films in a manner he found unacceptable. On a broader scale, Peckinpah saw economic considerations destroying the natural wilderness he loved so much. As Seydor notes, "the entertainment industry became for him both the fact and symbol of...corporate America" (Seydor, 361). Peckinpah regarded studio executives as "whores" who thought only of money and whose commitment to friendship was governed by the bottom line. In those sentiments there are echoes of 1960s college-aged baby boomers!

As one watches Sam Peckinpah's Westerns, one is struck by another similarity with college baby boomers of the 1960s. The boomers could talk endlessly about the poor and the economically and culturally oppressed, and some true to their views went to work among those people; for most baby boomers, however, the poor and oppressed remained an abstraction or a people incapable of ordering their own lives. Rather, they needed the superior intellect and skills of the boomers who would, in an elitist fashion, teach the poor and oppressed the "right" way to live. Like the baby boomers, Peckinpah appears to have a low opinion of the average person. Character actors such as L.Q. Jones, Strother Martin, and John Anderson appear frequently as ignorant, unwashed, bigoted human beings. The composite character type of the Hammond brothers in *Ride the High Country* appears in nearly all of Peckinpah's Westerns. The Hadley brothers in *Major Dundee*, Bowen and Taggart in *The Ballad of Cable Hogue* (Warner Brothers, 1970), and the Gorch brothers in *The Wild Bunch* all suggest that Peckinpah was doing more than creating characters; he was making a comment about the human condition!

Jon Tuska believes that Sam Peckinpah was fascinated with "alienated heroism" (Tuska, 1976, 574), and he titles his chapter on Peckinpah, "Sam Peckinpah and the Western with Only Villains." Tuska's characterization is on the mark; beyond *Ride the High Country*, Peckinpah's Westerns are films without heroes. The descent of the hero reaches its apotheosis in Sam Peckinpah and Clint Eastwood's Westerns, and it is the first of several themes in Peckinpah's Westerns that the remainder of this chapter explores.

In *Major Dundee*, Major Amos Dundee, Charlton Heston's character, resembles Henry Fonda's Colonel Owen Thursday in *Fort Apache*—except that Thursday has an elitist sense of social standing and superficial civil behavior that is utterly lacking in Heston's Dundee. Heston's Dundee is a hate-driven, crude human being. Sent to New Mexico Territory to guard Confederate prisoners of war, Heston understands that he is being disciplined for inappropriate conduct in battle. An egocentric officer with an authoritarian mentality, Heston is out of control, obsessed with his personal goal of getting back in the good graces of his military superiors. He believes that if he crosses into Mexico and captures the Apache leader Sierra Chariba, his superiors in the East will have to restore him to command. And he is prepared to pursue that goal irrespective of the human cost.

In the process of killing Sierra Chariba and his band of Apache Indians, Heston sacrifices nearly all of his command and becomes embroiled in a potential international crisis as he clashes with the French troops of Emperor Maxmillian. Heston loses most of his soldiers and ignores geopolitical realities in order to fulfill his personal ambition. Far from being a hero, Heston seemed to fit the increasingly popular 1960s perception of authoritarian military officers who were prepared to sacrifice all to realize their objectives in Vietnam. And as the war in Vietnam dragged on, American public opinion became increasingly suspicious of military personnel and motives. Sam Peckinpah's *Major Dundee* anticipates that attitude in the person of Charlton Heston's Major Amos Dundee. Whatever may be said about Heston's Dundee, it is clear that he is no hero.

Nor are there any heroes in *The Wild Bunch*. William Holden (playing Pike Bishop), leader of the Wild Bunch, is a killer and a thief. Not only does he rob banks and trains, he kills innocent bystanders. A telling moment is the film is occurs as the remaining members of the gang escape from a border town after a brutal shootout with the railroad posse. One of the Bunch is badly wounded, nearly blind in fact, so Holden kills him rather than risk having the man slow down their escape. And the gang does not even stop to bury their now dead comrade. Holden leaves behind Edmund O'Brien's (Old Sykes) grandson (Bo Hopkins as Crazy Lee) to face certain death while the gang escapes from the border town after the botched robbery that opens *The Wild Bunch*. Later, viewers learn that Holden also had an affair with a married woman, and barely escaped with his life when the woman's husband caught them together. Whatever he is, William Holden's Pike Bishop is no hero.

Neither is Deke Thornton, Robert Ryan's character, a hero in any traditional sense. Ryan once rode with the Wild Bunch and was Holden's close friend. One evening while they were frolicking in a bordello, detectives broke into the room and wounded and captured Ryan while Holden escaped. Sentenced to life in prison, Ryan will receive a pardon if he can capture the Wild Bunch. Determined not to go back to prison, Ryan pursues the Wild Bunch with dogged determination. While Ryan respects and never underestimates his adversaries, he is no less determined to capture them. There is something unsettling, something unheroic, about turning on one's former friends, even if it is to keep from being returned to prison!

Jason Robards' Cable Hogue is surely not in the same category as Amos Dundee, Pike Bishop or Deke Thornton, but it is difficult to see in him many qualities of the traditional hero. Stranded in the desert by two friends, Robards discovers water and establishes a prosperous rest station for stagecoaches and other travelers. But he is a self-centered person. He charges for the water and food he provides, even to his most trusted friends. Robards' mercenary nature is evident in an exchange with Stella Stevens, playing the prostitute Hildy. The respectable citizens chased Hildy out of town, and she has come to stay with Robards. One night at dinner, Robards reminds David Warner, playing Joshua the preacher, that he will have to pay for what he eats. When Stevens observes that he doesn't charge her for food, Robards' reply that he doesn't charge her because Stevens

Bo Hopkins, in his first film, plays Crazy Lee of *The Wild Bunch* (1969). Hopkins had kind words for Sam Peckinpah at a recent film festival.

does not charge *him* (for sex) underscores his venal nature. And he dies a distinctly unheroic death, run over by an automobile.

Beyond a lack of heroic qualities in Peckinpah's main characters, a second theme emerges as central to his Western films. Peckinpah's heroes are men who have outlived their time and are grappling with the new realities in which they find themselves. William Holden projects that condition in *The Wild Bunch*. When the Bunch discovers that they have been tricked (the sacks contain not money but iron washers), Holden laments that this was going to be his last job. He recognizes that the old days are going fast and that the Bunch (particularly himself and Ernest Borgnine) are not getting any younger. He observes, "We have got to start thinking beyond our guns." The tragedy of the film is that the Bunch never go beyond their guns. It seems to me that the final shootout with Mapache (Emilio Fernandez) and his forces is only in part motivated by the desire to rescue and then revenge the death of Angel (Jaime Sanchez). The Bunch provoked the shootout, at least in part, because they recognized that their way of life had no future, and it is better to die fighting than to live in a repressive, unintelligible world. Edmund O'Brien (Old Sykes) catches that perspective when he invites Robert Ryan to join him after the Bunch have been killed. O'Brien comments, "Ain't like it used to be, but it will do."

Changing times also destroys Jason Robards in *The Ballad of Cable Hogue*. Robards' rest station has been successful. Providing food and water for weary travelers and horses has guaranteed Robards a modest living and the acceptance and respectability that he always sought. Then one day Robards sees an automobile, the newest modern marvel. He correctly understands that the automobile spells the end of Cable Springs. An automobile can traverse the desert much quicker, and it does not need to stop for feed and water as do stagecoach horses. Technology has ended Robards' good life. He is as much a victim of changing times as was the Wild Bunch. And, just as the changing times destroyed the Wild Bunch, so technology kills Robards' Cable Hogue. When Stevens returns to him in an automobile, Robards prepares to leave with her for New Orleans. But when the brake fails, the automobile runs over Robards and he dies from the injuries. In both *The Wild Bunch* and *The Ballad of Cable Hogue*, death is the only escape from the changing times.

James Coburn, as Pat Garrett in *Pat Garrett and Billy the Kid*, chose to capitulate rather than die. Coburn had been a friend of Kris Kristofferson (Billy the Kid), and surely Coburn had done illegal things. But at the beginning of the film he appears as a lawman determined to run Kristofferson out of the territory, down to Mexico. Coburn's former friends are confused; what caused him to change? Coburn's response is straightforward: the times have changed. Politics has changed and the people in power want Kristofferson and his kind out of the territory. Businessmen are now in control, and there is no more room for free spirited hellraisers such as Kristofferson. As Jim Kitses suggests, "The only design that the film bleakly maps is that of the increasingly destructive impact on the West of a squalid capitalism" (Kitses, 223). Coburn's sense of self-preservation and personal ambition leads him to switch sides. Times have changed, and Coburn understands he must change with them or become an anachronism like Kristofferson and his friends. So Coburn begins to hunt down and kill those who had been his friends in order to ensure himself a more prominent role in the new power arrangement. The new power wielders are not people that Coburn likes or respects, but he recognizes in them the future, and in order to ensure his own future, Coburn is prepared to betray his former friends. Kitses defines Coburn's Pat Garrett as living "in a world defined by compromise and betrayal, where the genre's mantle of heroic identity is a lie" (Kitses, 224). And Kitses concludes that Peckinpah's basic strategy always insisted on the closing of the frontier; the times are changing (Kitses, 237).

Peckinpah's focus on changing times is a commentary on American life in the ten-year period after 1965. As one watches Peckinpah's Westerns thirty and more years after they were made, one is struck by the manner in which they reflect their times. The political system was changing in the 1960s. Just as James Coburn in *Pat Garrett and Billy the Kid*, Americans were turning their backs on the political liberalism that had dominated the country since the Great Depression and were becoming more economically conservative. Corporate America was on the verge of entering a period of political power that would last through the end of the century. Also, technology was looming on the 1960s horizon. In retrospect, the computers of that decade resemble the early automobile in *The Ballad of Cable Hogue*, but most Americans understood that this new technology would profoundly reshape the world of work and leisure. The violence, citizen anger and alienation from power structures, all elements in Peckinpah's Westerns, are glimpses of problems with which Americans would wrestle for the rest of the century. It is as though Peckinpah's Westerns hold up a mirror and permit Americans to see reflections of their culture in the 1960s, and to anticipate the future.

If Peckinpah's Westerns are films in which the main characters, not heroes in any conventional sense, grapple with changing times, they are nonetheless males. By and large, women have very little to do in Westerns; that is generally true of Peckinpah's films as well. But one can go further.

Jason Robards, as Cable Hogue, scrubs Stella Stevens' back in *The Ballad of Cable Hogue* (1970). Stevens plays the prostitute Hildy.

Even if they played only marginal roles, most traditional Westerns had a heroine. She was a "good" girl, often a loyal daughter, sometimes the hero's sweetheart, but always of a woman of virtue and character. In many traditional Westerns, the heroine's opposite was the dance-hall girl, or even the "whore with a heart of gold." Normally the latter two character types died at the film's end as suitable punishment for their wayward behavior. Just as Peckinpah's Westerns lack heroes in the traditional sense, so too the "good" girl heroine generally is missing from his Western films. Like the males of his movies, Peckinpah's female characters are flawed persons who often are either prostitutes or women made to function in that role.

In *Ride the High Country*, Mariette Hartley (Elsa Knudsen) is trapped on an isolated farm by her abusive father. Her father (R.G. Armstrong) beats her (there even may be hints of incest). Hartley longs to escape the harsh confines of the farm, and she entices Joel McCrea, Randolph Scott and Ronald Starr to take her to the mining camp with them so she can marry James Drury (Billy Hammond). At the mining camp she is nearly raped by the ignorant, unwashed, crude Hammond brothers. Clearly Hartley is a naive woman whose longing to escape an intolerable home threatens to create an even harsher life elsewhere. Scott and McCrea rescue Hartley from that fate, and they start back to the Knudsen farm. On the ride back, Hartley and Starr grow fond of one another, and the film ends with the certainty of their marriage. Mariette Hartley is a naive heroine, an innocent victim. She is as close as Peckinpah comes to a more traditional heroine in the Western films he directed.

Senta Berger's Teresa Santiago in *Major Dundee* also possesses some of the qualities of a traditional heroine, but not to the same extent as does Mariette Hartley in *Ride the High Country*. Heston discovers Berger living and working in a poor, small Mexican village that has been pillaged and oppressed by Indians, guerillas and French soldiers. Berger is the only character in *Major Dundee* to express any sympathy for Heston. Heston speaks to her of the burden of command, and Berger is attracted to him. Berger talks of her sympathy for the plight of the poor Mexican villagers. One night Heston and Berger slip outside the camp and have sex. But when Dundee is badly wounded by an Indian arrow and goes to Durango for medical care, he wallows in self-pity and with a prostitute. Berger leaves him when she discovers Heston with the whore. However, Berger's role is marginal at best, and she disappears entirely from the film after she finds Heston with the prostitute.

Stella Stevens' Hildy is also reminiscent of the traditional Western's "whore with a heart of gold," but she is a whore nonetheless. Stevens runs a thriving business in a room over the town saloon, and Robards visits her several times. When the "respectable" element in the community runs her out of town, Stevens moves in with Robards at Cable Springs. They become friends and lovers. Stevens' assumption that Robards loves her and that their relationship transcends the commercial is dashed when Robards tells her that he does not charge her for food because she does not charge him for sex. At that point, Stevens decides to leave Cable Springs. Robards realizes his mistake and that he loves her, but it is too late; Stevens has made up her mind to go. But at the film's end she returns to Cable Springs in an automobile. Clearly Stevens has become a successful New Orleans prostitute and madam. Robards and Stevens reunite, and Robards prepares to leave with her for New Orleans when he is run over by the runaway automobile and dies from his injuries. Throughout the film, however, Stevens' Hildy is much like Claire Trevor's Dallas in *Stagecoach*—both are the traditional "whores with a golden heart."

Women in *The Wild Bunch* lack any of the redeeming qualities of Mariette Hartley, Senta Berger or Stella Stevens. In fact, the only females in the film are either women of low moral character or Mexican women forced to provide entertainment for the Bunch. Women appear as prostitutes in the bordello at the time Ryan is captured. Aurrora Clavel plays the unfaithful wife with whom William Holden has an affair. Sonia Amelio's Teresa is like the Bunch itself, self-serving. She had been Jaime Sanchez's (Angel) girl, but when Mapache's (Emilio Fernandez) troops raided Sanchez's village, they not only took all the horses and cattle and killed Sanchez's father, they also took Amelio with them. The village elder assures Sanchez the she was not molested; rather, she went with Mapache of her own free will. Sanchez discovers her at Mapache's headquarters, and she makes it clear to him that she intends to stay with Mapache. She has become Mapache's girl, one of the camp whores. Sanchez kills her and thus helps to establish the reason for the final fatal shootout with Mapache's troops, the shootout in which the entire Bunch die. The only other women in the film are Mexican women given to the Bunch (particularly, but not exclusively, to the Gorch brothers) after they agree to steal guns that Mapache wants and needs.

As in *The Wild Bunch*, the only women in *Pat Garrett and Billy the Kid* are ones who provide sexual entertainment for the men. They have secondary, and in most cases, marginal roles in the film. Peckinpah's world, then, is a world of men, for the most part, and women exist to serve men. The best of them may be Stella Stevens' Hildy, and the worst is Sonia Amelio's Teresa in *The Wild Bunch*. Like the male characters, the women in Peckinpah's work are generally either amoral (and in many cases immoral), self-serving individuals or, as in the case of Mapache's camp women, victims who must do as they are told. The irony in that during the 1960s, when Peckinpah did his best work, the role of women in American society was on the verge of changing dramatically (see Chapter 11).

One of the most disturbing elements in *The Wild Bunch* illustrates a fourth theme: the destruction of childhood innocence. Children often played pivotal roles in traditional Westerns, particularly the B Westerns of 1930s and 1940s cowboy heroes. Enthusiasm, innocence, openness and vulnerability are characteristics one associates with the children of B Westerns. The violence of the 1960s in the civil rights struggles, the war in Vietnam and on urban streets and in the schools, all prominently displayed by the evening news on television, coupled with increasingly adult oriented motion pictures, changed American children during the decade. They grew up faster; they became, in many ways, little adults.

Two images in *The Wild Bunch* point to that change. The film opens with scenes of children torturing two scorpions caught in a bed of ants. The laughing, giggling faces of the children as they watch the scorpions try to escape the ants contrasts with the intense look on the faces of the Wild Bunch as they ride into town. The Bunch is about to create mayhem in the town as they engage the railroad posse in a violent, bloody shootout. And the children, in their own way, create the same sort of mayhem in the pit-like community of ants and two scorpions. The children's cruelty suggests not only the loss of childhood innocence, but Peckinpah's view that just beneath the veneer of civilized man lies the savage. That point is brought home dramatically in *Major Dundee* as the troopers remark on the savage cruelty of the French troops, noting that they are just like the Apaches. In *The Wild Bunch* the children behave with the ants and scorpions just as the Apaches and French soldiers in *Major Dundee*, and the Bunch and the railroad posse in *The Wild Bunch*. The children are as cruel as the adults. As the remnant of the Bunch escapes from town, the children even set fire to the pit, killing both the ants and the scorpions. Just as the Bunch had killed and would kill, so the children — in destroying the scorpions and ants — imitate adults.

In traditional B Westerns, children imitated adults as well. But the role models in those films usually exhibited positive qualities and heroic traits. *The Wild Bunch* demonstrates how childhood socialization changes as children's role models change. Films without heroes, urban violence, drug trafficking, and increasing numbers of single parent families — all elements beginning to emerge in 1969 — impacted children. They were loosing their innocence and wonderment, replaced by the need to grow up fast in an increasingly unsafe world!

That point is brought home dramatically in another poignant scene in *The Wild Bunch*. Mapache's troops are under attack by the revolutionaries, and, in the midst of exploding shells, a young boy brings a telegram to Mapache. The lad stands at attention, proud to be wearing a uniform and proud to be close to his (in his eyes) great leader. When Mapache finishes reading and dismisses the boy, the kid salutes and waits until Mapache returns the salute. One is struck by the glow on the young boy's face; he may be young, but he is proud to be a soldier, or at least to imitate one. *The Wild Bunch* recalls the image of mere children serving with the Viet Cong and attacking United States soldiers, an image all too familiar to Americans watching the war in Vietnam unfold on their television screens. And in the gory shootout that marks the violent climax of *The*

Wild Bunch, children not only wield weapons (as in Vietnam), they are also victims of the violence. Children have always been victims of war's brutality, but since 1969, in Vietnam, in Afghanistan, in the Palestinian resistance and in uprisings and wars around the world, children have become soldiers. Whether Peckinpah realized it or not, *The Wild Bunch* anticipates that trend.

Young women are also exploited in *The Wild Bunch*. At the time of their initial visit, Mapache gives the Gorch brothers older women for their sexual use, but Holden and Borgnine sleep and drink while the brothers cavort in the wine cellar with the women. Upon their return to Mapache's camp after the Bunch deliver the guns, Mapache again provides women to the Bunch, this time including Holden and Borgnine. What is striking is that the women with Holden and Borgnine — even though Holden's consort has a young child — are not much more than children themselves.

Films of the 1970s and 1980s such as *Taxi Driver* (Columbia, 1976) and *Pretty Baby* (Paramount,1978) highlight the sexual exploitation of children. The rise in teenage pregnancies and increasing abortions throughout the period, as well as the emergence of child abuse as a serious social problem, suggest that the place of children in American society had changed dramatically. The images of runaway children, alone on the streets and easy prey for pimps and drug dealers; youth gangs terrorizing entire neighborhoods and cities; and abused children began to challenge the image of childhood fashioned so carefully in popular television programs such as *Father Knows Best, Leave It to Beaver,* and *The Brady Bunch*. The childhood that Tom Brokaw so nostalgically wrote about in his autobiographical *A Long Way from Home* seemed as much out of place at the end of the twentieth century as did the Sioux wars of his South Dakota childhood. Sam Peckinpah's *The Wild Bunch*, rather than Brokaw's autobiography, described the fate of many young boys and girls at the end of the twentieth century.

Earlier in the chapter I noted Paul Seydor's comments about Peckinpah's ambivalence to religion. While Peckinpah rejected his parents' focus on biblically-based moral absolutes, he carried a well marked Bible with him. Not surprisingly, religion is a fifth theme that appears in several of Peckinpah's Westerns.

Some see the Christian Old Testament emphasis on God's law and judgment on a disobedient people being tempered by the Christian New

Testament stress on God's love, grace and redemption of the human race through the death of Jesus Christ. To a great extent, twentieth century Protestant Christianity engaged in an ongoing dispute over which of these elements to emphasize. The so-called "fundamentalists" are more likely to stress God's law and judgment, and to insist on fidelity to their understanding of the Bible as the only means of salvation. Protestant theological "liberals," on the other hand, preach mostly about God's love and His grace. Unlike fundamentalists, whose focus on law and judgment requires a specific salvation experience and a turning away from worldly habits and practices by the repentant individual, liberals believe that God's love and redemption is universal, and that His grace permits individuals to live and work in the world without renouncing it.

Peckinpah turns to the theme of religion in four of the five Westerns he made in the 1960s and 1970s (*Ride the High Country, Major Dundee, The Ballad of Cable Hogue,* and *Pat Garrett and Billy the Kid*). In three films he chose veteran character actor R.G. Armstrong to personify the place of faith in the human condition. According to Paul Seydor, Armstrong grew up in the deep South, the product of a fundamentalist Christian mother and a violent father. As Armstrong said, "Sam saw the depth of my hostility" (Seydor, 351).

In both *Ride the High Country* and *Pat Garrett and Billy the Kid*, Armstrong's characters (Joshua Knudsen in the former and Deputy Ollinger in the latter) are Bible-spouting, harshly judgmental individuals. As Joshua Knudsen, Armstrong will not permit his daughter, Mariette Hartley, to enjoy anything smacking of worldly pleasures. One is even led to believe that his moral absolutism and his biblical judgmentalism drove his wife to an early grave. Joel McCrea is Armstrong's opposite in *Ride the High Country*. McCrea is equal to Armstrong in quoting the Bible, but McCrea's Bible is less harsh, more reflective of the human condition, more understanding of human sin.

Armstrong as Deputy Ollinger in *Pat Garrett and Billy the Kid* is able to see none of Kris Kristofferson's humanity. The important thing to Armstrong is for Kristofferson to be judged harshly, to come to an awareness of the depth of his sin (mostly because of drinking and hellraising rather than murder), and to seek forgiveness and then be executed. In the persons of Armstrong's Joshua Knudsen and Deputy Ollinger, one surmises that Peckinpah was still resisting the lectures from his father at the Peckinpah family dinner table! In that, he caught the temper of the times as baby boomers rebelled against the Bible-based culture of their parents and grandparents.

Armstrong's character in *Major Dundee* is different from the above two roles. When Sierra Charriba kidnaps children, giving Dundee a reason to cross into Mexico in pursuit, he enlists help from civilians. Armstrong's Reverend Dahlstrom is a civilian volunteer. When Heston initially rejects him, remarking that they were not going in order to save souls, Armstrong replies that he had married the children's parents, and that, "Whosoever destroys my flock, I will so destroy."

Heston's column is a mixture of civilians, Confederate prisoners of war under the command of Richard Harris, white troopers and a contingent of African American soldiers. The first night in camp, one of the Confederates tells a black soldier to come over and pull off his boots. The remark fuels an already explosive tension in the camp and a fight appears imminent, when Armstrong's Reverend Dahlstrom intervenes with the remark, "Here, let me do it." He proceeds to pull off the man's boots, and when the Confederate pulls a knife on him, Armstrong gives the man a thrashing, throwing him back among his Confederate comrades. Harris further eases tensions when he walks to the black soldier and compliments him on the professional manner in which he crossed the river that day. However, it is Armstrong's preacher who is most responsible for defusing the situation by using his strength and restrained violence to prevent bloodshed. One can only think that Jesus' words "Blessed are the peacemakers, for they shall be called children of God" aptly describe Armstrong's character in *Major Dundee*.

David Warner, playing the preacher Joshua in *The Ballad of Cable Hogue*, suggests an entirely different view of faith. Warner is the personification of preacher as hypocrite for much of the film. He wears a cleric collar, but he is quick to turn the collar around when there is opportunity to seduce a pretty woman. His purpose of getting the woman in bed is masked by a superficial concern for whatever problem she faces. Piety for Warner hides his real motive and disarms the victim. Yet there is a serious side to Warner's Joshua.

At the end of the film, as Robards lay dying after being run over by Stella Stevens' automobile, he asks Warner to preach his funeral. After all, Robards remarks, most people don't get to hear their funerals, and he (Robards) wants to enjoy his. So Warner begins preaching what most "fundamentalists" would regard as an outlandish "liberal" sermon. There is no judgment or call to repentance. Warner reminds God of Robards' shortcomings— overcharging, stealing — but acknowledges that he was a man (to which Stevens utters "amen"). Warner hopes God will have room for Robards, but if not, Warner assures God that Robards, having lived on the desert, will not find Hell too hot. As they leave the grave, Warner prays for God to take Robards, but not "to take him too lightly." One suspects that Warner's eulogy is the sort of sermon Peckinpah would liked to have had preached at his own funeral.

Dub Taylor's character in *The Wild Bunch* offers a different view of faith, showing religion as being irrelevant. Taylor's temperance preacher rails against the evil of drink and leads his flock on a march to protest its diabolical influence in the world. The cutting between the Bunch riding into town, the children torturing the scorpions with the ants, and the temperance rally suggests that Taylor has little comprehension of the real evil in the world. The murder of innocent bystanders that is about the befall the community, as well as the merciless torture of the scorpions by the children, suggests something more sinister about the human condition than consuming liquor. The temperance marchers, however, are blissfully ignorant of the world around them and the world about to descend on their quiet community.

Again Peckinpah seems to echo an increasing criticism coming from diverse quarters of the American community. What did the church and the Christian faith have to say about the carnage in Vietnam? Why were so many "fundamentalists" silent about the treatment of African Americans? Why did the church not condemn the oppression of the poor, as did the Old Testament prophets? How could the best known evangelist of the day be so friendly with men like Lyndon Johnson and Richard Nixon? Certainly, within the Christian community in the United States, as well as among those who did not associate with that community, the role of the church in America was being openly debated. Provoked by such criticism, and in response to other concerns (such as pornography, abortion and homosexuality), fundamentalists and fundamentalist churches began to engage in politics in a manner that has substantially transformed the political landscape since 1969, the year in which *The Wild Bunch* first screened.

A final theme in Peckinpah's Westerns reflects the growing national disillusionment throughout the 1960s with counter-insurgency. *The Magnificent Seven* is a celebration of counter-insurgency on horseback (see Chapter 3). Initially, the seven gunfighters ride to the poor Mexican village for adventure and profit, but they are quickly won over by the cause. They return, after being run out by Eli Wallach, and destroy the bandits preying on the village. By their sacrifice, the seven gunfighters make the village (read Third World) a safe place in which democracy and economic progress could thrive.

While continuing that same general support posture, *Major Dundee* is a transitional film, less sure of the nobility and ultimate success of counter-insurgency. When Heston's column rides into the poor Mexican village, Senta Berger comes to meet them with the comment, "There seems to be no end to it." Apaches, guerillas, the French and now the Americans seem ready to pounce on the impoverished villagers. She tells Heston that the village has no food, no guns, no women. And if Dundee doubts it, she will show him the children with their nakedness and sickness.

Rather than taking, however, Heston orders two mules to be slaughtered and the meat shared with the people. The next few minutes of the film depict a now-happy populace celebrating with the Americans. Dancing, eating, drinking and sexual liaisons between the villagers and the soldiers all reflect the image of the United States as liberator, freeing the village from French oppression and sharing scarce food with them. To a generation raised on images of G.I.s sharing chocolate bars with German, Italian and Japanese children during World War II, and to a population convinced of the rightness of counter-insurgency, the behavior of Heston and his troopers was the only possible response.

As the film unfolds, however, the futility of counter-insurgency becomes apparent. The French return and destroy the village once the Americans leave. Counter-insurgency works only if the landscape is freed of those forces that oppose the American version of democracy and economic development. Counter-insurgency must give way to long term occupation so that democratic and economic transformation can unfold. Americans quickly grow restless with that approach, however. Go in, get the job done and get out is much more in keeping with American understanding of war. By the middle of the 1960s, Americans were beginning to grapple with the limits of counter-insurgency in Vietnam, and ultimately to condemn it as an ineffective military strategy. Senta Berger catches that realization when she visits Heston in Durango while he recuperates from his leg wound. She tells Heston that she has come to say goodbye; she is going to join the Juaristas. The fight against the French will not be one won by United States counter-insurgent forces, but by native resistance led by Mexican leaders who will remain after the French have been defeated.

By 1969, the transitional ambivalence about counter-insurgency in *Major Dundee* had disappeared. *The Wild Bunch* demonstrates that Americans can support national elements as self-serving and treacherous as those forces ostensibly opposed to democracy and economic progress. Initially, the Bunch tries to sell horses to Mapache (Emilio Fernandez) but ends by agreeing to obtain guns for him. Mapache, on the surface, represents the legitimate government, but in reality he is just a bandit preying

Ben Johnson, Warren Oates, William Holden and Ernest Bognine head for their final showdown with Mapache in *The Wild Bunch* (1969).

on the people. He had raided Angel's (Jaime Sanchez) village, stealing their food and gold and enticing their young women away. Mapache, in a number of ways, is a surrogate for the image Americans were beginning to form of the government of South Vietnam. South Vietnamese leaders appeared to many Americans to be more interested in self-aggrandizement and gaining power than in defeating the Viet Cong and North Vietnamese regulars. Richard Slotkin describes Mapache's Mexico (and, by implication, South Vietnam) as "a society ruled by force and money in which the strong lord it over the weak, taking the best of food, drink and women" (Slotkin 1992, 600). For some Americans, United States forces fighting for a corrupt South Vietnamese government were no better than the Wild Bunch stealing guns for Mapache.

To acquire the guns, the Wild Bunch attacks both the railroad and the United States Army, an army and country, admits William Holden to Mapache, with which they "share very few sympathies." As Slotkin observes, the Wild Bunch are not agents of democracy; their sympathies do not lie with the people of Mexico. Rather, they are merely mercenaries fighting for the side that will give them the most money. In Slotkin's words, the Wild Bunch are "agents of despotism" (Slotkin, 1992, 600).

The Bunch agree to let Jaime Sanchez have one case of guns for the guerrillas fighting Mapache. That sets up the final confrontation, because Mapache accuses Sanchez of stealing the guns and takes him from Ernest Borgnine, who, along with Angel, brings the last case of guns to Mapache's camp. The remaining members of the Bunch ride into camp to rescue Sanchez from Mapache's torture, and in the ensuing gun battle the Bunch is killed. The Bunch did not ride into Mapache's camp to destroy him in the name of democracy, the people or anything else; they went back for very personal reasons. They wanted to avenge the treatment of their friend, and they knew that their day, the day of the gun, had ended.

By 1969, substantial segments of the American population had rejected counter-insurgency as a means of overthrowing oppressive regimes. Sympathy for the plight of oppressed peoples had abated; Americans were coming to believe that some important national interest ought to be at stake before young Americans are asked to sacrifice their lives. The idealism that had supported much of American post–World War II foreign policy came crashing down in the jungles of South Vietnam and Cambodia. From 1969 to the end of the twentieth century, most Americans were willing to disregard the internal conditions of a country if the regime of that country, no matter how oppressive it might be, supported American national interests. Even the celebrated Gulf War was understood by most Americans as a war to prevent Iraq from destabilizing the region and jeopardizing the flow of Middle Eastern oil to the United States.

The Wild Bunch can be viewed as a metaphor for reshaped American foreign policy. Counter-insurgency was rejected as a policy for bringing democracy and economic progress to the world. Henceforth, the United States would concentrate on it national interest. It would intervene around the world when that interest was in danger, and it would support any regime — no matter what its internal policies — that supported American national interests. *The Magnificent Seven* of 1960 had given way to *The Wild Bunch* of 1969.

In *Gunfighter Nation: The Myth of the Frontier in Twentieth-Century America*, Richard Slotkin quotes extensively from a 1982 *Foreign Affairs* article by William A. MacNeill. In that essay, MacNeill commented on the importance of a "public myth" for a society. Some writers prefer "public philosophy" (Lowi; Loy), while others employ ideology to express the same idea (Slotkin 1992, 626). However it is expressed, it means that every society needs common beliefs and an understanding of how the world works that are shared widely by all segments of the society and serve as a base for making decisions about the public good. A public philosophy or public myth allows a society to achieve consensus on current and future policy. Without consensus on a widely accepted public philosophy, society "degenerates into a conflict among interest groups, each playing by its own rules for its own advantage" (Slotkin, 1992, 626).

Western films had been crucial elements in expressing the public philosophy that had evolved from the signing of the Declaration of Independence and the drafting of the Constitution of the United States. That public philosophy had been reshaped in the harsh days of the Great Depression, sharpened during World War II and refined during the often traumatic events of the Cold War. During the last thirty-five years of the twentieth century it was largely rejected. In its place emerged a new public philosophy based on single-issue interest groups, entrepreneurial politicians freed from the constraints of political parties and prepared to use any tactic that would get them elected, and a population that had forsaken civic engagement in lieu of the pursuit of personal wealth and security.

Not surprisingly, Westerns began to reflect this slowly emerging public philosophy. The Westerns of Sam Peckinpah are early indicators that the world, as well as the Western film genre, marched to the drum beat of a different public philosophy. The Westerns of Clint Eastwood would enlarge and enhance that difference. Only one voice of any major consequence challenged the outlook and assumptions of the public philosophy that began to take shape in the mid-to-late 1960s, developed in the 1970s and dominated American politics and culture from 1980 to the end of the century. That individual, of course, was John Wayne, and his Westerns— with some exceptions— must be viewed as dissents from the culture of the 1960s and early-to-mid 1970s. The next two chapters will first consider the work of Clint Eastwood and then John Wayne as the United States put the turbulent 1960s behind it and entered the last thirty years of the twentieth century.

Chapter 5

CLINT EASTWOOD:
"MAN WITH NO NAME"

When the CBS television program *Rawhide* premiered on January 9, 1959, Clint Eastwood, who was chosen to play the part of Rowdy Yates, was an unknown actor. Prior to *Rawhide*, like many other wannabe actors, Eastwood worked at odd jobs and accepted whatever roles he was offered, no matter how minor. He had small parts in a few Universal horror flicks; and up to the time of *Rawhide*, his biggest role was in the distinctly second-rate Western *Ambush at Cimarron Pass* (Regal Films, 1958). However, after eight seasons of playing Rowdy Yates on *Rawhide*, Eastwood was no longer an unknown, and he wanted to broaden his career by working in feature films as well as television. Initially, CBS would not agree. After a particularly strong Eastwood threat to boycott the series and go to Europe to make motion pictures, CBS relented and agreed to allow Eastwood to appear in feature length films (Zmijewsky and Pfeiffer, 17).

Eastwood accepted an offer from the Italian director Sergio Leone to star in *The Magnificent Stranger* (Zmijewsky and Pfeiffer, 17). In 1964 the film was released in Europe as *A Fistful of Dollars*, and Clint Eastwood became an overnight sensation on the Continent. Eastwood made two more films for Leone, *For A Few Dollars More* and *The Good, the Bad, and the Ugly*. United Artists bought the rights to show the films in the United States, and while the critics generally panned them, audiences flocked to theaters where they were showing (Zmijewsky and Pfeiffer, 21). Clint Eastwood was on his way to becoming one of the most popular actors of his day!

The three Westerns Eastwood made for Sergio Leone are important for this book because they established Eastwood's film image. Whether he was appearing in a Western or as "Dirty Harry," the qualities exhibited by Eastwood's Leone character, "the man with no name," became what audiences expected from a Clint Eastwood film. Eastwood offered motion picture patrons a new kind of hero, a man with characteristics largely unknown to previous Western heroes.

Zmijewsky and Pfeiffer describe "the man with no name" as a "human being who was seemingly devoid of the simplest emotions or sympathetic actions." He is a "no-nonsense figure who could take the law into his own hands and get away with it" (Zmijewsky and Pfeiffer, 7). To that, Richard Harmet adds that Eastwood's characters were "unconcerned about a higher moral order, he shot those who stood in his way. Above all, he was in complete control of his environment, certain of his actions and sure there was no obstacle he could not overcome and no human he could not dominate" (quoted in Zmijewsky and Pfeiffer, 7).

Eastwood's "man with no name" is far removed from the B Western cowboy stars prior to the early 1950s, and he has little in common with others, such as Joel McCrea, Randolph Scott and John Wayne, who appeared in bigger budget Westerns. The "man with no name" appeared on the silver screen at the right place and at the right time; he appealed to an American audience looking for a different type of hero, and to an audience frustrated by rapid social change that made it less possible for individuals to control their lives and that cheapened personal achievement.

It was the era of youth rebellion as well. Baby boomers opposed nearly all types and symbols of authority. Their battle cry "Don't trust anyone over thirty years of age!" shaped that generation. The "man with no name," a man who always did things his own way, a man who ignored the authority of traditional morality, and a man who often shunned legal authority as irrelevant or as part of the problem, appealed to baby boomers disaffected by traditional institutions and morality.

Zmijewsky and Pfeiffer summarize Eastwood's appeal as they explain United Artists' decision to buy the rights to his Sergio Leone Westerns:

> While Clint was away those years working in Europe, America was in the midst of a social upheaval. Youth riots, anti–Vietnam-war demonstrations, civil rights protests, and the drug culture swept America. With people so dissatisfied with tradition, United Artists thought the time was appropriate to introduce a new form of hero to the public [21].

The one element that shaped the youth rebellion and those who then–President Richard Nixon labeled the "silent majority" was the fact that both groups believed that they no longer controlled their own lives. While they disagreed (radically and violently at times) about the cause, both baby boomers and their parents, survivors of the Great Depression and World War II, believed that individuals had become pawns to forces beyond their personal control. Clint Eastwood's "man with no name" refused to accept that state of affairs; he asserted his individuality in the face of great personal and institutional resistance, and he won! No wonder Clint Eastwood's appeal crossed age and social boundaries. He voiced the concerns of many Americans of the time, and he did what many of them longed to do but couldn't because of social, career and legal constraints; he acted!

Eastwood's major contribution, then, to Westerns is the appearance of a new kind of hero, one with some distinctive characteristics. The "man with no name" is a man of few words. Eastwood says very little; he does not have much dialogue in his films. And when he speaks it is in short, declaratory sentences, such as "I reckon so" or "Is that so." Often his response is little more than a grunt. Certainly the "man with no name" is not one to speculate about cause and effect, or one likely to engage in philosophical speculation. When Inger Stevens, who is looking for the men who murdered her husband and raped her in *Hang 'Em High* (United Artists, 1968), objects to Eastwood's unrelenting search for the men who very nearly lynched him, he replies, "We all have our ghosts. You hunt your way, I hunt mine." That is about as philosophical as any Eastwood character ever gets.

Rather than speak, Eastwood stares. Viewers are frequently drawn to his eyes for clues about future action. They are hard eyes, eyes seemingly unmoved by fear or any other emotion. For example, in *The Outlaw Josey Wales* (Warner Brothers, 1976), Eastwood is cornered by two buffalo hunters set on claiming the reward for him, dead or alive. As the two men have their pistols leveled at Eastwood, viewers are drawn to his eyes. Eastwood's hard stare makes it clear that in a matter of seconds the two men are going to die. Eastwood says nothing to the men as he kills both of them; Eastwood's eyes and his stare replace words.

If Eastwood's characters speak little, they act quickly. Cowboy heroes of the silver screen were all men of action — and in that, Eastwood is no different. But there is something remarkably different about Eastwood's actions. For one, Eastwood's "man with no name" is arrogantly sure of himself. The few words he speaks, joined to the Eastwood stare, present a character with unfailing confidence in himself and his ability to master any situation. All cowboy heroes from 1930 until the mid–1950s were able to see relationships between people and events, an understanding that escaped the average citizen; hence the hero knew how to choose the appropriate action (Loy, 130–131). But cowboy heroes of yesteryear did so with a sense of humility that is lacking in Eastwood's character.

The "man with no name," with few exceptions, is a loner. Apart from Chief Dan George in *The Outlaw Josey Wales* and Morgan Freeman in *Unforgiven* (Warner Brothers, 1992), Eastwood lacks anyone who resembles the sidekick of previous Westerns. In *Hang 'Em High* he rides out by himself in search of the men who tried to lynch him. In *Joe Kidd* (Universal, 1972), Eastwood acts alone as he keeps Robert Duvall from murdering the villagers. And in both *High Plains Drifter* (Universal, 1973) and *Pale Rider* (Warner Brothers, 1985) he rides into town alone, dispatches the bad guys and rides away alone.

The traditional cowboy hero not only had a sidekick, he also depended on community support; he had allies who helped him round up the bad guys. With the exception of *Two Mules for Sister Sara* (Universal, 1970), Eastwood dismisses such support. A priest gives Eastwood a gun in *Joe Kid*, but it is Eastwood alone who kills Duval and his murderous henchmen. The climaxes of *High Plains Drifter*, *Pale Rider* and *Unforgiven* are the same: Eastwood faces and destroys the bad guys without any assistance from others in the community (with the lone exception of Michael Moriarity killing Richard Dysart in *Pale Rider*).

As a loner, Eastwood's characters often appear to be norm-less; rules and codes of behavior that apply to other citizens are ignored by Eastwood. When he is brought before the judge in *Joe Kidd*, the sheriff recites several laws that Eastwood has broken. Yet Eastwood seems to have no remorse, and may even be proud of the disturbances he has provoked and the trouble he has caused the sheriff. The judge's comment to Eastwood, "You do just about whatever you feel like," is a commentary on many of the characters Eastwood played in his films.

In *Two Mules for Sister Sara* Eastwood has hired out to the Juaristas, Mexican guerrillas fighting the French. Shirley MacLaine, playing Sister Sara, is surprised that Eastwood does not support the Juaristas' cause even though he has agreed to fight for them. It is only the money that attracts Eastwood. His reply that he does not believe in their cause or anybody else's cause dramatizes the loner role Eastwood played in nearly all of his Westerns.

In most respects, Eastwood's "man with no name" is amoral. He kills without remorse. Surely, in the context of the Western genre, the men he killed needed killing, but the traditional cowboy heroes killed reluctantly and with regret, no matter how evil the bad guys. Eastwood's "man with no name" lacked those traits. Two films in particular highlight the brutality of an Eastwood killing. In *Joe Kidd*, Eastwood has brought John Saxon (playing Luis Chama) into town, but Saxon is a Mexican revolutionary whom Robert Duvall intends to kill rather than permit to stand trial. In the shootout that climaxes *Joe Kidd*, Eastwood catches Duvall in the courthouse and, while sitting in the judge's chair, kills Duvall. The striking thing about the scene are the eyes of the two men — the Eastwood stare before he pulls the trigger, and the fear that leaps from Duvall's eyes as he realizes he is about to die. Maybe Duvall deserved to die, but the cold, amoral Eastwood stare makes viewers understand that hate, not justice, triumphed.

Probably the ultimate amoral killing in any Eastwood film is the murder of Gene Hackman in *Unforgiven*. Hackman's Little Bill is unquestionably a bully who runs the town with a capricious iron fist. On the other hand, Eastwood, Morgan Freeman (as Ned) and Jaimz Woolvert (the Wolverine Kid) are on a mission to kill for money. When Hackman catches Freeman (who decided to quit after Eastwood killed the first cowboy), tortures him to death and displays his body in front of the billiard hall, Eastwood rides into town for revenge. After shooting several men, Eastwood realizes that the badly wounded Hackman is not yet dead. Pointing his Sharp's rifle at Hackman's head, Eastwood simply grunts "Yeah" in response to Hackman's "I'll see you in Hell." Eastwood then shoots Hackman between the eyes and rides out of town. In traditional B Westerns the hero used violence for noble purposes and with restraint. Those characteristics are lacking in Eastwood's Westerns; he offers a new kind of hero and a new understanding of the role of violence in human affairs.

Although Eastwood's first post–Leone Westerns—*Hang 'Em High, Two Mules for Sister Sara* and *Joe Kidd*—include many of the "man with no name" characteristics, they lack the amoral tone of his later films. Jon Tuska agrees, and writes in *The Filming of the West*: "By the time of *Hang 'Em High*, the crude brutality was altered somewhat, although the relentlessness of Eastwood as an avenger was retained" (563). However, from *High Plains Drifter* to *Unforgiven*, Eastwood's character lacks many normal moral qualities. *High Plains Drifter* is particularly troublesome in that respect. It makes little difference whether Eastwood's "Stranger" is a ghost, the murdered sheriff returned from the dead or an avenging angel; his behavior in the town is, at best, amoral. He kills three gunman at the beginning of the film, rapes the town prostitute and exploits the willingness of the town to give him whatever he wants if he will protect them. At the film's end, with the town of Lagos in shambles and many of its citizens dead, he rides away. The "Stranger" takes what he wants, does what he wants and leaves. There is no hint that the people of Lagos are better citizens because he rode their way, nor is there much sympathy on the part of the "Stranger" for the plight of the people living in Lagos. In *High Plains Drifter*, Eastwood's "Stranger" is about as far removed from the hero of traditional Westerns as one can get.

Although Clint Eastwood's "man with no name" characteristics shaped his persona in all of the Westerns Eastwood made after Leone, the films themselves changed over time. The first three American-produced Eastwood Westerns—*Hang 'Em High, Two Mules for Sister Sara* and *Joe Kidd*—are more traditional Westerns (with upbeat conclusions) than are Eastwood's films after *High Plains Drifter*.

Hang 'Em High's theme of revenge versus justice is one familiar to traditional Westerns of the 1930s and 1940s. The film opens as Eastwood is nearly lynched by a group of vigilantes, led by veteran character actor Ed Begley, who decide Eastwood is guilty of murdering a rancher and stealing his cattle. As the vigilantes ride away after hanging Eastwood, Ben Johnson (playing a marshal) gallops up in time to cut him down. Thrown into a prison wagon, Eastwood is carted to a prison at Fort Grant where Pat Hingle (as Judge Adam Fenton) determines that Eastwood is innocent. Because Eastwood had been a lawman once upon a time, Hingle offers him a badge and the opportunity to track down and arrest those who lynched him.

The heroes in *Hang 'Em High* are traditional Western heroes, lawmen who have to enforce the law throughout the Oklahoma Indian Territory. Ben Johnson, who almost always played one of the good guys in Westerns, is one of those lawmen. As Hingle describes it, theirs is a difficult and dangerous job; they are a handful of marshals who must enforce the law throughout the vast Oklahoma Indian Territory. Only a few men stand between decent, law abiding citizens and the thieves and killers all too ready to prey on them. If he takes the job, Eastwood will become one of them, but he must commit himself to doing justice rather than pursuing vengeance. Hingle tells him, "Pick up the badge or leave justice to me and my men." And he warns Eastwood to bring nine men back alive. Eastwood agrees to those conditions and begins his quest.

Zmijewsky and Pfeiffer note in their synopsis of *Hang 'Em High* that Hingle warned Eastwood to bring the men back for trial. But they write that Eastwood ignores the order and begins to kill the men one by one (74). That is not a very accurate description of the film, nor of Eastwood's character. Eastwood kills Reno, the first would-be lyncher and the one who took his saddle, in a gunfight precipitated when the man refuses to surrender. But Eastwood makes sure that witnesses in the saloon give the sheriff a written account of what they saw; Eastwood wants to establish that he shot in self-defense. He arrests Alan Hale Jr., and Bob Steele turns himself in to Hingle. Eastwood kills Begley and two others when they try to ambush him as he rides up to their ranch house. On the other hand, Eastwood brings Bruce Dern back for trial and hanging, and at the film's end rides out to arrest the remaining culprits. Eastwood even insists that Hingle free a dying Bob Steele (who was against the lynching) before he will put the marshal's badge back on and go after the final two members of the lynching party. Far from engaging solely in personal revenge, Eastwood follows the law, and he insists on compassion for a dying Steele — even though he had been a member of the lynching party.

Hang 'Em High is not a movie about unfettered revenge. Eastwood uses violence just as would any other frontier marshal in a Western film. But he kills none of the men unless he is forced to do so. Quite the contrary, he goes to extraordinary measures to bring Bruce Dern back for trial. In the late evening, as an exhausted Eastwood slowly rides with Dern and his two fellow rustlers down the main street of Fort Grant, Hingle runs out to greet him, shouting to the town that Eastwood is "the best there is." As "the best there is" Eastwood brought his man back for trial; he did not take personal vengeance by killing him. In *Hang 'Em High*, Eastwood's character has many of the "man with no name" traits, but not all. There is also much in common with the heroes of traditional Westerns, who sought justice over personal revenge.

As Eastwood brings Bruce Dern and the two younger rustlers back to Fort Grant for trial, Dern turns out to be an exceptionally difficult prisoner. At one point Dern frees himself from the rope binding his hands and jumps Eastwood. In the ensuing struggle, Dern almost chokes Eastwood to death before Eastwood is able to subdue him. The two younger rustlers make no move to help Dern, and Eastwood, out of gratitude to them, believes he can convince Hingle and a jury not to hang the young men. But he is mistaken, and the two— along with Dern — are sentenced to die.

Surely one of the elements that marks *Hang 'Em High* as a modern Western is the circus-like atmosphere of the town on the day that several men are to be hanged (the only thing remotely resembling that atmosphere in a B Western appeared in *Firebrands of Arizona*, a tongue-in-cheek, Western-like comedy starring Sunset Carson). Hawkers flog their wares, beer sales flourish, and men and women jostle for a good viewing spot to witness the event. Scenes gravitate between the revelry of the crowd and the solemn prayers and hymns of James MacArthur, playing the preacher who must prepare the accused for eternity.

Eastwood is angry that his pleas for clemency for the two younger rustlers were ignored, and he is sickened by the crowd's behavior. He taunts Hingle with the question of who is worse — a judge with little sense of compassion or a crowd eager to see a hanging. And Eastwood tells Hingle that there is no difference between judging and a lynching. Hingle's response is that if Eastwood can't see the difference he ought to take off his badge. Eastwood removes the badge and goes out into the crowd. He grabs Arlene Golonka, playing the prostitute Jennifer, and takes her to a room where they have intercourse while the condemned men are hanged. It would appear that Eastwood is through with the law and more than ready to seek his personal brand of revenge. But, as he is dressing, Ed Begley and two of his fellow lynchers sneak into the house and shoot Eastwood several times from behind, leaving him for dead.

However, Inger Stevens nurses Eastwood back to health. But when Eastwood tries to kiss her while they are picnicking, she draws back. It is then that viewers learn that her husband had been murdered and she had been gang raped. She, like Eastwood, is unable to forget the past and establish new, intimate relationships. He then rides to Bitter Creek to get Begley and the other two who tried to kill him. He kills the two, but Begley hangs himself before Eastwood can shoot him.

Arguably the most intriguing part of *Hang 'Em High* occurs after Eastwood returns to Fort Grant. Hingle has learned the whereabouts of the final two men who tried to lynch Eastwood. He offers Eastwood his badge back, but Eastwood will not take it. He still does not see the difference between hanging a man after judging him, and a lynching. They are just as dead. "How many men do you have to hang to heal your scars?" Eastwood asks Hingle. Hingle's reply is much like that in *The Virginian* (Paramount, 1946) when Mrs. Taylor defends the Virginian to Molly. In a country without courts, the Virginian had no choice. He had to hang his best friend, Steve, in order to prevent further rustling. Hingle longs for government that will turn this "God forsaken territory into a state." When that happens, Hingle assures Eastwood, there will be appeals courts to make sure that he, Hingle, gets the law right. But until then the only thing standing between the decent people and the barbarians are Hingle and his handful of marshals. He pleads with Eastwood, "the best there is," to remain one of those marshals. Eastwood gives in and puts on the badge. The film ends as Eastwood rides out of town to arrest the last two men, and with the hope that both he and Inger Stevens gave buried the ghosts of their pasts.

Hang 'Em High has become my favorite Clint Eastwood Western. The "man with no name" traits do not overwhelm the film. Although Eastwood's character is a hard, driven man, he is also a man with compassion. He has pity for Bob Steele, tries to keep the two young men from being hanged and, in the end, responds to Hingle's plea to aid the cause of civilization in a harsh land. With a few lapses, Eastwood honors the badge he wears. And the film ends with the hope that he and Inger Stevens will get together. With Hingle's insistence on due process rather than revenge, *Hang 'Em High* also has much in common with traditional Westerns of the 1930s, 1940s and 1950s. Archer Winsten, of the *New York Post*, was on target when he called *Hang 'Em High* "a western of quality, courage, danger and excitement which places itself squarely in the procession of old fashioned westerns made with the latest techniques" (quoted in Zmijewsky and Pfeiffer, 74).

Two Mules for Sister Sara and *Joe Kidd* have much in common so they will be treated as tandem films. Unlike with *Hang 'Em High*, the "man with no name" traits are more visible in these two Westerns. In both *Two Mules* and *Joe Kidd*, Eastwood's dialogue is sparse, and (as noted above) when he does speak it is usually in short, declaratory sentences. And the Eastwood stare is employed often. For example, in *Two Mules for Sister Sara* the camera draws viewers' attention to Eastwood's eyes as he glares down at the men preparing to sexually assault Shirley MacLaine. He kills all three, hardly uttering a word! In *Joe Kidd* the Eastwood stare takes center stage on numerous occasions. When he appears before the judge, for example, Eastwood says very little, but he stares intently at the man who has the power to jail him, fine him or both. The taunts of Duvall's murderous henchmen are met with Eastwood's icy glare. He says very little to them, but viewers understand from the stare that when the time comes, those henchmen, so sure of their ability, will all die!

For the most part, Eastwood plays an emotionally detached loner in both films. That is particularly true in *Joe Kidd*. In the words of the judge who sentences him, Eastwood does just about whatever he pleases. Even though he agrees to serve as a guide for Duvall, Eastwood is never part of the group. He remains aloof from it, serving notice that he has his own reason for going after John Saxon, and that he does not approve of Duvall's bloodthirsty tactics. Even when he escapes from Duvall and forces Saxon to go back to stand trial, there is a peculiar detachment to Eastwood's demeanor. It is as if he were some sort of outside spectator to the action unfolding before him, rather than one of the combatants.

Eastwood's loner status is also apparent in *Two Mules for Sister Sara*.

Clint Eastwood believes that Shirley MacLaine is a nun in *Two Mules for Sister Sara* (1970).

He is a mercenary who helps the Juaristas because they pay him well. He has no commitment to their cause, as does MacLaine. When she reminds him that as an ex–Confederate soldier he too once fought for a cause, Eastwood replies, "Everybody has a right to be a sucker once." Now he fights for whoever will pay him the most; he doesn't worry about the cause. MacLaine throws that comment back in Eastwood's face when she volunteers to be arrested by the French, a mechanism designed to get Eastwood inside the French fort.

Yet, like *Hang 'Em High*, both *Two Mules for Sister Sara* and *Joe Kidd* end on a positive note, one that underlines relationships and affirms community. Once the French forces have been defeated and Eastwood gets his share of the gold, he and Shirley MacLaine (her true identity as a prostitute now revealed) ride off together. Once John Saxon has been delivered to the sheriff in *Joe Kidd*, Stella Garcia, once Saxon's lover, and Eastwood ride out of town together. The promise is that Eastwood will no longer be alone; he will be part of a family, or at least a relationship.

Community plays an important part in *Two Mules for Sister Sara*. Eastwood cannot defeat the French alone; it will require help from all the Juarista elements. So, for example, Mexican women and children deliver a piñata loaded with dynamite to the main gate of the fort, an act that the French commander misinterprets. Defeating the French requires the Juarista guerillas to fight and die; Eastwood could not have done it by himself. And as Eastwood and MacLaine traveled to the Juarista hideout and the fort, they needed information from the Mexican peasants, information that MacLaine could get because they thought her a nun.

In the first three Westerns Eastwood made in the United States, his "man with no name" image, though always present, is softened a great deal from the Leone films. Furthermore, the upbeat ending and the triumph of communal values distinguish them from later Eastwood Westerns. In addition, *Two Mules for Sister Sara* and *Joe Kidd* are both notable for the similarity of their villains. In both, Anglos are trampling the rights of innocent, powerless Mexicans. And in both, Eastwood is on the side of the oppressed Latinos.

Clint Eastwood is a mercenary in *Two Mules for Sister Sara*; he aids the Juaristas only for his share of the gold when they capture the French fort. Yet, as the film unfolds, one senses Eastwood's attitude softening. MacLaine's hatred of the French and her love for the Mexican people do not go unnoticed by Eastwood. The execution of a young Mexican revolutionary by the French, witnessed by Eastwood from a hilltop, and the brutal prison treatment of Mexican prisoners inside the fort, have an impact on him as well. If that interpretation of the film is accurate, Eastwood's dilemma reflected that of the larger American public opinion in 1970. By the time *Two Mules for Sister Sara* was released, American public opinion had turned against the war in Vietnam.

The year 1970 saw widespread college campus unrest and urban protest against the war. For many Americans, the war in Vietnam lacked any connection to American national interest. What difference did it make to citizens of the United States who controlled Vietnam? In that sense, public opinion on Vietnam paralleled Eastwood's mercenary impulse. In Eastwood's case, he was in it for the gold; American public opinion wanted some vital national interest at stake before young men were sent to die in a strange land. Yet there lingered in the United States of 1970 an anti-communist attitude and a concern for the oppression of people living under communist regimes. One senses that confusion articulated in *Two Mules for Sister Sara*, and many Americans in 1970 agreed with Eastwood's resolve to participate in the attack, one for which he was being paid, on the French fort, even in the face of great odds. Many Americans agreed with Senator Richard Russell from Georgia that we should never have been in Vietnam in the first place, but now that we were there we must finish the job. Eastwood finished the job. That is what made his films so attractive to many Americans.

If Eastwood's character in *Two Mules for Sister Sara* reflects the tension and uncertainty over Vietnam that gripped American public opinion in 1970, *Joe Kidd* can be viewed as a commentary on the civil rights movement in the country at the time. In the film, innocent Latino property owners in New Mexico are being forced off their land because their ancient land grants either have been destroyed or are thrown out of court. Anglos, with the courts behind them, are moving in and taking over. John Saxon playing Luis Chama, a Latino revolutionary who uses violence to stop the Anglos. He raids ranches, chases off livestock and burns buildings. *Joe Kidd* opens as Saxon and his band raid the town, break into the courthouse, and burn Anglo land deeds and titles.

By 1972, white Americans were alarmed at the militancy and violence characteristic of a portion of the civil rights movement. Martin Luther King Jr. had been dead for four years, and the civil rights movement had splintered. Younger African Americans were less supportive of peaceful resistance; they were more assertive of their rights and more inclined to use whatever tactics necessary to secure those rights. White Americans, in turn, continued to support the elimination of segregation while condemning the strategies and attitudes of younger African Americans. *Joe Kidd* uses a turn-of-the-century New Mexico setting to explore that dilemma.

As Saxon burns the Anglo land deeds and titles, the judge tries to assure them that if their claims to the land are valid the court will uphold them. Saxon scoffs at the judge's promise of due process; Mexicans know they have little chance of a fair hearing in an Anglo court. After Saxon and his band ride away, a train bearing Robert Duvall and his party steams into town. Duvall is the judge's opposite. Duvall is a large property owner who wants more land and takes what he wants. He respects no one's rights, particularly those of the poor and powerless Mexicans. Duvall's attitude is that, "If the sheriff can't stop him [Saxon], I will. I am not going to waste time arguing in court." Duvall intends to kill Saxon and put an end to all of the nonsense about Mexican property rights.

Duvall pays Eastwood's fine and sends for him. He offers Eastwood $500 to guide his party of killers up into the mountains to get Saxon. Eastwood refuses. When Duvall reminds Eastwood that the latter had once been a bounty hunter, Eastwood replies, "That was a long time ago." However, when Eastwood returns to his ranch he discovers that Saxon has stolen his horses and whipped his Latino hands with barbed wire. Eastwood now has a personal score to settle with Saxon and agrees to serve as Duvall's guide — for $1,000.

Once in the mountains Eastwood begins to more clearly understand Duvall's mission. Duvall's paid killers gun down several of Saxon's men. They also take Stella Garcia, playing Helen Sanchez, Saxon's girlfriend, with them. Duvall's party rides into a small Latino village at the foot of the mountains in which Saxon is hiding. When Saxon's men fire on Duvall's party, he calls up to Saxon, "If you hit one of my men, I will kill ten of your people." Duvall then warns Saxon that if he doesn't surrender by daybreak, he, Duvall, will kill five Latinos at a time until Saxon comes down.

Duvall imprisons Eastwood in the church with the rest of the townsfolk, but the priest slips him an old pistol. Eastwood escapes and, with Stella Garcia, rides into the mountains to convince Saxon to return to town with them to stand trial. Reluctantly, Saxon agrees to go, but not before he tells Garcia that he doesn't want her advice. He keeps her around not for advice but for cold nights. That comment, I am sure, did not go over well with the women in the audience influenced by the emerging feminist movement.

The remainder of *Joe Kidd* is filled with action as Eastwood fights off Duvall's men when he returns Saxon to town to stand trial for his illegal acts. Once in town, Eastwood engages in a running firefight with Duvall and his men that climaxes with the shootout in the judge's chamber. Duvall — the exploiter of poor, defenseless Latinos — is dead, and Saxon — the violent revolutionary — is in jail. Hopefully, Saxon will get a fair trial and Latino property rights will be validated. At least that is the hope *Joe Kidd* conveys as Clint Eastwood and Stella Garcia ride off together, presumably to his ranch to start a new life together.

Joe Kidd ends, then, on an optimistic note. The film maintains that if all parties in the struggle over civil rights will use the peaceful and lawful mechanisms of judicial due process, justice will be done. Unlike many of his other films, Eastwood's belief in *Joe Kidd* is that violence will not solve the issue of Latino property rights. Eastwood counsels Saxon to give up his guns and use legal and lawful processes to make his claims. That is exactly the argument one heard with greater frequency and urgency from white Americans in 1972.

Clint Eastwood made four Westerns after *Joe Kidd*. *High Plains Drifter, The Outlaw Josey Wales, Pale Rider* and *Unforgiven* are different in tone from those previously discussed. In the films following *Joe Kidd*, Eastwood's characters have more of the "man with no name" attributes. Two of them, at least, if not all four, offer a less-than-upbeat ending. And these Eastwood Westerns increasingly reflect the influence of New Western History.

Patricia Nelson Limerick, a New Western historian, begins her recent book, *Something in the Soil*, with the comment, "The land of the American West isn't what it used to be" (13). Well, the study of the American West isn't what it used to be, either! In fact, Limerick herself deserves much of the credit — or blame (depending on one's intellectual orientation) — for reshaping the study of the American West. Her 1987 book *The Legacy of Conquest: The Unbroken Past of the American West* quickly became one of the best known works of an orientation and subculture of American West historians called New Western History. Even though Limerick regards New Western History as "untamed and badly groomed" (Limerick, 16), it is nonetheless true that the movement and the historians who are part of it have achieved a level of recognition unusual in the world of academia. However, recognition is not synonymous with clarity; New Western History means different things to different audiences.

Cognizant of that diversity, Limerick developed "a four-word summary, exemplary in brevity and directness, of the changes in this field of history" (Limerick, 18). **Continuity** is the first of the words. Limerick rejects the notion that the end of the frontier meant that the West lost its distinctiveness. She observes, "Most of the issues that had agitated the nineteenth-century West continued to stir things up a century later" (Limerick, 19). **Convergence** describes the New West historians' recognition that the history of the West is more than the activities of white people. Indians, Mexicans, Asians and African Americans all moved westward, eastward and northward. Theirs is a history too long overlooked. **Complexity** describes Limerick's belief that the West was "morally complex." She describes it in a marvelous sentence: "The deeply frustrating lesson of history in the American West and elsewhere is this: human beings can be a mess — contentious, conflict loving, petty, vindictive, and cruel — and human beings can manifest grace, dignity, compassion, and understanding in ways that leave us breathless" (Limerick, 21). Finally, she suggests the word **Conquest** to describe the expansion of whites of European origin into the West, imposing social, political and economic dominance while seizing the land's resources.

One does not have to see many Westerns produced over the last twenty-plus years to recognize that Limerick's themes of convergence, complexity and conquest have been driving elements in plot and character development. *Dances with Wolves* (Columbia Tri-Star, 1990) skillfully integrates all three themes into a highly entertaining — if controversial — film. *Tombstone* (Buena Vista, 1993) and *Wyatt Earp* (Warner Brothers, 1994) offer much more complex portraits of Wyatt Earp and his brothers — including their wives and lovers — than did earlier cinematic efforts such as *My Darling Clementine* (20th Century–Fox, 1946) and *Gunfight at the OK Corral* (Paramount, 1957).

New Western historians are part of a broader movement (including popular culture) that aims to draw a new, revisionist portrait of the American West, one different (radically so in some cases) from the images carried by most Americans living in the nineteenth century and the first eighty years or so of the twentieth century. As Gene M. Gressley, a New Western historian himself, writes, "The new western, in a mirror of New West historiography, demythologizes the West" (Gressley, 15).

Gressley maintains that the West of earlier Western movies starring the likes of Roy Rogers, Gene Autry and John Wayne have given way to films that highlight the "democratic spirit trampled," "the environment ruined" and "the aborigine toyed with in a brutal vanquishment" (Gressley, 19). In Gressley's words, "the West of John Wayne is being transformed into the West of Clint Eastwood" (Gressley, 19).

The importance of that comment cannot be overstated, because after the death of John Wayne in 1976 (he appeared in ten Westerns after 1968), Clint Eastwood was the sole American actor doing much with the genre. Ben Johnson had supporting roles in a number of Westerns from the late 1960s to the early 1990s, but Eastwood was the only major Hollywood personality to consistently star in Westerns. From the release of *Hang 'Em High* in 1968 through the widely acclaimed *Unforgiven* in 1992, Eastwood appeared in ten Western films, by far the most of any actor in the last thirty years (Zmijewsky and Pfeiffer). For younger cohorts, Clint Eastwood defines the genre!

Employing Limerick's concepts of convergence, complexity and conquest, the rest of this chapter focuses on the last four Eastwood Westerns. Complexity best describes *High Plains Drifter*. According to Zmijewsky and Pfeiffer, when Eastwood read a nine-page idea for the film he thought it would make a "memorable, offbeat Western" (149). They conclude that, "*High Plains Drifter* is every bit the offbeat western Eastwood had hoped it would be" (150). But Zmijewsky and Pfeiffer suggest further that it "is not a likable film. There isn't one single character who is not either a killer or a sniveling coward" (150).

Complexity enters the film immediately as viewers are left to ponder the identity of the Stranger. Is he a ghost, the murdered sheriff returned from the dead, or an avenging angel? Eastwood even suggested that the Stranger was the murdered sheriff's brother (Zmijewsky and Pfeiffer, 150). Whoever he is, one thing is certain: the Stranger's demeanor is closer to Leone's "man with no name" than in any of Eastwood's other American-made films.

Eastwood has very little dialogue, and when he does speak, he speaks in the short declaratory sentences noted earlier. In *High Plains Drifter*, eyes, not words, communicate. The Eastwood stare pervades the film (as do the eyes of nearly every other actor). Insolence, pleasure, fear and other human emotions are captured in the eyes of all the players. Clearly this is a technique Clint Eastwood learned from Sergio Leone, and he uses it to advantage in *High Plains Drifter*.

The Stranger is amoral. He rapes the town prostitute, and when the town agrees that he can have whatever he wants if he will remain to protect them, the Stranger literally takes them at their word. With an arrogant attitude seldom seen in a Western hero, the Stranger takes and takes from the town all the while making clear his contempt for them! The Stranger's arrogant self-assuredness is more prominent in *High Plains Drifter* than in any other Western Eastwood made. The Stranger lacks any of the redeeming qualities of Eastwood's characters in *Hang 'Em High*, *Two Mules for Sister Sara* or *Joe Kidd*. From the time he rides into town and kills the first three gunmen, to the end when he rides away after killing the last three gunmen, the Stranger displays an arrogance and an aloofness that makes one dislike him as much as one dislikes the townsfolk. Tuska summarizes Eastwood's Stranger as "anything but a conventional hero," and concludes, "He had few, if any, admirable traits and almost no humanity" (Tuska, 563).

What is most striking about this film, however, is its depiction of the citizens of a frontier community. With few exceptions, they are all inept, cowardly hypocrites. Compared to the citizens of Lagos in *High Plains Drifter*, the residents of Hadleyville in *High Noon* seem a courageous lot. The sheriff, early in *High Plains Drifter*, assures Eastwood that Lagos is a good town with good people, but viewers quickly learn the contrary. All citizens in the town share a secret. They had the sheriff murdered when he discovered that the Lagos mine was on government land and was about to notify the authorities of that fact. That secret unites, divides and terrifies

Clint Eastwood as the Stranger takes whatever he wants in *High Plains Drifter* (1973), including Mariana Hill.

them. When Verna Bloom, playing Sarah Belding, warns Eastwood to be careful because "you are a man who makes people afraid and that's dangerous," Eastwood's reply that "it's what people know about themselves inside that is dangerous" accurately describes the citizens of Lagos.

Not only are they hypocrites (with the minister — a man of God — the foremost hypocrite among them), they are cowards. When the three men they hired to guard the mine began to steal from it, the town helped send them to prison. But the three vowed to get even when released from prison. In the meantime, the town hired three more gunmen to guard the mine and protect the town should the three previous gunmen return after being released from prison. Eastwood ruined that plan when he killed the three would-be town protectors. When the inhabitants ask Eastwood to take on the job of protecting the town from the three soon-to-be-released convicts, Eastwood tells the sheriff that the "only problem you got is a short supply of guts," an apt description of the entire town.

When Eastwood agrees to help them, he begins to teach them tactics to use when the three ex-convicts arrive, but the townsfolk, Westerners all, prove totally inept. They can't hit anything they shoot at. And they are shaking in their boots all the time they try! That is a remarkably revisionist view of citizens of western towns. Historical evidence suggests something quite to the contrary. The citizens of Northfield, Minnesota, and Coffeyville, Kansas, displayed a great deal of courage and proficiency with firearms as they fought off the outlaw bands trying to rob banks in their towns (Smith, 1996; Smith, 2001).

The only two people in the town who merit any respect are Paul Curtis, playing Mordecai, a midget who is treated by the rest of the town as a freak who deserves little respect, and Verna Bloom, playing Sarah Belding, wife of the town hotel owner and one of the conspirators responsible for the sheriff's murder. Eastwood makes Curtis sheriff, and the little man becomes Eastwood's main ally. Bloom, on the other hand, expresses contempt for both Eastwood and the town until she sleeps with him. That leads her to reclaim her self-respect. Bloom decides she can no longer live with the secret, and she decides to leave both her husband and the town.

Other than Curtis and Bloom, no characters worthy of respect appear in *High Plains Drifter*, not even the Stranger. When Eastwood rides away after killing the three ex-convicts bent on revenge, nothing has changed. Several townsfolk are dead, and the Stranger, whoever he is, has exacted his personal revenge. The town has been burned to the ground, but the townsfolk are generally as they were before. Zmijewsky and Pfeiffer are correct; it is an offbeat Western — bleak, in fact. Its lack of hope and any shred of optimism, combined with its consistently spooky nature, marks *High Plains Drifter* as an unusual entry in the Western genre.

Eastwood's next Western, *The Outlaw Josey Wales*, is regarded by many as his best Western, and Zmijewsky and Pfeiffer note that it is one of Eastwood's "most popular and profitable films" (189). By far the longest of Eastwood's Westerns, the movie bogs down at times, seemingly awash in its own violence. And the level of violence is the one thing striking about *The Outlaw Josey Wales*. From the initial killing of Eastwood's wife and son by the Redlegs, through the chasing down and killing of Bill McKinney (who plays Terrill, the Redlegs commander), viewers lose track of the body count. In fact, the murder of the two bounty hunters and the two buffalo hunters seem to be included just so Eastwood would have somebody to kill. They are an unnecessary intrusion into what could have been a taut story.

Clint Eastwood in his classic two-gun pose from *The Outlaw Josey Wales* (1976).

Unlike *Joe Kidd*, which denigrated the role of violence in solving human problems, *The Outlaw Josey Wales* seems to revel in it. Only after the purging influence of violence, first in the Civil War, and then after escaping to Oklahoma Indian Territory and Texas from Terrill and Fletcher, could Eastwood's Josey Wales walk away from his past and start a new life with Sondra Locke.

Other than William Munny in *Unforgiven*, Josey Wales may be the most complex character Eastwood portrayed in any of his Westerns. At times Eastwood's Josey Wales could exhibit compassion and understanding, and then just as quickly become conflict-loving, vindictive, and even cruel. The loving care of the young wounded comrade, his genuine affection for Chief Dan George and his friendship with Paula Trueman (Grandma Sarah), even though her son had ridden with the Redlegs during the Civil War, are instances of compassion and understanding. On the other hand, the seeming indifference to human life and the obsession for revenge throughout much of *The Outlaw Josey Wales* represent a darker side of his personality.

John Vernon, who plays Fletcher, is also complex. Initially viewers hate him because, as a commander under "Bloody Bill Anderson," he betrayed his own men by convincing them to surrender to Union forces. When they are slaughtered, Eastwood, not Vernon, tries to stop the mass murder. And when Eastwood becomes an outlaw, Vernon rationalizes that he must help capture him if the region is to have real peace. While Vernon always tries to soften McKinney's obsession with capturing and killing Eastwood, Vernon is nonetheless part of the pursuing Redlegs. Yet at the film's conclusion, after Eastwood has killed McKinney, Vernon does not betray Eastwood to the two Texas Rangers hunting him. For Vernon, the war is over, and, along with Eastwood, Vernon understands that everybody died a little bit during the war. Vernon permits the wounded Eastwood to ride away, presumably back to Trueman's ranch to start a new life with Locke.

New Western History is most apparent in the film's portrayal of the Indians. Rick Worland and Edward Countryman suggest that two qualities are central to New Western history. The first rejects the notion that there ever was free empty virgin land to be settled. They contend, "If that land seemed 'free' it was because white Americans did not have to pay the price of its purchase. That price was borne by Indians and by conquered South-western Hispanics" (Worland and Countryman, 185). The second quality understands that Indians and Latinos had occupied the land for centuries (Worland and Countryman, 185).

Both of those qualities are strikingly displayed in *The Outlaw Josey Wales*. Chief Dan George, playing Lone Watie, is a Cherokee transplanted to Oklahoma Indian Territory on the Trail of Tears, a journey in which his wife and children perished. When he fails to sneak up on Eastwood at one point, but permits Eastwood to sneak up on him, Chief Dan George notes that they were called the "civilized tribes" because they were easy to sneak up on.

When viewers first meet Chief Dan George he is dressed in the black formal coat and top hat that he wore when he and other chiefs went to Washington, D.C. But their pleas for assistance were largely ignored. The Indians, he tells Eastwood, were told, "Endeavor to persevere." The Cherokee and other Oklahoma Indians soon learned that the government's words contradicted its actions. Chief Dan George represents conquest. He was moved out of his Georgia homeland to Oklahoma by whites who wanted his land, and now he is kept impoverished in Oklahoma Territory by those same Indian policies. He decides to leave with Eastwood, and in a symbol of his newly declared independence and desire to reclaim his Indian ways, Chief Dan George burns the top hat and black coat.

Chief Dan George does not have a horse, so he and Eastwood head for a trading post where the chief is sure he can buy one. It is at the trading post that Eastwood kills the two buffalo hunters and viewers meet Geraldine Kearns, playing the Indian girl Little Moonlight. Kearns symbolizes the further conquest of Indians by white men. She is little more than property, and is beaten by the trading post owner when she drops a jug of liquor. The two buffalo hunters are in the act of raping her when Eastwood enters the room. Like Chief Dan George, Kearns decides she has no place to go and follows the chief and Eastwood as they head for Texas. During one night of their journey, Eastwood discovers the chief and Kearns engaging in sexual intercourse. Chief Dan George smiles at Eastwood and remarks that he is not as old as he thought he was. Kearns has become the chief's woman!

Will Sampson, playing the Comanche chief Ten Bears, is also an interesting character. According to white opinion, Ten Bears had given up all the land to the whites that he was going to give. When Ten Bears captures two of the men working on Trueman's ranch, Eastwood knows that the Indians will likely attack the ranch house. After preparing everyone to fight off an Indian attack, Eastwood rides into Ten Bears camp. Eastwood tells Ten Bears that they can either have war, in which case both Eastwood and Ten Bears will surely die, or they can live together like brothers. Eastwood promises Ten Bears that his people can have some cattle from which to make beef jerky if they will let the ranch live in peace. Ten Bears replies that there is iron in Eastwood's words and that peace is possible between them. The two men then become blood brothers and the captured ranch hands are freed.

The image of Ten Bears is striking. He is an Indian open to reason and willing to live in peace with the whites—if they are willing to let him live as well. The implication is clear: greedy whites who wanted all of the land and its resources, and who wanted the Indian destroyed, are the root cause of the so-called Indian troubles. When a white man, like Eastwood, is willing to live in peace with the Indians rather than become enemies, Indians will be good neighbors.

Unlike *High Plains Drifter*, *The Outlaw Josey Wales* concludes on an optimistic note. Eastwood has subdued his Redlegs pursuers; Vernon has decided to end the war and let Eastwood leave unmolested; and the ranch is at peace with the Comanches. Eastwood and Locke are now able to put the past behind them and start a new life together.

By 1985, Westerns were assumed to be passé; the time when the genre dominated the big screen and nightly television was long past. Not a few heads were raised in surprise when Eastwood announced that his next project would be a Western. *Pale Rider* was filmed in Sun Valley, Idaho, with much anticipation (Zmijewsky and Pfeiffer, 243–244). While it did not lead to a resurgence of the Western genre, *Pale Rider* did acceptably well at the box office. *Pale Rider*, then, is not important as the film that saved Westerns, nor as a film that set box office records. However, it is an important film in terms of New Western history.

The theme of conquest is central to *Pale Rider*, and receives expression in several ways. Richard Dysart, playing Coy LaHood (the main villain), pursues wealth by conquering the environment. But then, so too do the small-time miners. However, rather than use the slow, labor-intensive methods of the individual miners, methods by which nature rewards hard labor by yielding its gold in small quantities, Dysart employs hydraulic mining. Hugh chunks of earth are blasted away by pressured streams of water, laying bare gold deposits and creating gravel for sale.

Because hydraulic mining quickly uses up the land, it creates a nearly insatiable drive to mine even more land. Dysart must not only conquer — devastate is probably a more apt description — the surrounding landscape, he must also overcome any other obstacle, including human beings who stand in the way of his monstrous hydraulic pumps.

Pale Rider begins as Dysart's men ride down on the mining camp in an effort to scare the miners off their claims. The conquest of human beings is well under way at the start of the film. The conflict between large capital and small business (LaHood versus the small miners), and between capital and labor, is as old as post–Civil War America. Westerns of the 1930s and 1940s touched on facets of those conflicts (large cattle ranches dependent on the open range versus homesteaders), but *Pale Rider* elevates the conflict to a starkness and harshness seldom matched in the genre.

Since the small miners have a lawful right to their claims, Dysart cannot use legal procedures to force them off. Viewers quickly learn that Dysart has already tried (and failed) to conquer government as a means to getting what he wants.

When Dysart first appears in *Pale Rider* he has just returned from Sacramento; but he has not achieved his goal. Quite the contrary, he has learned that hydraulic mining is not popular with politicians. Scornfully, Dysart remarks to his son Christopher Penn that politicians in Sacramento regard hydraulic mining as rape of the land, and probably within two years will make it illegal. Dysart has not been able to conquer the state political landscape; therefore, it is even more imperative to run the miners off of their claims so he can begin hydraulic mining in their valley immediately — before the politicians in Sacramento make it illegal.

At this point in *Pale Rider*, Dysart learns that a preacher has ridden into the valley. The preacher prevented the attempted beating of Michael Moriarity (playing Hull Barrett, leader of the miners), and had stiffened the miners' resolve. When Dysart's efforts to have the preacher frightened off prove unsuccessful, he attempts to bribe him. That too fails! It is then that Dysart tries his final conquest, that of legal authority. John Russell, playing Stockburn, and his so-called deputies represent the ultimate degradation of lawful authority. They hide behind marshals' badges, but, in fact, their guns are for sale! The law they enforce is the will of those who hire their guns. The Dysart-Russell alliance is the ultimate conquest of democratic rule of law; it represents the merger of self-serving, oppressive capital with degraded legal authority.

The factual history of Colorado mining conflicts and Wyoming cattle wars is laden with alliances between capital and degraded legal authority, conflicts in which powerful capital, employing dubious legal authority, was able to conquer small ranchers and prevent mine laborers from organizing unions. One might guess, therefore, that Eastwood (as the preacher) and his miner friends in *Pale Rider* are doomed to defeat. The demythologized West of popular culture and New Western History would seem to require it.

However, Eastwood cannot bring himself to that conclusion, so he reaches back into the mythological West of *Shane* (Paramount, 1953). (*Pale Rider*, of course, draws much of its inspiration and plot from that earlier Western.) Just as Alan Ladd, after he kills Wilson and the Riker brothers, sends young Joey Starrett home to tell his mother that there are no more guns in the valley, so Eastwood rids his valley of Dysart and his henchmen, and Russell and his gunfighters, before riding away, never to return.

Pale Rider ends with the triumph of the mythological West, not its rejection. *Pale Rider*, just as does *Silverado* (Columbia,1985), that other Western released in the Summer of 1985, reaches back to the genre's roots and ends on a note of triumph. Justice has been done, the rape of the land thwarted, and the miners can now work their claims in peace; the bodies of the villains lying in the street are proof of it.

Seven years later, Eastwood returned to the genre with an entirely different view of the Western in *Unforgiven*. It is a film that more than any other Western represents the demythologized West. *Unforgiven* opens as an irate cowboy badly slashes the face of a prostitute who giggles at the size of his penis. Gene Hackman, as Little Bill, arrives on the scene and is prepared, as punishment, to bullwhip the two cowboys who participated in the slashing when Anthony James — owner of the billiard hall/brothel — protests.

The issue quickly turns from justice, punishment of the guilty, and restitution to the victim, to commerce. James holds up a legal contract that Strawberry Alice, the slashed prostitute, had signed, and James maintains that the slashing has ruined his property; nobody will want to be with a whore with a badly cut face. Concern for the victim gives way to an emphasis on property rights. It is James who deserves restitution, not Strawberry Alice. She is part of James' capital, no different, really, from one of his billiard tables. Strawberry Alice is like a factory machine that has broken down and needs to be replaced. In the West of *Unforgiven*, property rights trump the pursuit of justice.

Hackman makes his decision. He will not bullwhip the culprits; but come spring, the two cowboys must deliver horses to James as payment for damaging his property. When Anna Thomson, playing the prostitute Deliah, protests, Hackman makes clear the degradation of legal authority in the town of Big Whiskey. He reminds Thomson that the two cowboys are good people, hard working men who are just a little wild. Hackman's law is enforced with the "good ol' boys" in mind. Whores, it would seem, do not possess legal, enforceable rights in Hackman's town.

As *Unforgiven* unfolds, the beating and humiliation of English Bob, the severe beating administered to Eastwood, and the torture of Morgan Freeman all demonstrate how degraded is Hackman's law. Just as in *Pale Rider*, law in Big Whiskey works for capital, as well as Hackman's personal revenge. The source of Ordinance 14, prominently displayed at the entrance to town ("No Firearms in Big Whiskey"), is not even clear. Did a town board enact it? Or did Hackman enact it via fiat? There is no reference to courts in *Unforgiven*; Hackman's word is law.

When viewers meet Eastwood's William Munny, a notorious gunman/
killer now reformed, he is working his impoverished Kansas farm. Eastwood stands mud-splattered in his hog pen trying to separate hogs with
the "fever" from the rest of the herd when Jaimz Woolvert, playing the
Wolverine Kid, rides up. It seems that if the prostitutes can't obtain justice from Hackman, they will get it from somebody else; so they offer $1,000
to anyone who will kill the two cowboys who cut Strawberry Alice's face.
Ironically, just as Hackman before them, the prostitutes turn the slashing
into an issue of commerce. They will pay for revenge. In the final analysis, the prostitutes are not much different from bordello owner James. They
reduce their search for justice to a commercial transaction.

Eastwood tells Woolvert that he is not like that anymore; his now-
dead wife had reformed him from drinkin' and killin'. But Eastwood suc-
cumbs to his poverty; the $1,000 offers the chance to give his children a
better life, so Eastwood visits his friend and former associate Morgan Freeman (Ned Logan), and together they ride after Woolvert and the reward
money.

Eastwood kills one of the cowboys, and Woolvert kills the other one;
but in the process, Woolvert learns he has no stomach for killing. In the
meantime, Freeman has come to the same conclusion and has left them to
go back home. Before Freeman can get away, however, Hackman and his
posse capture, torture and kill him, displaying Freeman's body, lighted by
torches, in front of James' brothel.

When Eastwood learns of Freeman's torture and death from the prostitute who delivered the reward money to him and Woolvert, Eastwood
takes his shotgun and Woolvert's revolver and rides into Big Whiskey to
avenge Freeman. He murders James, Hackman and several of the deputies,
and rides out of town with a shouted warning to bury Freeman and not
to harm or cut up no more whores—or he will come back and "kill all of
you sons-of-bitches." Commerce, however, remains triumphant. Eastwood killed for his share of the reward, and viewers are led to believe at
the end of the film that he relocated to San Francisco and opened up a dry
goods store. The West of the merchant displaced the West of the gunman—the gun replaced by dry goods!

Unforgiven offers the ultimate conquest, the conquest of the Western
film genre. Eighty-nine years after the genre began with *The Great Train
Robbery*, and a century after Frederick Jackson Turner declared the frontier closed, *Unforgiven* ends the Western film as it had existed for nearly
all of the twentieth century. Like the frontier, the genre is now closed!
Frontier marshals have been reduced to torturers like Gene Hackman's Little Bill, and gunmen have become like Eastwood's William Munny, who

could kill only when drunk and who continually protested that he could not remember what he had done in the old days.

John Cawelti describes violence in the traditional Western as seeming to be "graceful, aesthetic and, even, fun" (Cawelti, 120). None of those descriptors fit the final shootout in James' billiard hall/brothel. Furthermore, as Cawelti notes, the schoolmarm dance-hall girl antithesis no longer holds for most Westerns. It surely does not for *Unforgiven*. Whores are about the only women in Big Whiskey.

In years to come, films that resemble earlier B Westerns (more recent films such as *American Outlaws* [Warner Brothers, 2001] and *The Crossfire Trail*) may be made for either the big screen or for television. But if any major Westerns are made in the future, one thing seems certain; they will not be like they were before *Unforgiven*. Clint Eastwood has done to the Western film genre what Limerick, Gressley and others have done to the study of the American West. Michael Coyne writes in *The Crowded Prairie: American National Identity in the Hollywood Western* that Eastwood helped to "bastardize the genre." Coyne's comment, "His 'man with no name' persona helped to take the heart out of the Western," is true up to a point (Coyne, 173).

Unforgiven won Clint Eastwood Academy Awards and, as just stated surely changed the genre forever. But it is also unlike most of his earlier Westerns. While the "man with no name" part of Eastwood's persona (beginning with the Leone films and transposed to his American productions from *Hang 'Em High* on) presented a new type of Western hero, it does not follow that he bastardized the genre. With the exception of *High Plains Drifter* and *Unforgiven*, careful analysis of Eastwood's Westerns make it clear that he retained traditional elements of the genre — principally the upbeat, optimistic conclusion. Worland and Countryman's words appear most relevant to *Unforgiven* when they note, "Newer historiography is more complex, both socially and morally. So are newer Westerns, and that is where intersection between the two streams of understanding finally appear to be possible" (Worland and Countryman, 185).

Chapter 6

JOHN WAYNE: "THE AMERICAN"

One man's disdain for Sam Peckinpah's Westerns without heroes, and for Clint Eastwood's "man with no name," thundered across American motion picture screens from the middle 1960s until his final film, *The Shootist* (Paramount), appeared in 1976; that man was John Wayne. In the prologue to *John Wayne's America: The Politics of Celebrity*, Garry Wills writes:

> When he was called *the* American, it was a statement of what his fans wanted America to be.... He stood for an America people felt was disappearing or had disappeared [Wills, 14].

Even though Wills does little with that idea throughout the rest of the volume, it is an important one. The notion that John Wayne came to be identified as *the* American at that moment in American history (when many Americans believed that the country they loved was passing away) is seminally important for understanding Wayne's impact on the country during the last twenty years that he lived.

But it had not always been that way! From the early 1940s on, Wayne was a popular motion picture star who was well known for his politically conservative views; but so were other prominent Hollywood personalities. Gary Cooper appeared as a friendly witness before the House Un-American Activities Committee; Wayne did not. Robert Young, Robert Taylor,

Walter Brennan and Ward Bond were as outspoken in their conservative views as was Wayne. From the end of World War II to the late 1950s, John Wayne was one among a number of politically conservative Hollywood personalities caught up in the great drama over the "blacklists" and a country preoccupied with ferreting Communists out of every nook and cranny of American life.

However, by the early 1960s, John Wayne's political views had become much more prominent. He disliked the Kennedys (see Chapter 3), and he was critical of Martin Luther King and the Civil Rights movement. As the war in Vietnam became an American war, Wayne energetically supported it and argued that the government ought to deal more forcefully with war protestors.

Garry Wills contends that Wayne, by the early 1970s, had become an "impressive anachronism," respected by even those who disagreed with his political views (Wills, 287). While there is a fair amount of truth in that assessment, it does a great disservice to Wayne. By the 1970s Wayne was more than an anachronism, he had become a symbol of an America that many people thought had been destroyed by the turmoil-laden 1960s.

By the late 1960s, people were going to see (or staying away from) Wayne's movies precisely because the man had become a symbol of the values held by people former President Richard Nixon labeled the "silent majority." America was caught up in great currents of political, cultural and social change, and John Wayne became a symbol for those resisting that change. Actually, Wayne had modified his views very little; American popular culture and politics had changed a great deal.

The end of ideology and the emergence of consensus politics that Daniel Bell and other scholars proclaimed at the beginning of the decade did not survive the 1960s. The Civil Rights movement and, above all, American involvement in Vietnam divided Americans, not only over specific political issues, but also over the idea of America itself.

If the United States had emerged from World War II, in the words of Winston Churchill, "at the pinnacle of the world," and if citizens of the country had the enjoyable task of living fifty percent better than they had ever lived before, the international leadership and domestic prosperity which followed reinforced Americans' propensity to see their country as a special place, one which possessed a peculiar destiny in the world.

At the end of the World War II, a wing of the Republican Party most closely identified with Senator Robert Taft of Ohio had wanted to dismantle the New Deal. They were unsuccessful in their efforts because the Republican Party until 1964 remained firmly in the hands of moderates who were committed to most of the New Deal's domestic objectives.

Republicans and Democrats often disagreed over the most efficient means to carry out those objectives, and on how to identify and root out political subversives. At times, disputes between the two political parties became rancorous. However, beyond those moments of political wrangling, a remarkable political and cultural consensus ruled the day.

If the 1950s, under the leadership of President Eisenhower, saw the federal government undertake few new social obligations, neither did it witness a dismantling of New Deal policies. The foreign policy of containment that President Harry Truman had so skillfully crafted from 1947 through 1951 thrived throughout the 1950s and 1960s under both Presidents Eisenhower and Kennedy. The 1960 Presidential campaign, one of the most closely contested in American political history, was not marked by a great deal of substantive disagreement between the candidates over important issues. Looking back, the years from 1945 to the early 1960s were not trouble-free, nor were they years without significant political disputes; but one does not do much damage to historical accuracy in describing them as years dominated by social and political consensus rather than as years of strident political and social conflict.

However, the 1960s had barely commenced when the African American struggle for civil rights in the South began to divide the country regionally and along class and racial lines. Those differences intensified as the civil rights conflict spread north and became intertwined with welfare and crime-related issues in the minds of many white working class folks. Turmoil in Southeast Asia quickly followed, first in Laos and then in South Vietnam.

By the mid–1960s, the first wave of "baby-boomers" enrolled in college, more than prepared to dispute traditional morality, and eager to reshape the world in their own, often utopian, images. Certainly all of these elements merged in the minds of the older generation that had suffered through the Great Depression and fought World War II. Campus unrest throughout the last five years of the 1960s—whether over black power, free speech, free love or in opposition to the war in South Vietnam—caused many older Americans to believe that something was terribly and tragically amiss in the country.

Political leaders became increasingly suspect. President Lyndon Johnson's "credibility gap," Governor George Wallace's extremism, and lingering suspicions of Richard Nixon left millions of Americans puzzled about whom they could trust. Into that cauldron of political and social turmoil strode John Wayne with public pronouncements accusing the Civil Rights movement of being communist inspired, and lecturing college students on everything from manners to responsibility. He made motion pictures such as *The Green Berets* (Warner Brothers, 1968) that supported the war in Vietnam, and a number of Westerns that highlighted traditional values of manliness and responsibility. It is precisely during the tumultuous 1960s that John Wayne became a symbol both of an America many thought was vanishing and of an America others regarded as racist, repressive and confining.

During the twenty years prior to his death, years in which Wayne became a spokesperson for an America many thought was endangered, he was not a symbol without substance nor one engaged in what most Americans regarded as atavistic wishful thinking. He represented a view of America that emerged from the troubled 1930s and the triumphant 1940s, a view that had millions of adherents.

Two of Wayne's Westerns from the 1940s help to put into perspective the man and his films after 1965. *Fort Apache* (RKO, 1948) expresses a perception of the military emerging from World War II that yet dominated public sentiment at the time of Vietnam. It is most aptly expressed in two pieces of dialogue in the film. As the troop marches out to its fatal confrontation with Cochise, Anna Lee, playing Emily Collingwood, and the other wives watch them ride away. Lee then utters her most thought-provoking line in the entire film: "I can't see them, all I can see is the flags."

At the film's conclusion, John Wayne, as Captain Kirby Yorke, briefs news reporters who will accompany him on the upcoming campaign against the Indians. The reporters ask about Colonel Thursday. In spite of the fact Wayne knows that Thursday was an arrogant martinet who led his troop needlessly to their deaths, Wayne describes him as a great soldier, "none finer." When one of the reporters laments the good men who died with Thursday in his gallant charge, Wayne's reply is that they are not really dead. They yet live, he insists, embodied in the regiment. Surely Collingwood, Mulcahy and all of the others were physically gone, but their spirits would live as long as the regiment lived.

That contention — that the spirits of dead soldiers live in and through their comrades in arms — is a reminder of the closing scenes in *To Hell and Back* (Universal-International, 1955), based loosely on the story of Audie Murphy, the most decorated soldier in the European Theater of Operation during World War II. Against the backdrop of the song "Dogface Soldier" appear the faces of all those friends of Murphy who had died in Italy and France. Yet they don't seem to be dead, rather they are alive in the persons of the troopers lined up in review as Murphy is awarded the Congressional Medal of Honor. Even though they are dead, they live in and through the regiment; we can still see the flag!

A generation of Americans who had lost fathers, sons, brothers, uncles and neighbors during World War II and in Korea believed that message. "The boys" had not died needlessly; they died protecting freedom, and their spirits live on in those young men guarding the frontiers of freedom in outposts all over the world. To honor the dead, one supported living soldiers. Whether the policy was right or wrong, Americans had a moral — even spiritual — obligation to support the regiment. Senator Richard Russell of Georgia caught that sentiment when he observed, "We are there now." Although a skeptic of the war, Russell believed we had to support the troops — we could not cut and run (Shesol, 380).

But the view of America embraced by Wayne's films of the 1940s did more than honor the American military. *Red River* (United Artists, 1948) suggests two other important elements. Tom Dunson, Wayne's character in the film, was an empire builder. In the years prior to the Civil War, he had built up the Red River D into a large cattle ranch. He was successful, and then the collapse of the Southern economy following the war brought him to the edge of ruin. Organizing a great cattle drive, Dunson starts for Missouri and better prices. Along the way he becomes single-minded and mean-spirited. He kills three of his punchers when they want to quit the drive, and he pushes the men at an unreasonable pace. When he tries to hang two punchers who had tried to leave the herd, his adopted son Matthew Garth intervenes.

Viewers understand Matthew has to intervene because all recognize that Groot, Walter Brennan's character in the film, is acting as Dunson's conscience when he tells him, "You was wrong, Mr. Dunson." Yet there is a great deal of ambivalence in the character of Tom Dunson. Americans have always given grudging admiration to the Dunsons of this world, men who endured great hardships to build things, men who were risk-takers. Even though the public did not always approve of their policies, Americans have always respected leaders who were not afraid to lead, men who stood firm in the face of public opposition. Such men engendered public sympathy and often public support.

Tom Dunson exhibited another American characteristic — a respect for God. It was an inter-faith, atheological, amorphous conception of God to be sure, but it was no less sincere. In a time of aggressive evangelical and fundamentalist Christianity, many tend to forget that Americans remain the most religious people of all the western nations, even though the popular understanding of God is much less rigorous than many religious conservatives desire.

After Tom Dunson killed the Mexican who protested his taking the land, and after he killed the three punchers, he "read" over them. In *She Wore a Yellow Ribbon* (RKO, 1949) he performed the same rite over the dead relay station attendants and a fallen trooper. Even in acts of violence, one acknowledged God as the creator, sustainer and final judge of human life. To be a true American, then, one respected this civil religious conception of God.

That was Wayne's understanding of God. Randy Roberts and James S. Olson, in the biography *John Wayne American*, describe Wayne's faith as "more inductive than deductive." They note that he once told a reporter, "There must be some higher power or how does all this stuff work?" (Roberts and Olson, 639). He didn't believe in miracles—even at the end of his life when he needed one—and he more often than not found God in the mountains and in solitude (Roberts and Olson, 639). In short, Wayne's faith was one that made sense to millions of Americans.

These two Westerns (as did nearly all of Wayne's films) projected a view of the social and political order believed by millions of Americans in the late 1960s and early 1970s. Honor the flag, support troops stationed around the world (particularly those engaged in combat), respect leaders, and pay homage to God were among the core ideas of "Americanism." The title of the Statler Brothers song "Whatever Happened to Randolph Scott" suggests the dilemma many Americans of that era faced. *True Grit* was the last motion picture many of them understood.

By the mid-to-late 1960s, both respect for leadership — the American Presidency, campus administrators or nearly any other authority figure — and religion was rejected by many of "the young." Presidents were booed and ridiculed, campus leadership was challenged, and sexual behavior incompatible with Judeo-Christian morality was practiced openly. War protestors burned both their draft cards and the flag. Others broke into draft boards and poured blood on the records. Even some notable Americans, such as Jane Fonda, visited North Vietnam and appeared (to the public mind, at least) to support North Vietnamese regulars and the Viet Cong.

Again, older Americans were confused, believing that something was terribly wrong in the country. John Wayne articulated those concerns as he lent public support to beleaguered Presidents and campus administrators, criticized those who opposed the war, and spoke of having made his peace "with the man upstairs."

In a decade when Americans were deeply troubled and generationally divided, John Wayne became an important cultural spokesperson for those who no longer understood what was happening to America, or, in some instances, even recognized their own children. Film critic Andrew Sarris wrote in 1979: "John Wayne is not one of us, if by us we stipulate the kind of people who read and contribute to *The New Republic*. Wayne was the

Other... (Roberts and Olson, 645). In those tumultuous years from the middle 1960s to the middle 1970s, Wayne was a symbol of Americanism to the "Other." To them, John Wayne was the constant — the one who expressed an America they understood — in rapidly changing times.

Roberts and Olson suggest that, "Those who hope to understand America must understand John Wayne's appeal" (Roberts and Olson, 647). They note:

> He preached individuality in an age of bureaucracy and laissez-faire in an era of social engineering. When others called for détente and pacifism, he insisted that evil exists in the world and must be crushed with righteous violence. John Wayne's feet were firmly planted in the American bedrock [Roberts and Olson, 648].

While their praise may be overdone, it is clear that John Wayne emerged as an important cultural symbol for the "silent majority" of the 1960s and 1970s. For a brief moment, Captain Kirby Yorke and Tom Dunson strode tall across the American landscape, ready to do battle with those who, it seemed to Wayne, were trying to destroy America. For that moment there was a John Wayne's America, and to it, John Wayne was and always will be simply "John Wayne, American."

However, that image of John Wayne got off to a shaky start in 1956 when he appeared as Ethan Edwards in *The Searchers* (Warner Brothers, 1956). Clearly, *The Searchers* has more in common with the descent-of-the-hero films discussed in Chapter 2 than with later Wayne efforts. The actor Harry Carey Jr. and Wayne biographer Ronald Davis consider *The Searchers* Wayne's greatest role and performance (Roberts and Olson, 420; Davis 1998, 203). Wayne, in truth, is a villain-like character for much of the film. He intends to kill Natalie Wood (Debbie) because he hates Indians so much and she has lived with them after being kidnapped. However, Wayne did not consider Edwards a villain; rather, "He was a man living in his times" (Roberts and Olson, 420).

That is an interesting observation. If by his times Wayne meant Texas of the 1870s, there is merit in his comment. Post–Civil War frontier settlers lived under continual harassment from Indians, and, more often than not white settlers demanded either the removal of Indians to reservations or, better yet, their total extermination. As a matter of historical assessment, Wayne is probably correct; Ethan Edwards was a man of his times.

On the other hand, Wayne's Ethan Edwards is not a hero in the sense that his western characters had been prior to (with the notable exception of *Red River*)— or after — *The Searchers*. The Searchers is an important film for the present study because it stands as an exception to all other post–1955 Wayne Westerns.

Viewers first meet Wayne as he rides up to his brother's cabin after a long absence during the Civil War and a self-imposed exile in Mexico. There are even hints that during his sojourn in Mexico, Wayne had been a bandit of sorts (he had a lot of unexplained gold coins). The racism that shapes his character throughout the film emerges early when he makes a comment about Jeffery Hunter being of mixed blood. It is also clear that Wayne and his sister-in-law are fond of one another, probably in love. *The Searchers* hints that Wayne lost her because he was unwilling to commit himself to a domestic life. Wayne's Ethan Edwards is not only a racist, he is emotionally repressed!

When Ward Bond and his band of Texas Rangers come to the ranch, Wayne and Hunter go with them to track down a band of marauding Comanches thought to be stealing cattle. But the cattle theft is a Comanche ruse designed to pull the Rangers away from the isolated homesteads. As the rangers, including Wayne and Hunter, chase the Indians, Scar (Henry Brandon) and his Comanches raid the homestead, kill Wayne's brother and sister-in-law, and kidnap the two girls. Wayne, Hunter and Carey Jr. begin the long search for the girls that gives the film its name.

Roberts and Olson observe, "During the course of the five year quest, Ethan's commitment hardens into something ugly" (Roberts and Olson, 422). They observe that Wayne's personality develops a sharp edge, and that he becomes quick to anger (Roberts and Olson, 422). "His hatred of Comanche blossoms into a megalomanical compulsion, a racism of frightening proportions" (Roberts and Olson, 423–24). Ronald Davis concurs with that assessment and notes that Wayne in *The Searchers* is "obsessed to the point of fanaticism" (Davis 1998, 205). "Edwards is a racist full of hate, uncomfortable with domesticity and sexually repressed" (Davis 1998, 205). Davis concludes that Wayne's Ethan Edwards is "incapable of modifying his values" (Davis 1998, 206).

Roberts and Olson note that in *The Searchers* Wayne turned the westerner into an antihero "worthy of the James Dean and Marlon Brando rebels of the 1950s" (Roberts and Olson, 425). As Roberts and Olson observe, throughout the film Wayne responds to criticism by replying, "That'll be the day." The comment quickly became part of 1950s teenage slang (Roberts and Olson, 425). *The Searchers* has much in common with Westerns that James Stewart made for Anthony Mann, and those in which

Glenn Ford appeared throughout the 1950s. Even though, at the end, Wayne redeems Ethan Edwards when he picks up Natalie Wood (playing Debbie) and, instead of killing her, says simply, "let's go home," his character throughout the film remains a complex, unappealing person. If Ethan Edwards in not a villain in any traditional sense, Roberts and Olson are surely correct in saying that Wayne's Ethan Edwards is at least an antihero!

Yet Robert C. Sickels accurately describes *The Searchers* as a bellwether film that illuminates "the social mores of the era in which it was made" (Sickels, 220). Wayne's description of Edwards as a man of his times applies to the United States in the middle 1950s as well as post–Civil War Texas. Surely Wayne's Ethan Edwards believed in white racial superiority, and he hated Indians. If one substitutes African Americans for Indians, that sentiment aptly describes millions of people in the United States of 1956. The South, as well as large sections of the North and West, was still segregated. Most children went to school with a majority of their same race, and African Americans and Hispanics were still denied access to public accommodations (restaurants, hotels, etc.). Sickels observes, "*The Searchers* reveals mainstream American culture's relative conservatism as concerns its understanding and tolerance of race and gender issues in the 1950s" (Sickels, 227).

The Searchers represents its time — the United States in the middle 1950s— both in terms of racial and gender issues and the changed view of the hero that shaped Westerns from the time *The Searchers* was released to the end of the century. John Ford, who directed *The Searchers*, would rethink racial attitudes in 1960s films such as *Sergeant Rutledge* (Warner Brothers, 1960), *Two Rode Together* (Columbia, 1961) and *Cheyenne Autumn* (Warner Brothers, 1964), and his heroes would remain more complex (adding elements of the antihero)— in contrast to Wayne's Kirby York of *Fort Apache* or Henry Fonda's Wyatt Earp of *My Darling Clementine* (20th Century–Fox, 1946) in the Ford films of the 1940s.

On the other hand, while Wayne softened his racism after *The Searchers*, he emphatically disavowed the antihero. Surely his characters were more complex than the heroes of traditional B Westerns, and often he employed the good-bad man theme that William S. Hart had used so effectively; but never again would Wayne play an antihero like Ethan Edwards. And, more often than not, his characters were men like Sheriff John T. Chance in *Rio Bravo* (Warner Brothers, 1959), John Chisum in *Chisum* (Warner Brothers, 1970) or Big Jake McCandles in *Big Jake* (National General Pictures, 1971). From 1959 through his last film, John Wayne offered Americans a hero more in keeping with traditional B Western heroes than the antihero favored by the younger moviegoers of the last twenty-five years of the twentieth century. It may be that Wayne expressed his attitude best in *Rooster Cogburn* (Universal, 1975) when he tells Katherine Hepburn, "I am what I am." Hepburn, at the end of the film, in turn spoke for many older Americans when she tells Wayne, "You're a credit to the whole male sex, and I am proud to have you for my friend." It is *that* Wayne, the Wayne of John T. Chance, John Chisum and Rooster Cogburn, that left an indelible impression on American popular culture in the last forty years of the last century. And it is to that body of work that we now turn.

For analytical purposes, Wayne's Westerns after 1959 are grouped into four categories as a convenient way to relate them to American culture as it changed in the last forty years of the century. Other studies of the man and his work will order the films differently. In no sense is the present typology anything other than a convenient way to think about the manner in which Wayne sought to come to grips with both his own aging and a rapidly changing American culture.

Most striking is that while many films in diverse genres consciously raised social issues and sought to intellectually challenge viewers from the mid–1960s onward, year after year Wayne made action-oriented Westerns. First and foremost, viewers were entertained. They were not encouraged to take the morning newspaper headlines into the theater with them (of course, *The Green Berets* is a striking exception to that observation). Westerns such as *The Sons of Katie Elder* (Paramount, 1965), *War Wagon* (Universal, 1967), *The Undefeated* (20th Century–Fox, 1969), *Big Jake* and *Chisum* drew from the rich plot and character heritages of the genre. Wayne's Westerns, more often than not, fit traditional Western genre expectations. Of Wayne's predominately action-oriented Westerns (the first of the four Wayne Western categories), *Chisum* is the most intriguing. Not only is it, in my opinion, the best Western he made after 1965, it also raises important questions about how a man is supposed to conduct himself in changing times.

Certainly *Rio Bravo* is an action Western, but since it was remade twice (as *El Dorado* [Paramount, 1967] and *Rio Lobo* [National General Pictures, 1971]), the *Rio Bravo* story is treated as a second type of Western in which Wayne appeared. Of the three, *Rio Bravo* and *El Dorado* are the most interesting because their motifs fit traditional genre expectations, and they explore the importance of friendship, loyalty and collective action in an increasingly impersonal, individualistic American culture.

The third and fourth categories of analysis are interrelated. In *True Grit* (Paramount, 1969) and *Rooster Cogburn*, Wayne's Rooster Cogburn is a man who refuses to adapt to changing circumstances and values. These two films can be viewed as largely autobiographical. In them, Wayne makes a statement about his dislike of contemporary culture and his insistence on doing things *his* way, the old tried and true method. Rooster Cogburn is the crotchety old man most of us have met at one time or another. The world has passed him by, but he won't admit it, nor will he change his habits or attitudes. That Wayne persona also appears, to some extent, in *The Train Robbers* (Warner Brothers, 1973) and reaches its zenith in *The Shootist*.

Closely related to this theme of a man who has outlived his times is the old man who mentors younger men. That element is present in *The Shootist, Chisum, True Grit* and *The Train Robbers*, but is most obvious in *Cahill United States Marshal* (Warner Brothers, 1973) and *The Cowboys* (Universal, 1972). One senses that by the late 1960s, as a result of his bout with cancer, John Wayne understood his own mortality and felt an urgent obligation to teach younger men and women the truths in which he believed. As he neared the end of his film career and his life, John Wayne was doing more than protesting the changes in American culture that he abhorred; he also wanted to ingrain in younger cohorts a respect for the values around which he had built his public persona.

However one categorizes Wayne's Westerns after 1965, one thing is certain. The values they offer are strikingly different from those that increasingly dominated the work of Sam Peckinpah and Clint Eastwood. Beginning with *Rio Bravo*, John Wayne tendered viewers a different view of the West, one that would dominate his films for the rest of his life, and one that was at odds with a rapidly changing film industry in the late 1960s and 1970s.

A number of film critics and Wayne biographers have commented on Howard Hawk's and John Wayne's reactions to *High Noon* (United Artists, 1952) and *3:10 to Yuma* (Columbia, 1957). Neither Gary Cooper in the former nor Van Heflin in the latter demonstrated those qualities that Hawks and Wayne associated with frontier lawmen. Wayne, in particular, objected to *High Noon* because he correctly understood it as an attack on Hollywood's timidity during the McCarthy era. *Rio Bravo* was fashioned as a response to *High Noon* (Tuska 1976, 512; Roberts and Olson, 439).

John Wayne, as Sheriff John T. Chance, arrests Claude Akins for a brutal murder, but Akins' brother (played by John Russell), a prominent cattleman, vows to free him from jail. In his determined stance against

John Wayne as the determined Sheriff John T. Chance in *Rio Bravo* (1959).

Russell, Wayne's friends rally to his aid. Dean Martin (Dude), Walter Brennan (Stumpy) and Ricky Nelson (Colorado) become his closest allies. But Angie Dickinson, Pedro Gonzalez-Gonzalez and Estelita Rodriguez all provide assistance. Unlike the citizens of Hadleyville in *High Noon*, Wayne's friends do not desert him.

In *El Dorado*, John Wayne is the gunman Cole Thornton, and Robert

Mitchum his old friend Sheriff J.P. Harrah. Wayne refuses Edward Asner's offer to become one of his hired guns and to help him to drive R.G. Armstrong off of his land because Wayne does not want to go up against Mitchum. Some months later, Wayne learns that Mitchum has become a drunk after being jilted by a woman, and that Asner has hired more fast guns. Wayne and his young protégé— James Caan — ride back to El Dorado to lend a hand to Mitchum. In *El Dorado,* Caan assumes Ricky Nelson's role in *Rio Bravo* and Arthur Hunnicutt (as Bull Thomas) is Walter Brennan's counterpart. And in the final showdown with Asner and his gunmen, R.G. Armstrong (playing Kevin MacDonald) and his family ride into town, prepared to lend a hand. Rather than be cowed, as were the citizens of Hadleyville, Armstrong and his family are prepared to fight for their land!

Roberts and Olson's comment about Wayne's character in *Rio Bravo* applies equally to *El Dorado.* They note that Wayne "does his job stoically and without fuss. In the process, his friends respond" (Roberts and Olson, 439). Wayne is a man who understands duty, and he possesses the personal integrity that allows him to persist even in the face of great odds. Wayne, as John T. Chance in *Rio Bravo*, was prepared to stand his ground even if his friends had not come to his aid. In *El Dorado*, Wayne and Caan ride to help Mitchum even though both men understand that they will be going up against more guns than they can muster.

Both films are also about leadership. Neither Sheriff Chance in *Rio Bravo* nor Cole Thornton in *El Dorado* shirk their responsibilities, even though the odds are against them. In modeling courage and determination to duty, they rally support —from some quarters of the community, at least. The not-so-subtle theme in each film is that leaders must lead. Watching *El Dorado* in motion picture theaters or *Rio Bravo* on television during the war in Vietnam, viewers must have been struck by the similarity between the sheriff's office in both films and the Johnson and Nixon White Houses during war protests. Both were buildings under siege, and the occupants had to move with care when they left either the sheriff's officer or the White House.

Yet neither Presidents Johnson nor Nixon could permit opposition to their policies, or the noisy clamor of war protestors, to compromise their leadership obligations. Nor could fear for their lives excuse Wayne and Mitchum in *El Dorado*, nor Wayne and Martin in *Rio Bravo*, from doing their duty (apprehending murderers and holding them for trial). In an era when leaders in all types of public and private institutions were being berated and challenged, *El Dorado* and *Rio Bravo* applauded individuals who do their duty in the face of a hostile environment. John Wayne did more than preach responsibility; he modeled it in his films, because in all of Wayne's Westerns after 1965, including *El Dorado*, allegiance to duty remains a dominant theme.

Both films are about second chances, as well. Dean Martin (Dude) in *Rio Bravo* portrays an ex-deputy and former gunman. Now he is the town drunk. For two years or so, Martin has scrounged drinks in the town saloon, even retrieving coins from spittoons (where cowboys who wanted to humiliate him had tossed them). Martin is unshaven and dirty. Yet Wayne gives him a chance to reform, and Martin agrees to try. A sub-theme in *Rio Bravo* is Martin's (successful, it turns out) effort to dry out and wean himself away from alcohol dependence.

A similar concern pervades *El Dorado*. When Wayne and Caan ride back to El Dorado, they find Mitchum the laughing stock of the town. Men in the saloon poke fun at him because, like a baby, he needs a bottle before he goes to sleep. Wayne and Caan discover Mitchum sleeping off a drunk in one of the jail cells. At Caan's suggestion, Wayne and Hunicutt mix a concoction that will sober him up and cause him to become physically ill if he drinks more whiskey. Like Martin in *Rio Bravo*, Mitchum has to fight his alcohol dependence, and will need to do his duty even though he has the shakes.

John Wayne gives both Dean Martin and Robert Mitchum a second chance, but it is their responsibility to exercise self-discipline and to change their behavior. In *Rio Bravo* and *El Dorado*, alcoholism is not a disease — it is the result of human weakness that leads to fleeing one's responsibility and to self-degradation. In the films, alcoholism is not overcome by therapy or medical treatment — it is corrected by an act of will. Loyal, understanding friends must reinforce effort, but ultimately it is the responsibility of the alcoholic to change his behavior.

In *El Dorado*, Caan's concoction helped Mitchum sober up, and it helped him for the moment to overcome his desire for whiskey; but it was not a long-term treatment. Mitchum had to fight through the shakes and the physical illness prompted by his withdrawal from alcohol dependence. The lesson here is that once an individual acknowledges his need to behave responsibly, it is easier to overcome the addiction. Viewers learn that from the climax of *El Dorado*. Still suffering from the shakes, Mitchum nonetheless does his duty as sheriff and goes to the saloon for the final showdown. The film ends with a renewed and reformed Mitchum, now cleaned up and sober, who has reclaimed his sense of responsibility and the respect and gratitude of the town.

A different responsibility highlights both *The Sons of Katie Elder* and *War Wagon*. The message in both films is that a man ought to insist on justice for himself and those whom he loves, and that corrupt individuals who have murdered and stolen property must be held accountable for their illegal actions.

The four sons of Katie Elder (John Wayne, Dean Martin, Earl Holliman and Michael Anderson Jr.) return home to attend the funeral of their mother. They learn that their mother died impoverished. Supposedly their father had gambled away the ranch while drunk, and then was killed the same night. The only witnesses, James Gregory and Dennis Hooper (as Morgan Hastings and his son Dave), now own the Elder ranch. When Gregory fears that Wayne will learn the truth, he has the sheriff (Paul Fix) murdered and then pins the murder on Wayne and his brothers. After a good deal of exciting action unfolds, Dennis Hopper, as he lay dying, confesses that Gregory killed the senior Elder. Wayne kills Gregory in a showdown, and the brothers (with the exception of Earl Holliman, who had been killed) reclaim the homestead. Wayne, Martin, Holliman and Anderson Jr. avenge their father's death and regain their stolen property. In short, they behave like sons in traditional Westerns had always behaved!

Bruce Cabot is the personification of evil in *War Wagon*. He saw to it that John Wayne was sent to prison on false charges, and then Cabot took his gold mine–rich property. Cabot runs the town, and the sheriff (and presumably all of the other town officials) answers to him. The film opens with Wayne (playing Taw Jackson) out of prison and plotting revenge against Cabot. Cabot transports his gold dust in an armor-plated wagon known appropriately as the war wagon. Wayne plans to hijack the wagon and steal the gold dust. With little hope that a corrupt political system will help him, Wayne intends to seek justice any way he can. He enlists the aid of Kirk Douglas (as Lomax), Howard Keel (Levi Walking Bear), Robert Walker (Billy) and Keenan Wynn (Wes Catlin) to help him steal the gold.

War Wagon is an enjoyable mixture of humor and action, but the pervasive theme is that Wayne intends to exact a measure of justice from Cabot by stealing his gold — and killing him if the opportunity presents itself. Both happen. Cabot shoots two of his own men as they try to escape the runaway war wagon, but one of them shoots and kills Cabot in turn. As Douglas looks into the overturned and wrecked war wagon, he sees Cabot's dead body. Douglas tells Wayne, "I guess you got your ranch back."

Chisum, a fable of the Lincoln County (New Mexico) war, is arguably one of John Wayne's best post–1965 Westerns. The opening credits run over painted frames of a cattle drive that link knowledgeable viewers to *Red River*. *Chisum* might even be viewed as an alternative to the cattle drive in *Red River*. Rather than drive the herd to Missouri, Chisum takes them to New Mexico and a fresh start. Or *Chisum* might be seen as the ultimate ending of *Red River*. Once the cattle market in Texas goes bust, Chisum moves his herd to New Mexico.

At one point, Wayne even acknowledges that he left a girl back in Texas. That reminds one of the opening scenes in *Red River* when Wayne refuses to take Coleen Gray with him as he leaves the wagon train. Gray and all the others in the wagon train are killed when Indians attack it. Throughout *Red River* Wayne appears to be haunted by the girl he left behind, just as he seems lonely in the midst of all that he has built in *Chisum*.

Chisum opens with a stirring song and the painted frames of a cattle drive, with its storms, stampedes and Indian attacks. The lyrics describe Chisum as the brave and resolute hero of a "hundred battles," struggling doggedly against great odds. The song and the painted frames make clear that it took a determined man to build the great cattle ranch that Chisum had built. The opening frames then give way to the silhouette of a solitary horseman (Wayne) sitting on a hill looking over the ranch.

The scene shifts to a cowboy, who says to Ben Johnson (he had been with Wayne from the beginning), "He's been up there an hour; what's he doing?" Johnson replies, "You wouldn't understand," as he rides his horse up the hill to Wayne. As Wayne looks over what he has built, Johnson asks, "Thinking about the beginning?" "The beginning and before," Wayne replies. Johnson can only observe, "Everything is different now." Wayne's response is startling to those familiar with John Wayne's political views: "Things usually change for the better." That comment may say something very important about John Wayne's outlook on life. Even though in 1970 (when *Chisum* was released) the country was deeply divided over Vietnam, and the social, political and moral values that he hated seemed triumphant, Wayne remained optimistic. One suspects that he trusted the common sense of the American people and believed that the country would right itself.

Forrest Tucker (as Lawrence Murphy) is the main villain, intent on grabbing all of the land he can. He owns the town sheriff (Bruce Cabot) and the largest dry goods store, as well as the only bank. His store charges exorbitantly high prices, and the bank imposes steep interest rates for its loans. Tucker's aim is to use debt as leverage to drive out the small ranchers so he can buy up their land. Wayne is one of the few men he can't buffalo. The other is Patrick Knowles (playing Tunstall), another cattleman. Geoffrey Deuel, playing Billy the Kid, is one of Tunstall's riders. Deuel's loyalty to Knowles goes beyond loyalty to the brand; Deuel regards Knowles much like a second father.

Wayne's determination and courage emerge early in the film. He has ridden into Lincoln to meet his niece, who is coming to live with him, when one of his riders gallops into town and tells Wayne that a herd of his horses are being rustled. Wayne and Johnson chase after the herd. When they catch them, Deuel and some of Tunstall's other cowboys ride up. In the ensuing shootout, Wayne gets his horses back and viewers witness Deuel's skill with a gun.

Andrew Prine (as Alex McSween) and Lynda Day (Sue McSween) came to Lincoln to work for Tucker, but Prine can't stomach Tucker's dishonesty. As the couple prepares to leave town, Wayne and Knowles offer Prine a job. The two men decide to use their considerable resources to open a store and a bank. They will give the folks in Lincoln honest businessmen with whom to deal. Knowles even decides to go to the capitol to see if the governor can stop Tucker's lawlessness.

On the way to the capitol, Knowles is waylaid by two of Tucker's self-appointed deputies (really gunmen), and one of them accidentally shoots and kills Knowles. Geoffrey Deuel intends to take his own, personal, revenge on Tucker and the men who killed Knowles. He tells Wayne that he is going to do "what you would have done twenty-five years ago." But Wayne talks Deuel out of seeking personal vengeance; wait for the law, he counsels.

Ben Johnson puts it in perspective when he tells Deuel, "Mr. Chisum has changed with the time." Now he cares; he cares about the people in Lincoln and he cares about the Indians. Johnson concludes that Deuel wants revenge, but Chisum wants justice. And Wayne appears to get his justice. A sympathetic judge swears him in as a lawman, and Wayne and a posse track down Knowles' two killers and begin the journey back to Lincoln. Near Lincoln, Wayne leaves Glenn Corbett (playing Pat Garrett) to take the two killers on into town. After Wayne rides away, Deuel canters up and greets his friend Corbett. Before Corbett can stop him, Deuel pulls his revolver and kills the two men who had murdered Knowles. Deuel rides away, now a hunted outlaw.

Deuel and his friends decide to attack Tucker with dynamite, so they go to Prine's store to get it. Tucker and his men discover Deuel in the store and the shootout begins. Lynda Day is allowed to leave the store, now under siege by Tucker's gunmen, and she rides to Wayne for help. When

Ben Johnson asks Wayne what he is going to do, Wayne's reply, "what I would have done twenty-five years ago," ties the film into the values of loyalty to one's friends, responsibility and commitment to justice that highlight nearly all of Wayne's post–1965 Westerns.

Wayne and his cowboys ride into town and lift the siege, but not before Prine is gunned down by Tucker's men. Wayne beats Tucker in a brutal fistfight, and the latter dies when he is run through by a steer horn. Deuel rides away from Lincoln, and the film ends with Corbett becoming a United States marshal, thus setting up the saga of Pat Garrett hunting down and killing Billy the Kid.

Chisum, maybe more than any other of Wayne's post–1965 Westerns, brings together the values that John Wayne affirmed. John Chisum is a man who worked hard, took risks and endured hardships to build something of which he could be proud. Wayne's Chisum is a hard man who protects his property, but he is also a man who believes in fair play and wants to give other people a chance to be successful. Decency, neighborliness and hard work are the values that Chisum affirms. He will protect his property and demand justice for himself and others. Revenge is beneath John Wayne's Chisum!

Near the end of the film, Ben Johnson and John Wayne engage in a bit of dialogue that suggests a good deal about Wayne's view of life. Johnson recounts the saying that there is no law west of Dodge and no God west of the Pecos. Walking away, Wayne responds, "No matter where people go, sooner or later there's the law, and they discover that God has already been there." I cannot think of any other film that better distinguishes John Wayne's view of the human condition from those of Sam Peckinaph and Clint Eastwood.

Values that are showcased in *Chisum*, *El Dorado*, *Rio Bravo* and nearly every other John Wayne Western are not innate in human beings; they are learned. Older adults must take the time to teach and model for younger people proper behavior, skills that will help them succeed in life, and values that give life meaning and permit people to live together civilly. The responsibility to transmit values to younger cohorts (what social scientists call socialization) assumes urgency in times of social and political turmoil. The massive impact of the baby boomers, turmoil over the war in Vietnam, sordid political scandals (the most prominent of which — but by no means the sole example — was Watergate), increasing numbers of Americans on welfare, and rising crime rates combined to create change and crisis in the American social and political landscape of the 1960s and 1970s.

For a conservative such as John Wayne, it was imperative to give voice to those who, like himself, believed that there was something terribly amiss

in the country. Set in the context of the Old West, John Wayne's Westerns appealed to conservatives—and were disliked by many liberals—who agreed with him. But Wayne also understood the need to transmit the values in which he believed so strongly to younger generations. Beginning with *The Cowboys*, all of his remaining Westerns in some fashion touch on teaching younger folks important value lessons.

The Cowboys opens with John Wayne (as Will Anderson) needing to get a large herd of cows to market in Belle Fouche. But his cowboys have all quit to try their hand at the gold fields in Idaho. Slim Pickens suggests that he wait until next year to market the cattle. When Wayne asks how he will pay this year's bills, Pickens tells him to wait like everyone else and pay them next year. But Wayne's code requires him to honor his debts ("I won't go on the take"). Even his wife tells him it is futile: "Give it up Will, you can't move heaven and earth."

Pickens had suggested hiring young boys, but Wayne scoffed at the idea. He needed men, real cowboys who knew how to handle cattle. When Pickens wants to know how old Wayne was when he went on his first drive, Wayne admits he was only 13 years old, but then he quickly adds that times have changed. But Wayne is desperate, so the next morning when the boys show up at Wayne's ranch, he hires them!

Under Wayne's tutelage, the boys learn to tame horses, rope and brand calves, and round up cattle on the open range. As the boys are getting a balking steer out of a wash, Bruce Dern (playing Long Hair) and a couple of his friends ride up looking for a job. They claim to have been in the Idaho gold fields and to have worked for all of the big ranchers in the area. Wayne questions them closely, and Dern finally confesses that they have been in jail, and Wayne refuses to hire them. When Dern asks if the reason he won't hire them is because they have been in jail, Wayne replies, "I don't hold jail against you, but I hate a liar." Wayne's refusal to hire Dern and his friends sets up the plot of the film.

Before Wayne and the boys start out on the trail, Roscoe Lee Browne (playing Jebediah Nightlinger) pulls his chuckwagon into the ranch and becomes the trail herd cook. An African American, Browne is also Wayne's conscience. He insists on being treated with respect and often challenges Wayne's treatment of the boys. One night while they are drinking a bit of

Opposite: John Wayne poses with the young actors who played the cowboys, young men whom Wayne mentored in *The Cowboys* (1972).

whiskey together, Wayne tells Browne that he had two sons, now both dead, who would have been about forty years old now. But, Wayne adds, they went bad on him — or he on them, he didn't know which. Browne then reminds Wayne that the boys on the drive could be another chance; they could become like Wayne's sons.

Wayne seems to take up the challenge of treating the boys as if they were his sons. When one of the lads with a bad stutter can't yell for help when one of his friends nearly drowns in the river driving the cattle across, Wayne tells him to either get over the stutter or go home. For Wayne, curing a stutter was a matter of will, not medical treatment. The view of alcoholism that permeated *Rio Bravo* and *El Dorado* reemerges in *The Cowboys* as a stutter. The boy is so angry he yells at Wayne, "You no-good goddamn son-of-a-bitch!" But he yells it without a stutter, and when Wayne asks him what he said, the boy employs the same phrase again without a stutter. And he does it a third time! Wayne chuckles; walking away, he tells the lad not to get in the habit of calling him that, but the boy's stutter is cured.

On the cattle drive, the boys grow up. They take their first drink — and get sick! While Wayne is away at Fort Smith checking on Indians, the boys stumble across a wagon of prostitutes and learn about women and sex. And when one of the boys is killed, they learn about death. They begin to develop a special bond with Roscoe Lee Browne as his gruffness gives way to warmth and caring for the lads. But, most of all, the boys are learning to work hard (Wayne reminds them he expects a full day's work for a full day's pay) and to take responsibility for the cattle. In short, they are learning to value the things that John Wayne regarded as important. And he allows them to try whiskey — and the inevitable morning hangover!

That John Wayne's lessons were not lost on the boys becomes apparent when Bruce Dern and his gang ride up, intent on rustling the herd. Browne's chuckwagon had broken down back on the trail and he had remained behind to fix it, so he is not around to help; and Wayne had locked up the boys' guns before they began the drive. Dern kills Wayne and rides off with the herd. When Browne finds the boys the following morning, they bury Wayne on the trail and start back to the ranch, or so Browne thinks. But the boys jump him and hold him down while they break into the locked box containing the guns.

When Browne asks what they think they are doing, one of the boys tells him they are going to get the herd back — "We are going to finish the job." They track the rustled cattle, and, with Browne's help, kill Dern and his gang, taking the cattle on to Belle Fouche. Wayne has been successful. He has taught the boys the importance of hard work, of finishing a job, of being men. Maybe Wayne was wrong when he scoffed at Slim Pickens' suggestion that he hire boys, noting that times have changed. Maybe the times had not changed as much as Wayne thought; maybe boys still could learn to work hard and act responsibly if they had a good teacher! That is the important lesson coming from *The Cowboys*.

The Train Robbers includes a mentoring theme as well. John Wayne, Ben Johnson and Rod Taylor are old hands, long-time friends who fought in the Civil War together, and they are joined by young Bobby Vinton on an expedition to help Ann-Margret recover gold from a wrecked train deep in Mexico. Around the campfire at night, Johnson and Taylor reminisce about the scrapes they have been in and how they owe their lives to each other and to Wayne. In short, they teach Vinton about friendship, loyalty and the need to stick with your friends. When the four arrive at the wrecked train and find the gold, they dig in to wait an attack from a large gang following them who also want the gold.

As he stands his post, Vinton tells Wayne that somehow he has changed. Wayne replies that he is just becoming a man. Being a man, Wayne reminds Vinton, means standing your ground instead of running. It requires speaking up when it would be safer to keep one's mouth shut. But, above all, being a man requires one to get up after being knocked down. *The Train Robbers* is not one of John Wayne's better films, but embedded in it are these little scenes in which older men take the time to teach younger men valuable lessons about being a man. And it even extends to Ann-Margret. When she wants to turn back after the gang of riders has attacked them, Wayne won't let her. Later on, when she expresses a sexual interest in him, Wayne deflects her with the observation, "I've got a saddle that is older than you are."

Cahill, United States Marshal, in many respects, continues the dialogue that Wayne had with Roscoe Lee Browne in *The Cowboys*. There Wayne had wondered whether his sons went bad on him or he on them. *Cahill, United States Marshal* suggests that the blame extends to both parties. The film opens as John Wayne brings a band of crooks back to Valentine, Texas, only to learn that the bank has been robbed and his friend the sheriff killed. What Wayne does not realize is that his two sons, played by Gary Grimes and Clay O'Brien, helped George Kennedy and his gang rob

In *Cahill: United States Marshal* (1973), John Wayne must face the consequences of permitting his sons to grow up without him around to help them learn right from wrong.

the bank. The boys had been promised that no one would get hurt, and they become frightened when the sheriff is murdered.

Wayne's Cahill is much like the fathers of the baby boomers who went to see the film; he wasn't around a lot while the children were growing up. In fact, Wayne's Cahill could best be described as an absentee father. He barely knew his sons, and they resented the fact that he was seldom there for them. To the boys, that was an indication that he really didn't love them. The oldest — Gary Grimes — had begun to run with a wild crowd, and was arrested for public drunkenness, leading to his participation in the bank robbery.

Wayne says to the boys, "Things seem to happen to you two when I am not around." Grimes reminds him that he is never around. Wayne acknowledges there is truth in that: "I've been gone a lot of time when you kids really needed me." And he concludes, "There is no excuse for negligence."

Wayne understands his failure as a parent, but he can't bring himself to fully acknowledge it. His response is a comment that many baby boomers heard from their fathers: it is not just a job, but part of my life. Wayne's Cahill, just like many fathers of the baby boomers, was devoted to his career. Career, not family, was the source of meaning in life for him, and his children suffered as a result. If the boys went bad, part of the blame lies with a father who went bad on them.

In a bit of irony, Wayne makes Grimes a deputy, but Grimes' resentment and the generational difference makes it hard for father and son to communicate. Furthermore, the boys' behavior convinces Wayne that they know more about the robbery and murder than they will admit. With the help of Neville Brand, playing the Indian tracker Lightfoot, Wayne tracks down four individuals and arrests them for the robbery and murder. Even though Wayne is convinced that the four are innocent of the crimes, a jury sentences them to hang. Wayne is now desperate to prevent a miscarriage of justice, to keep four men from hanging for a crime they did not commit.

The boys decide to return the money and confess the crimes to their father; but before they can do that, Kennedy forces them to give a share of the money to him. In an exciting climax, Wayne kills Kennedy and rides back into town to prevent the hanging. In the end, the boys acknowledge the wrongness of their actions, and Wayne protects his sons as any father would. The boys, in turn, gain a new respect for the man whom they thought did not love them. On the other hand, Wayne can promise them little. They did participate in a bank robbery and they were accessories to a murder. Wayne promises them he will do all he can to help them, but part of growing up is being held accountable for mistakes. Wayne's Cahill learned an important parental lesson: correct values and proper behavior have to be taught by parents who are present to help their children through the difficult years of growing up. Absentee fathers can neither teach nor model, and often they must live with the consequences of their failures as a parent.

John Wayne as mentor reaches a climax in *The Shootist* when he takes young Ron Howard under his wing. Wayne, as John Bernard Books, rides into Carson City in 1901, a man out of place in a city with telephones, indoor plumbing, paved streets and automobiles. Wayne has come to see James Stewart (playing Dr. Hostetler) for a second opinion. Stewart gives him the same diagnosis; Wayne has a cancer and only a short time to live.

Wayne takes a room at Lauren Bacall's boarding house and prepares to die with dignity.

Initially, Wayne is very authoritarian. He calls Howard "boy" and tells him to take his horse to the stable. Howard explodes. He responds that his name is not "boy," it is Gillom, and that he is not a servant. Wayne replies, "Fair enough," and the two begin to get along better. Howard is ecstatic when he discovers Wayne's identity. J.B. Books, the famous gunfighter, is living in his house! Howard focuses his attention on Wayne in what can only be described as hero worship.

Wayne responds to Howard's affection in his own way. He tells Howard the code by which he (Wayne) lives:

> I won't be wronged.
> I won't be insulted.
> I won't be laid a hand on.
> I don't do these things to other people and require the same from them.

When Howard asks Wayne to show him how to shoot, Wayne obliges the boy. Wayne is surprised at how well Howard can shoot. The boy tells him that his friend Bill McKinney (playing Cobb) taught him to shoot. McKinney struts around like a tough guy, but Wayne understands that he is really nothing but a punk, so Wayne reminds Howard that "There is more to being a man than handling a gun."

Stewart had told Wayne that if he possessed the courage that Wayne did, he would never let the cancer kill him. Near the end, Stewart advises, the pain will become intense, nearly unbearable. With the laudanum that he drinks to ease the pain having less and less affect, Wayne decides to take Stewart's advice. He has Bacall dry clean his best suit. He visits the barbershop and he arranges to have his remains cared for by the local undertaker. He sends word to his final three adversaries — Richard Boone (as Sweeney), Hugh O'Brian (Pulford) and McKinney — to meet him in the local drinking and gambling emporium.

In the subsequent shootout, Wayne kills all three men, but the bartender shoots him in the back, mortally wounding Wayne. Howard had run into the emporium in time to see Wayne shot. He picks up a revolver and kills the bartender. But Howard is appalled at his act. He has used a gun, he has killed, but rather than feeling like a man, Howard is scared and sick. He throws the gun away. Wayne nods his approval as Howard tosses the gun aside. With that nod of approval, Wayne continued to mentor Howard. As the final act of his life, he taught a young man that there was more to being a man than handling a gun.

Even in the calmest of times, surely one of the realities of aging is that one must come to grips with change. Ever-advancing technology requires older persons to master new gadgets, something not always easy for the elderly. Old landmarks disappear as familiar urban and country settings change. Evolving social and sexual behavior make common practices deemed inappropriate in one's youth. The heroes of one's childhood are dissected by later generations, and their flaws held up to public scrutiny. Issues and personalities that shaped the politics of one's earlier years give way to newer, more nuanced problems.

Born in Midwestern Iowa in May 1907, John Wayne lived through a great deal of change in his seventy-two years before breathing his last in a June 1979 California substantially different from the world he had known most of his life. He had been critical of much of the change, but he never appeared bitter. In his later films, Wayne offered two different models for dealing with change — and, ultimately, death. John Bernard Books in *The Shootist* offers one approach, while Rooster Cogburn in *True Grit* and *Rooster Cogburn* suggests an entirely different tack.

As noted previously, the Carson City into which Books rides is an emerging modern city. Automobiles, electric lights and indoor plumbing present a world far different from the world the famed gunfighter had known. As Wayne prepares to celebrate his birthday, the day he has decided that he will die in a gunfight rather than let the cancer slowly kill him, he asks Lauren Bacall to brush clean his suit. She suggests that she have it dry cleaned instead. Dry cleaning, she explains, is a new procedure for cleaning clothes. Wayne agrees to try it, and he dies in a suit cleaned by the latest technological innovation.

Wayne bought a paper the day he rode into Carson City to see James Stewart. The paper was filled with articles about the death of Queen Victoria. Wayne's comment about the queen's death might very well have been a comment about his own. He remarks, "Maybe she outlived her time, but she never lost her dignity." Throughout the film, Wayne's John Bernard Books is a man who has outlived his time and who is painfully aware of his impending death, but he is also a man who never loses his dignity.

Wayne continues to live by his code throughout the film. When Bacall invites him to attend church with her, he declines: "My church has been the mountains and the solitude. My soul is what I have made of it." No late-in-life religious conversion for Wayne; he will face death with the same belief system by which he lived life.

He does not want to die, but Wayne is determined to live by his own code and to die with dignity. And he is offered any number of opportunities to forsake his dignity, because throughout the film Wayne is surrounded by any number of near-buffoons. Henry Morgan's Marshal Thibido is far removed from the brave frontier sheriff, and he constantly cackles with delight at the thought that Wayne is going to die. Sheree North, as the old girlfriend, wants to marry him so that as his widow she can make money exploiting his life in dime novels. Even the undertaker, John Carradine, will make a profit off of his corpse! Yet, confronted by all of this silliness and exploitation, Wayne does not lose his dignity.

There is something noble about Wayne's John Bernard Books. One can surmise that if Books had not been stricken with cancer he would have adjusted to the times; he would not have become a disillusioned old man. Roberts and Olson write, "He found it easier to express some of [his] emotions on film than in real life" (Roberts and Olson, 596). Wayne, as he neared the end of his real life, was much more like John Bernard Books than Rooster Cogburn. Witness the self-depreciating humor and the fun he had with Harvard University students when he appeared at the invitation of the *Harvard Lampoon* (Roberts and Olson, 616–617). Wayne angered conservatives — including Ronald Reagan — when he became friends with President Jimmy Carter and supported the Panama Canal Treaty.

Rooster Cogburn, on the other hand, may be a man with "true grit," but he is also a man whom the world has passed by. Wayne's Cogburn drinks excessively, complains loudly about everything, and is self-obsessed. In *True Grit*, Wayne is berated by a lawyer who makes him acknowledge the number of men he has killed. By implication, he contends that Wayne's idea of enforcing the law is outdated. Wayne is an anachronism; the West he knew has vanished.

That evening, in Chen Lee's back room while eating with Kim Darby (playing Mattie Ross), Wayne spies a rat. Drawing his revolver, he shoots the rat dead. Wayne then goes off on a drunken soliloquy comparing outlaws to rats and how easy it used to be to kill rats. Judge Parker, he claims, had a good court until the lawyers came and insisted that the rats had a right to due process of law.

On the ride into the Indian Territory with Kim Darby and Glenn Campbell (as La Boeuf) to track down Robert Duvall (Ned Pepper) and Jeff Corey (Tom Chaney), Wayne continually rejects Texas Ranger Campbell's advice. At one point, Wayne reminisces about charging into a band of outlaws, reins in his mouth and blazing away with a gun in each hand. While he repeats that scene when he charges Duvall and his outlaws,

John Wayne as Rooster Cogburn, a man whom the modern world has passed by.

Rooster Cogburn is a man who lives in the past; he is a man who won't admit his own aging or acknowledge the changing times.

Wayne's portrayal of the Cogburn character continued (to an even more exaggerated degree) in *Rooster Cogburn*. At the beginning of the film,

Wayne returns the bodies of four dead outlaws draped over their horses. As he rides into town, people shake their heads in disapproval at his wanton use of violence.

John McIntire (playing Judge Parker) takes him to task and makes Wayne give up his badge. "The West is changing and you haven't changed with it," McIntire tells Wayne. And, he continues, "You have let yourself go. You have gone to seed." Wayne leaves the courthouse, muttering, "Ain't no justice in the West no more." But when outlaws kill Katherine Hepburn's missionary father and a number of Indians, Parker sends for Cogburn. He knows the Indian Territory and is the best man to track down the killers. Wayne can only smirk, "See who they come to if they have a real job to do."

Wayne sets out with Hepburn and Richard Romancito (as Wolf) in tow. Romancito's parents had been killed by the outlaws, and he insists on joining the hunt. Besides, he aspires to be a lawman. When Wayne discovers the boy's courage and determination, he tells him, "I'll help you up the trail and be proud to."

Hepburn and Wayne engage in numerous delightfully witty exchanges throughout the film. After Wayne has come up on the short end of one such exchange, he exclaims, "If they [women] ever get the vote, God help us!" And the run down river on the raft, by itself, makes *Rooster Cogburn* worth watching.

In the final frames, Wayne and Hepburn make peace with one another, for as Wayne tells her, "I am what I am." And as quoted earlier in the chapter, Hepburn tells Wayne, "You're a credit to the whole male sex, and I am proud to have you for my friend." Even though Wayne's Cogburn gets his badge back, the reality is that the world has passed Rooster Cogburn by. His methods are outmoded in the new West, the civilized West of due process of law. It's not a place in which Wayne's Rooster Cogburn feels at home. In that, he is vastly different from John Bernard Books in *The Shootist*.

There may be more than a little bit of irony in the fact that John Wayne's leading ladies in his last two films were Katharine Hepburn and Lauren Bacall. Both women had been closely identified with the politically liberal Hollywood community that John Wayne despised. Yet, on *Rooster Cogburn*, Hepburn and Wayne discovered they enjoyed working with one another. Hepburn admired his talent, and Wayne appreciated her determination and her willingness to ride horses and the raft, things she really didn't enjoy doing (Roberts and Olson, 619).

Wayne had worked with Bacall once before, in *Blood Alley* (Warner Brothers, 1955). According to Ronald Davis, the two actors got along very well. Davis notes, "Duke admired Bacall's backbone, her confidence in her beliefs, her humor, and her ability to express her convictions" (Davis 1998, 202). While filming *The Shootist*, Bacall knew that Wayne felt bad, but she said, "He never complained" (Davis 1998, 316). One day while they were waiting for the set to be lit, Wayne even took Bacall's hand and held it (Davis 1998, 316).

Clearly there was a great deal of professional respect between Wayne and the two women, but there may be more to it than that. By 1975 and 1976, when *Rooster Cogburn* and *The Shootist* were made and released, the world had changed for everybody. Vietnam, civil rights and rising crime rates destroyed the old New Deal coalition on which American liberalism had been based since the 1930s. New left radicals rejected Hubert Humphrey in the 1968 Presidential elections. Humphrey was the essence of New Deal liberalism and the Cold War warrior outlook of the Truman era. The new liberals who had rejected Humphrey were instrumental in the disastrous nomination of George McGovern in 1972. The liberalism of Katharine Hepburn and Spencer Tracy, and of Humphrey Bogart and Lauren Bacall, was mostly dead. American liberalism and the Democratic Party were in a time of crisis, searching for an identity. John Wayne, too, was renounced by many conservatives for his support of the Panama Canal Treaty. And Richard Nixon had betrayed them all when he permitted himself to become entangled in Watergate. So, as he made his last two films, John Wayne shared much of the same antipathy about America of the middle 1970s as did Katharine Hepburn and Lauren Bacall. By the time they appeared together in *Rooster Cogburn* and *The Shootist*, Wayne, Hepburn and Bacall may have had more in common than even they realized.

In June 1979 John Wayne died at the UCLA Medical Center. Praise was heaped upon him at his passing, and he remains popular with older adults twenty-five or more years after his death. While Congress awarded him a medal, John Wayne's films are his best legacies. In particular, the Westerns he made after 1965 offer an interpretation of the genre vastly different from those of Clint Eastwood and Sam Peckinpah. Younger viewers who want to understand what Westerns had been like but don't care for black and white movies can watch *The Sons of Katie Elder*, *Chisum* or any number of other John Wayne Westerns. In the final analysis, that may be John Wayne's lasting gift to America!

PART II

Changing Images

Chapter 7

"NOBODY GETS TO BE A COWBOY FOREVER"

With the release of John Wayne's *The Shootist* (Paramount, 1976), Wayne's long and illustrious film career came to an end. In many ways, Wayne's passing appeared to signal the eclipse of the Western as well. However, the genre did not disappear completely. A number of Westerns were produced and distributed from 1977 to 1990; some of them were good films. *Comes a Horseman* (United Artists, 1978), *Goin' South* (Paramount, 1978), *The Mountain Men* (Columbia, 1980), *Barbarosa* (Universal, 1982) and *The Grey Fox* (United Artists, 1983) were all worth the cost of ever escalating ticket prices. Nineteen-eighty-five was even heralded as the year that Hollywood rediscovered the Western. Clint Eastwood's *Pale Rider* (Warner Brothers, 1985) and Lawrence Kasdan's *Silverado* (Columbia, 1985) were both released with a great deal of box-office fanfare, but neither turned out to be films that rejuvenated the genre. Hence, by 1990, one could ask, "Is the Western dead?" While the answer was "probably not," one thing was obvious. Compared to its earlier twentieth-century glory years, by 1990 the previously robust Western had transformed into a 95-pound weakling. And by 1990 one had to confront the possibility of its demise entirely. But just as with Mark Twain's death, the passing of the Western had been greatly exaggerated. In fact, the last decade of the twentieth century saw a remarkable resurgence in the production of Westerns. The following films, while not an exhaustive list, document the increase in Western production during the 1990s.

1990   *Dances with Wolves* (Columbia Tri-Star)

1991   *Young Guns II* (20th Century–Fox)

1992   *Unforgiven* (Warner Brothers)

1993   *The Ballad of Little Jo* (Fine Line Features)
         Geronimo: An American Legend (Columbia)
         Posse (Gramercy Pictures)
         Tombstone (Buena Vista Pictures)

1994   *Bad Girls* (20th Century–Fox)
         Maverick (Warner Brothers)
         Wyatt Earp (Warner Brothers)

1995   *Dead Man* (Miramax Films)
         The Quick and the Dead (Columbia Tri-Star)

1998   *The Mask of Zorro* (Columbia Tri-Star)

1999   *Ride with the Devil* (Universal)
         The Wild Wild West (Warner Brothers)

But older viewers of pre–1955 Westerns, though pleased that Hollywood had rediscovered the genre, were bound to be disappointed. The 1990s Westerns continued to reflect the images and themes that had been emerging since 1955. They mirrored the United States at the turn of the century, not mid-century, and they were produced with a younger audience in mind, not older viewers. The chapters that follow examine the changing images of cowboys, outlaws, frontier marshals, Indians and women that emerged in Westerns of the last quarter of the twentieth century, and that dominated 1990s Westerns. One of the most striking of those changes is the shifting nature of the western film landscape after the early 1970s.

Whether or not they knew where the California locations were, viewers of pre–1955 Westerns were as familiar with the western town streets on the Universal, Warner Brothers, Columbia and Republic studio lots as their own neighborhoods. Iverson Ranch, Corriganville and the Monogram town set at Newhall appeared in countless Westerns, and the rocks, ridges and roads at these places were familiar sights to a generation that grew up on Westerns.

Those locations communicated order and civilization. The towns (with some exceptions) were places in which the houses, businesses and sidewalks were well-maintained. The dirt streets were usually just right —

no mud and very little dust. In short, the frontier towns of pre–1955 Westerns were the idyllic small towns of Main Street America transferred to the American West.

The Andy Jauregui ranch location offered attractive barns and corrals, and a ranch house surrounded by large trees, typical of Midwestern farms. The mountains of Southern California and the tree-lined roads of Corriganville, Walker Ranch and Iverson Ranch were appropriate places for the action to unfold in this Edenic West of the pre–1955 American imagination. Southern California filming locations became *the* American West, and the various town sets shaped popular understanding of frontier settlements. The handful of ramshackle buildings and the mud street situated on a treeless prairie in *Shane* (Paramount, 1953) are notable exceptions in pre–1955 Westerns.

Slowly the image of the frontier began to change. Towns became primitive places of unpainted buildings and muddy streets. Small, with nothing more than a handful of structures, the towns communicated not a new Eden, but the harshness and struggle for survival, as well as the impermanence that characterized the real West. Often the small settlements lacked social amenities, such as a hotel, and one had to travel miles to find the nearest sheriff or doctor. Towns in *Fire Creek* (Warner Brothers, 1968), *Will Penny* (Paramount, 1968), *High Plains Drifter* (Universal, 1973), *The Train Robbers* (Warner Brothers, 1973), and *Unforgiven* (Warner Brothers, 1992) are small, unkempt places that suggest a raw frontier far from eastern amenities—a place where life is hard.

Ranches changed as well. Far from tree-lined oases, the products of solid middle-class folks building a new civilization, the ranch became a group of undistinguished buildings situated on a treeless prairie. The ranches in *Monte Walsh* (National General, 1970) and *The Cowboys* (Warner Brothers, 1972) are a far cry from the ones familiar to fans of pre–1955 B Westerns.

Westerns of the last two or three decades of the twentieth century offered viewers a different visual West, a bleaker, harsher, starker West. This new West, with its dust and dirt, and its ordinary people trying to survive drought, blizzards and the land itself, was a less optimistic place than the West of the pre–1955 Westerns, and no film better captures that difference than does *Dead Man*.

Dead Man opens as Johnny Depp, playing accountant William Blake from Cleveland, journeys to Machine (somewhere in the West) to begin working as a bookkeeper in the Dickerson Metal Works. The very name of the town, Machine, suggests a corruption of the Edenic West by eastern industrialism, and that image is reinforced by the fact that Depp goes West not to fulfill an ambition to become a cowboy, but to be an accountant.

Viewers are introduced to Machine as Depp, in his eastern duds, detrains and walks through the town to the mill. Machine is a place of unpainted buildings and mud streets. Some animals root in the filth, while others wander untended along the street, bumping into passers by. As Depp walks toward the mill, townsfolk stare at him with a vacant, far-off look that suggests dullness and stupor rather than wonderment at a young man in his eastern clothes, obviously out of place in Machine. Machine is also a place of moral degeneracy, for as Depp passes by an alley, viewers see a woman on her knees in front of a man performing a sex act. Machine is a mill town, and the mill has corrupted all who work and live in the town. Machine represents industrialism at its worst; it has changed the western landscape.

Once at the mill, Depp discovers that he has no job, even though he has an employment letter. Viewers are reminded of a conversation on the train in which Depp showed his employment letter to a person and was warned not to trust words on a paper. In this new West, the West of Machine, commitments have been corrupted by industrialism. In the West of the imagination, a man's word was his bond; one honored one's commitments. But Machine has been corrupted by industrialism; new sets of values dominate the new West.

Despondent, Depp wanders into a saloon and purchases a bottle and winds up sleeping with a prostitute (or maybe a former prostitute). But her former lover, a man who has been away for two years, comes to her room; when he finds them together, he shoots the woman and wounds Depp. Depp escapes Machine on a stolen horse.

Depp is discovered by Gary Farmer, playing an Indian named Nobody. While Depp's wound will ultimately prove fatal, it is Farmer who gives the film the structure that is relevant here. Farmer had been kidnapped by British soldiers and sent to England to boarding school. There he discovered the poet William Blake. Farmer tells Depp that when he read the words of William Blake they jumped off the page at him, and they gave Farmer the courage to escape the boarding school and return across the ocean (how remains uncertain) to the United States. Farmer innocently believes that the accountant William Blake from Cleveland (Depp's character) is the English William Blake whom Farmer had read in boarding school.

The poet William Blake was an unmitigated opponent of the industrial revolution. Gregg Rickman writes that Blake was, "In his day a foe of both the ancient regimes of Europe and of the oncoming Industrial Revolution, which he saw as based in the deplorable rationalism of the Enlightenment and thus destined to destroy the balance between humanity and nature" (Rickman, 382).

In several of his poems, Blake suggests the destructive qualities of industrialism for both the environment and the human spirit. In *Milton*, Blake writes of "satan's mills" (Keynes, 483). And in his "Songs of Innocence and Experience," Blake asks:

> Is this a holy thing to see
> in a rich and fruitful land
> babes reduc'd to misery
> fed with cold and usurous hand?
>
> Is that trembling cry a song?
> Can it be a song of joy?
> And so many children poor
> it is a land of poverty!
>
> And their sun does never shine,
> and their fields are bleak & bare,
> and their ways are fill'd with thorns;
> it is eternal winter there [Keynes, 211–212].

The line "And their sun does never shine" reminds one of the misery of early industrialism, with its 12–16 hour work days. For most of the year, workers trudged to their jobs in the dark, and the sun had set before they went home. For them the sun never shone!

By confusing Depp's William Blake with the William Blake he had read as a youngster, Farmer's Nobody frames one way to view *Dead Man*. Progressives such as Theodore Roosevelt, and populists like William Jennings Bryan, feared the destructive qualities of industrialism, and they saw in the West the spirit of individual achievement on which the country had been founded. But if eastern industrial values were able to penetrate and ultimately dominate the West, that spirit would dissolve, as it has in the East. *Dead Man* is about the fall of that Edenic West, brought about by Robert Mitchum's (in his last screen role) Dickinson Metal Works!

With the fall of the Edenic West comes environmental degradation. It was hydraulic mining in *Pale Rider*, and it was the senseless destruction of the buffalo and wolf in *Dances with Wolves*. Surely no film has more graphically depicted that wanton destruction than *Dances with Wolves*. The skinned carcasses of buffalo taken for their hides and tongues, then left to rot on the prairie, and the needless killing of the wolf that Kevin Costner had partially tamed are lasting memories from *Dances with Wolves. Dead Man*, too, depicts the destructiveness of white behavior on the pristine West. As Depp journeys west, the dress and visage of his fellow travelers change as the train moves ever closer to Machine. At one point, the car is full of buffalo hunters, and they jump to the windows and begin randomly shooting at a passing herd of buffalo. They could not even get the furs or meat; they simply killed for the sheer joy of killing!

By 1995's *Dead Man*, the western landscape had changed. Frontier towns were small, isolated places, and some of them, such as Machine, verified the evils of primitive industrialism. Ranches were lonely places, places in which life was a struggle. One unknown cowboy claimed that, "The cow business is a damn fine business for men and mules, but it's hell on horses and women" (Marriott, xiii). Ever increasingly, Westerns after 1955 conveyed that sense. And, ever increasingly, the West of the movies acknowledged the wanton destruction of animal wildlife and the ravaging of the landscape in search of minerals.

But what about the cowboy? No other figure is as closely identified with the West and Westerns as the cowboy. How did popular understanding of cowboys change as the western landscape was reexamined? How was that understanding affected by the civil rights, the women's and the war protest movements that challenged traditional notions of the country as a land of equal opportunity and justice for all?

The cowboy is not a North American creation. As Holly George-Warren notes, the cowboy was adapted from the Mexican vaquero (George-Warren, 10). Furthermore, the dress, language and accoutrements (saddle, lariat, etc.) all reflect the south-of-the-border origin of the North American cowboy. But it is in the United States that the cowboy became a public icon.

The North American cowboy was born in the years immediately following the American Civil War. As the eastern demand for beef increased, cowboys rounded up great herds of free ranging wild Texas longhorns and started them for Missouri and Kansas railheads. The cowboy, then, is a product of the roundup and trail drives. But his existence was not limited to that short-lived period of American history. As ranches sprang up throughout the Southwest, Montana, Idaho, Wyoming and other parts of the Trans-Mississippi West, the men who worked those spreads and developed better breeds of short-horned cattle were called cowboys.

But the word "cowboy" quickly became a more generic expression, used to describe any group of unruly troublemakers. According to Casey Tefertiller, the citizens of Tombstone, Arizona, began to broaden the term cowboy to include others than those who worked cattle. Tefertiller writes that people in Tombstone referred "to all backcountry troublemakers as cowboys, distinct from the ranchmen who raised cattle" (Tefertiller`, 40). Surely, by the turn of the twentieth century the word "cowboy" had taken on this broader, more generic meaning.

During the last fifteen years of the nineteenth century, western ranching changed dramatically. The cattle business was consolidated and concentrated in the hands of a relatively few cattle barons and eastern syndicates. The open range was fenced and the need for roundups diminished. The harsh winter of 1886–87, with its blizzards that killed millions of cattle, was the crowning blow (George-Warren, 25). The winter forced untold numbers of ranchers to sell out and move on. Certainly, by 1890 when the Census Bureau declared the frontier closed, the cowboy as an occupation was a mere shadow of its former self.

But it is not the cowboy of history that left his mark on the American imagination; it is the mythic cowboy of popular culture. At the time that real cowboy life was fading, the cowboy as a popular culture hero emerged full bloom. It began with the post–Civil War dime novels and was nourished by the artwork of Frederick Remington and Charlie Russell. The wild west shows (Buffalo Bill's Wild West Show and Congress of Rough Riders of the World, and the Miller 101 Ranch are the two best known) transformed the hard, dusty work of real cowboys into an exciting life that young boys yearned to experience. The cowboy had become America's new hero!

Owen Wister's novel *The Virginian* continued the transformation. Wister's cowboys represented the ideal of American manhood and rugged individualism. Zane Grey and dozens of other Western novelists continued to foster that image, and newsstands featured row after row of Western novels and pulp magazines. Then, of course, motion pictures capitalized on the cowboy image and churned out thousands of Westerns during the course of the twentieth century.

And, the cowboy image is very much alive in the first decade of the twenty-first century. Though expressed in different ways, the cowboy remains a prominent figure. Rodeos have never been more popular. Since the sport is television-friendly, it has attracted millions of viewers around the country. Western dress and western clothing stores dot eastern metropolitan areas; cowboy clothing has become a national phenomenon rather than a regional one. And, of course, the cowboy image is still used in advertising for all sorts of products.

The cowboy also has become a surrogate for grappling with social change and political conflict. For example, in order to voice their disapproval of Hollywood cowardice in the face of the blacklists and charges of communist infiltration of the motion picture business, Carl Foreman wrote a screenplay set in the Old West, and Fred Zinneman directed it; the film was titled *High Noon* (United Artists, 1952). While *High Noon* yet represents the best example of using a Western to address contemporary issues, four films from the late 1950s to the early 1970s reexamined the image of the cowboy in the unsettling climate in the United States as it was buffeted by controversy over the Civil Rights movement and the war in Vietnam. Those films are *Cowboy* (Columbia, 1958), *Will Penny* (Paramount, 1968), *Monte Walsh* (National General, 1970) and *The Hired Hand* (Universal, 1971).

Prior to 1955, Westerns rarely depicted cowboys working. According to most Westerns, roundups took only a few days, calves were branded effortlessly (with very little sweat), and the West was remarkably free of dust and dirt. Nights were balmy and it almost never rained or snowed. While the cowboys often complained about the food, there was enough of it to satisfy even the most ravenous appetite. Singing cowboys, with their colorful shirts, ornate saddles and bridles, glamorized the West even more as they trailed a herd of cattle crooning a song! The West of pre–1955 films seemed to be a place where cowboy life resembled a continuous Boy Scout jamboree.

Jack Lemmon (as Frank Harris) in *Cowboy* believes in that myth. Stuck behind a Chicago counter as a hotel clerk, Lemmon longs for the excitement of the open range. When Glenn Ford (playing Tom Reece) brings his wild pack of cowboys to the hotel to celebrate after they sell their herd, Lemmon is spellbound by their behavior. Because he yearns to be a cowboy, Lemmon decides to join them. He uses his savings to buy a share of Ford's next herd and joins the group as they ride to Mexico to buy cattle to sell on the Chicago market.

Rather than the wise old trail boss who takes the young tenderfoot under his wing, Ford is short-tempered and impatient with Lemmon. Ford does not want him along on the drive, and he is not very tolerant of Lemmon's inexperience. The cowboys give tenderfoot Lemmon a green horse, and when the horse throws him, Ford tells Lemmon, "If you can't ride that horse, you are going to have to carry him." Lemmon experiences his first lesson that cowboy life is not all glamour.

In fact, on the trail Lemmon discovers that a cowboy's life is a lot of hard work. While it is cold and rainy at times, dust is an ever-present reality. Balky steers need to be herded. Life on the trail, working with real cowboys, is nothing like Lemmon imagined it would be. At one point he remarks, "I never thought life on the trail would be like this." And after one particularly hard day of work, Lemmon desperately asks, "Don't you ever get a day off?'

Will Penny depicts the harsh, lonely life of the cowboy even more than *Cowboy*. It is cold in the morning as the cowboys roll out of their bedrolls. It is dusty riding drag, but as Charlton Heston (as Will Penny) notes, "Riding drag is better than pushing a plow." For cowboys, life holds few options, and riding drag is better than most of them! Heston does real work — slopping hogs, tending difficult cattle and darning his socks.

Monte Walsh and *The Hired Hand* continue that image. *Monte Walsh* in particular emphasizes the hard work and uncertainty of cowboy life. Lee Marvin (playing Monte Walsh) and Jack Palance (as Chet Rollins) get only one month's pay for a winter's worth of work. The film stresses the hard, dusty job of rounding up cattle and horses, particularly when they don't want to be herded. And not all horses can be broken! One of the stars of *Monte Walsh* is a white horse that Mitch Ryan (Shorty Austin), the horse wrangler, can't break.

The Hired Hand suggests that there is little difference between ranching and farming. When Peter Fonda (as Harry Collings) decides to return to the wife he left several years before, she takes him and Warren Oates (Arch Harris) on as hired hands. The place itself looks more like a farm that a ranch, and Fonda and Oates work more like farmers than cowboys! They repair a windmill, grease a wagon wheel, and clear away and burn brush. One scene shows the two men trudging back to the house as the sun sets, carrying an axe and scythe. Clearly, it has been a long hard day of back-breaking work. Verna Bloom (as Hannah Collings) and her young daughter Megan Denver (Janey Collings) engage in the typical hard and hot work of women doing the baking and laundry by hand.

If these four Westerns countered the notion of cowboy life as one of leisure, even more did they question the cowboy code. The code required cowboys to be loyal to their friends, to be respectful toward and protective of women, to fight fair, and to be loyal to the brand for which they rode. In *Cowboy*, Lemmon learns to his disbelief and dismay that cowboy behavior does not follow the code. One evening the cowboys find a rattlesnake and begin playfully tossing it among themselves, but the snake bites one of the cowboys and the man dies. Lemmon cannot believe Ford's restrained response; the culprit who began the prank goes unpunished.

When Lemmon protests, Ford merely remarks that you don't correct a mistake already made by committing another one. And when the cowboys won't ride back into a town to help rescue a fellow cowboy who Lemmon believes is about to be set upon by a group of saloon toughs, he calls them "the most miserable group of men I have ever seen." Ford's notion that a man ought to take care of his own problems anticipates John Wayne's posture toward James Stewart in *The Man Who Shot Liberty Valance*, but it does not square with the popular notion that the cowboy code required helping out one's friends.

In *Will Penny*, Charlton Heston finally turns on the younger cowboy who had been jawing him. When Heston strikes him repeatedly with his hat, the younger man falls to the ground, protesting, "You ain't fightin' proper." But Heston reminds the man that he is the one who is down. Fighting, it would seem, is not a manner of honor and manly conduct — it is a means of protecting oneself, and anything is fair in a fight. Lemmon discovers the same harsh truth in *Cowboy*. After he accuses the group of being the most miserable lot he has ever seen, Lemmon and Ford start to brawl. Ford grabs Lemmon and holds his back over the campfire until Lemmon gives up. Lemmon, too, protests that Ford does not fight like a proper cowboy. Ford responds, like Heston, that fighting is not a game; there are no rules.

Peter Fonda in *The Hired Hand* violates the cowboy code when he shirks his family responsibilities. The film opens as Fonda (playing Harry Collings), Warren Oates (Arch Harris) and Robert Pratt (Dan Griffin) camp by a river. When their fishing line snags the body of a dead little girl floating in the river, Pratt is confused when Fonda cuts the line rather than bury the body or try to find out who she had been. As they sit by the campfire, the men talk of going to California and the coast. Later, when they sit around the table in a saloon in a small, dirty, nondescript town (really just a group of adobe brick building), viewers learn that Fonda is married and has a child.

He had left his wife and daughter several years back and had been drifting from place to place, first with just Warren Oates and then with Pratt. Fonda announces that he is not going to the coast, he is going home. What is striking, however, is Fonda's irresponsible behavior. Contrary to the cowboy code, which required one to be respectful toward and protective of women, Fonda left his wife and daughter to wander the countryside with his friends. He did not even know if they still lived on the ranch. He had forsaken his responsibilities as both a husband and a father — behavior far from what one would expect from a cowboy.

Pratt is killed by a man who accuses him of raping his wife, and then the man steals Pratt's horse. Before they return to Fonda's ranch, Fonda and Oates get the horse back. Fonda shoots the man in the feet while Oates rescues the horse; then they start for Fonda's ranch. His wife (Verna Bloom as Hannah Collins) still lives on the ranch with their daughter, but she won't take him back as a husband, only as a hired hand. So both men begin working on the ranch as hired help. Gradually, however, Fonda and Bloom renew their marital relationship.

But then the man they shot in the feet kidnaps Oates and sends word that he will cut off one of Oates' fingers each day until Fonda comes to rescue his friend. The code that Fonda had betrayed in his relationship with Bloom requires Fonda to attempt to aid his friend. And, though he frees Oates, Fonda is killed in the process. The film ends with Oates riding back to the ranch with Fonda's horse.

The Hired Hand sends all sorts of mixed signals. Fonda acted irresponsibly toward his wife and daughter, and even toward the dead little girl in the river. He reminds viewers of an immature man, one who is unable to fulfill his obligations as a citizen, husband or father. Fonda seems to live for the moment, satisfying a whim to see some part of the country that he has never seen before. Yet, the little girl in the river pricks his conscience and he returns to his wife and daughter. For the most part, however, his behavior is the opposite of what one expects from a cowboy. On the other hand, Fonda understands his obligation to try to rescue his friend. Only as a reaffirmation of male bonding does Fonda honor the cowboy code in *The Hired Hand*.

Marriage has always been problematic in Westerns. The cowboy-hero on occasion rode off into the sunset with the pretty girl, with marriage looming on the horizon. The ranch owner might be married (although more often than not he was a widower), and his son might be wooing an intended bride, but the rest of the cowboys lived, unmarried, in the bunkhouse. In Westerns, marriage was not the cowboy way. However, it was not until *Will Penny* and *Monte Walsh* that the topic was explored in depth.

When Charlton Heston's Will Penny is hired by Ben Johnson as a line rider who will spend the winter encamped far from the ranch house, he is admonished not to permit squatters to settle on any of the ranch land. However, once at his line cabin, Heston discovers that Joan Hackett and her son have taken up residence there. Before heading out to ride line, Heston tells Hackett that she will have to be gone by the time he returns.

Charlton Heston is the lonely cowboy *Will Penny* (1968), who can't marry Joan Hackett and become a farmer.

While riding line, Heston is ambushed by Donald Pleasence (playing Preacher Quint) and his sons. Left to die, Heston makes it back to the cabin where he is nursed back to health by Hackett. Even though she has a husband who is yet likely alive in California, the two fall in love. And Hackett's son treats Heston like a father. But Heston rejects the idea of marriage.

It is not clear whether Heston believes he can't or he simply won't settle down. He tells Hackett that he does not have the years to start and improve a homestead. Heston tells her that he "don't know nothin' about farming, always been a cowhand. I lived one way all my life." Heston cannot change. In his words to Hackett, "I came close with you, but it's too late for me."

There is tragedy in *Will Penny*, irrespective of how one reads it. When Heston rides away from the line cabin with his friends, does he go because he is too old to learn a new trade (farming) and start a family? Or is he going because he refuses to change? Cowboying is all he has ever known, and in a moment of decision, he chooses the familiar rather than the unknown (love). It is at the end of the film that viewers catch the sadness of Don Cherry's theme song "The Lonely Rider." Cowboys, particularly older cowboys, the film suggests, are not the carefree range riders of myth; they are really very lonely people!

Monte Walsh makes that point even more poignantly than does *Will Penny*. Jeanne Moreau (as Martine Bernard) is the love of Lee Marvin's life. She is a prostitute, but Marvin loves her nevertheless. He even calls her a Countess. One day Moreau informs Marvin that she is going to Charleyville, forty miles away. Nobody is left in their little settlement, and she reminds Marvin that one has to take what one can get.

After Jack Palance's wedding, Marvin wanders into an empty saloon and then goes to Moreau's deserted house. There is nothing left of the old cowboy way. Feeling alone, he rides to Charleyville to see Moreau. Marvin finds her waiting tables, the only work she could find. After they have sex, he asks her why they never got married. When Moreau tells him, "You never ask me," Marvin only replies, "Cowboys don't get married unless they stop being cowboys."

As they talk, Marvin vows to try something new, but he acknowledges, "I don't know what else I can do." Finally, unable to stop being a cowboy, Marvin assures Moreau that he will save his money and come back and marry her. Moreau tells him that she will wait, but her face informs viewers that she understands that Marvin's good intentions will never come to fruition. Moreau dies before Marvin can see her again, and *Monte Walsh* ends with Marvin as a lonely cowboy whose only companion is his horse. In the words of the theme song, Marvin is searching for a place where he belongs. He hopes the good times will come back, but he and the viewers know they never will. The cowboy life that Marvin had known will never return.

Monte Walsh is an excellent film, maybe one of the ten best Westerns produced after 1955. The acting is strong throughout, the characters are

Lee Marvin as *Monte Walsh* (1970) finds it difficult to adjust to the end of the open range and the close of the cowboy way of life.

realistic, and viewers are captivated by the raw emotions of individuals trying to adjust to changing times that they can't understand. It is the latter element that makes *Monte Walsh* a compelling film for contemporary viewers.

The film opens as Lee Marvin and Jack Palance ride into town in the spring after a long winter riding line. However, the town is full of cowboys looking for work. The harsh winter has killed off the cattle, driving many ranchers out of business. Consolidated Cattle Company, an eastern firm, has bought up all of the ranches, but as Jim Davis, now working as a foreman for Consolidated, notes, they never mention money — they call it capital!

Marvin and Palance go to work for Davis, becoming two of the lucky cowboys who could find work. The film then settles down to a slower pace, depicting cowboys doing actual work and engaging in bunkhouse tomfoolery. One day they haul barbed wire out to an old cowboy who is repairing a fence. He informs them that he has had a good life; he had even ridden up Missionary Ridge with Fighting Joe Hooker during the Civil War. As they leave, Marvin and Palance comment on how the old man speaks as if his life was over; and they conclude it might as well be, since he is reduced to riding fence.

Later they meet Matt Clark (as Rufus Brady) who is just drifting from ranch to ranch looking for work. Clark tells them that he tried working on the railroad for a while, "but it wasn't for me." When the herd turns out to be smaller than expected, Jim Davis informs them that he will have to let two of the cowboys go. He chooses Mitch Ryan (Shorty, the horse wrangler) as one of them. Ryan's response captures the pathos of many caught up in a changing economy: "I wish I knew something besides cowboying."

An important lesson from *Monte Walsh* is that individuals react differently to changing circumstances. Jack Palance marries a hardware store widow, gives up being a cowboy and runs the store. When Marvin confesses that he does not understand how Palance can give up being a cowboy, Palance tells him to look around. Palance reminds Marvin that there are fewer cowhands than there were ten or fifteen years ago. And, he continues, there will be ever fewer in the years ahead. The times are changing and a man has to change with them. In one of the great lines from *Monte Walsh*— or any Western — Jack Palance tells Lee Marvin, "Nobody gets to be a cowboy forever." For Palance, that change required him to settle down with a wife and a steady job.

Clark, on the other hand, robs a bank in Miles City, and Ryan kills a marshal when he comes looking for Clark. Both Clark and Ryan turn to robbing and stealing as their response to the changing economy. Ryan justifies rustling by telling Palance that the cows don't belong to the Slash Y, "but to somebody we don't even know." And when Ryan and another outlaw come to Palance's hardware store asking for a stake, they rob and kill Palance when he won't give them one. In the difficult times of a changing economy, friendship does not count for much!

When Marvin is in Charleyville talking marriage with Moreau, he sees the white horse, the one Shorty could not break, that Davis had sold to a wild west show. Marvin decides to break it, and even though he wrecks the town in the process, he tames the beast. The owner of the wild west show watches Marvin tame the horse and offers him a job. He offers Marvin $30 per week and all expenses. With that kind of money, Marvin could marry Moreau. He will get to travel all over the country and walk on paved streets— no mud for a year. The wild west show owner assures Marvin it will change his whole life. The only catch is that Marvin will have to adopt a stage name, Texas Jack Butler. Marvin refuses. Walking out, he comments, "I ain't spittin' on my whole life."

Lee Marvin remains the unrepentant cowboy. He loses the love of his life when Moreau dies, and his best friend, Palance, is murdered by another friend. The only thing left for Marvin is to kill Ryan. When he does that, his life becomes aimless. And so the film ends with Lee Marvin and his horse trudging alone up some cow path toward an uncertain future.

By the early 1970s, many Americans, like Lee Marvin, were facing an uncertain future. Watergate and the war in Vietnam had unnerved American self-confidence. The steel industry had collapsed. Automotive jobs were shrinking. The electronics industry had been captured by Orientals. Drug sales boomed and crime statistics rose. Old neighborhoods disappeared. Like Lee Marvin, men who had spent their productive years working in steel mills or automobile assembly plants could only utter, "That's all I know, I don't know how to do anything else."

Once again the Western was a vehicle for expressing contemporary concerns. If *Will Penny* and *Monte Walsh* were set in the Old West, a changing West trying to come to grips with the end of the open range and the cowboy way of life, they spoke to a public trying to understand the deindustrialization of the American economy. Like Will Penny and Monte Walsh, a lot of over-fifty-year-old men were trying to figure out where they belonged in the new economy.

Chapter 8

JESSE JAMES AND BILLY THE KID: OUTLAWS OR POPULIST HEROES

Nearly all of the images of the American westerner were developed prior to the Civil War and before scholarly-trained, professional historians in colleges and universities claimed the writing of history as their special province. James Fenimore Cooper's Leatherstocking Tales, and verbal and written legends about Daniel Boone, David Crockett, Kit Carson, and Jim Bridger, created the traits and qualities of the archetype westerner. Between 1865 and World War I, dime novels, newspaper accounts of western badmen, lawmen, the Indian wars, and western boom towns, the wild west shows of Buffalo Bill, Pawnee Bill, and the Miller 101 Ranch, the popular histories of Francis Parkman and Theodore Roosevelt, and, after about 1903, western novels and pulp magazines continued to elaborate and refine the pre–Civil War image of the westerner.

However, for twentieth century Americans, the image of the westerner was forever shaped by motion pictures. Edison Company's *The Great Train Robbery*, Essanay's one and two reel "Broncho Billy" films, and William S. Hart's square-jawed, resolute badman-turned-good enshrined the westerner as a genuine pre–World War I celluloid hero. Tom Mix, Hoot Gibson, Ken Maynard, Buck Jones and a host of lesser-known actors continued to popularize the westerner as a man of decisive action throughout the 1920s. They were followed by William Boyd, Charles Starrett, the singing cowboys, and a host of other actors and actresses who took their turns at interpreting the image of the westerner to the end of the twentieth century.

Surely, the frontier — and the men and women who pushed across the eastern mountain ranges, the Mississippi River, and the Great Plains to the Pacific Ocean — preceded the writing of popular or scholarly history. The stories and legends about Daniel Boone, David Crockett, the mountain men, and post–Civil War badmen, lawmen, women, and Indians, shaped popular perceptions as they were told in sensationalized newspaper stories and dime novels, and dramatized in stage plays and wild west shows. Academically trained historians did not make these men, women, and events significant because they chose to write about them; rather, the men, women, and events were important because they caught public fancy in popular culture genres.

Academic historians were late arrivals to the enterprise of writing about the West. To a large extent, as Richard Maltby notes, "The history exists because the legend exists" (Maltby 1996, 39). Kevin Brownlow, in his influential *The War, the West, and the Wilderness*, echoes Maltby when he writes: "So affectionate have we grown toward the Western that to suggest it reflects more wishful thinking than history seems blasphemous" (Brownlow, 224).

Jesse James, Bill the Kid, Butch Cassidy and the Sundance Kid, Wild Bill Hickok, Crazy Horse, Calamity Jane, and a host of other westerners, and events such as the gunfight at the O.K. Corral, the Battle of the Little Bighorn, and the Lincoln County War, are not ensconced in the American lexicon because of professionally trained historians writing academic history. Western personalities and events achieved heroic and legendary status because of popular genres such as dime novels, wild west shows, and, above all, motion pictures.

Popular genres, as part of popular culture, usually reflect an ideological perspective. Richard Slotkin defines ideology as the "basic system of concepts, beliefs and values that define a society's way of interpreting its place in the cosmos and the meaning of its history" (Slotkin, 5). *The American Heritage Dictionary* refines Slotkin by describing ideology as "the body of ideas reflecting the social needs and aspirations of an individual, group, class, or culture." Political scientists tend to stress consistence and coherence. For example, Janda, Berry and Goldman, in their widely used text on American government, define political ideology as a "consistent set of values and beliefs about the proper purpose and scope of government" (Janda et al., 18). Ginsberg, Lowi and Weir, in another widely used text, suggest that a single variable can provide coherence for an ideology. For instance, many fundamentalist and evangelical Christians, and some

Moslems, use religion as a single variable that unites the elements of their belief systems. Race served the same function for Nazis (Ginsberg 1999, 252).

The history — more often legend than factual history — of Jesse James and the James gang cannot be understood apart from its ideological component. From the days of John Newman Edwards, editor of several different Missouri newspapers and a James apologist, through the dime novels and to the latest Jesse James film's interpretations of the man, his gang, and their motives, images of Jesse James are laced with ideological overtones.

"Lost cause" was the variable that drove the earliest ideological interpretation of Jesse James. While the Civil War had formally ended by the late spring of 1865, tension continued to flare in Missouri. Northern "victor" justice was in place, and Yankee "carpetbaggers" appeared to enrich themselves at the expense of the defeated Southerners. Neighbor was pitted against neighbor on the Missouri-Iowa and Missouri-Kansas borders. Many Missourians, including Frank and Jesse James and Cole Younger, were unrepentant rebels, reluctant to surrender in 1865, and they continued to chafe under hated Yankee rule during the rest of the decade and the 1870s.

William C. Davis, in *The Cause Lost: Myths and Realities of the Confederacy*, writes that the "cause lost became the Lost Cause" (Davis 1996, X). Myths quickly surrounded the leading personalities and events of the conflict as Southerners sought to account for their defeat. Davis observes, "Mythology sprouts like crabgrass whenever strong passions on important issues command the attention of large numbers" (Davis, 175). Those myths reflect the social, cultural, and political needs of individuals and social groups; they become part of an ideology. Early interpretations of Jesse James reflected that ideology.

Partisans of the defeated South, such as John Newman Edwards, either denied that James committed the crimes for which he was accused, or they sought to justify his behavior when the evidence of Jesse's criminality proved incontrovertible. On the other hand, victorious Northerners argued that Jesse and Frank James, as well as the Younger brothers, were "bushwhackers," not regular soldiers, and that they had simply continued their thieving and murdering ways once the war ended. Yankee oriented newspapers were just as likely to attribute every criminal act in Missouri, Iowa, and Kentucky to the James gang as was Edwards in denying any illegal activities on their part.

Sensationalized and romanticized dime novels from the 1880s to the early twentieth century turned the James gang into heroes of sorts by opting for another ideological perspective. The Lost Cause of Edwards gave way to agrarianism versus industrialism, and East versus West, as populism swept the prairie and Rocky Mountain regions. The debate was over the newly emerging industrial order, with its power and wealth locus in the East (Slotkin).

In the dime novels, Jesse James became a symbol of traditional agrarian virtues, such as proper, gentlemanly behavior toward women and concern for the poor and downtrodden. The Pinkerton Detective Agency, on the other hand, was a symbol of industrial wealth and power hiding behind eastern industrial-formulated laws and using arbitrary legal methods to subdue hard-working peoples of the heartland. In short, the Jesse James of dime novels was both a symbol and defender of traditional agrarian society and values, while the hated Pinkertons epitomized the arbitrary use of law by the noxious eastern industrial elite.

In his remarkable *Gunfighter Nation: The Myth of the Frontier in Twentieth-Century America*, Richard Slotkin demonstrates how that concern over industrialism fueled both populist and progressive ideologies. Progressives such as Theodore Roosevelt, and populists such as William Jennings Bryan, sought to preserve Anglo-Saxon, Teutonic values and virtues on which the country had been built. They opposed the eastern industrial society increasingly fueled by the labor of Eastern Europeans, Italians, and Russian Jews. And both progressives and populists voiced increasing alarm at the rise of a softer managerial class that had not experienced the character hardening struggles of those who had been part of the economic conflicts that led to a survival of the fittest.

Jesse James became a populist hero to those longing for a resurgence of Anglo-Saxon, Teutonic values and virtues, and for those who sought to protect American society from the harsher aspects of industrialism. Individuals who reveled in the prosperous new industrialism regarded James as a public enemy who robbed banks and held up trains, a menace to private property. In their eyes, the myth and image of Jesse James as a populist hero was at least as threatening as the labor organizers and reformers who challenged the wealth and power of the eastern industrial elite.

The debate between populists/progressives and conservatives over the fundamental nature of the economy and American culture, and contrasting perspectives over real, imaginary, and quasi-imaginary figures (such as Jesse James), shaped ideological exchanges up to 1930. By 1930, the Lost Cause had slid into the background, and industrialism had emerged triumphant. So-called "Coolidge prosperity" and Herbert Hoover's optimistic assessments of the economy in 1929 underscore President Coolidge's belief that, "The business of government is business." What Arthur M. Schlesinger Jr. termed "the old order" reigned supreme (Schlesinger).

However, its supremacy proved short-lived. The Great Depression, the New Deal, and increasing criticism of the industrial-based ideology (which many blamed for the current hard times) shook the industrial order in ways unimaginable in 1924, the year Calvin Coolidge was elected President. Ultimately, however, the New Deal accepted much of the industrial ideology and sought to control it via consumer-oriented Keynesian economics, a pluralism that recognized the legitimacy of labor unions and farm organizations, and a host of regulations and regulators (Kennedy; Brinkley).

Interestingly, as New Deal proponents and opponents debated both the desirability and means of containing industrial wealth and power, Hollywood rediscovered Jesse James. Silent westerns had not ignored Jesse, but neither did they do a great deal with him. In 1921, Mesco Pictures produced two films about Jesse James' life starring his son, who was billed as Jesse James Jr. The films melded the Lost Cause and industrial ideologies. In the first Mesco production, *Jesse James Under the Black Flag*, James joins Quantrall after Union soldiers have abused his family. In the second effort, *Jesse James as the Outlaw*, Jesse tries to live peacefully after the war, but the Union supported home guard won't let him — when railroad agents kill his half-brother and blow off his mother's arm, Jesse becomes an outlaw (Rainey 1998, 71). In 1928, Paramount produced *Jesse James*, starring the then popular western actor Fred Thomson. While no print of this film has existed for years, plot summaries indicate that Lost Cause was the dominant ideology that explained James' motives (Rainey 1998, 72).

Between 1939 and 1995, about eight major A Westerns, numerous B Westerns, a handful of serials, and some television episodes featured Jesse James, the Younger brothers or the James gang. Films and television episodes in which Jesse appeared as a marginal character, one among a number of bad men, are too numerous to consider. Four variables help to understand the ideological orientation of each film. First, what is the context of the film? Do Jesse and Frank James and the Youngers become outlaws as a result of the Civil War legacy, or because of the railroads as symbol of the newly emerging industrial order? Or are there other reasons? Second, what is the image of Jesse James? Is he a good man victimized by railroad and Yankee abuse, a restless young man bored with peace, or a cold-blooded killer and thief? Third, is there progression in the film? Does Jesse go from being good to bad to good, or is he generally unchangingly restless and bad overall? Fourth and finally, who are the villains? Are they railroad personnel, Union soldiers, Missouri neighbors or the Pinkerton Detective Agency?

The first major sound western about Jesse James, and the one most highly regarded by critics, *Jesse James*, was released by 20th Century–Fox in 1939. It reflects dominant public opinion during the New Deal 1930s and employs the industrial ideology to explain Jesse's motives. The film's context is railroad expansion in Missouri. The St. Louis Midland Railroad is buying up right-of-ways, and the railroad does not care how it obtains the land. Brian Donlevy, playing Barshee, heads up a gang of bullies. They use any tactics—including murder—to obtain the right-of-way. When Jesse and Frank prevent Barshee from taking the family farm, they go into hiding for their own safety. But when Barshee kills their mother, the brothers vow revenge and become outlaws. They kill Barshee and declare war on the railroad. At this point in the film, McCoy, the head of the railroad, played by a badly miscast Donald Meek, puts a price on their heads. Clearly, the culprits in this film are McCoy and Barshee, as representatives of the emerging industrial order who run roughshod over rural folks and agrarian values.

Jesse James, on the other hand, is a good man victimized by abusive industrial leaders who have no sense of honor, and who are prepared to destroy anyone who threatens their wealth and power. Even the promise of amnesty for Jesse, Frank and the rest of the gang is merely one of McCoy's ruses to entice Jesse to surrender so that he can be imprisoned. Not even McCoy's word is trustworthy!

But Jesse begins to change. Initially driven by a sense of justice, he begins to delight in his reputation; robbing banks and stopping trains become ends in themselves. Frank and the rest of the gang urge caution. Jesse explodes, reminding them that he runs the gang, and if they don't want to conform they can leave. In the film *Jesse James*, it is Jesse who masterminds the raid on the Northfield bank, and he bullies Frank and the rest of the gang into going along, even though they believe it to be a foolish endeavor.

During the disastrous raid on the bank in Northfield, Minnesota, Jesse is badly wounded, and, while at home recovering, he recognizes the futility of his life; Jesse decides to reform. He has just told Zee, his wife, of his decision to go to California and start a new life when the Ford brothers come visiting. While Zee is upstairs packing for the trip, Bob Ford kills Jesse. Ford, forever immortalized in "The Ballad of Jesse James" as "that dirty little coward who shot Mr. Howard" is a tool of the railroads. From the opening frames to the final scene, the villains are industrialists, and Jesse James is the populist hero who, in the name of agrarian values and virtues, opposes them.

The 1939 film is one of two or three major Westerns to employ the industrial ideology. The next two, *The Great Missouri Raid* (Paramount, 1950) and *The True Story of Jesse James* (20th Century–Fox, 1957), rely on the context and ideology of the "Lost Cause." In *The Great Missouri Raid*, Frank kills Major Trowbridge's (played by Ward Bond) brother, a Union officer, after he beats Jesse and threatens to hang their stepfather. Major Trowbridge vows revenge. So when Jesse, Frank, and others who rode with Quantrall try to surrender, Trowbridge orders them ambushed. Portrayed as peaceful Southerners driven to outlawry by a spiteful Yankee, the boys become heroes to their friends and neighbors. After the war, Trowbridge heads a detective agency and unrelentingly pursues the gang, motivated by personal vengeance.

MacDonald Carey, playing Jesse James, interprets Jesse as did Tyrone Power in the 1939 film. Initially the victim of victor's justice, Carey begins to enjoy the glamour and excitement of their lives. However, after the Northfield raid, Wendell Corey, playing Frank James, decides to take his wife on a tour of Europe and forsake his outlaw ways when they return. Frank and his wife, along with Jesse's wife (named Bee in this film), convince Jesse to join them. Jesse is packing for the trip when the Ford brothers arrive. Trowbridge, who promises a ten-thousand-dollar reward and a general amnesty, has encouraged Bob Ford to kill Jesse James.

Jesse dies a good man temporarily driven outside the law by a revenge-minded Yankee. As a symbol of the "Lost Cause," Jesse James upholds traditional Southern values and virtues that were threatened by the Northern victory and the onslaught of eastern industrial values and virtues.

The True Story of Jesse James opens with the raid on the Northfield, Minnesota, bank, and Jesse and Frank James' lives are told in a series of flashbacks as the two hide in a cave, eluding the posse hotly pursuing them. The two ideological interpretations of Jesse James are reflected in a conversation between the editor of a newspaper and his assistant. The assistant is sure Jesse is dead, and he wants the editor to print an obituary. He tells the editor that he can use one of the several already prepared, one that blames the war or one about Jesse being a modern-day Robin Hood.

That point arises again as the gang robs a bank. Cole Younger (played by Alan Hale) grabs a dime novel from a desk in the bank. As the gang hides in a farmhouse, Younger reads from the novel about how they rob from the rich in order to give to the poor. The gang laugh at that assessment of their motives. Clearly, in 1957 *The True Story of Jesse James* rejects the industrial ideology as an explanation for Jesse's behavior.

Like *The Great Missouri Raid, The True Story of Jesse James* shows Union soldiers interrogating Jesse's mother and stepfather when soldiers

This title card from the film highlights Robert Wagner's interpretation of Jesse James.

drag Jesse into the yard. The commanding officer assures Jesse and his mother that Frank will not be harmed; they only want to question him. That is not enough for Askew (played by Chubby Johnson), a Unionist neighbor who grabs Jesse and begins to beat him with a belt. Only the Union officer prevents Askew from beating Jesse to death.

At the war's end, Frank and Jesse try to surrender, but they are ambushed and their Unionist neighbors constantly harass them. Jesse takes revenge when he meets Askew on the road and shoots him; that act drives Jesse further outside the law. Like MacDonald Carey's interpretation of Jesse, Robert Wagner's Jesse, though initially the victim, soon begins to enjoy the life to which he has been driven. He plans the raid on the Northfield, Minnesota, bank as the gang's most ambitious endeavor, even though the gang remains skeptical about pulling a job so far away from home.

With the gang destroyed at Northfield, Jesse begins to reassess his life. He promises Zee that they will buy that farm in Nebraska that they have always wanted and settle down — no more robbing banks and trains. At that point the Ford brothers come calling...

The True Story of Jesse James is less of a sympathetic interpretation than the previous films, but even this one elicits sympathy for Frank and Jesse. After all, the film suggests, if their neighbors would have let them live in peace, the boys might not have been driven down the road they chose. While Jesse is less of a populist hero in *The True Story of Jesse James*, he is not much less of a sympathetic figure.

By the early 1970s, "New West" historians were offering new interpretations of Western history, and traditional views of western individuals and events were reexamined in light of the civil rights and feminist movements and a general abhorrence to violence prompted by the war in Vietnam. Psychological explanations replaced earlier ideological orientations. *The Great Northfield Minnesota Raid* (Universal, 1972) has more in common with films such as *Doc* (United Artists, 1971), *Bad Company* (Paramount, 1972), and *Dirty Little Billy* (Columbia, 1972).

Robert Duvall plays Jesse James as a psychopathic killer in *The Great Northfield Minnesota Raid*. On their way to Northfield, the gang stops at a farmhouse not far from the Minnesota town. They discover that granny, who lives on the farm, may lose it because she can't pay her debts, but she tells the gang that her husband had always told her not to sell the children. The children turn out to be dolls. Jesse convinces her to loan him one of the dolls in return for enough money to pay her debts. As the gang rides toward Northfield they encounter the banker on his way to granny's house. Jesse kills the man and leaves the doll to throw suspicion on granny.

After the raid has failed, the gang hides in the unsuspecting granny's house. She leaves with Frank and Jesse, but a few scenes later we see them driving her wagon. Jesse is wearing granny's shawl and bonnet as a disguise. Clearly they have murdered the old woman. There is nothing heroic nor sympathetic about Duvall's portrayal of Jesse. He is a cold-blooded killer, much like James Cagney's Tommy in *Public Enemy* (Warner Brothers, 1931) or Edward G. Robinson's Rico in *Little Caesar* (Warner Brothers, 1931). Jesse James in *The Great Northfield Minnesota Raid* is a public enemy, a threat to the life and property of everyone, including a harmless old woman.

In many ways *The Long Riders* (United Artists, 1980) is a return to the action-oriented Westerns of yesteryear. It is a film filled with exciting horse chases and excellent stunts, particularly during the attempted robbery of the Northfield bank. While the Civil War serves as context for the James and Younger brothers, there is no effort to invoke memories of the "Lost Cause." The brothers—and the emphasis is on the sets of brothers in this film—are portrayed as restless young men bored with peace. One of the Younger brothers observes that if it had not been for the war they might all have taken different directions, and David Carradine as Cole Younger tells a Pinkerton detective that they played a hard game both during and after the war, and they lost.

Riding with Quantrill and Bloody Bill Anderson had been an exciting time for men scarcely out of their teens. Farming and ranching proved inadequate substitutes for the war; the brothers began to rob banks and hold up trains as a means to obtain quick money and ease the boredom of their lives. While one can understand their restlessness in the aftermath of combat—many young men following World War II, Korea and Vietnam experienced the same sense of loss—that is not a satisfactory explanation, let alone justification, for their actions.

James Keach as Jesse James never reforms. He vows to put a new gang together after the failed Northfield raid. In fact, the Ford brothers approach the Pinkerton detective with an offer to kill Jesse for fifteen thousand dollars. Jesse, it seems, has sent for the Fords to discuss a new bank robbery with them, so they know where he is. The image coming from *The Long Riders* is of men who are generally bad; they are public enemies. In contrast, the chief field officer for the Pinkertons, the one in charge of apprehending the James brothers, is a polite human being. Unlike in the other films, his task is a job, not a vendetta.

Frank and Jesse (Trimark Pictures, 1994)—the last Jesse James film to be considered—returns to the industrial ideology. The movie opens with pictures from the Civil War, and Frank and Jesse taking the oath of allegiance. The next scenes are of Frank and Jesse trying to pry a large tree stump from a field. Jesse is restless and objects to this kind of work, complaining it offers none of the excitement of the war. A rider, a paid assassin from the Rock Central railroad of Chicago, interrupts their work. He wounds Frank and heads for the James farm. When his offer for one dollar an acre is rejected, he shoots the elder James and throws a bomb into the house. Frank and Jesse's younger brother is killed and their mother's arm is blown off.

Jesse vows to kill the assassin. Frank—echoing populist sentiment—tells Jesse that the soldiers, railroad, and politicians are all in it together. Not to be deterred, Jesse and Frank kill the assassin, and begin to rob banks and stop Rock Central trains. The head of the railroad hires the Pinkerton Detective Agency to bring in Jesse and Frank James—dead. He notes

The Carradine brothers portray the Younger brothers in *The Long Riders* (1980).

that dime novels are presenting the two as heroes, and that the only way to stop that sort of thing is to kill the two of them!

Later in the film, Jesse remarks that the only job that he has ever been good at is robbing banks. The excitement of the chase seems to satisfy Jesse's restlessness, which not even marriage and a family can expel. After the Northfield raid, the Pinkertons give the Ford brothers a choice — either kill Jesse James or be hanged. They choose to kill Jesse.

Rob Lowe's portrayal of Jesse James is multi-faceted. In large part he is a populist hero, driven to extreme measures when the political system appears to countenance the exploitation of rural folks by the industrial East. But Lowe's Jesse is also a psychologically troubled individual whose restlessness following the war made him easy prey for a life punctuated by episodes of bank and train robberies, followed by the excitement of the chase.

To a great extent the career of Jesse James remains a mystery, as much myth as fact. Even during his life the James gang was accused of crimes they surely did not commit (Brant; Rainey, 1998). As Jesse James caught the fancy of popular genres such as dime novels and motion pictures, interpretations of his life and motives conformed to the ideological perspective of the moment. Richard Maltby writes: "The ideological framework provided by the myth governed the choice of material for Western history. Then the procedures of narrative fiction operated on the now-legendary events to transform them into the material of Western myth, which wrote itself as history" (Maltby, 39).

The first ideological perspective derived from the myth was to see Jesse as a fine example of the Lost Cause, upholding the nobility of Southern manhood. In the words of Frank James in *Frank and Jesse*, the railroads and the politicians were in it together. The next ideological orientation imposed on the myth was derived from the political and social conflicts that fueled populism and viewed Jesse as a hero striking out against those railroaders and industrialists who oppressed hard-working rural folks (the carriers of the true Anglo-Saxon, Teutonic values and virtues upon which the country had been founded). The other side saw Jesse and Frank James a bushwackers, murderers and thieves who had supported slavery and now threatened private property. In the words of the head of the Rock Central Railroad in *Frank and Jesse*, dime novels distorted the true character of the outlaws; they had to be killed to stop perpetuating the myth.

Late twentieth century views of Jesse are more varied. The 1995 film *Frank and Jesse* opts for conflict over emerging industrialism as the incipient cause, the motive behind their actions. But the picture also includes a psychological explanation. Rob Lowe's Jesse is a restless young man, bored with peace and eager for adventure reminiscent of the exciting days of war. *The Long Riders* includes that element as well.

Marley Brant, Jesse James' most recent biographer, suggests this view when he writes in *Jesse James: The Man and the Myth*:

> Jesse James was a career rebel. His future was decided once he swore the mysterious oath that aligned him with the Confederate guerrillas....Their conventional lives were over before they reached the age of thirty. They were bored — and broke. So they did what frustrated desperate youth have often done. They roamed the country in an effort to participate in adventures of their own creation. They robbed banks and trains and created a chaotic stir of excitement wherever they made their presence known. They thought little of defying the accepted moral practices of their nineteenth-century society [Brant, 2].

One thing seems certain, neither the last word has been written nor the last film produced about Jesse James. How he is presented in the future will depend on which existing ideology or what new ones serve the social needs and aspirations of groups or classes in the early twenty-first century.

Historian Robert Utley acknowledges that the myth of Billy the Kid preceded efforts by historians to find the "real" Billy. Utley writes, "Common outlaw, uncommon personality, inspiration for a giant in the pantheon of American heroes— such was Billy the Kid. So all-encompassing is the giant of legend that he has buried the man of reality" (Utley, X). In fact, there is a great deal of confusion surrounding the life of the real Billy the Kid.

The Kid was probably born in New York City in 1859, the son of Catherine McCarty (who may or may not have been married at the time Billy was born). Named Henry McCarty, he lived with his mother for a time in Indianapolis, Indiana, until they drifted West with many other Americans in the years following the Civil War. When his mother married William Antrim, young Henry took the name Henry Antrim. As an adolescent, young Antrim was continually in trouble. By 1878, he lived in New Mexico and worked for John Tunstall. Tunstall and Alexander McSween opposed the Irish clique of Lawrence Murphy and James Dolan. The latter two individuals were part of the so-called Santa Fe Ring that controlled the politics and economics of the New Mexico Territory.

Tuntsall's opposition to the Santa Fe Ring and his determination to challenge Murphy for a contract to sell beef to the Indian reservations led to his murder and precipitated the Lincoln County War of 1878. Henry Antrim, who had by then taken the name William Bonney, participated in that war, but unlike most of the other participants he never stopped fighting. Bonney, known simply as the Kid, became a celebrated outlaw, the subject of outlandish dime novels. The legend emerged and, as Utley observes, it is virtually impossible to separate the real Kid from the one fashioned by dime novels and Leon Metz's famous (or infamous) *Pat Garrett: The Story of a Western Lawman.*

Other than the fanciful Republic and PRC "B" Westerns, the Billy the Kid story was told in four major films prior to 1955. *Billy the Kid* (MGM, 1930) stars Johnny Mack Brown as the Kid and Wallace Berry as Pat Garrett. It is a highly imaginative tale in which Garrett allows Billy and his sweetheart to escape over the border into Mexico. *Billy the Kid* (MGM, 1941) stars Robert Taylor as the Kid and makes no pretense at historical accuracy. None of the prominent figures from the Lincoln County War appear, and Billy is killed at the end of the film by Pat Garrett for reasons having little connection to the real Billy the Kid. *The Outlaw* (RKO, 1943) is most remembered for Jane Russell's ample breasts. Pat Garrett (Thomas Mitchell) permits the Kid (Jack Beutel) to ride away rather than be shot. Finally, in *The Kid from Texas* (Universal, 1950), Audie Murphy plays the Kid, and Frank Wilcox as Pat Garrett kills him at film's end.

The Left Handed Gun (Warner Brothers, 1958) was the first post–1955 version of the Billy the Kid story. Paul Newman plays the Kid as a Western version of James Dean. Billy is introduced in the opening scenes of the film as he staggers along a dusty prairie trail carrying his saddle. Lyrics sung over the opening credits ask viewers to view him with tenderness. They describe Billy as "death's child," and equate his name with sorry. The lyrics conclude that he belongs to all men.

Colin Keith-Johnston as Tunstall takes in the wandering Newman, gives him a job and teaches him to read. But Tunstall, who has become a father figure for Billy, is killed on his way to the Army quartermaster to set a price for beef he hopes to sell to the Indian reservations. At his funeral, McSween (John Dierkes) describes Tunstall as a model citizen. He did not lie, he did not hurt and he listened to any man who spoke to him. In short, McSween concludes, he lived like a man ought to live. When Billy vows to seek vengeance, McSween warns him that revenge is against God's way. Revenge is childish, and a man puts away childish things. McSween reminds Billy that those were the truths that Billy learned as Tunstall taught him to read.

When McSween advises Billy to use the law, Billy replies that Brady, the sheriff played by Robert Foulk, is the law and he does what he is told. Billy enters into a pact with Charlie (James Congdon) and Tom (James Best) to kill Brady and Murphy. When they escape to McSween's house after killing Brady, a crowd gathers to burn the place down. McSween resents Billy's lawless act and is angry that Billy sought shelter from the mob in his house; so he and Billy fight as the building burns, but Billy, badly burned, escapes and is taken to Saval's (Martin Garralaga) place to recover. Pat Garrett (John Dehner) is the town blacksmith.

When amnesty is extended to Billy, he refuses it. He has become arrogantly psychopathic. "I don't run, I don't hide, I go where I want, I do what I want" is the Kid's attitude. When Billy, Tom and Charlie return to the town for Garrett's wedding, they find Hill (Bob Anderson), the last of the gang that killed Tunstall, among the wedding guests. Even though Billy gives his word to Garrett that they will leave Hill alone, the Kid breaks his promise and kills Hill.

An irate Garrett vows to track them down. Garrett kills both Tom and Charlie, and captures Billy. But the Kid escapes and heads once again for Saval's place. But when Saval discovers that Billy has had sex with his wife (Lita Milan), he threatens to kill the Kid. A contrite Billy hands him his gun and tells him to go ahead and shoot him. At that point, Garrett arrives and orders Billy out of the house. Garrett shoots and kills Billy when he believes the latter is going for his gun, but the holster proves to be empty.

At first glance, *The Left Handed Gun* seems to lack purpose or coherence. That Garrett became angry at Billy for killing Hill at the wedding seems too farfetched; it is an inadequate reason for Garrett to agree to become a sheriff in order to kill the Kid. Paul Newman's Billy the Kid is simply a troubled youth who has a difficult time adjusting to the death of Tunstall, the man — maybe the only man — who had been a source of stability in his young life. Without that adult role model, Billy drifted from trouble to trouble. In that, *The Left Handed Gun* resembles the troubled youth films that became prevalent in the 1950s.

But there is surely something more to the movie than the troubled youth theme. *The Left Handed Gun* also challenges the traditional understanding of the hero. Hurd Hatfield as Moultrie, a newspaper man, always lurks in the background. It is he who writes the dime novels extolling the heroic exploits of Billy the Kid. But in the end, Moultrie discovers the great distance between the Kid of dime novels and the real Kid. Moultrie dejectedly exclaims to Billy, "You are not like the book, you don't stand up to glory. You're not him, you're not him!" Disillusioned with the real Kid, Moultrie tells Garrett where to find the Kid. In *The Left Handed Gun*, Newman's Billy the Kid dies because he does not fit the heroic image of the westerner fashioned in dime novels and later films. *The Left Handed Gun*, the 1958 version of the Billy the Kid story, fits well with other Westerns of the late 1950s. They are invitations to viewers to reassess the traditional American image of the hero.

If anything, *One Eyed Jacks* (Paramount, 1961) is more confusing than *The Left Handed Gun*. Marlon Brando plays a Billy the Kid–like character (the film was adapted from Charles Neider's *The Authentic Death of Hendry Jones*). The movie's plot revolves around Brando's desire for revenge. Karl Malden (Dad Longworth) had run out on Brando, permitting him to be captured and sentenced to five years in a Sonora, Mexico, prison. Brando escapes and tracks down Malden, finding he has become the elected sheriff— and a respectable citizen — of a California town.

Brando plays a moody Kid (one is constantly reminded of his role in *A Streetcar Named Desire,* and fully expects to hear him cry out "Stella" at any moment). When Brando kills a man in the town, Malden viciously bullwhips him and warns Brando, "If you ever come back here, I will shoot

Marlon Brando plays a moody version of a Billy the Kid–like character in *One Eyed Jacks* (1961).

you down like a dog in the street." Of course, Malden is far less interested in law and order than he is in keeping Brando from disclosing that he (Malden) ran out on his partner. The beating intensifies Brando's hatred, and he vows that he "will not forget it as long as I breathe."

Partially as an act of revenge, Brando spends the night with Malden's stepdaughter (Pina Pellicer), and she becomes pregnant. But Brando discovers that he loves the girl, so after he has killed Malden, he rides away to Oregon or somewhere with the promise to return for her.

Even more than *The Left Handed Gun*, *One Eyed Jacks* is a confusing film. Brando seems miscast, and his moody, introspective Kid seems out of place in a Western movie. But the film continued the trend toward a less-than-heroic (even antihero-like) main character.

Unlike many of the films about Jesse James, ideological overtones are largely absent in both *The Left Handed Gun* and *One Eyed Jacks*. Paul

Newman and Marlon Brando play the Kid as a troubled youth, a Western film version of James Dean's cinematic image. They also continued the trend, discussed in chapters 1 and 2, toward rethinking the traditional image of the Western hero. Certainly, whatever Newman and Brando's Kids were, they were not heroes in any traditional sense. However, ideology would resurface in both *Chisum* (Warner Brothers, 1970) and *Pat Garrett and Billy the Kid* (MGM, 1973).

John Wayne's John Chisum is no member of the Santa Fe Ring. Quite the contrary, he is an unrelenting foe of Forrest Tucker's Lawrence Murphy, who *is* a member (although the Santa Fe Ring is never mentioned in the film). Furthermore, Wayne's Chisum stands for fair play and equal opportunity for all New Mexico settlers. He defends the sort of economic development that benefits all hard-working folks, no matter their economic level, rather than the market control of Murphy's economic exploitation.

Geoffrey Deuel's Billy the Kid is a good-looking young lad who sets all the ladies hearts to throbbing. Employed by Patrick Knowles' Tunstall, he, too, stands for economic and political justice for all the peoples of New Mexico territory. When Billy is first introduced in the film, one senses that, though a fast draw, he is not the killer of his reputation. Chisum is grateful when Billy and other Tunstall riders help him fight off a gang of horse thieves, and the Kid becomes a welcome guest at the Chisum ranch. Chisum grows concerned, however, when a romance blossoms between Billy and Chisum's niece (Pamela McMyler). Chisum knows of the Kid's reputation, and he forbids Billy to see his niece or visit the ranch after the Kid kills Tunstall's assassins.

When Tunstall is killed (see Chapter 6), Billy takes the law into his own hands, becoming an outlaw. *Chisum* ends with John Chisum killing Lawrence Murphy, and Billy riding out of Lincoln to become a hunted man. But the underlying ideology in *Chisum* is clear. Economic development based on a free market benefits all citizens and will permit New Mexico to become one of the United States. Even though he became an outlaw, Geoffrey Deuel's Billy the Kid embraced those values. And, as the Great Depression receded from memory by 1973, most Americans eagerly endorsed free market economics unfettered by government regulation.

Kris Kristofferson's Billy the Kid plays a different role in *Pat Garrett and Billy the Kid*. First, Kristofferson's Billy is simply a killer; he may smile a lot, but he is a killer nonetheless. As Paul Seydor observes, when Kristofferson's Billy the Kid kills, it is nearly always from ambush or from the back. In Seydor's words, "Virtually nothing Billy does is heroic, noble, or honorable" (Seydor, 289). One is struck by the grin on Billy's face as he

Kris Kristofferson, as Billy the Kid, sits in jail awaiting execution while R.G. Armstrong, as the Bible-spouting Deputy Ollinger, holds shotgun at the ready in *Pat Garrett and Billy the Kid* (1973).

kills R.G. Armstrong (playing the despicable Bible-spouting Ollinger), asking, "How does Jesus look to you now?" Furthermore, Billy's motives for killing are not clear. There is no suggestion that he was avenging Tunstall's murder (it is not even mentioned in the film), nor does he steal to help others or enrich himself. As Seydor writes, "Billy has no desire to become rich, but that is chiefly because he has no ambition at all"(Seydor, 289).

Second, in *Pat Garrett and Billy the Kid*, Kristofferson's Billy is a man who will not acknowledge changing times. By the late 1960s and early 1970s, youth rebellion had eclipsed the troubled youth of 1950s American culture. That the Santa Fe Ring intends to bring economic development (as corrupt as it might be) to New Mexico and rid the state of its wild element is of no concern to Kirstofferson. In their meeting at Fort Sumner that opens the film, Garrett tells Billy that he must leave the territory. When the Kid suggests that he does not understand, Garrett tells him that the times have changed and that the new power brokers want his kind out of New Mexico. Billy only replies to Garrett's comment that the times have changed by protesting that *he* has not changed and that he *won't* change.

The Santa Fe Ring represents the new order. As corrupt and power hungry as are its members, including John Chisum, they are the forces of progress and economic development. Just as Jesse James opposing the railroad stands as a symbol of the agrarian culture opposing eastern industrial power, so in *Pat Garrett and Billy the Kid* does Billy stand as a symbol of the Wild West now threatened by the ever encroaching might of eastern industrial finance.

Films of the 1950s often featured troubled youth or outright juvenile delinquents. Actors such as James Dean and films such as *The Blackboard Jungle* (MGM, 1955), typify the period. Interpretations of Jesse James and Billy the Kid often mirrored those themes. However, by the late 1960s and early 1970s, rebellious youth had replaced the J.D. themes. For example, *Easy Rider* (Columbia Pictures, 1969) and *The Graduate* (Embassy Pictures, 1967) offered different views of young cohorts. Kris Kristofferson's Billy the Kid has much in common with the youth rebellion films of that period. Just as Kristofferson's Kid rejected the changes that were unfolding in New Mexico territory, so too did many baby boomers reject the corporate work culture and moral values of their parents and grandparents.

By the late 1980s much of the youth rebellion had disappeared from the American landscape. Generation X did not exhibit generational distinctives, as had their baby boomer parents. The eastern industrial economy stagnated as power and wealth shifted west and south. Watergate, Iran-Contra and congressional scandals intensified the widespread disgust and disillusionment with politics and politicians that had begun in the Vietnam era. As a result, by the late 1980s Americans expressed diminishing confidence in many types of public institutions, including the federal government. And high on the public agenda was a concern for widespread drug usage. In the midst of those changes and controversies, two new films about Billy the Kid, *Young Guns* (20th Century–Fox, 1988) and *Young Guns II* (20th Century–Fox, 1991) appeared, and both reflected American culture of the last decade of the twentieth century.

A number of themes in *Young Guns* and *Young Guns II* continued the interpretation of events and personalities that had appeared in earlier Billy the Kid films. Pat Garrett's motive is one of those continuities. William Peterson appears as Pat Garrett in *Young Guns II*. While Garrett had not ridden with Billy the Kid (Emilio Estevez) and the other Regulators in *Young Guns* (Patrick Wayne played Pat Garrett in the first film), he had been the Kid's friend. But after Billy kills two of John Chisum's (played by James Coburn) ranch hands in *Young Guns II*, Chisum vows to get the Kid and his gang. In *Young Guns II*, Chisum convinces his partners in the Santa Fe Ring to offer Garrett the job as sheriff. Garrett accepts, and he

Emilio Estevez, as Billy the Kid, and the rest of the young guns in *Young Guns II* (1991).

even takes along his personal newspaper reporter to record the events as he tracks down the Kid. Even thought he is a law officer, Garrett's desire for social acceptance and fame, not a regard for justice, taint his dogged pursuit of Emilio Estevez's Billy the Kid.

Garrett's hypocrisy is made even more poignant when he raids a bordello in which the Kid and the rest of the remaining Regulators are holed up. The Kid escapes, but Garrett prepares to burn down the house. Garrett had been a regular customer, as had other so-called respectable male members of the community, but he tells the madam as he prepares to torch the place that he does not sleep with whores anymore.

The image of Pat Garrett in *Young Guns II* as a fame-seeking hypocrite tracks well with public opinion of the time. Increasingly, Americans questioned the motives and tactics of law enforcement officers, and suspected that many so-called reformers were merely trying to hide shameful past behavior. As divorce rates climbed and stories of male marital infidelity increased, one suspected that most males, even the most respected community leaders, were not faithful to their spouses. *Young Guns II* reflects those views.

Young Guns and *Young Guns II* also continue to reject the myth that Billy the Kid was driven to the violent behavior that shaped his young life. In *Young Guns*, after Tunstall (Terence Stamp) is murdered, McSween (Terrance O'Quinn) has the "boys" made deputies and charges them with the duty to arrest Stamp's killers. When the young deputies track Henry Hill (Gadeek) to a tavern, Dick Brewer (Charlie Sheen) sends Billy in to arrest Hill. The Kid waits for Hill in the outhouse and shoots him as Hill finishes relieving himself. Billy makes no effort to arrest Hill; he kills him in cold blood and shoves the arrest warrant into the dead man's mouth.

Killings pile on top of killings, many of them instigated by Billy. Soon the Regulators, as the band was known, are wanted men with a two-hundred-dollar bounty on their heads. As Doc (Keifer Sutherland) observes, "There is a whirlwind out there and when you are in it, you can't get out." But it was Billy's violent behavior, his desire for blood and revenge, and his fondness for his growing reputation as a gunman that created the whirlwind. It was Billy's behavior that turned a group of young men bent on using the law to capture those responsible for the death of their beloved employer into wanted men. In *Young Guns*, Estevez's Kid kills because he enjoys it. He revels in his notoriety, and he relishes his image as a dangerous killer. And the film ends with the suggestion that all of the Regulators except Billy have tried to resume normal lives.

Clearly that hope was not realized; hence *Young Guns II* brings the gang back together and follows them until each dies in turn. One of this sequel's segments in particular continues to deflate the Billy the Kid myth. Billy and the remaining Regulators are resting in a saloon when the Kid overhears a man proclaim that he intends to hunt down and kill Billy the Kid. That is too much for Billy, who engages the man in conversation and asks to see the gun with which he intends to kill the Kid. As the man busily talks with a girl, Billy empties the gun and gives it back to him. Then he kills the man.

Turning to Doc (Keifer Sutherland), Billy asks if that makes twenty five (men he has killed). When Doc answers five, Billy concludes, "let's call it ten." Certainly the point of this exchange is to demonstrate that Billy the Kid killed far fewer men than he claimed or others believed. Rather than being a young man driven to criminal activity, or one who killed a prodigious number of people, *Young Guns* and *Young Guns II* depict Billy the Kid as a brash young man taken with his own mostly undeserved reputation.

One of the most salient features of the two films is the pervasiveness of political corruption and dishonest politicians. In *Young Guns*, Lawrence Murphy (Jack Palance) explains to Tunstall (Terence Stamp) that he does not want him to have the beef contract, and neither does the territorial attorney general nor the governor. In short, the Santa Fe Ring controls the territory and uses that control for their personal economic benefit. Since Stamp's Tunstall is a threat to that control, he must die.

The extent of Murphy's political control is apparent at the end of *Young Guns*. Murphy's henchmen have Billy and the rest of the Regulators bottled up in McSween's house when a cavalry unit rides into town to arrest the Kid. But the cavalry commander defers to Murphy, and his men assist in burning down the house and driving out Billy and the Regulators. In New Mexico Territory, the Santa Fe Ring even controlled the United States Army. While Billy kills the evil Murphy at the end of *Young Guns*, *Young Guns II* makes it clear that Palance's death did not destroy the Santa Fe Ring; it continues to function effectively throughout the latter film.

Young Guns II opens in 1950 as a very old man consults with a lawyer in a sand dune next to a modern highway about receiving a pardon that had been promised him. The old man is Billy the Kid (continuing the myth that Garrett did not really kill the Kid), and he wants the pardon that Billy believes Governor Lew Wallace had promised him. As the film unfolds, viewers learn that Governor Wallace (Scott Wilson) convinces Billy to turn himself in, and that he will grant him a full pardon if he testifies that the Murphy/Dolan Irish faction stole Chisum's cattle.

As Billy sits in jail awaiting the trial, he learns that Wallace has tricked him. There is no pardon; Billy will be tried for murder — and likely found guilty and hanged. In *Young Guns II*, the governor's promises are of no value; he gave his word merely as a ruse to trick Billy into surrendering. The governor is just another lying, dishonest politician. That view of government officials tracked well with public sentiment in the 1990s.

The 1996 National Elections Studies conducted by the University of Michigan's Center for Political Studies found that fifty-five percent of the public believed that one could trust the government in Washington only some of the time, and forty-five percent of the sample agreed that people like themselves had no say in what government does. Another forty-three percent agreed that quite a few people in the government are crooked. *Young Guns* and *Young Guns II* capture that overall distrust of government felt by the American public in the last twenty years of the twentieth century.

One last element in *Young Guns* dates the film. After the Regulators become hunted men, Chavez Y. Chavez (Lou Diamond, playing a character of both Mexican and Indian lineage), ingests the hallucinogenic drug peyote as a means of discovering the course of action the gang should pursue. The rest of the gang follows Chavez' example, and they all get high. At the time *Young Guns* was playing in theaters and on television, media attention was focused on the Supreme Court case *Employment Division, Department of Human Resources of Oregon v. Smith* (494 U.S. 872, 1990). The case revolved around whether two Native Americans could be fired from their jobs as drug counselors because they had ingested peyote — an illegal drug in Oregon — during Native-American religious ceremonies. While the Court ruled against the two Native Americans, the case (as well as the film) made Americans aware of the role peyote played in Native-American culture.

Butch Cassidy and the Sundance Kid (20th Century–Fox, 1969) is, arguably, the best known "outlaw" Western of the twentieth century. Paul Newman (Butch Cassidy) and Robert Redford (Sundance Kid), two of the biggest box office draws of that time, play the two outlaws in a chic, quippy, tongue-in-cheek fashion that appealed to baby boomers and made *Butch Cassidy and the Sundance Kid* one of the most financially successful Westerns of all time.

Just as John Wayne, with his "That'll be the day" from *The Searchers*, gave 1950s Americans a new slang expression, so too did Newman's oft-repeated question, "Who are those guys?" as they try to elude their pursuers, give Americans of the early 1970s a new way to express their bewilderment or confusion. "Who are those guys?" became a standard way of expressing uncertainty about someone's identity, or lack of clarity about the significance of an event.

The overarching theme of *Butch Cassidy and the Sundance Kid* is one that emerged earlier in the chapter; the two outlaws are men who have outlived their times. The West is dominated by large corporations, such as the Union Pacific Railroad, and powerful individuals, such as E.H. Harriman. There is no room left for two free spirits, such as Butch and

Sundance in the corporate-dominated West. They are not bad guys—they just rob trains! They carefully try not to hurt anybody; Newman even acknowledges that he has never shot anyone. E.H. Harriman of the Union Pacific Railroad does not see it that way, however, so he organizes a special force to capture the two outlaws. In the new West of *Butch Cassidy and the Sundance Kid*, the railroad wins and the outlaws lose.

When Newman and Redford, eluding Harriman's special force, seek assistance from a friend, their friend lectures them on the changing times. "You may be the biggest thing around here," he warns them, "but you are still outlaws. ... Your times is over." Both Butch and Sundance recognize that if they remain in the United States they will be captured or killed, so they go to Bolivia.

Butch Cassidy and the Sundance Kid turns the history of the 1960s on its head. In the early years of the decade, idealistic Americans had gone to South America as Peace Corp. volunteers. Their goals had been to bring economic development and democratic institutions to that continent. Butch and Sundance go to steal and rob. However, their first effort to rob a bank fails when Cassidy realizes that neither of them speaks Spanish, and so no one in the bank will understand their commands. *Butch Cassidy and the Sundance Kid* resonates with an attitude prevalent in the late 1960s— that the "ugly American" who did not understand the indigenous language nor culture made things worse, not better. Surely Butch and Sundance have no intention of making things better; they are in Bolivia to rob banks. And they rob and steal until they are gunned down by Bolivian military forces. The 1960s, which began on the optimistic note of *The Magnificent Seven* (United Artists, 1960) defending a poor Mexican village from bandits, ends with Butch Cassidy and the Sundance Kid gunned down in a poor Bolivian village as outlaws by Bolivian soldiers.

Chapter 9

"NEVER MIND WYATT, IT HAPPENED THAT WAY"

No single event in the history of the American frontier has captivated public imagination as has the shootout near the OK Corral in Tombstone, Arizona, on October 26, 1881. The personalities involved in the dispute were real people, and the event surely happened, but the motives and circumstances of the shootout have generated a great deal of debate. That is not surprising, for as with many other personalities and events of the American frontier, the factual history of the gunfight at the OK Corral is much disputed. However, one thing is clear; the shootout itself was a relatively minor occurrence in the settling of the American West. Its importance pales in comparison, for example, to the Battle of the Little Bighorn that ultimately forced the entire Sioux Indian nation onto reservations.

While the story of the gunfight was covered widely by newspapers of the day, its significance for twentieth-century Americans comes from Hollywood's infatuation with the shootout. The gunfight at the OK Corral is a classic example of an event that transcends its historical significance because Western movies repeatedly chose to portray the shootout on the silver screen. Wyatt Earp, Doc Holliday and the gunfight at the OK Corral in Tombstone, Arizona, are excellent case studies of the extent to which popular culture shapes public understanding of frontier personalities and events, and the manner in which motion picture interpretations of the shootout and the combatants changed throughout the course of the twentieth century.

The central role that cinema played in elevating Wyatt Earp to a national hero and transforming a relatively minor event into one of some historical significance is underscored at the conclusion of *Tombstone* (Buena Vista, 1993). Narrator Robert Mitchum informs viewers that Wyatt Earp died in Los Angeles in 1929. Mitchum notes that movie cowboy stars William S. Hart and Tom Mix were among Earp's pallbearers, and Mitchum adds, "Tom Mix wept." According to Hart biographer Ronald L. Davis, Earp visited movie sets and tried to correct mistakes he saw in the representation of the West (Davis 2003, 150). By 1929, Wyatt Earp had become a well-known personality due to motion pictures, and his reputation was enhanced by the 1931 publication of Stuart Lake's largely inaccurate biography of Earp, *Wyatt Earp: Frontier Marshal*. By the early 1930s, Earp had come to embody the qualities of the frontiersman that filmmakers sought to inject into their productions. The myth had overtaken history.

Wyatt Earp (Warner Brothers, 1994) has a similar ending. While on a boat bound for the Alaska gold fields seventeen years after the events in Tombstone, Wyatt Earp (played by Kevin Costner) and Josie (Joanna Going) are approached by a young man (Mackenzie Astin) who recognizes Earp. The young man wants to know whether on not an incident in which Earp prevented the man's uncle from being lynched was factual. Earp remains noncommittal as the young man recounts his uncle's version of the story; Wyatt merely inquires about the uncle, only to learn that he was killed a short time after the incident.

After the young man leaves, Earp says to Josie, "Some people say it didn't happen that way." Josie replies, "Never mind Wyatt, it happened that way." Nick J. Swinhart, on his excellent website on Wyatt Earp, points out that, "The image of this man we have today has been blurred and misconstrued to the point we no longer think of him as being a real person with real feelings, emotions, and faults in character" (Swinhart, 1). Who knows whether or not the incident recalled on the boat happened that way or not — or, for that matter, who knows what really happened on that Tombstone street that fateful day in October 1881. The real Wyatt Earp and Doc Holliday, and the events popularly associated with their lives, have been so transfigured by popular culture that it is difficult to separate the flesh and blood individuals from those figures viewers have come to know through images on the silver screen.

Casey Tefertiller, a recent Earp biographer, made note of Los Angeles city councilmen Nate Holden's 1994 comments at the unveiling of a plaque designating Earp's former residence in the city. Holden remarked, "Frankly, we could use Wyatt Earp in America today. He was an incredible tall-in-the-saddle hero, a mixture of great myth and fact, who should never be forgotten" (Tefertiller, 344). Because the life of Wyatt Earp has become such a mixture of fact and fiction, it is helpful to begin with brief biographical sketches of both Wyatt Earp and Doc Holliday.

Readers who want brief biographical overviews of the lives of both men should consult Buck Rainey's *Western Gunslingers in Fact and Film* and Jon Tuska's *The American West in Film: Critical Approaches to the Western.* Casey Tefertiller's *Wyatt Earp: The Life Behind the Legend* offers a longer and more thorough study of the man. John Myers' *Doc Holliday* is the most recent biography of that famous Western personality. It was first published in 1955 by Little, Brown and Company, and subsequently republished by the University of Nebraska Press as a Bison Book.

Wyatt Earp was born in Illinois in 1848. Like many other families of that era, the Earps moved around a lot, first to Iowa and then to San Bernardino, California. Wyatt returned east however, and in 1870 he was appointed constable in Lamar, Missouri. There he met and married Urilla Sutherland. However, the marriage proved short lived. She died either from typhoid fever or in childbirth (accounts vary). In any case, Earp soon left Lamar, either out of grief over his dead wife or because of misappropriation of funds. He drifted to Oklahoma Indian Territory where he was indicted for stealing a horse, but he never stood trial. After a time working at various jobs (including buffalo hunting), Earp began his career as a Kansas lawman.

There is some dispute as to whether or not he was ever a peace office in Ellsworth, but he quickly made a name for himself in the Kansas cattle towns of Wichita and Dodge City. Although stories of gunfights and showdowns with outlaws and rowdy cowboys are overstated (Earp apparently killed only one person in Dodge City), he enforced the law with vigor. In fact, Tefertiller contends that Earp frequently did not carry a gun, and when he had one, he preferred to pistol whip miscreants rather than shoot them (Tefertiller, 1). However, residents of Dodge City eventually tired of his tactics and Earp was relieved of his duties.

In the late 1870s he migrated to Tombstone, Arizona, where he was joined by his brothers, James, Virgil and Morgan, and their families. The brothers speculated on mining claims and, along with Bat Masterson and Luke Short, ran the gaming tables at the Oriental Saloon. Tombstone was a wild frontier town, and soon the Earp brothers were back in law enforcement. The wild element, known as the "cowboys," resented the Earps and feuding soon erupted between them. In addition, Ike Clanton opposed the Earps' efforts to stop his lucrative rustling of Mexican cattle.

A number of events surely precipitated the gunfight. Rustling, the theft of some army mules, a stagecoach holdup and the murder of Sheriff Fred White by Curly Bill Brocius, one of the most notorious of the "cowboys," intensified the rift between the Earps and Ike Clanton and the other "cowboys." In addition, bad blood developed between Sheriff John Behan and the Earps.

Behan was a Democrat, Wyatt Earp a Republican. The Territorial Governor, a Democrat, appointed Behan as county sheriff, and Behan reneged on a promise to make Wyatt his deputy. Behan also had a mistress, Josephine Sarah Marcus, a Jewish actress, who left him when she realized he had no intention of marrying her. Soon Wyatt had forsaken his common law wife, Mattie, and had taken up with Josephine (Josie). Behan also was a friend and ally of the "cowboys," and apparently on several occasions had tried to convince Wyatt and his brothers to look the other way when Ike Clanton rustled cattle.

The thirty-second shootout at the OK Corral left Virgil and Morgan badly wounded and Doc Holliday slightly injured, but Frank McLaury, Tom McLaury and Billy Clanton were killed. In a process laced with politics, Wyatt Earp and Doc Holliday were exonerated of murder charges. But the bloodletting had just begun. When Morgan was murdered and Virgil crippled by the revenge-minded "cowboys," Doc and Wyatt started on a nearly two-year campaign of revenge, killing many of the "cowboys," until both men left or were forced to flee Arizona.

Wyatt married Josie soon after the gunfight, and together they moved to California. Wyatt continued speculating in mining properties, and they lived for a few years in Alaska during the gold rush, and in various places in Nevada and Arizona working gaming tables at saloons. Later in life, Earp was caught up in allegations that he was part of a plot to fix the Fitzsimmons-Sharkey heavyweight prize fight, and he actually stood trial for carrying a concealed weapon when he refereed the bout.

As Tefertiller writes, "Wherever Wyatt Earp appeared, the world seemed to go mad around him, and it forever baffled him that history would not just leave him alone" (Tefertiller, 1). And, Tefertiller contends, "Tombstone, with its web of ambiguities and uncertainties, would haunt Earp for the rest of his life" (Tefertiller, 1). Even with his 1929 death, Wyatt Earp could not escape Tombstone. Motion pictures and historians continue to mine the man and the event for new interpretations and continuing controversy.

John Henry "Doc" Holliday was born in Griffin, Georgia, in 1851 of well-to-do parents. As a young man he went to dental school and established an office in Atlanta, but in 1872 he contracted tuberculosis. The coughing fits brought on by the disease made continuing his dental practice impossible, and he was only given six months to live anyway. Thinking that the higher altitude and drier air of the West might be better for his lungs, Holliday left Georgia.

Holliday discovered quickly that he had an affinity for gambling, and soon began his second career — as a professional gambler. But it was a dangerous occupation, and Holliday had little previous experience with weapons. In fact, during an early dispute, both Holliday and his adversary jerked their guns and repeatedly fired away without hitting each other. But with practice he soon became a deadly shot. For most of the rest of his life, Holliday carried a knife, a shoulder holster and a waist gun.

Knowing that he was a dying man simply made Holliday more reckless. He killed his first man, a gambler in Dallas, in 1875, and other victims soon followed, forcing Holliday to move frequently from town to town. After he killed a man in Denver, he drifted to Fort Griffin, Texas. He dealt Faro at Shanessey's saloon, and there he met the two individuals who would play pivotal roles in his life — Kate (Big Nose Kate) Elder and Wyatt Earp. Kate Elder was a prostitute who lived and traveled with Holliday until just before the shootout in Tombstone. For reasons not immediately apparent, Earp and Holliday liked one another from the beginning and became close friends.

As with other towns, Doc and Kate were forced to leave Fort Griffin after Holliday disemboweled Ed Bailey, a local tough, in a vicious knife fight. They wound up in Dodge City, where Earp worked as a peace office, and Holliday dealt Faro at the Long Branch Saloon. Presumably Kate continued to work as a prostitute. In Dodge, the friendship between Wyatt Earp and Doc Holliday solidified when Doc saved Wyatt's life. A bunch of rowdy Texas cowboys had Earp alone and intended to kill him when Doc intervened, startling the leaders of the gang, and thus allowing Earp to pistol whip one of them and get the drop on the entire group. Wyatt Earp never forgot that Doc Holliday saved his life that day.

Doc and Kate followed the Earps to Tombstone. Kate set up a brothel in town and Doc earned his living gambling. Doc and Kate got along well unless one or both of them had been drinking. When they were drunk their fights were loud and violent. According to Allie Earp, Virgil's second wife, she saw Kate one day and "she looked as if an ore wagon had run over her. She had a black eye, one lip was swelled up, and her clothes looked like the wind had blown 'em on her ever which way" (Lackman, 58). On another occasion, Kate got drunk and threatened to kill Doc before he threw her out. Obviously intoxicated and egged on by Ike Clanton, she accused Doc of holding up a stagecoach and helping to kill the driver, Bud Philpot. Based on Kate's allegation, Doc was arrested for murder. But the charges were dismissed when Kate recanted, and Doc paid her expenses to leave Tombstone. She continued to work as a prostitute until she married George M. Cummings after Doc died in 1887. She lived with Cummings until 1930 and died in Prescott, Arizona, in 1940 at the ripe old age of 87.

Ike Clanton's use of Kate to get Doc Holliday was all the excuse Doc needed to join the Earp brothers in the gunfight. And he continued riding with Wyatt to revenge Morgan Earp's death. After the gunfight at Tombstone and the ensuing vendetta against the cowboys (a campaign in which Doc probably killed more men than did Wyatt Earp), Doc went to Colorado to seek medical treatment for his tuberculosis. But he was arrested on murder warrants from Arizona and jailed. However, the governor refused to extradite Holliday to Arizona, and he entered a sanitarium and died on November 8, 1887.

Numerous big-budget and B Westerns prior to 1955 employed characters like Wyatt Earp and Doc Holliday, and the gunfight in Tombstone, in their storyline, but two films, *Frontier Marshal* (20th Century–Fox, 1939) and *My Darling Clementine* (20th Century–Fox, 1946), established the baseline by which to compare post–1955 depictions of the two men and events of their lives.

In both films, Wyatt Earp is depicted as a brave, resolute frontier hero. Neither film deals with Earp's earlier life; both start with his arrival in Tombstone. Henry Fonda (in *My Darling Clementine*) and Randolph Scott (*Frontier Marshal*) as Wyatt gain public notice by entering a saloon to capture a drunken Indian (Charles Stevens in both films) who is shooting up the place. Both men initially reject offers to become town marshal. But both decide to accept the position for personal reasons, Fonda after he discovers that his younger brother has been murdered and their cattle rustled, and Scott after he has been kidnapped, taken out of town and beaten by Joe Sawyer (Curly Bill) and his gang of toughs.

Both Fonda and Scott are shown playing poker and drinking whiskey at the bar, but neither film even hints that the Earps were also professional gamblers with a large interest in the gaming tables of the Oriental Saloon. In fact, *Frontier Marshal* does not include the other Earp brothers. Both Fonda and Scott enforce a "no guns in town" rule, and both successfully turn Tombstone into a law-abiding, peaceful town.

The source of the dispute that leads to the gunfight (as well as the gunfight itself) differs in the two films. In *Frontier Marshal*, Ben Carter (John Carradine) is the saloonkeeper who wants to keep Tombstone a wide open town for gambling, and to hide his other illegal activities. Wyatt's imposition of law and order in Tombstone threatens Carter's financially lucrative rackets. Walter Brennan is exceptionally good as Old Man Clanton in *My Darling Clementine*. Clanton murders, robs and rustles without a hint of remorse. Earp is Clanton's opposite, and the town is literally not big enough for both men, thus setting up the inevitable shootout.

The gunfight is radically different in the two films. Wyatt Earp in *Frontier Marshal* goes it alone after Curly Bill's toughs kill Doc Holliday (Cesar Romero). And the shootout takes place at night, unfolding from behind buildings, in doorways and under staircases. In short, there is little historical accuracy in the shootout as depicted in *Frontier Marshal*. *My Darling Clementine* portrays the gunfight as it is traditionally understood — a standup affair in the daytime between the Earp brothers and Doc Holliday, and the Clantons and the McLaury brothers (in this film, Johnny Ringo appears as well).

Neither film suggests any events beyond the shootout. As "The End" flashes across the screen in *Frontier Marshal*, Earp appears set to marry Sarah Allen (Nancy Kelly) who had come to Tombstone in search of Doc Holliday, to whom she had been engaged back East. Although there are hints of a budding romance between Wyatt and Clementine (Cathy Downs) in *My Darling Clementine*, the films ends with Earp leaving Tombstone. He has accomplished his mission; Tombstone is now a civilized place where women and children can live in peace, and business and schools and churches can flourish.

In both *Frontier Marshal* and *My Darling Clementine*, Wyatt Earp meets Doc Holliday for the first time in Tombstone. In both films Holliday (played by Cesar Romero in *Frontier Marshal* and Victor Mature in *My Darling Clementine*) is a medical doctor, plagued by an unidentified disease (but one remarkably similar to tuberculosis), who tries to run from his past. Though known as a gambler and killer, Holliday is portrayed in both pictures as a remarkably cultured man. In one scene in *My Darling Clementine*, Mature even quotes Shakespeare when Alan Mowbray is unable to finish a recitation.

The women in both films reflect the polarities that frequently characterized pre–1955 Westerns. Chihuahua (Linda Darnell in *My Darling Clementine*) and Jerry (Binnie Barnes in *Frontier Marshal*) are the hot-tempered, sensual saloon entertainers who are Doc Holliday's lovers. Sarah Allen (Nancy Kelly in *Frontier Marshal*) and Clementine (Cathy Downs in

My Darling Clementine) are the virginal eastern women once engaged to Doc Holliday who arrive in Tombstone searching for the man they once knew. While both Darnell and Barnes's portrayal of Holliday's lovers bear some resemblance to the historical Kate Elder, neither of them is assigned that name in the films. And Kelly and Downs' characters have no basis in fact.

Near the beginning of each film, when Scott and Fonda catch Darnell and Barnes assisting a gambler who is cheating at cards, they punish both women by dumping them in horse troughs. Both women expect Doc to come to their aid when he discovers how they had been treated, but in both films the outcome, much to the displeasure of the women, is that Wyatt and Doc become friends.

In the films, Doc is a physician, not a dentist. In *Frontier Marshall* Holliday successfully removes a bullet lodged near the spine of a young boy accidentally caught in the crossfire of a shootout. Sarah Allen, who was a nurse, assists Doc, and one anticipates that the two will get back together, but Doc is murdered before anything more can happen.

Doc is not successful in his operation to save Chihuahua's life. She had been accidentally shot by Billy Clanton (John Ireland), who had become her lover after she left Doc in a fit of rage. Holliday had gone gunning for Billy and caught him escaping through Chihuahua's window. As the two men exchange shots, Chihuahua is fatally wounded. Doc blames Billy for Chihuahua's death, and that is his motive for joining the Earps in the shootout.

Introduced by Frankie Lane singing the catchy theme song, *Gunfight at the O.K. Corral* (Paramount, 1957) has a great deal in common with both *Frontier Marshal* and *My Darling Clementine*. It is an excellent example of the continuity between pre– and post–1955 Westerns.

The film opens as Wyatt Earp (Burt Lancaster) rides into Fort Griffin, Texas, in search of two outlaws he had been trailing. He meets Cotton Wilson (Frank Faylen) who had been a friend and a fearless peace officer. Sadly, Wyatt learns that the two outlaws had been in town, but that Wilson had not held them as Earp had expected him to do. Wilson has changed; he has aged. His new philosophy now of live and let live is foreign to Wyatt. Earp's reaction — telling Wilson that if he can't do his job he should step aside and let someone else do it — is one that resonated with 1950s audiences. 1950s viewers expected policemen to be honest and do their job of protecting the community.

Burt Lancaster, as Wyatt Earp, meets Kirk Douglas' Doc Holliday.

In Fort Griffin, Wyatt meets Doc Holliday (Kirk Douglas) for the first time. And even though Earp does not like Holliday, he warns him that Ed Bailey (Lee Van Cleef) carries a hidden gun in his boot. Doc is able to knife Bailey before he can draw the boot gun. The friendship begins, then, according to *Gunfight at the O.K. Corral*, because Wyatt first saved Doc's life, not the other way around.

Later in the film, in Dodge City, even though Earp proclaims, "I never needed anybody in my life, and I don't need Doc Holliday," he does, in fact, need him. Shanghai Pierce (Ted De Corsia) and his Texas cowboys have an unarmed Wyatt cornered after he has stopped them from breaking up a town dance. Pierce is set to kill Wyatt when Doc slips in the back door and gets the drop on the cowboys, thus saving Earp's life.

Laura Denbow (Rhonda Fleming), a lady gambler, is Wyatt's love interest. Wyatt prepares to give up his job as a peace officer and marry

Laura, when his brother telegraphs that he needs help in Tombstone. Wyatt tells Laura that he must go to Tombstone because Virgil is his brother. But Laura warns him that, "We are not going to start life together with a gun your hand. ... You have got to meet me halfway." Wyatt refuses. His sense of duty to his brother and his duty to his profession forces him to choose duty over love. That attitude surely made sense to a great many males in 1957. Only about a dozen years removed from the end of World War II, that generation of males possessed a keen sense of duty and of responsibility. They had flocked to military enlistment offices to help defeat two mighty military regimes, and they had returned victorious to create the most prosperous economy in the history of the world. They believed one was obligated to work hard and to acknowledge one's duty, irrespective of the personal cost.

Once in Tombstone, Wyatt discovers that Ike Clanton (Lyle Bettger) heads a gang of highly successful rustlers. The showdown between the Earps and Clanton becomes inevitable when Wyatt refuses Cotton Wilson's offer. Wilson has relocated to Tombstone and become county sheriff. He no longer makes any pretense of being honest, and openly works for Clanton. Wilson offers Wyatt $20,000 if he will look the other way while Clanton ships his stolen cattle. Wyatt refuses the bribe.

In the meantime, Doc Holliday has arrived in Tombstone without his mistress, Kate Fisher (Jo Van Fleet). She had left him in Dodge City for Johnny Ringo (John Ireland). Doc had promised Wyatt that he would not fight while in Dodge City, and he refuses Ringo's challenge to shoot it out. Doc won't fight, even when Ringo throws a glass of whiskey in his face. He leaves the room with both Ringo and Kate laughing at him, and with wounded pride.

Wyatt, as an upright lawman, takes a liking to young Billy Clanton (Dennis Hopper), and when young Clanton gets drunk, Wyatt takes him to the Clanton ranch. Mrs. Clanton (Olive Carey) is beside herself worrying about her young son. Wyatt tells Billy — and his mother warns him to listen — that no gunslinger ever lived long enough to celebrate his thirty-fifth birthday. All gunfighters, Wyatt lectures Billy, are lonely and die without a friend. As Wyatt leaves the ranch, Ike Clanton stops him and reminds him that he is out of his territory. But viewers learn that Wyatt has been appointed a United States marshal; he is *not* out of his territory.

Ike decides it is time to get rid of Wyatt and he plans to kill him when the lawman makes his night rounds. However, James Earp (Martin Milner) takes his brother's place and is murdered instead. Wyatt knows that Clanton has called the play and sends word that he is prepared to meet them. When the logic of that attitude is questioned, Wyatt replies, "To hell with logic — that is my brother lying there." Not even Virgil's wife, who reminds Wyatt that his "duty is to the town, not your own family pride," can dissuade Wyatt from the impending gunfight.

Doc goes to see Kate (who has arrived in Tombstone with Johnny Ringo) to find out who killed James Earp. Holliday is about to either beat her or kill her when he has a severe coughing spell that puts him in bed. Kate remains with him, nursing him throughout the night. But in the morning, Wyatt comes to a still sick and weak Doc imploring his help: "I need you Doc, don't let me down." Holliday gets out of bed, telling Van Fleet, "If I am going to die, let me die with the only friend I ever had." Doc really has two motives for joining Wyatt — his friendship for the latter; and because Ringo has joined forces with Clanton, and Doc has a lingering score from Dodge City to settle.

Young Billy Clanton is with his brother, and as the shootout unfolds, Wyatt can't bring himself to kill Billy; but Billy has his gun leveled at Wyatt and is prepared to kill him until Doc shoots the lad. Wyatt takes off his badge and drops it by Billy's body.

The film ends without offering a hint of any of the events that followed the real shootout. Doc remains in Tombstone, but the film concludes with Wyatt riding out of town, heading for California in search of Laura. But as he leaves, he tells Holliday, "I just want you to know I would never have made it without you."

Gunfight at the O.K. Corral continues the image of Wyatt Earp, Doc Holliday and the gunfight in Tombstone that began in films such as *Frontier Marshal* and *My Darling Clementine*. In that respect, the film mirrored the decade in which it was made (see Chapter 1), offering a great deal of continuity with the past. The images fashioned in *Gunfight at the O.K. Corral* were images Hollywood Westerns had been projecting on the silver screen ever since William S. Hart strapped on a pair of six-guns. But things were about to change.

Even though John Sturgis directed (and produced) *Hour of the Gun* (United Artists, 1967), just as he had *Gunfight at the O.K. Corral*, the two films are very different. The United States had begun to change in the ten years separating the two motion pictures. By 1967, the social and political consensus that had defined life in the 1950s was gone. The struggle over civil rights dominated the evening news as so-called freedom riders from the North flocked south during summers of the early 1960s to challenge racial segregation. Conflicts between federal authorities and the governors of several southern states over integration of public universities divided an already nervous public. The 1964 presidential election was the most ideologically divisive since 1932 and 1936. And if racial and ideological discord were not enough, the first waves of baby boomers were growing suspicious of the war in Southeast Asia. Their doubts were reinforced by Senate Foreign Relations Committee hearings led by its chairman, Senator William Fulbright of Arkansas. By 1967, the notion that politics stops at the water's edge was more fiction than fact. *Hour of the Gun* reflects a different country, a changing Hollywood and a more cynical, suspicious electorate than had existed when *Gunfight at the O.K. Corral* premiered.

As it opens with the famed shootout, *Hour of the Gun* proclaims, "This picture is based on fact. This is the way it happened." While Ike Clanton (Robert Ryan) bosses a gang of rustlers and thieves, politics appears to be the underlying motive for the shootout in *Hour of the Gun*. Early in the film, Clanton tells his gang, "Back East I could make law. Out here all I can do is buy it." Wyatt Earp (James Garner) is incorruptible and won't be bribed into going along with Clanton's schemes. Clanton stands for freedom of the range against easterners who want to restrict that freedom, and Clanton views Earp as an easterner.

The famous gunfight does not settle anything; the violence continues. Morgan Earp (Sam Melville) is killed the night he wins the election for town marshal, and Virgil Earp (Frank Converse) is crippled for life. But Wyatt becomes a United States Marshal and begins to use federal authority to hunt down those responsible for killing his brother. In his quest for vengeance, Wyatt is joined by Doc Holliday (Jason Robards).

Wyatt soon becomes obsessed with revenge, and regards the arrest warrants he carries as little more than licenses to kill. At one point a frustrated Doc Holliday tells Wyatt, "Those are not warrants, they are hunting licenses." And when Wyatt refuses a drink, Doc scoffs at him, "If you are going to kill like me, you might as well drink like me."

As *Hour of the Gun* unfolds, Wyatt becomes more revenge-minded. Enforcing the law by serving the arrest warrants becomes secondary to personal vengeance. In their last meeting at the sanitarium where Doc has gone for treatment of his tuberculosis, Wyatt vows to Holliday that he is going to find Clanton wherever he went. Symbolically, Wyatt trails Clanton to Mexico, a place where Earp has no authority, and kills him.

Hour of the Gun well reflects the United States in the middle 1960s. The Civil Rights movement, escalating conflict over American involvement in Vietnam, and increasing rancor between liberals and conservatives over the role of government in public life created a divisive political climate and the temptation to politicize every difference of opinion. Robert

Ryan's portrayal of Ike Clanton in *Hour of the Gun* underscores the increasing tendency by the mid–1960s to see every conflict, even historical ones, as politically motivated.

But in the film, Clanton is a bad guy, a criminal who wants political control in order to protect his illegal enterprises. James Garner's Wyatt Earp, on the other hand, is a federal marshal, committed to law and order. In the mid–1960s, public opinion still held generally positive views of public officials, and most citizens believed that law enforcement officers were honest and trustworthy. Yet, as stories about Martin Luther King Jr. and John F. Kennedy's personal lives began to surface, and as statements from President Lyndon Johnson and officials in the Pentagon about success in Vietnam became dubious, the American public began to doubt the veracity of men and women serving in government. James Garner's portrayal of Wyatt Earp as an increasingly revenge-motivated person, one willing to abuse his authority, became more acceptable to movie audiences. Garner's portrayal of Wyatt Earp as a complex man, as one who did not reflect the heroic qualities of Randolph Scott, Henry Fonda and Burt Lancaster in the earlier films about Earp, serves as a transition from those films to *Doc* (United Artists, 1971).

Unlike the films previously considered, the primary focus of *Doc* is on Stacy Keach as Doc Holliday. However, Harris Yulin's portrayal of Wyatt Earp is completely different from previous films. In *Doc*, Tombstone is a wide open town, and the Clantons, McLaurys and Johnny Ringo are bad people, but there is no suggestion as to why they are bad. But if they are bad (for whatever reason), Wyatt Earp is not much better. Earp hopes to be elected town marshal, and he proposes to Doc that he organize the gambling while Wyatt runs the law. Yulin's Wyatt Earp is corrupt; he intends to use the law for his own benefit.

When a stagecoach is robbed, Wyatt suspects Johnny Ringo of the crime, and he and Doc ride to Ike Clanton's (Mike Witney) ranch. But Wyatt has no authority outside of Tombstone, and Clanton gives him a severe beating in a fist fight, taunting Earp's inability to hide behind his guns. Rather than a brave man who is more than any man's equal in a brawl, Wyatt Earp is not very brave nor very good at fisticuffs. As Doc helps Wyatt clean up after the fistfight, Wyatt tells Doc, "I am going to have to kill him [Clanton]."

But as much as he wants revenge on Clanton, the corrupt Wyatt wants to win the election for town marshal even more. He sends word to Clanton that if he will turn over Johnny Ringo (Fred Dennis), Wyatt will make sure Clanton gets the $20,000 reward. Earp will get credit for capturing Ringo and undoubtedly win the election. Then Wyatt tells his brother Virgil (John Bottoms) that they will clean up Tombstone. Virgil replies, "You mean clean out Tombstone, don't you."

Doc Holliday begins to doubt this corrupt Wyatt. He tells Wyatt, "You've changed; I don't know you any more." Wyatt only replies that he does not understand Doc any more, and he blames Kate Elder (Faye Dunaway) for the change in his friend. Wyatt scolds Kate, "Ever since you hooked on to him, he ain't been himself. He can't think straight." (For more about Dunaway's Kate Elder and her relationship to Keach's Doc Holliday see Chapter 11.)

Doc becomes friends with The Kid (Denver John Collins). Holliday tries to talk the Kid out of becoming a gunfighter and siding with Clanton. Because Doc has begun to understand the emptiness of his life, he wants to redeem himself by saving the Kid. Doc tells Wyatt, "It's a different world." Holliday acknowledges that he is not going to live forever, and that he is sick of young kids gunning down old men. "I want to leave something behind," he tells Earp.

Ike Clanton appears to accept Wyatt's offer, but Clanton plans to take the money and then kill the Earps. When Wyatt learns of Clanton's treachery, he begins to work out a scheme to frame Ike for the robbery and murder of the stagecoach driver. That provides the motive for the shootout. According to *Doc*, the shootout occurred because Wyatt was going to frame Clanton for crimes he did not commit in order to enhance Earp's chances of being elected town marshal of Tombstone. Politics and personal ambition are the underlying motives for the shootout, and it was all arranged to get Wyatt Earp elected to public office.

In *Doc*'s version of the shootout, all of the Clantons and McLaurys are killed. Holliday kills the Kid, even after he holsters his gun, claiming that the Kid reminded him too much of himself. Morgan Earp (Philip Shafer) is also killed, and Wyatt uses his death as an opportunity to make a campaign speech, turning the ambition-driven killings into the triumph of law and order. Wyatt's speech reminds viewers that even before sound bites and spin doctors, politicians were inclined to hide personal ambition behind the cloak of public service.

For this book, *Doc* is an important film because of its revisionist image of Wyatt Earp. Harris Yulin's Wyatt Earp is a corrupt, glory-seeking human being who relishes power for its ability to enhance his personal wealth. Public-spirited speeches are mere ploys designed to cloak Earp's real motive of personal financial enhancement.

By 1971, Americans had begun to lose confidence in their elected public officials, and charges of police corruption and brutality were frequent. Richard Nixon had been elected in a bitterly fought 1968 presidential election, and he had never been able to shake the image of "tricky Dick" from earlier in his political career. The expansion of the war from Vietnam to Cambodia had ignited massive protests on college campuses and the streets of the nation's capitol. The siege of the American presidency that had begun during the Johnson years continued throughout Richard Nixon's first term in office! Certainly, the street riots in Chicago during the 1968 Democratic National Convention, with their allegations of police brutality, were yet fresh in the public's mind. *Doc* fits that climate of opinion.

Approximately twenty-two years would elapse between the release of *Doc* and the more celebrated *Tombstone* in 1993. In those intervening years, Americans continued to express little confidence in public officials, as scandals of all sorts shook national, state and local governments. Voting turnout plummeted as more and more citizens came to believe that elections changed very little because increasingly they were dominated by pollsters, sixty- and thirty-second television spots designed to manipulate the public rather than enlighten it, and slick public relations experts. In many ways Harris Yulin's portrayal of a politically corrupt Wyatt Earp in *Doc* fit better the public mood in 1993 than it had in 1971.

But more than political corruption was shaking public confidence in 1993. An ever-increasing urban and suburban population felt itself under siege from escalating crime rates and youthful gang violence. Casey Tefertiller notes that, "Crime emerged as a social issue again in the America of the late 1980s and early 1990s, with debates focusing on the same issues that had torn Arizona apart a century earlier" (Tefertiller, 343). And he continues, "It is inevitable that America rediscovers Wyatt Earp whenever lawlessness reigns" (Tefertiller, 343). Unlike *Doc*, *Tombstone* cast the showdown in Tombstone not as a contest between two equally corrupt power aspirants, but as a noble effort by Wyatt Earp, his brothers and Doc Holliday to stamp out the "cowboys," a functional equivalent of late-twentieth-century urban gangs.

Tombstone opens, as did *Pale Rider* (Warner Brothers, 1985), with the pounding hoofs of the "cowboys'" horses as they ride into a peaceful Mexican village celebrating a wedding. Curly Bill Brocius (Powers Booth), leader of the "cowboys," accuses the groom of killing two of his men. The "cowboys" then murder the groom and the assembled townsfolk, including

Kurt Russell's interpretation of Wyatt Earp in *Tombstone* (1993).

the priest. They drag the bride into the church as one of the "cowboys" pulls up her dress in preparation for the rape and murder surely to follow; all the while, Curly Bill and the other "cowboys" gorge themselves on the food of the wedding feast.

These opening scenes set the milieu of Tombstone and the surrounding countryside. Dominated by red-sashed "cowboys," Tombstone is a lawless, violent town where neither life nor property are protected. The Earps and Doc Holliday arrive in this milieu, not to establish law and order but to make money. Wyatt Earp (Kurt Russell) chases a tinhorn gambler and bully out of the Oriental Saloon, and he and his brothers run the gaming tables for one-quarter of the take. In addition, they buy up mining properties, but none of them turn out to be worth much.

The only law in Tombstone is Marshal Fred White (Harry Carey Jr.), a peaceful man who is powerless to stop the "cowboys" by himself. One evening Curly Bill goes to an opium den and gets high. When he starts to shoot up the town, Marshal White tries to take his gun from him, but Curly Bill shoots White (whether intentionally or by mistake is unclear). When the town leaders ask Wyatt (once again) to accept the marshal's position, he declines. Wyatt protests, as he had done before in the film, that he is through with guns and being a peace officer.

But when Virgil Earp (Sam Elliott) sees a little boy nearly run down in the street by a bunch of "cowboys," he accepts the marshal's badge and makes Morgan Earp (Bill Paxton) his deputy. That sets up the showdown with the Clantons and McLaurys. Wyatt, however, is a reluctant participant. He tells Virgil and Morgan that in all his days in Kansas he was only mixed up in one shooting. There is nothing very heroic about the shootout (just as one suspects was true of the real one), and Wyatt cynically tells the mayor, "Well I guess we did our good deed for the day, Mayor."

True to the history of the event, *Tombstone* does not end with the shootout. Wyatt and Doc Holliday (Val Kilmer) are indicted for murder, but the judge decrees that the evidence does not warrant charging them. The "cowboys," vowing revenge, kill Morgan and badly wound Virgil. Wyatt plots his own revenge, telling the "cowboys," "I am coming and Hell's coming with me." There is no hint of Wyatt becoming a U.S. Marshal; he is simply taking revenge on the "cowboys" for what they did to his brothers. Doc notes, "It is not revenge he [Wyatt] is after. It is a reckoning he is after." And he gets his reckoning. Wyatt kills Curly Bill, and Ike Clanton (Stephen Lang) escapes only after he throws away his red sash (which marked him as a "cowboy") while Wyatt chases him.

Kurt Russell's Wyatt Earp's vulnerability surfaces when Johnny Ringo (Michael Biehn) sends a challenge to meet him one-on-one. Doc Holliday is sick in bed at the time. Wyatt knows he is not fast enough to beat Ringo in a standup gunfight, an opinion that Doc acknowledges to be accurate. Nonetheless, Wyatt rides out to meet Ringo. Holliday, however, gets out of bed and meets Ringo before Wyatt. Earlier in the film, Ringo and Doc had had a confrontation at the Oriental Saloon. Doc reminds Ringo that they have some unfinished business, beats him to the draw, and kills him.

Tombstone ends with Wyatt visiting Doc in the sanitarium as Holliday lies dying from tuberculosis. The two men talk, and then Doc asks Wyatt to leave. Wyatt's parting words to the dying Holliday are, "Thanks for always being there, Doc." While the death scene in *Tombstone* does not parallel Doc Holliday's real-life death (for example, Wyatt Earp did not know his friend had died until some time had passed), there is one interesting parallel. Just before he died, Doc Holliday is reported to have said, "This is funny." Most biographers take that to mean that Holliday never thought he would die in bed from tuberculosis, but would be killed in a gun or knife fight. Val Kilmer's Doc Holliday (who, in my opinion, is the best characterization created by all the actors who ever played the famous gambler) catches that irony. Kilmer plays Holliday throughout *Tombstone* as a reckless, cynical man, one for whom life means very little.

Wyatt Earp leaves the dying Doc Holliday and goes to California in search of Josephine (Dana Delaney), who had left Tombstone before he and Doc started their killing rampage. Throughout *Tombstone* all Wyatt wants is a normal life, one free from the constant threat of some disgruntled "cowboy" trying to shoot him. As he goes to find Josephine, Wyatt acknowledges that he has nothing left — no pride and no money. He does not even know how he will make a living!

That sums up the last forty years or so of the real Wyatt Earp's life. He was a living legend constantly having to scratch for enough money to keep body and soul together! *Tombstone*, however, continually reminds viewers of the heroic nature of the Earp brothers. They brought law and order to the wild frontier towns and chased the "cowboys" out of Tombstone. Surely as urban viewers watched *Tombstone* in 1993 and 1994 they, too, wished that a Wyatt Earp would come along and clean up their urban communities. Tefertiller is surely right — as long as there are periods of lawlessness, the life and legend of Wyatt Earp will shine bright in American memory. It is no wonder that President Clinton took *Tombstone* with him on a visit to Russia to show Russians an example of American popular culture (Tefertiller, 343).

Wyatt Earp, with Kevin Costner in the lead role, is first and foremost a character study. Unlike the previous films about Earp that were mainly action pictures, from the beginning scenes in which young Wyatt attempts to run away from home to fight in the Civil War to the closing segments on the boat bound for Alaska, the key element which gives the film coherence (if indeed it has any) is probing Wyatt Earp's motivation. Why did Earp act the way he did? Why did he make the choices he made? What factors in his personality and social background shaped the man who would become a legend?

In approaching the man from that perspective, *Wyatt Earp* (Warner Brothers, 1994) tracks well with late twentieth century American fascination with homespun, do-it-yourself psychology. From publications such as *Psychology Today* to a plethora of talk show hosts who offered all sorts of advice to their guests (who in turn had all sorts of problems), Americans sought psychological explanations for every ill that befell them. And that preoccupation with psychology dovetailed with the urge to become intimate with heroes.

Americans no longer wanted public personalities, contemporary or historical, to possess an aura of mystery. Rather, public opinion insisted on knowing what made heroes tick. What motivated them to act as they did? What public masks hid private weaknesses? What personal secrets did public personalities try to hide from the light of public awareness?

By the mid–1990s the descent of the hero was complete. Americans no longer put their heroes on pedestals. They no longer shielded their idols' private lives from public scrutiny. Public personalities simply became like every other person as Americans disclaimed the sense of the heroic. The assault on the heroic appeared to abate after the attack on the World Trade Center on September 11, 2001. But appearances are deceiving. Rather than reclaim the heroic, the events of 9-11 further cheapened the concept. Everyone associated with the event became a hero, and two years later anyone who fought in Iraq was championed as a hero. As Americans enter the midpoint of the first decade of the twenty-first century, the concept of hero is an idea with little substance. It is the natural consequence of homespun, do-it-yourself psychology and the descent of the hero in popular culture that began fifty years ago.

Kevin Costner's interpretation of Wyatt Earp fits well that late twentieth century trend. Gene Hackman, playing Nicholas Earp — Wyatt's father — and a man about whom very little was known, offers a great deal of homespun psychological advice to his family. Nicholas tells young Wyatt (Ian Bohen), "When you take a job, you finish it." Sitting around the dinner table one night, the elder Earp advises his family, "Nothing counts as much as blood, the rest are just strangers." That view echoes later in *Wyatt Earp* when the now-grown-up Wyatt tells the Earp wives that they don't count as much as brothers. Wives, he says, come and go, they die; brothers remain forever.

Nicholas also advises young Wyatt that there is a great deal of viciousness in the world, and he warns him, "When you find yourself in a fight with such viciousness, hit first if you can, and when you do hit, hit to kill." That advice, too, is echoed when the adult Wyatt defends being a "deliberate man" to his friend and deputy Ed Masterson (Bill Pullman). Wyatt tells Masterson, "You are not a deliberate man, I do not sense that about you. You are too affable." When Masterson ignores Wyatt's warning, and after Wyatt has been asked by the Dodge City town fathers to turn in his badge, Masterson is murdered because he was not stern enough to maintain law and order in the famous cow town.

Surely one of the high points in *Wyatt Earp* occurs when Wyatt returns to Dodge City to resume his former position as town marshal. He bursts through the swinging doors of a particularly rowdy saloon, proclaiming,

Kevin Costner offered viewers a psychologically focused interpretation of the man in *Wyatt Earp* (1994).

"My name is Wyatt Earp!" Wyatt's motivation is psychological. He revels in being a "deliberate man" who acts promptly and often violently when confronted by vicious individuals.

Doc Holliday (Dennis Quaid) serves as Wyatt's friend, counselor and conscience. Doc, early in the film, tells Wyatt, "I know it is not easy being my friend, but I will be there when you need me." Wyatt in turn defends Doc. When Johnny Behan (Mark Harmon) accuses Doc of participating in a stagecoach robbery and killing the driver, Wyatt replies that Big Nose Kate (Isabella Rosselini) told him that only after Behan had gotten her drunk.

When Mattie (Mare Winningham) tries to kill herself with an over-dose of laudanum because she can't stand the thought of losing Wyatt to Josie (Joanna Going), Wyatt takes refuge in the Oriental Saloon, trying to console his guilty conscience with whiskey. Holliday assures Earp that he

[Holliday] confronts death every day, and that some people are better off dead than alive — and that might apply to Mattie. He adds that it "don't matter much whether we are here or not."

If Doc tries to assuage Wyatt's guilt over his behavior toward Mattie, he serves as Earp's conscience in the pursuit of the "cowboys." Wyatt is single-minded, driven in his determination to get them all. But Holliday reminds him that he can't kill them all, that his obsession with revenge will fail. And indeed it does, as the end of *Wyatt Earp* acknowledges.

Reasons for the shootout are murky at best in *Wyatt Earp*. The stage-coach holdup and the murder of Sheriff White highlight the hatred between the Earps and the Clantons and McLaurys. Clearly the latter are cattle rustlers, and Wyatt refuses Johnny Behan's offer of peace if he will coop-erate with them. But reasons for the intensity of the hatred between the two groups remain unexplained. And in *Wyatt Earp*, the shootout is pro-voked by Ike Clanton (Jeff Fahey) who is unarmed at the time. Virgil Earp (Michael Madsen) wants only to disarm the rest of them, but Morgan Earp (Linden Ashby) and Doc Holliday are looking for trouble. As the four men walk toward the showdown, Morgan tells Doc, who has a shotgun hidden under his coat, to kill them all.

In *Wyatt Earp* the shootout is pointless. It serves no purpose other than to underline the hatred — largely unexplained — of the Clantons and McLaurys for the Earps, a hatred the Earps heartily reciprocate. If it has no purpose, neither does it solve anything. The "cowboys" take revenge when they later murder Morgan and badly cripple Virgil. But that only escalates the violence. When Wyatt sees Virgil off to California (after he had been wounded) at the train station in Tucson, Virgil tells him to get them all. That sets Wyatt on a bloody trail of violence as Wyatt and Doc become wanted men when they murder those responsible for killing Mor-gan and wounding Virgil. But, as Doc warned Wyatt, they could not kill them all, so the drive for revenge falls short. In fact, the futility of vio-lence may be the whole point of *Wyatt Earp*. If so, that distinguishes the picture from other, more traditional, Westerns and gives it much in com-mon with *Unforgiven* (Warner Brothers, 1992). But there is another way of viewing the film.

In traditional Westerns, violence had to be legitimized in some fash-ion. Peace officers could use violence because it was their job to maintain law and order. The cowboy hero, even if he were not acting in any formal capacity, could use violence because he possessed a charisma that attracted people to him and validated his actions. But violence was also legitimate when avenging the murder of a parent or sibling, or to protect the family homestead. Tradition dictated such a response. No self-respecting father or son was expected to stand idly by while those responsible for murder of a family member, or theft of family property, went unpunished.

Costner's Wyatt Earp's response to the assault on his brothers is understandable as violence legitimized by tradition. And it is reinforced by Dennis Quaid's Doc Holliday. After Morgan Earp dies, Wyatt confronts a distraught Doc, who tells Wyatt that he loved that boy "like he was my own brother." At some point the pursuit of revenge becomes self-destructive, but up to that point the violence it perpetrates is legitimate. The murderers were not only hiding behind the law, they were being protected by it. In American culture, Costner's Wyatt and Quaid's Doc would have been regarded as less than men if they had simply ridden out of Tombstone without visiting retribution on those responsible for destroying their family.

But the violence in *Wyatt Earp* is more than tradition rooted in family; it is also a statement about how one must act when law enforcement agencies are corrupt. Johnny Behan is a corrupt cop. He is friends with criminals, and he tries to bribe Wyatt; hence, his warrants for the arrest of Wyatt and Doc are illegitimate, instruments designed to perpetuate his power rather than establish justice.

Increasingly in the last three decades of the twentieth century, Hollywood turned to the theme of urban vigilantes fighting criminals. Charles Bronson, Clint Eastwood, Sylvester Stallone and Bruce Willis became closely associated with that type of action motion picture. In one sense they are urban cowboy heroes (however, I do not regard the films as Westerns in any sense of the word) fighting corrupt legal bureaucracies and bringing justice to those protected by inefficient or powerless courts. Will Wright writes of these movies:

> These are films of urban paranoia where no one can be trusted and betrayal is everywhere. The hero must exist in a bureaucratic structure — the police, the government, a newspaper — where all his bureaucratic superiors are incompetent or corrupt. He must defy those superiors to defeat the villains, and he is commonly denounced and condemned as a "cowboy" — not a team player — by outraged bureaucrats [Wright, 22–23].

Yet because contemporary viewers recognize the corruption and the distortion of justice, the behavior of the hero (Eastwood, Bronson, Willis) remains legitimate. *Wyatt Earp* has more in common with films such as *Dirty Harry* (Warner Brothers, 1971) and *Die Hard* (20th Century–Fox, 1988) than it has with earlier films about the famous marshal. In *Frontier Marshal, My Darling Clementine* and *Gunfight at the O.K. Corral,* the hero is incorruptible, and he acts (as a peace officer) to protect lives and property. Even in *Hour of the Gun*, as James Garner's Wyatt Earp is consumed more and more by revenge, viewers understand that he is a United States Marshal and that he has a legitimate right to use violence. Even Val Kilmer as Doc Holliday wears a badge in *Tombstone*. That is not the case in *Wyatt Earp*.

Kevin Costner's Wyatt Earp has much more in common with Clint Eastwood's "Dirty Harry" and Bruce Willis' urban vigilante. He ignores warrants for his arrest after he kills two men in Tucson while seeing Virgil off to California, and he makes no pretense of legal authority when he goes gunning for the other "cowboys." There is a great gap separating Randolph Scott and Henry Fonda from Kevin Costner, and that gap speaks volumes about how much American culture had changed by the last decade of the twentieth century.

One other element in both *Tombstone* and *Wyatt Earp* is worth noting. While Mattie, Wyatt Earp's common law wife, had appeared as a marginal character in *Doc*, no film prior to the two released in the 1990s featured Josephine Marcus, the actress Earp would eventually marry. It is interesting that as social commentators, public officials, and popular culture rediscovered families in the last fifteen or so years of the twentieth century, both *Tombstone* and *Wyatt Earp* chose to explore that facet of the famous lawman's life.

In *Tombstone*, Dana Wheeler-Nicholson plays Mattie as a woman increasingly dependent on drugs, a mixture of opium and laudanum. Kurt Russell's Wyatt tries to maintain a relationship in the face of Mattie's erratic, drug-dependent behavior. Dana Delaney as Josephine is the one making a play for Wyatt in *Tombstone*. She makes a point of learning his identity when she arrived in Tombstone, and in the Oriental Saloon, after one of her performances, she invites Wyatt to dance with her, an invitation he declines.

At first, Wyatt brushes aside her obvious advances, but all of that changes one afternoon when he comes across Josephine while riding. She asks Wyatt what he wants out of life, and what is his idea of Heaven? Wyatt responds that he wants to make some money and to have children. Josephine, on the other hand, says that her idea of Heaven is room service. She wants to go places and to have fun. She tells Wyatt, "I am a woman; I like men."

Mattie becomes increasingly jealous of Josephine as she recognizes the growing attachment between Wyatt and her rival. But in *Tombstone*, the attraction is mostly one from a distance; Wyatt and Josephine are never shown being intimate. Mattie leaves Tombstone with the other Earp women after Morgan is killed and Virgil badly wounded. The last time Wyatt sees Josephine is at Henry Hooker's ranch as she is on her way to California. When Wyatt leaves Doc Holliday for the last time, Wyatt heads to California in search of Josephine. Mattie just fades into the background, no longer a part of Wyatt's life after she leaves Tombstone.

Wyatt Earp puts an entirely different spin on the relationships. According to this version, Wyatt sees Josephine (Joanna Going) for the first time as she performs in Dodge City, and he is infatuated by her. Mattie (Mare Winningham) is a prostitute who becomes Wyatt's common law wife. It is she who wants children, but Wyatt tells her that children were never part of the bargain. As in *Tombstone*, Mattie in *Wyatt Earp* is a suicide-prone, drug-dependent woman who grows increasingly jealous of Wyatt as she senses she is loosing him to Josephine. Mattie becomes violent, and at one point tries to shoot Wyatt. On other occasions she taunts him, urging Wyatt to return to his Jewish whore.

At first, after Johnny Behan (Mark Harmon) brings Josephine to Tombstone, she and Wyatt maintain an aloof, almost hostile relationship. But that changes when Behan begins to show a photograph of the bare-breasted Josephine around town. She leaves Behan and begins her association with Wyatt. Unlike Kurt Russell in *Tombstone*, Kevin Costner's Wyatt Earp makes no pretense of being faithful to Mattie; and when she leaves town with the rest of the women, it is clear that Wyatt is now with Josephine. Earlier in *Wyatt Earp*, Josephine asked Wyatt about his relationship with Mattie. Wyatt replied, "We have been together for a while. She uses my name." And *Wyatt Earp* includes at least one scene that shows Josephine and Costner becoming intimate before Mattie leaves Tombstone.

But in both *Wyatt Earp* and real life (and unlike in *Tombstone*), Josephine stays with Wyatt as he and Doc Holliday carry out their revenge-minded blood bath against the "cowboys." In real life, as well as the film, Josie (Wyatt called her Sadie) was with him until Earp died in 1929.

It is striking, however, with all the criticism leveled at unfaithful spouses and philandering public officials in the 1990s, that *Wyatt Earp* would deal straightforwardly with Wyatt's unfaithfulness to Mattie and the open manner in which Josephine became Earp's lover. That, along the utter lack of legal pretense as Wyatt and Doc kill "cowboys," makes *Wyatt Earp* a paradoxical film.

Chapter 10

"INDIANS ARE HUMAN BEINGS"

From the perspective of the first decade of the twenty-first century, it is difficult to imagine a country in which African Americans, Hispanics and Native Americans were denied access to the same public accommodations as Caucasians, and were not guaranteed equal protection of the laws in many other ways. That same America regarded persons of the Jewish faith as inferior to Christians, and established Jewish quotas at leading universities, and practiced discriminatory employment and housing policies. Even whites from parts of Europe other than Great Britain, Ireland and Germany were called Spics, Polacks, and Dagoes, or labeled in other demeaning ways. But that was the United States scarcely a half century ago, a country governed by white males of northern European extraction. Archie Bunker in the popular 1970s television series *All in the Family* may have been a caricature, but it was one reflected in the attitudes of many small towns across the width and breadth of America!

For the first sixty years or so of the twentieth century, popular culture reflected and reinforced those attitudes. Radio's long-time hit program *Amos 'n' Andy* utilized white-generated caricatures of African Americans: Andy Brown as not-so-bright, gullible stooge; George "Kingfish" Stevens as the lazy, conniving shyster; and Lightnin' as the slow moving, slurry speeched black male all fit pervasive white images of African Americans. Motion pictures, too, reinforced those caricatures, as the characters portrayed by African Americans, Hispanics and Indians reflected white stereotypes (for a full discussion of those stereotypes see Chapters 8 and 9 in my *Westerns and American Culture, 1930–1955*).

While public policies changed little in the 1950s, change, nonetheless, was in the air. Even though the Supreme Court's ruling in *Brown v Board of Education* (347 U.S. 483) had little immediate impact on policies that affected the lives of most racial minorities, it did energize the Black community. Congress responded with a weak civil rights act in 1957, but it proved a significant achievement because it was the first piece of civil rights legislation to clear Congress since the end of Reconstruction in 1876. In the South, the integration of Central High School in Little Rock, Arkansas, and the Montgomery, Alabama, bus boycott led by Dr. Martin Luther King, began a process of racial equality that, while not yet fully realized, would culminate in the passage of the Civil Rights Act of 1964 and the Voting Rights Act of 1965. In the North, public accommodations of all sorts (public swimming pools, restaurants, etc.) were effectively integrated by 1960.

Gradually, Westerns began to reflect the new emerging America, as the treatment of Native Americans on film changed dramatically from the mid–1950s to the end of the century. In fact, Indians became symbolic of other racial minorities, as Westerns began to assume a perspective different from that of white males. This chapter explores the shifting images of Indians in Western films after 1955 as an example of the manner in which Westerns grappled with the broader political and social movements toward racial and ethnic equality, and the ever increasing reality of cultural diversity in the country during the last forty-five years of the twentieth century.

The 1950s opened with the screening of *Broken Arrow* (20th Century–Fox, 1950). It is certainly not the first Western to project a positive image of Indians, but the inclusion of a major Hollywood personality such as James Stewart, and the film's "A" production qualities, gave *Broken Arrow* greater visibility than the average, run-of-the-mill Western. James Stewart and Jeff Chandler (playing the Apache Indian Cochise) establish a close friendship, and Stewart even marries an Indian maiden, Sonseeahray, played by Debra Paget. Although Paget dies before any children result from the union (that probably would have been asking too much of white audiences in 1950), the film makes no effort to deemphasize the marriage between an Indian woman and a white man. *Broken Arrow* shows Indians as a people who value family and want to live in peace with their neighbors.

That theme was reflected in another 1950 film, *Devil's Doorway* (MGM, 1950). In the latter, it is an Indian male and a white female who fall in love; and Robert Taylor learns that, as an Indian, he could not live as an equal to whites in their world. In both films, the culprits are irrational, Indian-hating whites.

If *Broken Arrow* and *Devil's Doorway* project positive images of Indians, *The Searchers* (Warner Brothers, 1956) offers viewers a negative one. Henry Brandon's (Scar) marauding Comanches raid, murder, burn, rape and kidnap because they are savages sworn to destroy all white people. John Wayne may have played an Indian-hating psychopath in the film, but his behavior is not totally irrational. How could one defend murder, rape and kidnapping? If the image of Indians in *The Searchers* is valid, the complete destruction of Indians is the only course for white people to choose. When Ward Bond and his band of rangers swoop down on Brandon's camp at the climax of *The Searchers*, the killing of Indians elicits little objection from white viewers. It is the appropriate response to Indian behavior in the film. *The Searchers* offers a view of Indians totally at odds with the two 1950 films.

So the issue is raised! Which view — that of *Broken Arrow* and *Devil's Doorway*, or that of *The Searchers* — would Hollywood choose as the 1950s evolved into the 1960s? Initially, and for the most part, Hollywood chose to stress the latter. Increasingly, Westerns focused on conflict between the two races and made little effort to understand either Indian culture or the white settlement of the western frontier from an Indian perspective. The dominant image of Indians is one of savage opposition to whites. Indians (increasingly Apaches) kill whites simply because they are there to be killed. And Indians kidnapping white women and children is a theme that appears with some regularity in Westerns between 1955 and the mid–1960s.

In *Dakota Incident* (Republic, 1956) Dale Robertson portrays an Indian-hating, yet frontier savvy bank robber. Robertson loathes Washington politician Ward Bond (as Senator Blakely). Bond is on a tour of the West to ensure fair treatment for the Indians, and he believes that they are a people who listen to reason. When Indians attack the stagecoach in which Robertson and Bond are riding, the passengers, with the exception of hero Dale Robertson and leading lady Linda Darnell, are all killed, including Bond. Bond had jumped from the ditch in which the Indians had the passengers pinned in order to reason with them. Clearly the Indians did not understand that they were an abused people and that Ward Bond was their friend! And there is no explanation for the Indian assault on the stagecoach other than it was carrying white passengers.

Guns of Fort Petticoat (Universal-International, 1957) and *Sergeant Rutledge* (Warner Brothers, 1960) include similar images of Indians. Audie Murphy, in the former, helps a group of Texas women learn how to handle firearms so they can beat off an Indian attack on the vacated mission in which they have taken refuge. Again, the only explanation for Indian hostility is that they use the Sand Creek Massacre as an excuse to raid defenseless women whose men are away fighting in the Civil War. The film also plays on the stereotype of superstitious Indians who will only fight when the medicine man says conditions are right to attack. In an absurd climax, Murphy kills the medicine man and hangs his dead body on the front door of the mission to force the rest of the Indians to give up their assault on the women.

Sergeant Rutledge includes remarkable images of black soldiers for a film made in 1960, but that understanding does not extend to Native Americans. The Indians in *Sergeant Rutledge* have left the reservation to raid and murder. They kill a railroad station master and would have killed Constance Towers, the leading lady in the film, had Woody Strode not arrived in time to save her. Later in the picture, the black cavalry unit engages in a running fight with the Indians, and the Indians kill Towers' father. Strode assures Towers he saw her father killed and that it was quick; he was not tortured.

Tomahawk Trail (United Artist, 1957) is a pedestrian, undistinguished B Western, but its image of Indians—Mescalero Apaches—reflects the notion of Indian as savage raider constantly at war with white soldiers. Chuck Connors, as Sergeant Wade McCoy, narrates the film. George Neise, as Lieutenant Jonathan Davenport, does not understand Apaches, even though he has fought Sioux in the Dakotas. Neise insists that the Apaches won't attack the soldiers because they are not at war. Connors replies to that sentiment, "I know Apaches. We are never at peace." And Connors assures Neise that the Apaches know where they are: "Mescaleroes can hear a butterfly ten miles away." Indeed, the Apaches do attack and steal the cavalry horses. But in a fight with a small band of Apaches, the cavalry unit captures two women, one a white woman who had been taken hostage when the Indians burned a fort, and the other a daughter of Victorio, the Mescalero chief.

Once the straggling band of survivors reach Fort Bowie, they discover that the Indians have attacked and killed all of the soldiers and salted the well. The only thing that saves them is that Lisa Montell, playing Tula the Indian girl, escapes and returns to her father, who lifts the siege and leaves the remaining soldiers alive.

Comanche Station (Columbia, 1960) and *Two Rode Together* (Columbia, 1961) focus on the theme of Indians kidnapping white women and children. Randolph Scott trades for Nancy Gates (Mrs. Lowe), who had been kidnapped by the Indians, in *Comanche Station*. Scott's wife had been kidnapped as well ten years before, and Scott has never given up looking for her. He also has to ward off an attack when the Indians try to take Gates back. In *Two Rode Together* (see Chapter 2 for more details about this film), James Stewart and Richard Widmark try to buy back white captives from Quannah Parker, the Comanche chief. Woody Strode, as Stone Calf, may be the most absurd image of an Indian in any Western ever produced.

Hollywood advertisements of their film productions throughout the 1950s highlighted conflict between Indians and whites. The title lobby card for *Fort Bowie* (United Artists, 1958) declares:

> When America's frontier fort became an Apache massacre-ground
>   no man surrendered....
>   no woman was spared...
> as the two nations clashed in the death-battle that shook the desert.

The title card for *Fort Yuma* (United Artists, 1955) began, "In all the blood-drenched annals of Apache warfare..." And the title card of *Blood Arrow* (20th Century–Fox, 1958) heralded the movie as a story about "Hired guns against Blackfoot savages."

Some films, however, built on the image of Indians seen in *Broken Arrow*. Three films in the mid–1950s are examples of a more positive treatment of Indians: *The Vanishing American* (Republic, 1955), *7th Cavalry* (Columbia, 1956) and *Walk the Proud Land* (Universal-International, 1956). *7th Cavalry* opens with Randolph Scott (playing Captain Tom Benson) returning to his post with his new bride, only to learn that Custer and his entire company have been killed at the Little Big Horn. Custer had granted Scott leave from the post in order to get married, but the fact that he inadvertently avoided the dire fate of his unit becomes a black cloud hanging over Scott's head. What makes *7th Cavalry* interesting is that both Michael Pate (as Captain Benteen) and Frank Wilcox (Major Reno) blame Custer for disobeying orders and unnecessarily dividing his command in search of personal glory. The Indians are not portrayed as unintelligent savages. Custer was simply overwhelmed by a superior force,

Title card from *The Vanishing American* (1955). Note the embrace between Scott Brady (playing a mixed race character) and Audrey Totter (lower left). It was unusual in 1950s Westerns for that sort of intimacy to cross racial bondaries.

Indians whose fighting ability Custer did not take seriously and who were defending their families and hunting grounds.

Scott volunteers to lead a burial detail to the valley of the Little Big Horn, but as the column enters the valley they discover that the Indians have marked it as sacred ground and will resist any effort to remove the bodies of the dead soldiers, particularly that of General Custer. As Indians surround the burial detail, Scott engages Pat Hogan (Young Hawk) in a revealing conversation. Hogan tells Scott that the Indians believe that if the body of Custer is removed, his spirit will go with the body and that the Indian victory will be lost. Hogan had been to white schools, but he rebuffs Scott's response that the Indian belief is superstition. It appears that the Indians will kill the burial detail — until Comanche, Custer's horse, the lone survivor of the fight, appears on a ridge. The Indians believe that it is the spirit of Custer, and they let the burial detail pass unharmed.

Even though the image in *7th Cavalry* is one of superstitious Indians, their humanity is also apparent. They honor the corpses of their dead enemies, and they have carefully buried Custer. When they become convinced that Custer's spirit is in Comanche, they permit the burial detail to leave the valley unharmed. While *7th Cavalry* includes many of the stereotypes that dominated Western movie presentations of Indians, it is not the harsh depiction of Indians found in a film such as *The Searchers*. In that sense, *7th Cavalry* is a transitional film, one that contains a more positive view of Indians.

The Vanishing American is a picture whose obvious sympathies are with Native Americans. Anticipating the end of the film, one in which Scott Brady, the half-breed hero of *The Vanishing American*, dies, Republic wrote in the prologue, "Today the forces of justice and tolerance are writing a new ending." *The Vanishing American*, a modest B movie, has a great deal in common with Tim McCoy's *The End of the Trail* (Columbia, 1932) and Gene Autry's *The Cowboy and the Indians* (Columbia, 1949), the two most pro–Indian B Westerns ever produced. Like the Autry programmer, in *The Vanishing American* the Navajos are being exploited by a corrupt Indian agent and a crooked store owner.

Audrey Totter (as Marian Warner), billed second to Scott Brady in the credits— but in many ways the *real* star of *The Vanishing American*, arrives on the Navajo Indian reservation to take possession of a waterhole that she inherited from her uncle. It is the only water in the area, and Totter intends to make money by fencing in the waterhole and selling the water. Initially, she treats Indians and whites alike — very rudely. Then she begins to understand that Gloria Castillo (Yashi) is held in literal bondage by trading post proprietor Forrest Tucker (Morgan), and that through violence, Tucker and Gene Lockhart (Blucher), the Indian agent, keep the Navajo in a constant state of fear. They murder, extort and kill sheep as ways to exploit and cow the Indians who are supposed to be their wards.

Scott Brady, playing the half-breed Blandy, is the one person Tucker and Lockhart can't control. Gradually Brady and Totter join forces to oppose Tucker and Lockhart, and to ensure just treatment for the Navajos. James Millican (Walker), a United States Marshal and a relative of Totter, arrives on the scene during the climactic gun battle between the Navajos (led by Brady) and Tucker's gunmen. Millican, a symbol of federal authority, stands for law, order and justice. Even though Brady dies at the end of the film, it is clear that Tucker and Lockhart, both of whom die as well, will no longer be able to prey on the Navajos who want only to raise sheep and their families on a peaceful reservation. Rather than bloodthirsty savages who hate all whites, the Navajos are merely victims preyed upon by evil whites.

Audie Murphy's John Clum in *Walk the Proud Land* is the opposite of Tucker and Lockhart in *The Vanishing American*. Sent by the Interior Department to serve as Indian agent at the San Carlos reservation in 1876, Murphy in *Walk the Proud Land* expresses the tension that existed between the Interior Department and the Army. Too often overlooked by historians, who regard Ulysses Grant as one of the weakest — if not *the* weakest — of all the American presidents, is Grant's genuine concern for the plight of American Indians.

As William S. McFeely notes, Grant had a "commitment to prevent the extermination of the Native Americans" (McFeely, 305). Grant favored a course that would civilize the tribes and ultimately make them United States citizens. Grant wanted to transform Indians from wandering nomads to Christian farmers. He honored their claims to the land on which they lived, and he rejected the notion that they were savages to be exterminated, if possible, and if not, to be completely controlled (McFeely, 311). Those sentiments were at odds with the views embraced by Generals Philip Sheridan and William Tecumseh Sherman, his old comrades-in-arms from the Civil War.

Murphy's Clum has a letter of empowerment from President Grant, as well as authority from the Department of Interior. His view, expressed to Morris Ankrum (General Wade) as "the problems of human beings are the same everywhere," is at odds with the military policy of harsh rule. Murphy discovers that Apache leaders are kept in chains as a warning to others who might want to leave San Carlos. He also learns that food supplies are inadequate, but that the Apaches are not permitted guns to hunt for themselves. Murphy unchains the leaders, forces the soldiers off of San Carlos, organizes an Indian police system, and returns guns to them so they can hunt their own food. He even becomes a blood brother to the Apaches. In short, Murphy treats Indians as human beings; he restores their pride and dignity. And they reward Murphy by helping him capture Geronimo!

John Ford's last Western, *Cheyenne Autumn* (Warner Brothers, 1964), continues several of the themes found in *Walk the Proud Land*. According to Ronald Davis, Ford had wanted to do a story that told the truth about Indians (Davis 1995, 321). As Davis comments about *Cheyenne Autumn*, "The Indians are no longer the savage enemies of an advancing civilization;

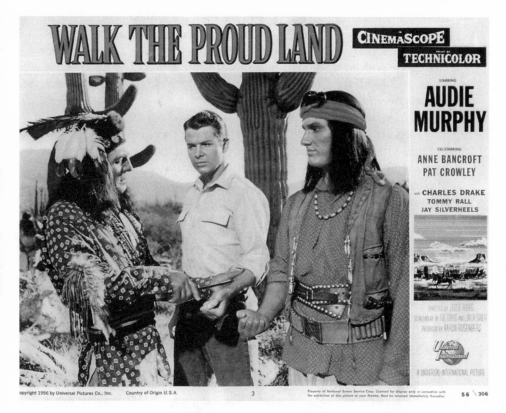

Audie Murphy plays Indian agent John Clum, who cares for the Indians' welfare and becomes a blood brother to Tommy Rall in *Walk the Proud Land* (1956).

they are the tragic heroes, the dispossessed. The cavalry has become the pawn of a remote and vindictive government" (Davis 1995, 328).

Although critics of the day did not like the film (Davis 1995, 327), Jon Tuska proved more perceptive when he labeled it "a sad and beautiful picture" (Tuska 1976, 519). Tuska maintains that the film rises to a "delicate elegy," depicting the tragedy befalling Indians as their numbers dwindled (Tuska 1976, 519).

Cheyenne Autumn unfolds on both a political level and a human one, in which viewers meet man's inhumanity to man. Edward G. Robinson, as Carl Schurz, the Secretary of the Interior, wants fair and humane treatment for the Indians (in that, he represents the Grant approach). Members of Congress and military officers disagree. They stand for the extermination, as much as possible, of all Indians so that white settlers can inhabit their lands. Sounding like Murphy's John Clum, Robinson asserts that, "Indians are human beings with the rights of human beings." But he is trapped by Washington, D.C. politics, and he must guard his steps so that his enemies will not politically destroy him and put in his place someone whose policies track with the aims of white settlers and the military. At the political level, *Cheyenne Autumn* highlights the conflict within the federal government over appropriate Indian policy, a conflict often overlooked in histories of the West.

Richard Widmark, as Captain Thomas Archer, narrates *Cheyenne Autumn*. Of the one-thousand Cheyenne removed to the barren Oklahoma desert, only 286 remain alive. Widmark concludes that they "are as far out of place as eagles in a cave." The Cheyenne are starving to death, and dying from small pox and malaria. But they are hopeful. *Cheyenne Autumn* opens as the Indians gather at a military outpost, eagerly awaiting a congressional delegation that they anticipate will permit the Cheyenne to return to their ancient homes in the north. But the congressional delegation fails to appear. They encountered dust storms and rough roads on the way to the reservation and decided to return to the fort in order to prepare for an upcoming officer's ball!

If the congressional delegation is indifferent to Indian suffering, the commander, played by former cowboy star George O'Brien, proves equally cold-hearted. He tells an outraged Carroll Baker (Deborah Wright), the missionary teacher at the reservation, that he only guards the Indians. He does not care whether or not the congressional delegation understands the Indians' sufferings. "When you have reached my age," O'Brien tells Baker, "You will have learned it pays to tend to your knitting."

White indifference to the Cheyenne plight is not lost on the Indians. Ricardo Montalban, as Little Wolf, tells Widmark, "Indians are asked to remember much. The white man remembers nothing." And Montalban orders the Indian children to no longer attend the reservation school: "White man's words are lies, better children not learn them."

Gilbert Roland (as Dull Knife) decides that there will be no more dying in this place, so the Cheyenne begin the long trek back to their ancient lands, an event that Widmark calls "a footnote in history." Yet it is an event that provokes military intervention and arouses white animosity. The Cheyenne trek north becomes a symbol of Indian resistance, and Washington politicians, frontier settlers, and the military want it crushed. But the Cheyenne make it to Fort Robinson in northern Nebraska, and it appears— momentarily, at least — that they have won.

Karl Malden (Captain Oscar Wessels) seems sympathetic to the Indian plight. He orders food and shelter for the survivors of the long march. Malden assures Widmark and Baker that he does not believe in a policy of extermination. However, Malden's sentiments change when he is ordered to hold the Cheyenne prisoners and return them to Oklahoma. Cheyenne resistance to returning to the barren land from which they fled clashes with Malden's Prussian authoritarianism. Malden will not tolerate opposition to his words, so he denies the Cheyenne food, blankets and warmth until they bend to his will.

In the end, the Cheyenne, at the cost of several dead, break out of Fort Robinson. They are only saved from extermination, however, by Edward G. Robinson's forceful intervention to circumvent the military decision to either return them to Oklahoma or exterminate the remaining members of the band.

Ford claimed that he wanted to make *Cheyenne Autumn* so that, "The audience not only met the Indian face to face, but got to know and admire him" (Davis 1995, 328). Ford tried to accomplish his goal by telling the story from the Indians' perspective. *Cheyenne Autumn* invites viewers to remember that the settling of the Trans-Mississippi West was not without social cost. There were people living on the land before the whites arrived. Those native people were displaced and their culture nearly destroyed. The lesson coming from *Cheyenne Autumn* is that while white Americans celebrate the settling of the frontier as a defining moment in American history, there is also much to mourn — and there is much of which to be ashamed. By the mid–1960s, white Americans were readier to reflect on that lesson. *Cheyenne Autumn* may not have been the first to make that case, but it does so more poignantly than most Westerns that preceded it. And as Ronald Davis observes, "In that regard it was a forerunner of New West history" (Davis 1995, 321).

Hombre (20th Century–Fox, 1967) offers an equally sympathetic — but different — view of Indians than *Cheyenne Autumn*. Paul Newman plays the central character in *Hombre*, John Russell, a mixed race man raised by a whites. John Russell Sr. gave him his white name, but Newman chose to live as a White Mountain Apache on the San Carlos reservation. He served as a member of the reservation police force.

Hombre opens as Newman learns that the stagecoach line for which they catch and tame wild horses is going out of business, to be replaced by the railroad. White civilization and progress has once again intruded on the Apache way of life. But Newman also learns that John Russell has died and left him a gold watch and a two-story boarding house in Sweetwater.

Martin Balsam (as Mendez) tells Newman of his inheritance. Balsam challenges Newman to come out of the mountains, speak English, cut his hair and live like a white man. Even though Balsam is Mexican, he assures Newman that he is closer to being white than any White Mountain Apache. Balsam wants Newman to put himself on the winning side for a change.

Newman does as Balsam suggests. The next time Newman appears on screen it is as a white man with short hair who speaks English. But he decides to sell the boarding house, and he winds up on an ill-fated stage-coach with a motley group of passengers, two of whom are Frederick March, playing Favor, the Indian agent from the San Carlos reservation, and Barbara Rush (Audrey Favor), his wife.

When March learns that Newman grew up on the reservation and served in the police force there, he considers it inappropriate for an Indian to ride in a coach with white passengers, particularly himself and his wife. So Newman rides on top with Balsam. But March is far from an upstanding person; he is absconding with several thousand dollars he has swindled from the reservation. March and Rush hope to get to Mexico and then take a boat for Europe.

Richard Boone (Grimes) and his gang know about March's plans, so they stop the coach, turn the horses loose, take Rush hostage and leave the remaining passengers stranded. Newman kills some of the gang, reclaims the money and starts off in pursuit of the rest of the outlaws. The irony is that the rest of the passengers need Newman's skills learned as an Apache to survive the desert and the outlaws, who want the money back. Newman, the social outcast, is their only hope of survival!

The last third of the film is familiar to those who know Westerns. Running gun battles and the search for water reach a climax, with the passengers and the outlaws holed up in an abandoned mine. Finally, Boone ties Rush to a post in the hot sun and threatens to let her die unless he gets the money.

In the shootout that ends *Hombre*, Newman and all of the outlaws are killed. The film surely had to end with Newman's death; white society was not yet ready for a mixed-race White Mountain Apache to live with it as an equal. In that sense, *Hombre* was symbolic of white attitudes toward both Native Americans and African Americans in 1967. For the most part, the days of demeaning segregation had passed, but the white community was still uncertain about the extent to which racial minorities ought to be accepted by white society. The passengers needed Newman's Apache skills to survive, but they were not yet ready to accept him as an equal. In the 1960s, whites could cheer the athletic exploits of racial minorities (such as baseball great Hank Aaron) and appreciate the artistic ability of African

Americans (such as Sidney Poitier and Nat King Cole), but many of those same whites were reluctant to embrace social and economic equality.

Custer of the West (Cinerama, 1967) offers a contrasting view of the conflict between whites and Indians. Early in the film, Lawrence Tierney (as General Philip Sheridan) offers Robert Shaw (Custer) several options for post–Civil War service. But Tierney warns Shaw, "They don't pin medals on you for killing Indians and stealing their lands." Shaw, Tierney counsels, will not find much glory in chasing the best light cavalry in the world. Tierney's words are complimentary to Indians, and viewers assume that they contrast with Shaw's glory-hunting motives. Because he wants action, Shaw ignores Tierney's advice and chooses a frontier command that puts him in the thick of the conflict with the Cheyenne.

Shaw is able to chase the Cheyenne back to the reservation and keep them there — until they raid and burn a town celebrating the Fourth of July. By now, however, Tierney's attitude toward Indians has changed; he wants the Cheyenne destroyed. Tierney even uses the well-worn phrase "the only good Indian is a dead Indian" to describe his policy. Furthermore, Tierney informs Shaw that it is election time and the administration needs a victory. It is up to Shaw to give the administration that victory. Custer's famed raid on the Cheyenne Washita River camp, a raid that killed mostly women and children, is explained in *Custer of the West* as provoked by Washington politics. In fact, Shaw is shown sitting on a white horse dictating a letter to Tierney as the raid unfolds. He notes that the raid was successful because the women and children offered little resistance. Politics, not Shaw's quest for glory or his Indian-hating manner, is the root cause of the Washita River raid in *Custer of the West*.

The film's ultimate point, however, is contained in an exchange between Shaw and Kierone Moore (playing Dull Knife). Shaw acknowledges that Indians have human rights, treaty rights and moral rights, but none of that concerns him. He [Shaw] is a soldier, not a philosopher, politician or moralist. It is his responsibility to obey orders and to keep the Cheyenne on the reservation. The rightness or morality of that policy is of no concern to Shaw. He reminds Moore that Cheyenne pushed other tribes off of their land without considering the moral consequences of such action. The Cheyenne are simply paying the price for being a backward people confronting a superior civilization.

In many ways, *Custer of the West* is a cynical motion picture. Its underlying philosophy is that right or wrong do not matter. Ultimately, might makes right; a law of history requires that inferior peoples and civilizations must give way to those with superior technology and methods. In the film, Robert Shaw is both the exponent and victim of that outlook! Social Darwinism was a dominant social theory in the latter part of the nineteenth century (and, to some extent, remains so today). The theory extended Darwin's survival of the fittest theory about the animal kingdom to social relationships in the human community. Only the fittest prospered and ultimately survived. From Shaw's perspective, the Cheyenne were an inferior people doomed to extinction when confronted by a superior people. Right and wrong had little to do with the conflict; it was simply the law of nature!

Shaw becomes a victim of his own words. The railroads advance west, and that provokes further Indian resistance. Shaw finds himself caught in a contradiction. On the one hand, he is encouraged to treat Indians as human beings and to enforce treaty rights. On the other, he is required to use military power to destroy Indians and ignore treaty obligations. Shaw begins to understand that the political process has been corrupted by profit seekers.

Money dictates policy. The Indians, as well as he himself, are victims of a two-faced policy of making treaties while at the same time killing Indians, all in the name of whatever is best for the railroads. When Shaw objects, he is relieved of command and returns to Washington under court marital. But, according to *Custer of the West*, Shaw is somewhat vindicated. He brings down Secretary of War Belknap and ties President Grant's brother into the railroad corruption. But Shaw pays a price for angering highly placed politicians; he is ignored by his military superiors and left to wallow in eastern obscurity.

While in Washington, D.C., Tierney arranges for Shaw to see a new invention, an armored, almost tank-like, vehicle mounted on railroad tracks. The inventor assures Shaw that it will change the nature of warfare. Machines will replace men as the ultimate fighting weapons. Shaw is incensed at the notion that men will become obsolete in warfare, that combat will no longer be an occasion for glory, merely for killing.

Shaw ultimately rejoins his command as part of the famous three-pronged military campaign against the hostile Sioux and Cheyenne in Montana. As the 7th Cavalry rides into the Little Bighorn Valley, Shaw divides his command. As his part of the command approaches a ridge, Shaw tells a young officer to keep the troop at that spot; they are not to advance further. Shaw then rides with a trooper to the top of the ridge, where he sees a long line of Indians ready for combat.

The Indians advance toward them, and Shaw engages Kieron Moore

(Dull Knife) in a conversation. Shaw acknowledges that his way of life is over, as well as that of the Cheyenne. Machines have replaced men; men are no longer relevant as combat instruments. Not only have Darwinian laws of survival of the fittest destroyed Indians, advancing technology has destroyed the way of life that Shaw values. If superior whites destroyed inferior Indian civilization, now whites with superior technology and capital are destroying and enslaving those whites who do not possess that technology and capital. In that sense, *Custer of the West* anticipates one of the themes addressed in *Dead Man* (Miramax, 1995) by some twenty-eight years.

When Moore's Indians reply to Shaw's pleas by shooting their guns in the air, the young officer ignores his orders and advances the troop. The end result is, of course, that Custer and his command are killed. In *Custer of the West*, both Custer and the Indians are victims; one is victim of an advancing superior white civilization, and the other is a victim of a profit driven, increasingly technological society, and of a young officer who disobeyed orders. But even if the young officer had not ignored Shaw's command, Shaw, like the Indians, had no future. Like the Indians, Shaw's way of life was bound to be replaced by its profit driven, technological counterpart. Ultimately, *Custer of the West* opts for a social Darwinistic explanation of the Indian wars.

Five years later, *Ulzana's Raid* (Universal, 1972) would employ a different interpretation of Indian behavior. Joaquin Martinez (Ulzana) and a handful of Apaches flee the San Carlos reservation and begin raiding the surrounding countryside. Burt Lancaster (McIntosh), a savvy Indian scout, accompanies Bruce Davison (Lieutenant Garnett DeBuin), fresh out of West Point on his first independent command, and a troop of cavalry intent on capturing Ulzana. *Ulzana's Raid* is most interesting for this study because it relies on cultural relativism and naturalism to explain the Apache's behavior.

In a conversation with Davison, Jorge Luke (Ke-Ni-Tay), an Apache scout accompanying the troop, explains why Apaches kill and torture. The troop have come across the body of a dead man and his wife, but fine that Ulzana had spared a young boy. Luke explains that Apaches believe that when they kill a man, that man's power flows to the one who killed him. There is no power in killing a woman or child. So Apaches kill to obtain power; it is part of the cultural expression of their worldview.

Lancaster adds to that perspective when Davison asks him if he hates

One man alone understood the savagery of the early American west from both sides.

BURT LANCASTER
In
ULZANA'S RAID

co-starring
BRUCE DAVISON   **RICHARD JAECKEL** Music by *FRANK DeVOL* · Written by *ALAN SHARP*
Directed by *ROBERT ALDRICH*   Produced by *CARTER DeHAVEN* · *A CARTER DeHAVEN-ROBERT ALDRICH PRODUCTION* [R]
    A UNIVERSAL PICTURE · TECHNICOLOR®
                                                                72/381

In *Ulzana's Raid* (1972), Burt Lancaster is the army scout wise in the ways of the Apache who helps hunt down Ulzana.

Apaches. Lancaster replies that hating Apaches would be irrational; it would be like hating the desert. Apaches, like the desert, are the way they are because of their nature. Apaches, like untamed animals such as lions or tigers, act the way they act because of their natural instincts. It is irrational to hate a lion that acts like a lion, and it is irrational to hate the desert for being the desert. Things such as lions and deserts are to be respected, even feared and caged, but not hated. So it is with Apaches.

White persons, with different cultural orientations and contrasting natures, are supposed to behave differently. Davison is angered when he discovers some of his troopers mutilating the dead body of an Apache; the white soldiers are behaving like Apaches, not whites. Davison orders them to stop the mutilation and bury the body. Lancaster observes that when whites behave like Apaches, "It kind of confuses the issue." Naturalism explains Apache behavior; it does not explain the actions of the white soldiers. But naturalism can ultimately lead to despair and inhibit the ability to render judgment. Lancaster voices that possibility when he responds to Davison's bewilderment. "Hell," Lancaster assures Davison, "ain't none of us right."

In the clash between the two cultures, naturalism suggests that it is appropriate for whites to fear Apaches; it may even be necessary for whites to defeat and destroy the Apache's culture and to contain his natural instincts. The Indian reservation, much like a zoo in which wild animals are caged, is an appropriate response to the Apache's natural instincts; it is a means to turn Apaches into peaceful farmers who are able to live among their white neighbors. The conquest of supposedly inferior Indian culture by supposedly superior white culture about which Shaw spoke in *Custer of the West* is the ultimate method of dealing with Indians. The reservation system, in which Indian culture is destroyed and native natural instincts modified, seems to be the only other option to the cultural relativism and naturalism which pervades *Ulzana's Raid*.

If *Custer of the West* and *Ulzana's Raid* present the Indian wars as a clash of cultures, a clash that the Indians are predestined to lose, *A Man Called Horse* (Paramount, 1970) offers a much more sympathetic interpretation of Indian culture. Richard Harris (playing Lord John Morgan) is an English nobleman captured by the Yellow Hand Sioux in the 1820s. Jean Gascon (as Batise), the son of a white mother and an Indian father, also has been captured by the Yellow Hand and crippled by them when he tried to escape captivity. Gascon acts as Harris' (and the viewers) interpreter of the Yellow Hand dialect and customs.

Although initially he is treated like an animal (hence his name: A Man Called Horse) and has to work with the women, he learns about the Yellow Hand from Gascon. And about a year into his captivity, Harris kills two Shoshone and scalps one. He returns to the Yellow Hand village, this time in triumph, and gives the two Shoshone horses in trade for a wife. But before he can consummate the marriage, Harris must prove himself as a man. So he participates in the Sun Dance ritual — in which he hangs suspended by his pectoral muscles. Harris proves himself a man and becomes a Yellow Hand warrior.

Gascon is ecstatic; now he believes they can escape the village together. But Harris becomes irate at Gascon's attitude. He tells Gascon, "Five years you have lived here and you have learned nothing from these people!" Harris, although white, has become a Yellow Hand!

Yellow Hand women are forced to serve the pleasures of their white captors in *The Return of a Man Called Horse.*

A Man Called Horse offers viewers a sympathetic understanding of diverse facets of Indian culture. Among them are self mutilation at the death of a loved one, the casual nature of marriage, and the Sun Dance (although the film notes that the United States government outlawed the ceremony). Viewers are invited to understand and appreciate Native American culture in a much more compassionate manner than in *Ulzana's Raid.* The film also makes clear that not all Indians are alike; they, too, fought among themselves. In *A Man Called Horse*, other Indians, not whites, are the Yellow Hand's enemies. In fact, the film climaxes with a Shoshone raid on the Yellow Hand village, a raid that kills many Yellow Hands, including Harris' wife. *A Man Called Horse* ends as the remnant of the tribe pack up to leave after the Shoshone raid, and Harris gallops over a ridge, returning to his life as an English Lord.

Six years later a sequel was produced, *The Return of a Man Called Horse* (United Artists, 1976). The opening scenes are of a raid on the Yellow Hand village by Indians led by a white man as punishment for the Yellow Hand raiding the traps of American fur traders. The Yellow Hand are told

In *The Return of a Man Called Horse* (1976), Richard Harris undergoes the Sun Dance Ritual again in order to purge himself of white cultural bias and reconnect with Yellow Hand culture.

they must leave the area or they will all be killed. A number of Yellow Hand women are taken prisoner to serve as workers and for the sexual pleasure of the white trappers.

Scenes then shift to England, with its fox hunts and concerts, but Richard Harris, surrounded by Indian artifacts, is a troubled human being. He longs to visit his Yellow Hand friends. Harris tells an assistant, "I am going back. I will be gone for one year, no more." The assistant can only respond, "I hope you find what you are looking for."

Once back, Harris finds the Yellow Hand camp deserted and the area overrun by white fur trappers. Harris assumes the disguise of an English traveler who has lost his way. At the fur trappers' fort he witnesses the brutal murder of a Yellow Hand woman. Fearing that Harris is a spy for the Hudson Bay Company, the leader of the trappers orders him tracked down and killed. But Harris anticipates that effort and instead kills several of his pursuers, and threatens to burn one of them alive unless he tells Harris where the Yellow Hand have gone.

When Harris learns that the Yellow Hand have fled into the badlands, he goes searching for them. Harris finds the remnant of the Yellow Hand an impovishered, beaten people. Gale Sondergaard (as Elk Woman) blames an evil spirit for their predicament, and they use the gifts Harris brought with him to appease the spirit that has brought so much misery to them. Harris reprimands the Yellow Hand, claiming that their belief in the evil spirit is mere superstition. But Sondergaard accuses Harris of thinking like a white man and not a Yellow Hand. She convinces him to undergo purification rights for four days and nights, which will permit Harris to identify with the suffering of the Yellow Hand, enable him to hold the sacred pipe, and empower him to lead the people out of the badlands. Harris seeks a vision, suffers for his people, and goes through the Sun Dance ritual with other young men of the tribe.

When the rituals are completed, Harris has become a Yellow Hand once again, purged of his white cultural biases and spiritually prepared to lead his people. Harris and the Yellow Hand leave the badlands, hunt buffalo and visit Red Cloud to plead for help against the fur trappers. However, Red Cloud will not help the Yellow Hand. The trappers by the rivers are his friends, and Red Cloud's people trade with them. When Harris insists that the Yellow Hand men are not strong enough or numerous enough to fight the white men, Red Clouds merely replies, "Let your women fight."

At that point, *Return of a Man Called Horse* becomes just another action Western. The women do indeed fight, and Harris leads the Yellow Hand as they defeat the trappers and reclaim their lands. There would be one more Horse movie, *Triumphs of a Man Called Horse* (Paramount, 1982), but it is a run-of-the-mill action Western with little effort to probe Indian culture, and need not concern us here.

Although *The Outlaw Josey Wales* (Warner Brothers, 1976) is not, strictly speaking, an Indian Western, its positive view of Indians parallels 1970s films such as *A Man Called Horse* and the later *Grayeagle* (American International, 1977). Chief Dan George (playing Lone Watie) and Geraldine Kearns (as Little Moonlight) are abused and impoverished reservation Indians who join forces with Clint Eastwood's Josey Wales (for a more elaborate discussion of *The Outlaw Josey Wales*, see Chapter 2). But it is Will Sampson's portrayal of Ten Bears that remains most compelling. Sampson has decided to fight rather than be pushed further off of his land. As Eastwood and his band prepare the ranch house for the anticipated

Indian attack, Eastwood decides to parlay with Sampson. Eastwood tells Sampson that they both can choose to die or choose to live. Eastwood will respect the Comanche, even permitting them to take a few cows for food, if the Comanche will let him work the ranch in peace. Sampson responds that there is iron in Eastwood's words, and the two become blood brothers. Sampson even frees two of Eastwood's cowhands that Sampson had captured and was preparing to kill. Will Sampson's portrayal of Ten Bears is one of an Indian leader who listens to reason, not a bloodthirsty savage who kills for the sheer joy of killing whites. *The Outlaw Josey Wales* suggests that whites and Indians could live in peace if each understood and respected the other.

Grayeagle is an excellent, heartwarming Western. Its top-notch cast includes Ben Johnson, Lana Wood, Iron Eyes Cody, Jack Elam, Paul Fix and Alex Cord. The story offers enough twists and turns to keep it interesting, and its upbeat ending makes *Grayeagle* stand out in a decade marked by political cynicism and economic turmoil.

When Lana Wood (playing Beth Collier) is taken from her 1848 Montana cabin by Alex Cord (Grayeagle), Ben Johnson (John Colter), Iron Eyes Cody (Standing Bear) and Jack Elam (Trapper Willis) begin the long quest to get her back. The film opened with Paul Fix (Running Wolf) pleading with the Great Spirit to help the Indians. The animals are leaving, and Fix fears that the whites are coming to destroy the Indian. Fix is an old man near death, and his hope for eternal peace lies with the mission of Cord's Grayeagle.

Although Wood does not know it, and viewers only gradually learn it, she is part Indian, Fix's daughter. Cord is returning the girl to the Cheyenne camp so her father can look upon her one time before he dies. Cord explains to Wood that when a child is born to a chief, his eyes must look upon the child once before he dies or his spirit will wander in the sky eternally. But it is a good day for Fix to die because now he has seen Wood and his spirit is free to join the Great Spirit forever. Fix tells Wood that her face is the one he has seen painted in the afternoon sky. Cord assures Wood that Fix had been a great chief and she would have been proud to be his daughter.

Iron Eyes Cody, playing the Cheyenne Standing Bear, knew Wood's birth lineage, although he had never told Johnson the truth, and Johnson had married Wood's mother after she was born. Cody appears at the Cheyenne camp as a sign that Wood will be returned to her people when

Fix dies. In the meantime, Wood comes to enjoy and respect Cheyenne culture. And she has fallen in love with Alex Cord!

In the meantime, Johnson and Elam have many adventures as they pursue Wood and Cord. Cord and Wood had slept overnight in the camp of some Shoshones who tried to buy Wood from Cord for two horses. When Cord refuses to sell the girl, the Shoshones pursue them, and Wood killed one of the Shoshones as he fought with Cord. Led by Charles B. Pierce, playing a renegade white called Bugler, the Shoshones track down and capture Johnson and Elam, whom Pierce blames for killing the Shoshone. Elam is killed in a fight with one of the Indians. Johnson, however, is freed after he kills his adversary. Ordered to return home, Johnson ignores the warning and is able to track down and kill Pierce, but Pierce wounds him in the fight, forcing Johnson to give up the search for Wood.

As Cody returns Wood to Johnson, they are attacked by Shoshones who want the white woman for themselves. But Cord comes riding to the rescue, and both Cody and Wood believe that he has sacrificed his life to save her. The film ends, however, when Cord appears on the horizon by Johnson's cabin, and all three — Johnson, Cody and Wood — run to greet him!

The image of the Cheyenne in *Grayeagle* is of a people living in peace with each other, their neighbors, and the environment. As part of their culture — their religion, to be exact — Wood is taken to their camp so the old chief can enjoy eternal peace. Although it takes much of the film for viewers to understand, the Cheyenne mean her no harm, and they pledge to return her to her people. It is a positive image of Indian culture, one that viewers admire. To watch *Grayeagle* is to be moved by the love the Cheyenne have for their old chief, and Alex Cord's courage as he fights off Shoshones and other impediments to Fix seeing his daughter before he dies.

Grayeagle is a delightful film because white viewers are invited to understand Cheyenne culture and to appreciate the nobility of their character. No social Darwinistic explanation, no resorting to naturalism, *Grayeagle* is a story about how one woman comes to understand and appreciate the nobility of her father's people. It is a film about the comradeship between an Indian, Iron Eyes Cody, and a white man, Ben Johnson. Ultimately it is a film about hope, the hope that peoples of different races and contrasting cultures can learn to respect each other and live together in

Opposite: Alex Cord is the Cheyenne brave *Grayeagle* (1977), who takes Lana Wood to her Indian father before he dies.

peace on an increasingly small planet. Of all post–1955 Indian-focused Westerns, *Grayeagle* is the best, in my opinion.

If *Grayeagle* is a heartwarming film with an upbeat ending, the same cannot be said for *The Stalking Moon* (Grand National, 1969). (For more about this film see Chapter 2.) Like *Grayeagle*, *The Stalking Moon* is a quest film, but in this one, it is the Indian who tries to rescue a captured son. Eva Marie Saint plays the white woman who, along with her mixed race son (Noland Clay), is taken prisoner by the cavalry. Gregory Peck (as Sam Varner) is an old retired army scout who takes Saint and Clay to his ranch. But the boy's Apache father, played by Nathaniel Narcisco, tries to rescue his son. Narcisco tracks them to Peck's cabin, and the last few minutes of the film are filled with suspense and terror as Narcisco tries to kill Peck and take back his son.

The *Stalking Moon* opts for a white perspective. Just as it seems natural that Ben Johnson would endeavor to rescue wood from the Cheyenne, so it seems natural that Narcisco would try to get his son back from his white captors. Yet there is no sympathy for Narcisco in *The Stalking Moon*. He is presented as a murderous Apache, not as a distraught father who wants his son back. Narcisco's behavior in *The Stalking Moon* is as natural as Ben Johnson's reaction in *Grayeagle*. But the possibility that an Apache is a human being driven by the same concern for the protection and well being of their children seems lost in *The Stalking Moon*. It is incomprehensible to Peck that Narcisco wants his son raised as an Apache. What else would he want? Morally, *The Stalking Moon* is a troubling film.

The Stalking Moon also causes white viewers to reflect on the growing concern that many from the non-white community in the last part of the twentieth century had for the adoption of children of color by white couples. While viewers feel sympathetic toward Eva Marie Saint's struggles to adapt to white culture, a culture in which she was raised but is now foreign to her, the film, for the most part, ignores the difficulty that Noland Clay will face as a mixed race youngster living in white society. Clay is an Apache, and he wants to go with his father; Apache culture is the only culture he has ever known. Learning to live in white society will be hard for the boy, and racially prejudiced whites will not make it easy for him.

Trooper Hook (United Artist, 1957) does a much better job than *The Stalking Moon* of addressing racial prejudice. Barbara Stanwyck (as Cora Sutliff) and her mixed race son are rescued when Rudolfo Acosta (Nanchez) is captured. (Stanwyck's role in this film is explored further in Chapter 11.) Acosta had taken the captured Stanwyck as his woman, and together they had a son. Joel McCrea (Trooper Hook) is the man charged with returning Stanwyck to her husband. On the return trip, people gawk at Stanwyck and speak of the boy as a mongrel kid. White folks hate the little boy because he is an Apache and, more specifically, the son of a feared Apache leader.

Acosta is correct when he tells McCrea that his son will be scorned and abused, and that he would be better off raised by Apaches. Even though Acosta understands that McCrea will try to protect the boy, Acosta tells McCrea, "You cannot speak for your people." Acosta's words are prophetic because Stanwyck's husband, played by John Dehner, will not permit the boy to live with them.

The film ends with little resolution. Both Dehner and Acosta are killed in the climactic gunfight, and Stanwyck and the boy are going to live with McCrea after his enlistment ends in four months. But that does not resolve the issue that, as a mixed race child, the boy will face a hostile white world for the rest of his life.

It is likely that the best known of the entire 1970s Indian-oriented Westerns is *Little Big Man* (Paramount, 1971), a film that anticipates the themes explored in *Dances with Wolves* (Orion, 1990) by nearly two decades. Both movies view white penetration of the Great Plains from the Indian perspective; both portray Indian assessments of whites; and both depict whites as a crude, unsavory race when compared to Indians, who live in harmony with each other and their environment. *Little Big Man* and *Dances with Wolves* are revisionist Westerns in which relationships between the two races are inverted from those found in nearly all traditional Westerns. But in the rush to correct perceived misrepresentations of Indians in traditional Westerns, both films overstate unsavory white qualities and ignore enmity that existed among diverse tribes of Plains Indians. In their preoccupation with cultural sensitivity (albeit a noble goal), *Little Big Man* and *Dances with Wolves* are as guilty of historical distortion as were many pre–1955 Westerns.

Dustin Hoffman (playing Jack Crabb) in *Little Big Man* is a white man who moves easily and repeatedly between the Cheyenne world to which he had been taken when he was ten years old and the white world to which he returns throughout the film. The Cheyenne call themselves "human beings," and in *Little Big Man* they are a tribe that practices tolerance and kindness toward all other people. For example, Hoffman, as he narrates, observes that one young boy does not want to become a warrior or go out on hunts or raids. No one in the tribe, Hoffman asserts, will think less of the lad.

Chief Dan George (as Old Lodge Skins), Hoffman's Cheyenne grandfather, judges whites as strange. They do not know where the center of the earth is located; hence they kill women and children, and ravage the landscape. Noting the social distinctions and social classes that shape white society, Chief Dan George tells Hoffman that whites believe that everything is theirs, even their own people. But, alas, there is no way to escape the inevitability of white incursion into Cheyenne lands, so Chief Dan George, now old and blind, assures Hoffman that dying is the only way to deal with whites.

As the film unfolds, Chief Dan George's words appear accurate. The sham marriage between Thayer David (Reverend Pendrake) and Faye Dunaway (Mrs. Pendrake), and the ultimate discovery of Dunaway working as a prostitute; the comical depiction of Wild Bill Hickok by Jeff Corey; and the arrogant stupidity of George Armstrong Custer, as portrayed by Richard Mulligan, makes one wish Hoffman would remain with the Cheyenne. In no sense does *Little Big Man* make one very proud of the whites who settled the Great Plains.

The same themes continue in *Dances with Wolves*. The white soldiers are ignorant, crude people, and their commanding officers are self-serving paper pushers who know nothing about the Great Plains or the Indians who populate them. The slaughter of the buffalo for their tongues and skins, and the unnecessary sport-like killing of the wolf that Kevin Costner had partially tamed merely add to the crudeness and environmental insensitivity of the whites in *Dances with Wolves*. Somehow Costner senses those qualities in his fellow soldiers, and he requests a frontier posting after being wounded in a Civil War engagement. His reason for requesting the new assignment is straightforward: he "always wanted to see the frontier before it is gone." Now settled in a lonely deserted post on the Great Plains, Costner is a firsthand observer of the frontier.

In contrast to the crude white soldiers, the Sioux (Lakota) are a people of reason. The number of times the Sioux men sit in council talking and reasoning with one another is one of the most striking elements in *Dances with Wolves*. Led by Floyd Red Crow Westerman (playing Ten Bears), each warrior is allowed to speak his thoughts. One of them describes whites as inferior to the Sioux. They are dirty and it is easy to steal their horses. He claims that they will never be able to take over the Sioux land.

Westerman agrees that whites are a "poor race and hard to understand," but he is not sure they can be easily turned back. He displays a Spanish Conquistador helmet and observes that his great grandfather defeated them and the Sioux have turned back other whites who sought to take their land. But, Westerman acknowledges, they just keep coming. Later, as Kevin Costner and Graham Greene (as Kicking Bird) talk, Greene wants to know how many white people there are. Costner assures him that they are greater than the stars in the sky, and that nothing can keep them from overrunning Sioux land. Indeed, *Dances with Wolves* ends with the acknowledgement that in only a handful of years after the Civil War ended, the vast majority of Sioux lived on government reservations.

I watched both *Little Big Man* and *Dances with Wolves* again soon after I watched *Custer of the West* for the first time. Shaw's contention to Kieron Moore (playing Dull Knife) in the latter film — that the Cheyenne took the hunting lands of other tribes— is a reminder that too often comments on the former two films overlook the fact that the Plains Indians were warlike. In *Custer of the West*, the massacre at Washita River by white soldiers is depicted in bloody detail, but so was the attack on the Cheyenne camp by their Indian enemies. And the Pawnee, long time enemy of the Sioux, attack Westerman's camp in *Dances with Wolves*. In fact, the Plains tribes often treated one another as the whites treated Indians, taking land by force. One should never forget that Blackfoot and Crow Indians did much of the scouting in the final campaign against the nonreservation Sioux, and in the fight with Geronimo, Apache scouts helped the army.

In many respects, *Dances with Wolves* and *Little Big Man* bring the genre full circle. Scott Simmon, in *The Invention of the Western Film*, maintains that Westerns shot in the East in the first decade of the twentieth century included noble Indians set upon by greedy whites who sought to disrupt the idyllic natural setting of the Indian abode. Tying that motif back to James Fenimore Cooper, Simmon notes that "pessimism about pioneering" diminishes optimism about America's future (Simmon, 14). To a great extent, both *Little Big Man* and *Dances with Wolves* leave the viewer disheartened. A noble people were being exterminated, and one could not be sure about the character of those who sought to replace them!

It is indeed fitting that the final Indian-focused Western produced by Hollywood in the twentieth century would be about Geronimo, the last great Indian leader to surrender. *Geronimo: An American Legend* (Columbia, 1993) is a curious film because it draws from both Hollywood Indian story traditions. There is no effort to gloss over the murder of women and children, or to make the Apaches appear as noble savages beset by irresponsible whites. Wes Studi portrays Geronimo as a complex personality, one that, at times, evokes audience sympathy, and on other occasions fear and mistrust. The United States Army is equally complex. Gene Hackman's depiction of General George Crook as a man who, though sympathetic to the Apache plight, had a job to do is historically accurate. Jason Patric and Matt Damon, as officers Gatewood and Davis, share Hackman's concern for Apaches and both respect Studi's Geronimo. Kevin Tighe, as General Nelson Miles, is their opposite. He is prepared to tell Geronimo anything in order to get him to surrender, whether or not it is the truth.

The film opens with the first surrender of Studi (Geronimo) and his rescue by Patric from a Tombstone posse that intends to hang the Indian leader. Turkey Creek, where Studi is held, is a barren place, a place poorly suited to teach Apaches how to be farmers. The soil will not grow corn, and, besides, Studi refuses to become a farmer. Soon Studi joins in on an Apache version of the ghost dance, a dance that promises to bring back the great leaders who will make war on the white soldiers. The shooting starts when soldiers try to arrest, but wind up killing, the holy man leading the dancers. Studi and his warriors escape from Turkey Creek armed with the weapons of dead soldiers.

The ghost dance episode is a figment of Hollywood imagination. Geronimo, according to Charles Robinson III in his excellent biography of General Crook, feared for his life and thought that Crook had abandoned him. Robinson contends, "Boredom almost certainly was a factor, as was vanity. He [Geronimo] was an active man. Raiding offered excitement, and gave power and prestige" (Robinson, 273). For whatever reason, in May 1885 Geronimo escaped the San Carlos reservation.

The rest of the film unfolds as the military endeavors to capture Studi. But since Hackman is unable to finalize the capture, he is relieved from command, replaced by Kevin Tighe. Tighe orders Patric and Damon to find Studi in Mexico and convince him to surrender. Studi is promised that he will be able to return to Arizona after a two-year confinement in Florida. But once Studi surrenders, none of the promises are kept. Patric is transferred to a post in Wyoming so that his presence in Arizona will not be a constant reminder of the Army's failure to capture Studi. Damon resigns his commission in protest over the failure of the military to keep its word. Damon mistakenly thought that the uniform he wore signified honor and truth, but he discovers that Tighe believes only in results. The military earned the gratitude of the nation when Studi surrendered. To Tighe it matters not that deception and lies were employed. Tighe describes Damon as an idealist, and notes that he hates idealists. Studi, the rest of his band, all Chiricahua Apache leaders and all of the Chiricahua Apache scouts who helped track Studi are sent to prison in Florida.

In the final analysis none of the promises made to the Chiricahuas were kept. In the last decade of the twentieth century, American culture thrived on ambiguity, so it is not surprising that there are no winners in *Geronimo: An American Legend*. Studi and his band raided, tortured and killed because they disliked whites in their land and they could not accept the inevitable. White bounty hunters who sold Indian scalps in Mexico were no better than killers. The military, with its deception and dishonesty, proved equally unsettling. Moral confusion abounds in the film, and in that sense, *Geronimo: An American Legend* reflects the decade in which it was made.

Geronimo's last words at his final surrender speak not only for Native Americans in the nineteenth century, they serve as an appropriate obituary for the Hollywood Indian story that first appeared at the dawn of American film and concluded with *Geronimo: An American Legend*: "Now my time is over."

The Hollywood Indian story remained a rich source for exciting Westerns over the last half of the twentieth century. As racial barriers toppled and sensitivity to non-white cultures increased, the Indian story became more complex than it had been in nearly all pre–1955 Westerns. Native Americans were viewed sympathetically, as a tragic people who deserved better treatment from whites. In turn, Westerns sought to probe the complexity of Indian life, as well as depict Indian culture more realistically. The same cannot be said for the portrayal of Hispanics and African Americans.

The descent of the Western after the mid–1960s from its place as one of the preeminent American film genres parallels the movement within the African American community from a rural southern majority to a northern urban majority. The migration north during the 1920s, rural displacement of sharecroppers and tenant farmers during the Great Depression, and the relocation west and north to higher paying factory jobs during World War II created an urban, street-savvy black population. Urban action and comedy films, not Westerns, depicted African American life in the last half of the twentieth century.

Westerns produced in the 1960s recognized that African Americans had lived in the real West, and they included black characters far more often than had pre–1955 Westerns. Jim Brown appeared in Westerns such as *Rio Conchos* (20th Century–Fox, 1964) and *100 Rifles* (20th Century–Fox, 1968); Sidney Poitier costarred with James Garner in *Duel at Diablo* (United Artists, 1966) and in *Buck and the Preacher* (Columbia, 1972); and Fred Williamson plays an escaped slave in *The Legend of Nigger Charlie* (Paramount, 1972) and *The Soul of Nigger Charlie* (Paramount, 1973). Danny Glover in *Silverado* (Columbia, 1985) and Morgan Freeman's role as Clint Eastwood's friend and conscience in *Unforgiven* (Warner Brothers, 1992) are more recent reminders that the West was not solely a white range. *Posse* (Gramercy Pictures, 1993) even opts for a black point of view of race relations on the frontier.

I do not want to diminish the importance of any of these films, but none of them probe racial relationships with the depth that John Ford did in *Sergeant Rutledge* (Warner Brothers, 1960). (See Chapter 3 for a complete discussion of that film.) Ford opened the door for Westerns to deal forthrightly and intelligently with racial prejudice. The genre, for the most part, declined the invitation. But, as I noted above, film genres other than Westerns are probably better venues for raising those issues.

It is also surprising that, as the Hispanic population increased rapidly in the United States during the last half of the twentieth century, Westerns did little to refashion the stereotypes that shaped the genre prior to 1955. Mexico remained a place of poor, semi-literate peasants who were exploited by banditos, corrupt Federales or French troops. And the women, for the most part, continued to be portrayed as sensual persons of easy virtue. Films such as *The Magnificent Seven* (United Artists, 1960), *Major Dundee* (Columbia, 1965) and *The Wild Bunch* (Warner Brothers, 1969) do not differ much in their depiction of Mexicans from earlier Westerns. In 1998, *The Mask of Zorro* (Columbia Tri-Star) sought to breathe new life into that character, but, for the most part, Hispanics (particularly Mexicans) continued to serve as the familiar characters of traditional pre–1955 Westerns. There are some exceptions, such as *Valdez Is Coming* (United Artists, 1971), but they are just that — exceptions.

The Hollywood Indian subgenre remains the one Western film type that sought to come to grips with changing race relationships in the United States during the last forty-five years of the twentieth century. Indians, more than African Americans or Hispanics, were the vehicle through which Westerns sought to explore changing American understanding of its history and culture, and to raise white awareness of peoples with diverse histories and cultures living among them.

Chapter 11

"Hard-Ridin' Woman with a Whip"

As 1955 dawned, American women who spent their school years during the Great Depression and who experienced both the fear and exhilaration of the war years must have felt themselves confused and constrained. Glenda Riley notes, "In 1956, *Life* magazine described the ideal American woman as a wife, hostess, volunteer, 'home manager,' and 'conscientious mother'" (Riley, 132). Yet, women made up 29 percent of the workforce in 1950 (Riley, 132). Riley comments, "Apparently, women had reservations about the post-war 'back-to-the-home' message" (Riley, 132).

On the one hand, many women had earned good salaries working in wartime industry. And without men around they learned to do things, such as change tires and balance the checkbook. Many of them managed to be caregiving mothers to young children while at the same time working eight hours or more each day in war-related jobs. American industry, as much as anything, had won the war, and women had been a vital cog in the industrial war machine.

Of course, much of that ended when the war concluded and the men returned home. Women lost their well-paid factory jobs, partly because of union rules that guaranteed returning veterans their old jobs, and partly because American culture in the mid–1940s believed that a woman's place was at home if her husband was capable of supporting the family. Many women gave up their jobs, got married and soon were pregnant, and the baby boomer generation that followed would occupy much of their time

271

for the next several years. In 1955, even the oldest of the baby boomers was barely ten years old. The female role as housewife to their career-oriented veteran husbands, and as mothers to their young children, displaced memories of independence enjoyed during World War II.

June Cleaver of *Leave It to Beaver* is often cited as the archetypal housewife of the 1950s. She may have been, but it seems to me that Lucille Ball's Lucy Ricardo of *I love Lucy* may be closer to the truth. Ignore the comedic nature of Ball's character and her propensity for getting herself, her husband and her friends into impossible situations. Reflect rather on the aspirations that usually lay behind her scheming. Lucy Ricardo wanted to be more than a housewife and mother. She wanted a career. She longed to appear on the stage with her husband, and to meet all of the famous people with whom he came into contact.

Lucille Ball's Lucy Ricardo, then, may be closer to the archetypal 1950s woman than June Cleaver. Lucy experienced the frustration of being left at home, of being denied voice to whatever talents she possessed. Unlike most 1950s women, Lucy did not accept her status; she rebelled. Oh, it was funny, and it always had a happy ending, but it was rebellion nonetheless!

Unlike Lucy Ricardo, most American women did not rebel; they managed their households and raised their children as apparently happy women. They also raised their daughters differently. The hallmark of baby boomer women is that they believed they could do whatever they wanted to do. They rejected traditional gender career distinctions—many of them majored in academic subjects that women had generally scorned—and they asserted their right to define their own lives as they wished. Of course, like all young people, they did some foolish things. Many of them regret their flings with sexual liberation, and most understand that their total rejection of the "establishment" was misguided. But those things have passed; however, young baby boomer women changed forever the role and place of women in American culture. That has remained, and it may be the most important revolution of the 1960s!

As an example, my first teaching job began in January 1965, and as a young faculty member I wanted to build a political science program at a midwestern Christian college. Up to that time not many women had graduated with a major in the discipline from that institution, and when I started teaching, there were no women majoring in political science. By the late 1960s change was in the air. As the century progressed, more and more women majored in political science, as well as other programs such as management, accounting and physics—disciplines that had not previously attracted many women. By the end of the century, women held Ph.D.s in diverse academic disciplines; and in any given law school women made up nearly half, if not over half, of the student body.

Surely the feminist movement which emerged in the 1960s and 1970s played an important role in awakening women to their potential as scholars, athletes, political leaders, scientists and corporate executives. Equally important is the Civil Rights Act of 1964 that made gender-based discrimination illegal. That legislation spawned, in turn, other federal and state laws that struck down gender-discriminating hiring and promotion policies. Important as they were, feminism and gender affirmative action programs must tip their hats to those post-war baby boomer mothers who raised their daughters to exercise their talents and not hide them for fear of alienating males, to step out into areas long thought inappropriate for women, to reject the notion that some careers were closed to women, and, above all, to accept the challenge of bringing a woman's perspective and values to diverse social, economic and political institutions.

Make no mistake, in 1955 the world still belonged to males, but change was reshaping American culture. It would take twenty or more years for that change to bear fruit, but bear fruit it did. It bore so much fruit that writing in the first decade of the twenty-first century it is as difficult to imagine a time when women were not lawyers, environmental scientists and Ph.D.s in political science as it is to imagine a time in the United States when racial, ethnic and religious segregation was openly practiced and defended. In retrospect, the last forty years of the twentieth century were extraordinarily revolutionary!

The emergence of women into nearly every facet of American life during the last forty years of the twentieth century impacted motion pictures as well. Female character types, motion picture themes and film plots began to reflect the increasing role of career women in American life, as well as the adventures of women who sought to balance their careers with their roles as wives and mothers. And female characters became much more independent, more assertive and less deferential to men. While Hollywood—from its earliest days with Mary Pickford and Lillian Gish, through women such as Bette Davis and Katharine Hepburn, to present celebrities such as Jennifer Aniston — always offered strong female leads, increasingly after 1955 women began to write, produce and direct films as well.

That was not necessarily good news for Westerns because women have always been the gender least attracted to the genre. While the stereotype of the heroine who waits by the garden gate to kiss the hero goodbye as he rides away into the sunset is overstated (as is 1940s and 1950s actress Noel Neill's oft-repeated assertion at film festivals that women had very little to do in Westerns), it is nonetheless true that Westerns are action films about men. Relationships are seldom probed in depth, and characters are seldom nuanced. Westerns are visual, not verbal, films. Women, even if they have substantial roles in the plot and action, are almost always subordinate to the hero and lead villain. That is because — at least according to Jane Tompkins in *West of Everything: The Inner Life of Westerns)* — women talk while men act. Westerns, Tompkins believes, don't like language. She notes, "Westerns treat salesmen and politicians, people whose business is language, with contempt" (Tompkins, 51). Tompkins suggests, "The Western hero's silence symbolizes a massive suppression of the inner life" (Tompkins, 66).

It is not really important whether or not Tompkins has it right (although I think she makes a valid case). Her underlying point remains that Westerns are not films that appeal very much to women. And the younger the woman, the less appealing is the genre. It is simply foreign to her world of experience; she did not grow up in an era when it was staple entertainment for her brothers and father, and she most certainly did not play cowboys and Indians with her brothers or male neighbors.

Westerns do not conform to most women's notion of good entertainment on a night out. They do not generate conversation over a cup of mocha after the movie has ended. For several years I have taught a class on the history of the United States during the 1930s and 1940s in which the students view films from those years in order to better understand the culture of that era. With only a handful of exceptions, women in the class turn up their noses at Westerns.

Even if women do not like Westerns, it is equally true that only a handful of Westerns lack female characters. So, if Westerns are primarily male-oriented entertainment, how have women characters in the films changed over the years since 1955? To what extent, if any, have Westerns produced since 1955 reflected the increasingly important roles that women play in public life? Have female character types changed from those that dominated the genre prior to 1955 (for full discussions of those character types see my *Westerns and American Culture, 1930–1955*)?

Before proceeding further, note must be made of an important change in the motion picture industry in the 1950s: the weakening of the Motion Picture Producer's and Distributor's Code. With the emergence of *film noir* after World War II, and the culturally liberating influences of the war, motion pictures began to deal more openly and frankly with marital infidelity, mental illness, rape, graphic violence, hypocritical clergy and a host of other subjects that had been forbidden by the Code. While the Code would not give way to an early version of the present motion picture rating system until the late 1960s, it lost its effectiveness after World War II. As the studio system declined (studio moguls, after all, had generated the Code) and independent producers emerged, Code enforcers were ignored more and more, and suggestions to remove objectionable content went unheeded. Having broken the dominion of B Westerns that had more or less defined the genre before the early 1950s, and having escaped the Motion Picture Producer's and Distributor's Code yoke, Westerns began to include previously forbidden themes and images (as did other genres). That is most evident in the treatment of women.

For the most part, however, women continued to play traditional roles in Westerns; they were faithful wives who stood beside their man, or loving daughters and sisters who deferred to the male(s) in their lives. As examples, Mala Powers (playing Laura Reno) in *Rage at Dawn* (RKO, 1955) is the loving sister of the Reno brothers and Randolph Scott's love interest. Even though she hates what her brothers do, she faithfully tends house for them, and as the film ends she rides off into the sunset as Scott's wife-to-be.

In *Lonely Are the Brave* (Universal-International, 1962) Gena Rowlands (Jerri Bondi) is the loyal wife increasingly distraught over Kirk Douglas and Michael Kane's unwillingness to accept the modern world. Nancy Gates (Mrs. Lowe) is the loving wife who eagerly awaits reunion with her blind husband after she had been kidnapped by Indians in *Comanche Station* (Columbia, 1960).

Jeanne Crain (Dora Temple) is the obedient wife who fled with Glenn Ford from town to town as he ran from his own cowardice in *The Fastest Gun Alive* (MGM, 1956). Crane's character, however, suggests that things were changing. Now pregnant with their first child, Crane believes that at last she has found a town in which to settle. Furthermore, she believes that Ford had thrown away his father's gun, and had made peace with his fear of violence and his remembrance of his cowardice when his father was murdered. However, her understandings explode as Ford becomes more and more restless with his life away from whiskey and guns, the two symbols, he believes, that define manhood in the Old West. Ford's fears return to haunt him when he straps on his father's gun and shows off. Rather than face the inevitable challenges to his claim as the fastest gun alive, Ford prepares to run again. This time, however, Crain is not the obedient wife. She intends to remain in Cross Creek, have her baby and establish a life for them in the town. She won't leave with Ford, and she holds fast to that conviction to the end of the film!

Jeanne Crain refuses to leave Cross Creek with Glenn Ford in *The Fasted Gun Alive* (1956).

Other examples of traditional images of women in Western films could be offered, but the point has been made. However, as Jeanne Crain's role in *The Fastest Gun Alive* suggests, women began to break free of the constraining roles in which they had been confined in Westerns. They began to talk back and became more assertive. Women were also more likely to become victims of violence!

More frequently after 1955, women were portrayed as victims of unwanted sexual advances and rape. *Man of the West* (United Artist, 1958) is a daring film for its day. Julie London (playing Billie Ellis) is a saloon entertainer who has to constantly ward off the probing hands of her boss and male customers. But when she is taken captive by Lee J. Cobb's gang, the probing hands turn into something more. Forced to strip in front of the men, London is saved from gang rape by the quick thinking of Gary Cooper, who turns Cobb's attention to the bank at Lassoo. By the end of the film, however, Cobb has raped London. She became a victim of actual assault.

Posse from Hell (Universal-International, 1961) may be the best example of the rape theme. Zohra Lampert (Helen Caldwell) is taken hostage

Audie Murphy tells Zora Lampert that as far as he is concerned she has never been touched in *Posse from Hell* (1961).

by the outlaws as they ride out of town after robbing the bank. When the posse, led by Audie Murphy, finds Lampert, she has been repeatedly raped by the outlaws. Throughout the rest of the film, Lampert has to deal with the social disapproval resulting from the assault. The ladies in town blame the victim, and Lampert believes herself a fallen woman, a social outcast. *Posse from Hell* deals with rape and its consequences forthrightly, and for that reason the film is different from nearly all Westerns that preceded it.

Inger Stevens in *Hang 'em High* (United Artists, 1968) had been the victim of gang rape — or, as she explains to Clint Eastwood, she was raped again and again after a group of toughs murdered her husband. Now each time a lawman brings a prisoner to Fort Smith, Stevens visits the jail to see if that man is one of her assailants. During much of the film, viewers are left wondering why Stevens visits the jail. It is during a picnic with Eastwood that she tells him about the assault. Again, in pre–1955 Westerns, Stevens would have been far less explicit about her motive. But with the development of the rating system and society's willingness to confront the severity of sex crimes, Westerns were willing to treat the issue openly.

Other Westerns dealt with women victimized by Indians. Barbara Stanwyck stars as a woman kidnapped by Apaches in *Trooper Hook* (United Artists, 1957; more about Stanwyck below). Eva Marie Saint is the white woman captured by Apaches in *The Stalking Moon* (National General, 1969). Chapter 3 focused on Saint's character as a woman who found it difficult to adjust to white society, but the manner in which her character discusses her captivity with Gregory Peck speaks volumes. Saint understands the white view that a woman should kill herself before she permits an Indian male to have sexual intercourse with her. As with the blame-the-victim attitude toward rape, Saint recognizes that white society will blame her for giving birth to and rearing a mixed race boy. She confesses to Peck that she was too weak, too afraid of dying to resist, so she did what she had to do to stay alive.

The woman-as-victim motif permeates *MacKenna's Gold* (Columbia, 1969). Camilla Sparv (Inga) is taken captive by Omar Sharif's gang. Her fate, he makes clear to Sparv, is to be given to one of the Apaches who rides with him or taken to Mexico and sold.

Mexican women in Sam Peckinpah Westerns were often depicted as whores when, in truth, they were victims. The Mexican women in *The Wild Bunch* (Warner Brothers, 1969) do not seem to have much choice when they are given to Ben Johnson and Warren Oates as sexual playthings. Neither do the younger women, who, near the conclusion of *The Wild Bunch*, are given to William Holden and Ernest Borgnine for the same purpose. Mexican women appear in the same roles in Peckinpah's *Pat Garrett and Billy the Kid* (MGM, 1973).

The third image of the Western female — that of an independent career woman as a force for either good or evil in the community — continues a trend that appeared in numerous 1940s Westerns. For example, Evelyn Finley and Betty Miles portrayed gun-totin' hard-ridin' women more than capable of bossing the ranch and competing with men; and Dale Evans in many of her mid–1940s films with Roy Rogers portrayed a competent career woman making her way in the world. Ruth Roman in *The Far Country* (Universal-International, 1955), Angela Lansbury in *A Lawless Street* (Columbia, 1955), Audrey Totter in *The Vanishing American* (Republic, 1955), Joan Collins in *The Bravados* (TCR, 1958), Verna Bloom in *The Hired Hand* (Universal, 1978) and Carrie Snodgrass in *Pale Rider*

(Warner Brothers, 1985) all continue the genre tradition of independent women capable of protecting their interests.

However, a variant of that theme became more pervasive and more explicit after 1955. The "whore with a heart of gold" was not an infrequent character in pre–1955 Westerns, but her profession, as such, was never stressed, and more often than not she died at some point during the film (or she forsook her profession for the love of a man, as did Claire Trevor in *Stagecoach* [United Artists, 1939]). After 1955, Westerns were inclined to treat prostitution more kindly. Stella Stevens' Hildy in *The Ballad of Cable Hogue* (Warner Brothers, 1970), Jeanne Moreau in *Monte Walsh* (National General, 1970), Faye Dunaway as both Kate Elder in *Doc* (United Artists, 1971) and Mrs. Pendrake in *Little Big Man* (National General, 1971), as well as the actresses portraying the prostitutes in *Unforgiven* (Warner Brothers, 1992) all bring a more sympathetic posture to the profession than appeared in traditional Westerns.

Other images of women appear at times in Westerns, but they are not as pervasive as the ones just discussed. Surprisingly, few post–1955 Westerns portray women as villains. It became somewhat common for B Westerns to employ women in that role during the 1940s. Jennifer Holt's villainy in the Jimmy Wakely programmer *Range Renegades* (Monogram, 1948) and Eddie Dean's *The Hawk of Powder River* (PRC, 1948) are excellent B Western examples, as is Jane Greer in the bigger-budget Western *Station West* (RKO, 1948). *Oklahoma Woman* (American Releasing Corporation, 1956) and *The Maverick Queen* (Republic, 1956) are among the few post–1955 Westerns that employed that convention. Although Valerie French (playing Mae Hogan) does not play an outlaw in *Jubal* (Columbia, 1956), she is surely an evil person. But, again, that sort of female character seldom appears in Westerns produced after 1955.

Finally, Mary McDonnell's role as Stands with Fist in *Dances with Wolves* (Columbia Tri-Star, 1990) represents a rather unique image of women. At first, she appears to have been a victim. As a child she was taken by the Sioux after they killed her family. But she has become thoroughly acculturated as a Sioux woman. She is even afraid of Kevin Costner the first time they meet.

But it is McDonnell who holds the film together. Costner cannot speak the Sioux language, and Graham Greene (playing Kicking Bird) does not understand English. Greene turns to McDonnell and asks her to interpret for them. Although she does not want to do so, and claims that she has forgotten the language, she finally agrees to act as interpreter. It is McDonnell who helps Greene understand Costner, and she is able, in turn, to help Costner understand and appreciate the Sioux people and culture.

Barbara Stanwyck strikes a pose as the gun-totin' title character in this lobby card from *The Maverick Queen* (1956).

While not the only factor, the deepening love that Costner and McDonnell feel for one another shapes the close bond between Greene and Costner. Those two relationships make *Dances with Wolves* a warmly sentimental film. And McDonnell is the linchpin that holds the film together in a remarkable role for a woman in a Western.

The images of women in Westerns after 1955 reflected both change as well as continuity with Westerns before that date. But the most appropriate way in which to examine the images is to consider them in the work of specific actors and actresses over the last forty-five years of the twentieth century, and the career of Barbara Stanwyck seems the most obvious place to start.

Dale Evans (as the leading lady in numerous Roy Rogers B Westerns and television productions) and Gail Davis (TV's Annie Oakley and frequent leading lady in Gene Autry Westerns) may rightly be considered the Queens of B Westerns. Barbara Stanwyck can claim that title for bigger-budget A Westerns. Stanwyck once described herself as "the best action actress in the world. I can do horse drags and jump off buildings, and I have the scars to prove it" (Schackel, 122). Equally important, as Schackel notes, "Stanwyck brought to the Western heroine a spunky determination and spirit of independence unusual for women in Westerns in this era" (Schackel, 113).

Beginning with *Annie Oakley* (RKO, 1935), Barbara Stanwyck appeared in a dozen Westerns (concluding with 1957's *Trooper Hook*), before she left the big screen to make guest appearances on numerous television Westerns, and to star as the boss-lady Victoria Barkley in the popular *The Big Valley* television show. As Schackel notes, her characters were always independent, free-spirited women.

In *Union Pacific* (Paramount, 1939), Stanwyck is as comfortable with the action as are the men, and she did much of her own stuntwork in the film (Schackel, 117). She even got her man in the end.

She was the loyal wife in *The Great Man's Lady* (Paramount, 1942) who defended her husband (Joel McCrea)—until she discovered that he was not an honest man; then she left him.

Stanwyck was not beneath playing disreputable characters, as she did in *The Furies* (Paramount, 1950) when she helps to destroy her own father, or in *The Violent Men* (Columbia, 1955), a film in which Stanwyck plays the unfaithful wife who lusts after her husband's (Edward G. Robinson) brother (Brian Keith). And in *Cattle Queen of Montana* (RKO, 1954) she demonstrates that she can shoot as well as any man, and that she is fully capable of protecting her property!

In both *The Maverick Queen* (Republic, 1956) and *Forty Guns* (20th Century–Fox, 1957), Stanwyck plays a conflicted woman. The traditional image of woman as wife (or one who longs to settle down with one man) vies with the image of an independent, assertive and ambitious woman more than capable of making her way in the world.

Viewers first meet Stanwyck's character, Kit Banion, in *The Maverick Queen* when Scott Brady (as the Sundance Kid) reports to her his failure to rustle Mary Murphy's herd of cattle. Brady regards Stanwyck as his woman, an affection Stanwyck does not share. She pushes him away when he tries to kiss her, telling Brady to take a bath. Even though Stanwyck is part of the Wild Bunch, she reminds Brady that she takes orders only from Butch Cassidy, and from *no one* in her private life. She is an independent woman who will love whom she wishes to love. Stanwyck has higher aspirations than settling for a man like Brady. With contempt dripping from her voice, she tells Brady, "Someday I will meet a better man and I will drop you like a poison snake." Brady only replies that he will kill Stanwyck before he lets another man have her.

The better man comes along in the person of Barry Sullivan. Sullivan is really an undercover law officer posing as Jeff Younger in order to infiltrate the Wild Bunch. In their first conversation, Sullivan identifies the unique position Stanwyck possesses in the town when he observes that she is a "big wheel in this town," adding, "That is unusual for a lady." Stanwyck falls in love with Sullivan, and in conversations with him the contrasting images emerge.

Stanwyck comes from a proud Virginia family who lost everything in the war. She had gone West and branded every unbranded calf she could find — hence her name the Maverick Queen. And she had fallen in with the Wild Bunch in order to make more money. But she recognizes that the days of her kind are ending (the film is set at the end of the nineteenth century).

The soft, feminine side of Barbara Stanwyck emerges when she pleads with Sullivan (who she mistakenly believes is Jeff Younger wanting to join the Wild Bunch) to leave the gang and go straight. The country is changing, she tells Sullivan, settlers are moving in. In a couple of years the Wild Bunch will be gone. But, although Stanwyck is in love with Sullivan, she is trapped. It is too late for her to get out of the gang; it is too late for her to change her ways. And "marriage is not for people in our business," she tells Sullivan.

So the outlaw Kit Banion can't have marriage, home and a family, the things she longs to have. But she can save Barry Sullivan. When Pinkerton operatives shut down her saloon and give her six hours to leave town, she rides to the Hole in the Wall to save Sullivan after she learns his true identity. In the end, Stanwyck dies, but only after she has helped to save Sullivan and destroy the Wild Bunch.

The opening song in *Forty Guns* sets the nature of Stanwyck's character. The song describes a "high-ridin' woman" brandishing a whip. The song reminds viewers that she commands and men obey. At the same time, the song challenges a man to take away her whip and tame her.

Viewers first meet Stanwyck (playing Jessica Drummond) dressed in black and mounted on a white horse as she leads her forty gunmen past the buckboard in which Barry Sullivan (Griff Bonnell), Gene Barry (Wes Bonnell) and Robert Dix (Chico Bonnell) are riding into town. Stanwyck's Jessica Drummond runs the town and the territory around it. She is powerful and she is dishonest. Stanwyck shields thieves and killers, and she has swindled the government out of thousands of tax dollars. Protected by her forty guns, a corrupt sheriff (Dean Jagger) and a town too afraid of her to resist her control, Stanwyck appears untouchable by any force.

Sullivan and Barry (two federal marshals), along with their younger brother Dix, ride into town to arrest a deputy sheriff for robbing the United States mail. Early on, Sullivan and Barry stop John Erickson (Brockie Drummond) and his cronies from wrecking the town. Sullivan quickly learns of Stanwyck's power when she gets Erickson off the next morning with a small fine for disturbing the peace.

When Sullivan goes to Stanwyck's ranch to arrest the man for whom he has a warrant, viewers see Stanwyck sitting at the head of a long table having dinner with all of the men who obey her. The warrant is served, and Stanwyck tells the other men to leave the room so she and Sullivan can talk. From that point on to the end of the film, a romance begins to blossom between the two.

One day, as they take shelter from a storm in an old shack, Stanwyck tells Sullivan of her past. She had been orphaned at a young age, and by the time she was eighteen years old she bossed her own spread. She became politically active and now runs the territory. But she tells Sullivan that this is the last stop, the frontier is over. Stanwyck recognizes that people like her are rapidly becoming a thing of the past.

Sullivan shares her notion about the changing West, and both he and Barry try to keep Robert Dix, their younger brother, from following in their footsteps as lawmen. Sullivan tells Dix, "My way of making a living is on its way out. I am a freak." Both Sullivan and Stanwyck are people trying to find their way in a rapidly changing world.

The film reaches it crisis point when Erickson murders Barry and is arrested for the crime. At the climax, Erickson uses Stanwyck as a human shield to break jail. Confronting him on the street, Sullivan shoots, but does not kill, Stanwyck and then kills Erickson. By that time, however, Stanwyck is willing to give up all that she had built for Sullivan. The federal government is preparing charges against her for tax fraud, and the town no longer does her bidding. Just before the jail break, she informed Erickson that he would have to hang — the judge and jury were no longer hers to control.

Forty Guns ends with Robert Dix ensconced in town as the new sheriff, Barry Sullivan driving his buckboard slowly out of town, and Stanwyck, now fully healed from her gunshot wound, running after Sullivan, yelling, "Mr. Bonnell, Mr. Bonnell!" The ending of *Forty Guns* is a compelling contrast to the beginning. In the beginning, Stanwyck was the black-clad assertive woman with a whip who ran the town. At the end of the film she is a broken woman in a dress running after her man, crying for him to wait for her as he rides out of town. Those two images tell us much about the conflicted role of women in the United States in 1957.

Phil Hardy, in *The Western*, calls *Trooper Hook* a "significant Western." And he notes that director Charles Marquis Warren "neatly and powerfully forces his characters to confront their previously unexamined attitudes" (Hardy, 260). Stanwyck gives a strong performance as Cora Sutliff, a woman who had been kidnapped by Apaches.

After Stanwyck was kidnapped, she became the squaw of Rodolfo Acosta, playing the Apache leader Nanchez, and had borne a son with Acosta. When she is discovered after Joel McCrea and his soldiers capture Acosta and his band, Stanwyck refuses to give up her son. In Chapter 10, I examined white attitudes toward her mixed race son. The pertinent element of *Trooper Hook* for this chapter is the manner in which Stanwyck endeavored to adjust to living in white society once again.

Mindful of white attitudes toward captive white women (and recognizing their blame-the-victim mentality, Stanwyck confesses to McCrea that she did what she had to do to survive. Acosta beat her when she would not work. But initially the Apache women were worse than the men. But then, Stanwyck says, she became Acosta's squaw. She became an Apache woman; she worked like them and even began to smell like them. But she did what she had to in order to survive. McCrea comforts her by relating a story of his existence at Andersonville prison during the Civil War. A demented old man liked dogs, and so McCrea pretended to be a dog in order to get part of the old man's meager rations. Each day, McCrea told Stanwyck, he pretended to be a dog until the old man died. People in crises, so it seems, will do what they have to do to survive.

Stanwyck's Cora Sutliff survived because she is a strong woman. She protects her mixed race son, and she remains quiet in the face of prejudiced taunts. But her strength is most poignantly displayed when she is reunited with John Dehner (playing Fred Sutliff), her husband. Dehner feels sorry for himself. He speaks of what he has suffered during the years of separation and has little understanding of what Stanwyck experienced. Dehner is appalled that Stanwyck brought her mixed race son with her. Dehner insists that the boy cannot remain with them, and Stanwyck is equally insistent that he will. She wants Dehner to give the relationship a chance.

At one point in their conversation Dehner tells Stanwyck that he was ready to forgive her. Stanwyck is flabbergasted. What is there to forgive? She jumps from her chair, indignantly proclaiming, "Forgive me?!" She goes into the other room, collects her meager belongings and prepares to leave the house. Clearly Stanwyck can't live with Dehner any longer because he, too, blames her for permitting herself to be captured alive and sexually tarnished by Acosta. Although Stanwyck will not remain without her son, it is also true that whatever love existed between her and Dehner has vanished. Dehner could not overcome his prejudice. When compared with the strong Stanwyck, Dehner is a weak male.

Trooper Hook ends with both Acosta and Dehner killed as Stanwyck, McCrea and the boy flee the attacking Apaches. But, in the end, two people who know what it means to do anything necessary to survive are united. McCrea is a strong man, a fitting mate for the survivor Stanwyck. Of all her Westerns, Barbara Stanwyck's role as Cora Sutliff remains my favorite.

While *McLintock* (United Artists, 1963) is clearly William Shakespeare's *Taming of the Shrew* transported to a western stetting, there is much more to the film than that. Viewing *McLintock* in the first decade of the twenty-first century, one is struck by the extent to which the 1960s leap from the screen. And recognizing the manner in which the film reflects the decade helps one to understand why Maureen O'Hara (playing Katherine McLintock) and, to a great extent, Stefanie Powers (Becky McLintock) behave like shrews.

Wayne's conservative political and economic views emerge more clearly in this film than in many other Westerns in which he appeared. Near the beginning of *McLintock*, Wayne points out to the homesteaders who hope to farm the mesa the impossibility of the task ahead of them. When one of the farmers protests that the government gave them the land, Wayne replies that the government never gives anybody anything. The homesteaders will have to improve the land, and that, Wayne contends, will be difficult. The mesa was made for buffalo, and cattle have done alright grazing there, but it is six thousand feet above sea level and will be hard to plow. Later, Wayne shakes his head in disbelief at fresh-out-of-college Jerry Van Dyke's (Matt Douglas Jr.) assertion that Wayne is a reactionary because he earns a profit from the beef he sells. And government officials (particularly Strother Martin, playing Agard the Indian agent) and Robert Lowery (as territorial governor Cuthbert Humphrey), are pompous human beings taken with their own authority and importance. They are not public officials concerned very much with the public good.

In *McLintock*, Wayne has little use for college kids. That surely anticipates middle America's bewilderment with, and anger at, college students as the 1960s wore on. Middle America did not understand the music, attitudes or behavior of the college generation. In 1960, middle Americans still affirmed the values and behavior shaped by the rigors of economic depression and world war. Theirs was a different America from the one baby boomers experienced. The split between the two groups widened in the 1960s because older Americans regarded college students as spoiled children who did not understand how good they had it.

Wayne speaks for older America in two ways during the film. First, in aiding Comanches, a people he had fought in his younger years, Wayne defends the old order. When Michael Pate, playing Puma, an old Comanche chief who has been imprisoned, and Wayne greet one another, it is as blood brothers and revered enemies.

Both Pate and Wayne have nothing but contempt for Strother Martin, who insists that the Indians are obligated to take orders from him. The Indians are a symbol in *McLintock*; they represent the old values and behavior patterns to which Wayne subscribed, and which he thought were dissipating in the 1960s.

Second, Wayne also represents the old order when he tells Stefanie Powers that she will not inherit his ranch once he dies. He has willed her a small spread on the upper Green River, but that is all. The rest of his ranch will go to the government for a national park, a place where the timber and buffalo will be protected, a place out of reach of those who want to destroy the Old West. Furthermore, Wayne tells Powers that he wants her to find the right man, get married and, together with her husband, build a life as he and her mother had done. In that, Wayne echoes the mothers and fathers of the baby boomers who worried that their children did not appreciate the importance of hard work and of building something for the future. Like Wayne, many of the men who had served in the military during the war and returned home to build successful careers feared that their children took success for granted; they feared that their children assumed that success was a right rather than a product of hard work.

It is this culturally conservative milieu that Maureen O'Hara rejects. She had separated from Wayne because she disliked the small town, the ranch and the people, whom she regarded as socially inferior. O'Hara lives in New York City and other places in the East, and she spends her summers at Newport. Culturally, she regards the East as superior, and Wayne's world as inferior and contemptible. O'Hara associates with the elite and powerful. She dislikes the vulgarity of familiarity, insisting that she be addressed as Katherine rather than Katie, and that her daughter be called Rebecca, not Becky. She treats all people in the town of McLintock and on the ranch as her social inferiors, even the old family friend. Jack Kruschen (Birnbaum, the general store proprietor).

O'Hara is a shrew because she developed a sense of social and cultural superiority after she and Wayne had overcome Indians and other obstacles on their way to wealth and power. In short, O'Hara is a shrew because she has forgotten her roots! She returns to McLintock only because their daughter is returning from college, and she wants to take her east to live with her. Wayne will not agree to let Powers live in the East, and a comedy of conflict follows as O'Hara moves back to the ranch and engages Wayne in a matrimonial tug of war over their daughter. As Wayne said to O'Hara on their first meeting after she returned to McLintock, "Indian fighting is good practice for our kind of conversation."

Stefanie Powers herself is a bit of a shrew. She is a shrew not because she has forgotten her roots, but because she has been to college. Powers has become an elitist who judges people by their educational and social pedigrees. For example, she calls Purdue an acceptable college for a backward place like Indiana, and she wants to know why Patrick Wayne (playing Devlin Wilson) only attended two years. In seems beyond her comprehension that anyone could be too poor to afford four years of college. She treats him with contempt, although she secretly admires his masculine demeanor (which contrasts sharply with that of the less manly Jerry Van Dyke [as Matt Douglas Jr., with whom she had gone to college]). The relationship between Patrick Wayne and Stefanie Powers parallels the ongoing conflict between Wayne and O'Hara. It culminate when Patrick Wayne turns Powers over his knee to spank her as Wayne hands him a coal shovel to use on Powers' posterior. Patrick Wayne returns the favor at the end of the film when Wayne turns O'Hara across his knee after he has chased her through the town — she in her bloomers. By the end of the film, both women are tamed.

John Wayne, on the other hand, is not totally free from responsibility for his marital difficulties with O'Hara. Yvonne De Carlo, playing Louise Warren, the ranch cook, and Wayne get drunk one night and fall down the stairs. De Carlo winds up sitting on Wayne's lap. When O'Hara finds them in the drunken stupor at the bottom of the stairs, De Carlo tells O'Hara not to draw any false conclusions because she is sitting on Wayne's lap. O'Hara replies that the first one-hundred women sitting on his lap bothered her, but the one-hundred-and-first one was of little consequence. There is more than a strong hint throughout the film that Wayne had been

something of a womanizer. That may explain Wayne's unwillingness to discuss the situation when Powers asked him why he and her mother had
separated.

   McLintock is as much a comedy as anything. The brawl in the mud
pit, the chase around town with O'Hara in her bloomers, and the Indian
raid to free their chiefs from military confinement (a raid that barely dis-
rupts the town's Fourth of July celebration) make the film enjoyable. In
the final analysis, however, the film's message is that women are meant to
be wives and mothers. Women are most contented following the traditional
roles that women have historically played. When they reject their true
nature, they become haughty; they become shrews. It is then obligatory
for strong males to tame them. One can be sure that as *McLintock* ends,
O'Hara will continue to speak her mind, that she will never be a submis-
sive little wife. But one can equally be sure that she will also continue
to live at the ranch and that John Wayne will move back into the master
bedroom!

   From the late 1960s to 1990, public attitudes and policies about the
place of women in American life changed dramatically. Discriminatory
gender attitudes and policies fell rapidly as women moved into corporate
and political leadership, as well as other careers (such as doctors, lawyers
and accountants) that had been closed to women for the most part. But it
was also a period in which the number of Westerns produced declined
substantially. For example, in the thirteen years after 1955 four-hundred-
and-sixty Westerns were released (an average of thirty-five per year), but
in the twenty-one years after 1968 only two-hundred-and-seventy-five
Westerns appeared on the big screen (an average of thirteen per year)
(Adams and Rainey; Rainey, 1990). If one considers only the ten years
between 1980 and 1989, a meager sixty-four Westerns were released (an
average of just over six films per year).

   Westerns probably were not the best films to express the changing role
of women in American culture, and the decline in the number of them
produced suggests the degree to which the genre had lost its hold on public affection. However, it is also true that diverse screen images of women
appeared in the few Westerns that *were* being produced, images that
reflected the changing role of women in American culture.

   Linda Hunt's role as Stella in *Silverado* (Columbia, 1985) is impressive. Owner of the Midnight Star, a saloon in Silverado, she takes in Kevin
Kline (playing Paden) as her partner. Both Hunt and Kline recognize that

Linda Hunt stares at the body of a man Brian Dennehy just killed while Kevin Kline and Scott Glenn look on in *Silverado* (1985).

Brian Dennehy (as Cobb) is a corrupt sheriff who must be stopped. It is Hunt, however, who expresses a philosophy of life that permeates *Silverado*. Hunt is a short woman who has a ramp built behind the bar so she can serve drinks. When Kline comments on the cleverness of the arrangement, Hunt only replies that the world is what you make it. Later, in a conversation in the saloon, Hunt tells Kline that she has observed that the big and powerful try to push other people around. But they can only do that if you let them, and then she reiterates her philosophy of life: "The world is what you make of it." Hunt's comment serves as the impetus for Kline and his compatriots (Scott Glenn, Kevin Costner and Danny Glover) to take on Dennehy and his gang.

Hunt's part in *Silverado* as a woman who plays a vital role in public life was anticipated in four of John Wayne's later films: *True Grit* (Paramount, 1969), *The Train Robbers* (Warner Brothers, 1973), *Rooster Cogburn*

(Universal, 1975) and *The Shootist* (Paramount, 1976). Kim Darby's Mattie Ross is a determined young woman in *True Grit*. She vows to avenge the murder of her father by Jeff Corey (playing Tom Chaney). She out-bargains Strother Martin in a horse trade, and she is more than Wayne's equal when she convinces him to help her find Corey. As Wayne, Darby and Glenn Campbell (as La Boeuf) pursue Corey, who has joined Robert Duvall's (Ned Pepper) gang, Darby proves herself to be a persistent and brave young woman; she will not be left behind. It is Darby who shoots Corey, gets herself captured, and falls into a pit of rattlesnakes. She only escapes death when Wayne makes a mad dash with her to a doctor. John Wayne would win his only academy award for *True Grit*, but Kim Darby's role as the girl with true grit is equally impressive.

Surely a man as macho as John Wayne would not permit himself to be taken in by a woman, but that is exactly the scenario in *The Train Robbers*. Ann-Margret (playing Mrs. Lowe) convinces Wayne and his three friends (Ben Johnson, Rod Taylor and Bobby Vinton) that her now-deceased husband had stolen half-a-million dollars in gold, which is now stashed in a wrecked train in Mexico. Ann-Margret will give Wayne $50,000 if he helps her recover the gold. *The Train Robbers* unfolds as Wayne's party (including Ann-Margret) travel to the wrecked train and fight off the remaining members of the gang (who want the gold for themselves). Ann-Margret continually plays on their sympathies as a helpless widow with a young son. As the party returns with the gold, the men decide to forgo their share in order to give it to her young son. It is then that Wayne learns that he has been duped. Ricardo Montalban, playing a Pinkerton detective, informs them that she is not Mrs. Lowe, but a whore who worked in the brothel in which Lowe had died, and that Lowe had never been married. The film ends with the men jumping on their horses in pursuit, or, as Wayne says, "to rob a train."

Rooster Cogburn is a delightful film in many ways. Just as Ann-Margret makes *The Train Robbers* an unusual Wayne Western, Katharine Hepburn, as the missionary spinster Eula Goodnight, makes *Rooster Cogburn* memorable. Just like Kim Darby in *True Grit*, Hepburn insists on accompanying Wayne as he tracks down her father's killers. Hepburn more than proves herself worthy of Wayne's respect. She demonstrates that she can shoot straight, and during an ambush she actually saves Wayne's life. Although she nags at him about his excessive drinking, she is remarkably tolerant when he lights up a cigar after they eat. And Hepburn (and not a double) rides the rapids during the film's exciting climax. In fact, Roberts and Olson write that Wayne admired Hepburn because she was willing to ride horses and the raft down the rapids, things she did not particularly like to do. Wayne commented, "She's a man's woman. Imagine how she must have been at age 25 or 30" (Roberts and Olson, 619). *Rooster Cogburn* is delightful for that very reason; Hepburn plays a woman every bit Wayne's equal. She symbolizes the new world into which women were entering, a world in which women would be respected for their courage, grit and ability, not merely for their sexual function.

Lauren Bacall (Mrs. Rogers) plays a similar, but different, role in *The Shootist*. Bacall runs the Carson City boarding house in which Wayne takes a room while he waits to die from cancer. Bacall is a widow who insists that her boarders follow her rules. She does not know Wayne's identify as the famous gunfighter J.B. Books, nor does she much care. She is a dignified woman who runs a quiet household, and she expects Wayne, who has spent all of his life giving orders and getting his way, to behave accordingly. Tense is an appropriate description of their relationship early in the film. But as *The Shootist* progresses, and once Bacall learns of Wayne's impending death, the two strike up what Ricci, Zmijewsky and Zmijewsky call "a platonic romance" (Ricci, 316). Increasingly, Bacall becomes more protective of Wayne as she senses his increasing pain from the cancer. And, as her last act of kindness, she has his best suit dry-cleaned on the day he has chosen to die in a gunfight rather than let the cancer kill him in a slow agonizing manner. In *The Shootist*, Lauren Bacall's Mrs. Rogers is a dignified, reserved woman, and it is these very qualities that permit Wayne's J.B. Books to live his last days with dignity as well.

Verna Bloom appeared in two Westerns in the 1970s—*The Hired Hand* (Universal, 1971) and *High Plains Drifter* (Universal, 1973)—in which she played a strong woman. Bloom, as Hannah Collings, is Peter Fonda's wife in *The Hired Hand*. She is some years older than Fonda, and he had abandoned her to spend several years wandering the West with Warren Oates. When Fonda and Oates return to his ranch, Bloom treats them like hired hands. They will work and they will sleep in the barn; Bloom will not permit Fonda to share her bed and renew marital intimacy as if nothing had transpired between them.

In his absence, Bloom had managed the ranch and hired men to help her with the work. Bloom's image in the film is one of a ranch wife, not a glamorous, well dressed urbanite. She is a hard working frontier woman who made her way in the world without relying on a husband to provide for her. Gradually, however, Bloom and Fonda renew their relationship, but on *her* terms. It is then that viewers discover something else, something startling for a film released in 1971. Verna Bloom's Hannah Collings is a woman with sexual desires. She acknowledges to Fonda that the hired help provided sexual services for her — although, again, it was on her terms; they were men who worked for her and helped her satisfy her biological drives. She tells Fonda that sometimes it would be in the barn, and sometimes in the open field, but never in her bed in the bedroom. In *The Hired Hand*, Bloom's character is a remarkable woman for an early 1970s film, but her character is a harbinger of the impending revolution in gender relationships.

Verna Bloom plays Sarah Belding in *High Plains Drifter*. She is the wife of Ted Hartley (playing Lewis Belding), one of the town leaders of Lagos. Hartley and the other town bigwigs are really part of a murder conspiracy. The rich mine they own sits on government property, and when the sheriff learned about it they had him murdered. Now they live in fear — fear that the three men they framed will kill them when released from prison, and fear that somebody will uncover their secret. In a town of cowards and hypocrites, Bloom's Sarah Belding is the only character with any sense of integrity. Bloom is the only one in town who does not readily cater to the Stranger's (Clint Eastwood) whims.

In the end, however, Bloom and Eastwood sleep together. But what is most striking, Bloom realizes that she can no longer live with a hypocrite such as Hartley. On the morning after the climactic shootout between Eastwood and the three ex-convicts who have returned to wreak vengeance on the town, Bloom loads a buckboard with her belongings, preparing to leave Lagos and her husband.

In neither film does Bloom play a glamorous woman. Rather, her characters are somewhat plain, no-nonsense females. They are serious-minded women who possess the necessary integrity to be true to themselves, and, in the case of *The Hired Hand*, honest enough to acknowledge their sexual needs.

If Darby, Hepburn, Bacall and Bloom represent determined, courageous women who are the hero's equal, their counterpart is the equally independent prostitute. Probably the best known of these is the drug dependent Julie Christie (Constance Miller) in *McCabe and Mrs. Miller* (Warner Brothers, 1971). Equally interesting, however, is Jeanne Moreau's portrayal of the prostitute Martine Bernard in *Monte Walsh*. Moreau wants to marry Lee Marvin (Monte Walsh), but she knows that it likely will never happen. However, she promises to wait for him while he makes enough money to marry her. Moreau is a realistic woman who understands that Marvin is both a dreamer and too set in his ways to give up being a cowboy and settle down with a wife. Moreau (along with Jack Palance) is the pillar that gives Marvin whatever emotional stability he has in life. When both Moreau and Palance die, Marvin is left to drift alone toward an uncertain future.

Shirley MacLaine (as Sister Sara) may be the real star of *Two Mules for Sister Sara* (Universal, 1970), even though the film is normally thought of as a Clint Eastwood vehicle. MacLaine is a prostitute masquerading as a nun. Eastwood is convinced that she is a woman of God after he rescues her from being raped and killed by three men. MacLaine plays a sassy, independent woman who is more than Eastwood's equal. She aids the Mexican people in their fight against the French; Eastwood has been hired by the guerrillas to help them get gold with which to buy arms.

Eastwood is completely taken in by MacLaine (reminiscent of the manner in which Ann-Margret fooled John Wayne in *The Train Robbers*), and he is speechless (even for Eastwood) when he learns her true identity. But MacLaine is also Eastwood's conscience. Initially, his intentions are mercenary; Eastwood helps the rebels because they pay him, not because he supports their cause. Gradually, however, MacLaine enables him to see how oppressively the French treat the Mexicans. And, gradually, Eastwood and MacLaine fall in love. The film ends with MacLaine on her donkey following Eastwood; she has given up her profession of entertaining many men to become a one-man woman!

Of all of the 1970s films in which the heroine played a prostitute, Faye Dunaway's portrayal of Kate Elder in *Doc* is the most intriguing. Stacy Keach (as Doc) wins Dunaway from Mike Witney (Ike Clanton) in a poker game at the beginning of the film. But Keach does not want to take her to Tombstone with him. "I don't travel with anybody," Keach tells Dunaway, but he ultimately changes his mind. The Tombstone to which they ride is a bustling city, and Dunaway is a well known, popular whore. As she dismounts from Keach's horse and walks toward the brothel in which she works, the men of the town treat her as if she were a victorious queen returning to her castle. Dunaway is a popular woman and proud of her profession!

Keach is quite taken by Dunaway, and one night he goes to the brothel and tears her away from a customer; they set up housekeeping in a small house in the Mexican neighborhood of Tombstone. Dunaway fixes up the place so that it becomes a home, and she becomes a common law wife to Keach. But she wants more; she wants real marriage and a child, things far removed from Keach's violent world. At one point, one of the good church ladies of the town stops by to scold Dunaway for living in sin, and the woman tells Dunaway that she should get on her knees and repent of her wicked ways. Dunaway rejects that notion and assures the woman, "When I am on my knees, it won't be in prayer."

However, life with Dunaway begins to change Keach; he must choose between her and his friends, the Earps. Harris Yulin (as Wyatt Earp) even tells Dunaway, "Ever since you hooked on to him, he ain't been himself. He can't think straight." Soon Keach and Dunaway begin to drift apart. One night, high on opium, Keach promises Dunaway that they will go away soon. Dunaway replies, "Soon ain't soon enough." That is the last viewers see of Dunaway in the film. She is a woman who discovers the stability and happiness of living with one man in a steady relationship. When Keach rejects that sort of life to join with the Earps in the shootout, Dunaway leaves him. The house Dunaway had made a home becomes a shack again. Throughout the film, Dunaway is a strong woman, first as a prostitute and then as Keach's partner. She is also a woman who knows what she wants, and she leaves Keach when he does not live up to her expectations of marriage and a family.

Raquel Welch offers viewers a different kind of heroine in *Hannie Calder* (Paramount, 1972) and *100 Rifles* (20th Century–Fox, 1969). In the first film, Welch plays a woman who has been brutally gang raped, and who hunts down and kills her three attackers. In *100 Rifles*, Welch plays a Yaqui Indian woman, Sarita, who fights with the guerrillas against Fernando Lamas (as Verdugo). Welch uses her female attractiveness to lure unsuspecting males into traps; then Welch becomes a warrior.

For example, near the end of the film, Welch is showering in a semi-transparent garment at a railroad watering tank. Of course, the soldiers whistle and gawk at her, and because they are looking at Welch they don't see the trap the Yaquis have laid for them. In the fight that follows, Welch switches from being a sex object to a fighter, shooting as effectively as the men. In *100 Rifles*, Raquel Welch continues the tradition of gun-toting heroines first begun by the likes of Evelyn Finely and Reno Browne in 1940s B Westerns. The major difference is that films had changed by the time Welch came along. Welch's sexuality could be used as a weapon in her fight for justice for her people in a way that 1940s censors would never have permitted.

One should not assume that Westerns in the 1970s and 1980s ignored the traditional role of women as wives and mothers, because they did not.

Two films can be cited as good examples of portraying more traditional roles for women. Dana Wynter's role as Valerie, Glenn Ford's (Santee) wife in *Santee* (Crown Productions, 1973), is impressive. Together, Wynter and Ford have developed a strong marriage, and they have built an excellent horse ranch. Wynter maintains a home to which Ford returns after his excursions as a bounty hunter. But once home, nothing is said about Ford's profession; home is an island of sanity for him, a place away from a violent occupation. In their married life, Wynter and Ford have lost a son, murdered by outlaws, and they hurt and healed together.

In short, they are two people deeply in love who have committed their lives to one another. Wynter's character supports her husband, but she is never afraid to speak her mind, to let Ford know her preferences. If any Western shows marriage as it ought to be, *Santee* could lay claim to being that film. *Santee* depicts marriage as it has increasingly come to be understood, a relationship between two equally important partners who have pledged to help each other as they build a life together, not as a relationship in which the male as breadwinner is the most important partner and the entire household revolves around his every whim.

Carrie Snodgrass assumes a traditional role as Sarah Wheeler in *Pale Rider* (Warner Brothers, 1985). She is a widow with a teenage daughter, Sydney Penny (playing Megan Wheeler). She probably will marry Michael Moriarty (Hull Barret) at some time, but it will be Snodgrass who decides when, not Moriarty! Snodgrass is a voice of caution and reason as the independent miners endeavor to keep their claims in the face of unrelenting opposition by the wealthy Richard Dysart (Coy LaHood). She takes in the Preacher (Clint Eastwood) as a border and tries to help Penny (along with Eastwood) understand that she is not yet a full-grown woman. Snodgrass' portrayal of a mother trying to help her teenage daughter work through her first love (and to understand that Penny's infatuation with Eastwood is merely a passing fancy) is an involving subplot in a very good film.

As the last decade of the twentieth century opened, the gender revolution was nearly complete. Affirmative action programs had assured women access to leadership positions and careers long denied them. Archaic laws that discriminated against women (for example, laws giving preference to men serving as estate executors) had been declared unconstitutional by the courts. Much remained to be done (equal pay for equal work, for instance), but state and federal laws were bound to change as more and more women were elected to State Legislatures and the Federal

Congress. In fact, by the 1990s the gender revolution had been so successful that college-aged women needed to be reminded that things had not always been the way they found them. Women taking my class on the history of the United States in the 1930s and 1940s are appalled at the image of women they see in films of the era, and they struggle to understand that it was only a few short years ago that women broke free from the constricting roles that tradition had defined for them.

It is not surprising that women in 1990s Westerns portrayed characters that further elaborate the changes that had begun in the 1970s and 1980s. The images of women in the two 1990s Wyatt Earp films are instructive of the manner in which domestic relationships changed.

Dana Delaney's Josephine in *Tombstone* (Buena Vista, 1993) is a woman who knows what she wants. She is the aggressor in her relationship with Kurt Russell (playing Wyatt Earp). From the moment she saw Russell (as she exits the stagecoach in Tombstone), Delaney is attracted to him. She ignores his many brush-offs until finally one day they meet on the trail while riding. It is she who pushes the conversation as they relax on a blanket in a meadow while their horses graze nearby. Delaney is frank with Russell: "I am a woman, I like men." She wants to travel, to live a life of luxury and ease. As she tells Russell, her idea of Heaven is room service. When Russell and Val Kilmer (Doc Holliday) commence their killing rampage after the shootout in Tombstone, Delaney leaves him. Again she takes the role of aggressor, walking away from a relationship she has cultivated because she abhors the violence in Tombstone. *Tombstone* concludes as Russell leaves a dying Kilmer to go search for Delaney.

Many young women of the 1990s are like Dana Delaney's Josephine in *Tombstone*. They do not sit at home or in their college rooms waiting to be asked out on a date by a male to whom they are attracted; they initiate the relationship. The modern male does not have to guess whether or not a woman is attracted to him; more than likely, she will tell him!

The wives in *Wyatt Earp* (Warner Brothers, 1994) are faithful partners, but they are also outspoken. They make clear to Kevin Costner (as Wyatt Earp) that they do not want to leave Dodge City for Tombstone. They have a good, prosperous life in Dodge City, and they don't want to give it up, but, as faithful wives have always done, they follow their husbands to Tombstone. But they also remind Costner that his big plans have not borne fruit. The mining claims have not paid off; all of his schemes to strike it rich have fallen through.

When the women insist that their voices count as much as the men's, Costner rejects that view. He tells the women that, "Wives don't count as much as brothers." Wives die; brothers are for always. One of the women merely replies, "You are a hard man, Wyatt Earp." But Costner is wrong; brothers don't last forever. One brother is killed and the other badly crippled. It is the wives who remain, one to mourn her dead husband and the other to nurse her mangled spouse. The wives' boldness surfaces later in the film when one of the women slaps Costner and snarls, "Damn you to Hell, Wyatt Earp!"

The image of the Earp women in the Costner film may be historically accurate if one can believe Ron Lackman. He claims that the Earps struggled financially while they lived in Tombstone. In order to supplement the family income, the Earp women took in sewing and did other odd jobs, possibly including prostitution (Lackman, 55). If that is the case, then more than likely they would have made known their views on family finance.

Bad Girls (20th Century–Fox, 1994) and *The Quick and the Dead* (Columbia Tri-Star, 1995) offer viewers a different image of women. *Bad Girls* is unlike traditional Westerns in that it contains some nudity and numerous sexual situations, and the central focus of the film is on four heroines, not heroes. But in other ways, *Bad Girls* has a great deal in common with traditional Westerns. The stunt work, the bravery of the four women, the bigger-than-life bad guys and the climactic shootout are all ingredients of a typical Western.

The film opens with the four women working as prostitutes in a saloon/bordello. Their counterpart is the preacher and his flock that condemns the drinkin', gamblin' and whorin' that goes on under their very noses. The girls are forced to flee town when Madeline Stowe (playing Cody Zamora) kills a respected town leader who insists on kissing Mary Stuart Masterson (Anita Crown). It is his birthday and he wants the kiss he paid for! Viewers learn that Masterson's husband had died of cholera as they were on their way to a western homestead; she had become a prostitute as her only means of surviving. She tells her dead husband at his gravesite that she is no longer his blushing bride, but Masterson adds that she never let another man kiss her.

The preacher organizes a lynch mob to hang Stowe. His gospel has no grace; it is all austere Hellfire, damnation and judgment. The preacher condemns Stowe to Hell; she has a scorpion between her legs that has ruined many a good man. But before the mob can hang Stowe, her sister prostitutes rescue her. As they gallop out of town, one of the horses tramples the Bible the preacher was carrying.

Above: Drew Barrymore, as one of the ***Bad Girls,*** demonstrates that a woman can survive in the wild west while retaining her femininity. ***Opposite:*** Madeline Stowe plays Cody Zamora, leader of the ***Bad Girls*** (1994).

On the run from Pinkerton detectives the dead man's wife has hired to track them down, the women begin to resemble traditional cowboy heroes—except they are women, and they use the attributes of their sex to influence men and escape difficult situations. Sitting around the campfire at night, the women agree they are done with being whores. They will settle on Masterson's homestead claim and start a sawmill with Stowe's banked savings. As one of them asks, "We sold our bodies, why can't we sell wood?"

In the adventures that follow, Drew Barrymore chases down and stops a runaway team of horses. They get caught in a bank robbery and lose Stowe's money to James Russo (playing Kid Jarrett), and the film unfolds as the women fight to get their money back. At one point, Andie Mac-Dowell (Eileen Spenser) is jailed, and Drew Barrymore uses her sex appeal to help free the prisoner. She visits the jail and claims that a man beat her. She shows the deputy marks near a breast and raises her skirt, displaying her thigh and garter. Needless to say, the deputy is kept occupied ogling Barrymore's bare skin while Masterson frees MacDowell from jail. They also learn that Masterson's homesteader claim is not valid because her husband is dead. "It's the law," a lawyer tells Masterson. Frustrated, Masterson proclaims that as a widow she is worthless, "but I had some value as a whore." The women have to come up with a new plan. Masterson does not have a homestead and Stowe has lost her money.

Near the climax of *Bad Girls*, Barrymore is captured by Russo's gang. They force her to strip and put on a red dress; she has to act as a prostitute for the gang. But she, in turn, is rescued by the other women; and in a shootout reminiscent of other Westerns, the four women kill Russo and his gang, and they get back Stowe's money. The film ends as MacDowell decides to marry and remain at the ranch on which they had settled, and as the other three women gallop across the prairie on their way to the Klondike and the gold fields.

Not surprisingly, critics did not care for *Bad Girls* very much. However, the overall theme of the film is interesting. Four women whom fate had turned into whores assert their independence from men (at least, three of them did) and demonstrate that they are able to take care of themselves (they are more than any man's equal in a shootout, for instance). Whatever else may be said about the film, the four bad girls are women of the 1990s.

So is Sharon Stone (as Ellen) in *The Quick and the Dead*. Stone plays a female gunfighter who returns to the town of her childhood, a town now controlled by Gene Hackman (playing Herod). Hackman is an evil man (note the biblical imagery of his name) who hanged Stone's father. He told the little girl that he would let her father go if she could shoot the rope using a pistol, but she killed her father instead. Now she is back to take her revenge on Hackman. Each year the town has a gunfight contest, and Stone enters the contest hoping to meet Hackman.

Stone, however, is not a killer. One evening Hackman invites her to dine with him and Stone appears in a long dress. She has a derringer tucked in her garter. But she can't bring herself to kill Hackman. However, Stone's image at the dinner is an interesting one. She is a lovely woman, and as she raises her skirt under the table to display the derringer, she also bares a lot of shapely thigh. Even though she dresses as a male in the gunfight contest, she remains a woman. By the 1990s, women could have it all. They could compete on near-equal footing with men in many facets of daily life, but they could remain feminine. Stone's role in *The Quick and the Dead* signifies the passing of an era in which women had to choose between being feminine and thus giving up competing with men, or becoming tomboys with little hope of marriage and family. The modern woman can be an athlete and/or outstanding student as well as an attractive person who appeals to men.

But Stone in *The Quick and the Dead* also demonstrates that a woman's value system differs from men. She finds it difficult to kill. She struggles to kill the pimp who raped the saloonkeeper's young daughter and intends to force her into becoming a whore. Finally, in a fit of despair, Stone rides out of town, but she stops by her father's grave. Reminded of who she is and of her mission, Stone returns to the gunfight and kills Hackman.

As they face one another, Hackman wants to know who she is. Westerns have a long tradition of a family member taking revenge on the person who killed one or both parents. Bob Steele and John Wayne made careers out of that theme in the 1930s. Therefore, one expects Stone to identify herself and claim revenge, but she does not. All she utters is, "You stole my childhood." For males, the moment of confronting Hackman would be a sweet moment of revenge, but for Stone, as a woman, it is a reminder of the relationship with her father that Hackman destroyed. Stone's response to Hackman focuses on relationship, not revenge.

That is an important difference. As women assume positions of political and corporate leadership, and move into significant research and teaching careers, it is becoming clearer that men and women process information differently, and that they value different things. For example, Cindy Simon Rosenthal in *Women Transforming Congress*, demonstrates that women in Congress understand their representational roles differently than do men, and they approach the legislative process in ways distinctive to their sex (Rosenthal). Sharon Stone's Ellen makes that same point in *The Quick and the Dead.*

Sharon Stone and the four ladies of *Bad Girls* are women who compete in a man's world as women. They retain feminine appeal while proving their worth in gunfights, ranch work and even chasing down runaway buckboards. Suzy Ames, as Little Jo Monaghan, in *The Ballad of Little Jo* (Fine Line Features, 1993) gives viewers a different perspective. In order to succeed on the raw frontier, really a man's world, she passes herself off as a man.

Ames' Little Jo is a victim of male predators. She is seduced by a photographer, and when she becomes pregnant, Ames' family throws her out of the house. She travels west, only to fall victim to Rene Auberjonois (playing Streight Hollander) when he sells her to two wandering ex–Union soldiers. She escapes from their clutches, buys men's clothing, cuts her hair, puts a scar on her face and rides into Ruby City masquerading as a man.

She digs for gold — hard work in the mud and rain — until Ian McKellan (as Percy) offers to let her rent a room from him if she will take a job at the livery stable. The work is no less arduous— Ames merely exchanges digging dirt in search of gold for shoveling manure. But she is a hard worker, and soon becomes a friend to all the men and women in town. She even stops McKellan from killing a prostitute. McKellan had told Ames that he "found women to be more trouble than they are worth." McKellan concludes, "Once a month I visit the girls in their tents." He found it to be cheaper and less trouble than being married. Soon after stopping him from killing the prostitute, Ames goes to work for Bo Hopkins (Frank Badger), tending his sheep during the winter. There she learns to shoot in order to kill coyotes that raid the flock.

Ames stakes out a homestead. She builds a cabin and runs a flock of sheep. She even rescues David Chung (Tinman Wong) from a potential lynch mob. Forced to take him on as an employee, Ames has Wong do the household work while she runs the ranch. Then one day Ames confesses that she is really a woman, and she and Wong become lovers; they establish their own little two-person family on the frontier. They are two social discards, both the objects of discrimination, who find happiness together in their isolated homestead.

Ames and Wong's happiness is threatened when an eastern cattle company begins to buy up all of the land. They murder a Russian family of homesteaders, and they try to buy — and then scare — Ames off of her land. Ames, however, is more than their equal. On her way to Ruby City with Bo Hopkins to vote, they are accosted by three gunmen. Ames kills two of them with her revolver and shoots the other one with her rifle as he tries to escape. She is a woman who knows how to handle firearms.

The tragedy of *The Ballad of Little Jo* is public reaction after she dies and the undertaker discovers her true sex. The people of Ruby City, all former friends, now talk of her as a freak. They even mount her dressed as a man on a horse and place that picture in newspapers next to the tin-type of her as a woman. In a fit of bitterness, Bo Hopkins, Little Jo's best friend, even wrecks her cabin! In order to survive in a man's world, Suzy Ames, as Little Jo Monaghan, had masqueraded as a man. She had proven herself capable of doing men's work, and she had become a success on the frontier, a man's world.

The three films—*Bad Girls* and *The Quick and the Dead* on the one hand, and *The Ballad Little Jo* on the other — suggest the dilemma for contemporary women. Can they continue to be women who bring a woman's perspective to positions of leadership, or must they ultimately become like men in order to earn promotions and move into higher leadership positions? The first two films suggest that women can succeed in a male-oriented world without compromising their femininity.

The Ballad of Little Jo represents the opposite. The cover of the box for the videotape of the film proclaims, "In the wild west, a woman had only two choices. She could be a wife or she could be a whore." Suzy Ames' Little Jo Monaghan could not have prospered on the frontier as a woman. If she had not masqueraded as a man, more than likely she would have been the woman wearing a transparent nightgown paraded into Ruby City on a horse by a pimp to be used for the pleasure of men. Only time will tell which model, the one of *Bad Girls* and *The Quick and the Dead*, or of *The Ballad of Little Jo*, will dominate gender relationships over the next decade or so.

Epilogue

The first three years of the twenty-first century continued the decline of the Western. Though at least two Westerns appeared in 2001, *Texas Rangers* (Miramax, 2001) was a box-office fiasco because it was not a good film; and *American Outlaws* (Warner Brothers, 2001), a retelling of the Civil War experiences of the James and Younger brothers, only played to larger crowds because its stars, all young heartthrobs, attracted a younger audience. But there is little to suggest that *American Outlaws* encouraged the production of more Westerns. As Scott Simmons notes, no Westerns were released in theaters during 2002 (Simmons, xv).

There is a strong temptation to pronounce the Western dead. But that happened several times in the twentieth century, and the genre always demonstrated its resilience by bouncing back into public affection. And, as these words are being written, there are signs of life reappearing in the genre. Tom Selleck starred in *The Darkening Trail* and *Monte Walsh*, both produced for television by TNT. In 2003, the USA television network is running a new Western series, *The Peacemakers*. Fans of Westerns eagerly await HBO's miniseries *Deadwood*, and in August 2003 Kevin Costner's latest Western, *Open Range* (Buena Vista, 2003), opened in theaters.

Open Range questions the conclusion made at the end of Chapter 5 that Clint Eastwood's *Unforgiven* closed the Western genre. *Unforgiven* is such a powerful post-modern film that I thought it would influence whatever Westerns came after it. Kevin Costner, however, has given motion picture patrons a Western different from the post-modern *Unforgiven*. *Open Range* draws on the twentieth century's rich tradition of the genre.

305

Its villains are not nuanced; they are just plain mean! Robert Duvall (as Boss Spearman) and Kevin Costner (Charley Waite) are heroes in the tradition of Randolph Scott and Joel McCrea. Annette Bening (Sue Barlow) is a heroine reminiscent of 1940s and 1950s heroines. She has more in common with Vera Miles (Hallie Stoddard) from *The Man Who Shot Liberty Valence* than she does with the whores in *Unforgiven* or *Bad Girls*. And the townsfolk who rally behind Duvall and Costner in the final shootout with Michael Gambon (Denton Baxter) and his hired guns are more like townsfolk in traditional Westerns than the inept cowards in *High Plains Drifter*.

As these words are written in 2003, the Western now has two models from which to draw (if, in fact, many Westerns are produced in the future). However, before those who enjoy more traditional Westerns become too hopeful, a word of caution: Only a handful of patrons under thirty years of age attended the screening of *Open Range* at which I was present. It is not clear that the film appeals to younger age cohorts.

There may be life left in the genre, but that remains to be seen. One thing is certain, however. As new Westerns appear they will continue to reflect American culture as it exists at the time of production. Westerns have always been roadmaps that tell viewers more about the contemporary United States than about the country as it existed in the last half of the nineteenth century. I doubt that twenty-first century Westerns will be any different.

BIBLIOGRAPHY

Adams, Les, and Buck Rainey. *Shoot-em Ups: The Complete Guide to Westerns of the Sound Era*. Metuchen, N.J.: Scarecrow Press, 1985.

Bignell, Jonathan. "Method Westerns: The Left-Handed Gun and One-Eyed Jacks," in Ian Cameron and Douglas Pye, editors. *The Book of Westerns*. New York: Continuum, 1996, pp. 111–122.

Blottner, Gene. *Universal-International Westerns, 1947–1963: The Complete Filmography*. Jefferson, North Carolina, and London: McFarland & Company, Inc., Publishers, 2000.

Brant, Marley. *Jesse James: The Man and the Myth*. New York: Berkley Books, 1998.

Brinkley, Alan. *The End of Reform: New Deal Liberalism in Recession and War*. New York: Alfred A. Knopf, 1995.

Brokaw, Tom. *A Long Way Home: Growing Up in the American Heartland*. New York: Random House, 2002.

Brownlow, Kevin, *The War, the West, and the Wilderness*. New York: Alfred A. Knopf, 1979.

Cawelti, John. *The Six-Gun Mystique Sequel*. Bowling Green, OH: Bowling Green State University Popular Press, 1999.

Coyne, Michael. *The Crowded Prairie: American National Identity in the Hollywood Western*. London and New York: I.B. Tauris Publishers, 1998.

Davis, Ronald L. *Duke: The Life and Image of John Wayne*. Norman: University of Oklahoma Press, 1998.

_____. *John Ford: Hollywood's Old Master*. Norman: University of Oklahoma Press, 1995.

_____. *William S. Hart: Projecting the American West*. Norman: University of Oklahoma Press, 2003.

Davis, William C. *The Cause Lost: Myths and Realities of the Confederacy*. Lawrence, Kansas: University Press of Kansas, 1996.

Everson, William K. *The Hollywood Western*. New York: A Citadel Press Book, 1992.

Fenin, George N., and William K. Everson. *The Western: From Silents to Cinerama*. New York: The Orion Press, 1962.

Frye, Northrop. *The Anatomy of Criticism*. Princeton: Princeton University Press, 1957.

Gallafent, Edward. "Four Tombstones 1946–1994," in Ian Cameron and Douglas Pye, editors. *The Book of Westerns*. New York: Continuum, 1996, pp. 302–311.

_____. "Not with a Bang: The End of the West in *Lonely Are the Brave, The Misfits* and *Hud*," in Ian Cameron and Douglas Pye, editors. *The Book of Westerns*. New York: Continuum, 1996, pp. 241–25.

George-Warren, Holly. *Cowboy: How Hollywood Invented the Wild West*. Pleasantville, New York, and London: The Reader's Digest Association, Inc., 2002.

Ginsberg, Benjamin, Theodore J. Lowi and Margaret Weir. *We the People*. New York and London: W.W. Norton & Company, Second Edition, 1999.

Graham, Don. *No Name on the Bullet: A Biography of Audie Murphy*. New York: Viking Penguin, 1990.

Gressley, Gene M., editor. *Old West/New West*. Norman and London: University of Oklahoma Press, 1994.

Grist, Leighton. "*Unforgiven*," in Ian Cameron and Douglas Pye, editors. *The Book of Westerns*. New York: Continuum, 1996, 294–301.

Halberstam, David. *The Fifties*. New York: Villard Books, 1993.

Hardy, Phil. *The Western*. New York: William Morrow and Company, Inc., 1983.

Janda, Kenneth, Jeffrey M. Barry and Jerry Goldman. *The Challenge of Democracy*. Boston and New York: Houghton Mifflin Company, Sixth Edition, 2000.

Kazan, Alfred. *On Native Grounds: A Study of American Prose Literature from 1890 to the Present*. Garden City: Doubleday & Company, Inc., 1956.

Kennedy, David M. *Freedom from Fear: The American People in Depression and War*. New York: Oxford University Press, 1999.

Keynes, Geoffrey, editor. *Blake Complete Writings*. London Oxford New York: Oxford University Press, 1966.

Kitses, Jim. "An Exemplary Post-Modern Western: *The Ballad of Little Jo*," in Jim Kitses and Gregg Rickman, editors. *The Western Reader*. New York: Limelight Editions, 1998, pp. 367–380.

_____. "Peckinpah Re-Visited: *Pat Garrett and Billy the Kid*," in Jim Kitses and Gregg Rickman, editors. *The Western Reader*. New York: Limelight Editions, 1998, pp. 223–244.

Lackman, Ron. *Women of the Western Frontier in Fact, Fiction and Film*. Jefferson, North Carolina, and London: McFarland & Company, Inc., Publishers, 1997.

Lentz, Harris M. III. *Western and Frontier Film and Television Credits 1903–1995*. Jefferson, North Carolina, and London: McFarland & Company, Inc., Publishers, Two Volumes, 1996.

Limerick, Patricia Nelson. *Something in the Soil*. New York. London: W.W. Norton & Company, 2000.

Lowi, Theodore J. *The End of Liberalism: The Second Republic of the United States*. New York London: W.W. Norton & Company, Second Edition, 1979.

Loy, R. Philip. "Politics and the Environment: Toward a New Public Philosophy," in Edwin R. Squiers, editor. *The Environmental Crisis: The Ethical Dilemma*. Mancelonia, Michigan: The Ausable Trails Institute of Environmental Studies, 1982, pp. 209–226.

_____. *Westerns and American Culture, 1930–1955*. Jefferson, North Carolina, and London: McFarland & Company, Inc., Publishers, 2001.

McFeely, William S. *Grant: A Biography*. New York and London: W.W. Norton & Co., 1981.

Macksoud, Meredith C. *Arthur Kennedy, Man of Characters*. Jefferson, North Carolina, and London: McFarland & Company, Inc., Publishers, 2003.

Magers, Boyd, and Michael Fitzgerald. *Western Women*. Jefferson, North Carolina, and London: McFarland & Company, Inc., Publishers, 1999.

Maltby, Richard. "A Better Sense of History: John Ford and the Indians," in Ian Cameron and Douglas Pye, editors. *The Book of Westerns.* New York: Continuum, 1996, pp. 34–50.

Manchester, William. *The Glory and the Dream: A Narrative History of America 1932–1972.* New York: Bantam Books, 1975.

Marriott, Alice. *Hell on Horses & Women.* Norman: University of Oklahoma Press, 1953.

Matthews, Leonard. *History of Western Movies.* New York: Crescent Books, 1984.

Meyer, William R. *The Making of the Great Westerns.* New Rochelle, New York: Arlington House Publishers, 1979.

Myers, John. *Doc Holliday.* Lincoln and London: University of Nebraska Press, 1973.

Neale, Steve. "Vanishing Americans: Racial and Ethnic Issues in the Interpretation and Context of Post-War 'ProIndian' Westerns," in Edward Buscombe and Roberta E. Pearson, editors. *Back in the Saddle Again: New Essays on the Western.* London: British Film Institute, 1998, pp. 8–28.

Nott, Robert. *Last of the Cowboy Heroes: The Westerns of Randolph Scott, Joel McCrea, and Audie Murphy.* Jefferson, North Carolina, and London: McFarland & Company, Inc., Publishers, 2000.

Place, J.A. *The Western Films of John Ford.* Secaucus, N.J.: The Citadel Press, 1974.

Putnam, Robert D. *Bowling Alone: The Collapse and Revival of American Community.* New York: Simon & Schuster, 2000.

Pye, Douglas, "The Collapse of Fantasy: Masculinity in the Westerns of Anthony Mann," in Ian Cameron and Douglas Pye, editors. *The Book of Westerns.* New York: Continuum, 1996, pp. 167–173.

_____. "Ulzana's Raid," in Ian Cameron and Douglas Pye, editors. *The Book of Westerns.* New York: Continuum, 1996, pp. 262–268.

Rainey, Buck. *The Reel Cowboy: Essays on the Myth in Movies and Literature.* Jefferson, North Carolina, and London: McFarland & Company, Inc., Publishers, 1996.

_____. *The Shoot-Em-Ups Ride Again: A Supplement to Shoot-Em-Ups.* Waynesville, North Carolina: The World of Yesterday, 1990.

_____. *Western Gunslingers in Fact and on Film.* Jefferson, North Carolina, and London: McFarland & Company, Inc., Publishers, 1998.

Ricci, Mark, Boris Zmijewsky and Steve Zmijewsky. *The Complete Films of John Wayne.* New York: A Citadel Press Book, 1983.

Rickman Gregg. "The Western Under Erasure: *Dead Man,*" in Jim Kitses and Gregg Rickman, editors. *The Western Reader.* New York: Limelight Editions, 1998, pp. 381–404.

Riley, Glenda. "Barbara Stanwyck: Feminizing the Western Film," in Richard W. Etulain and Glenda Riley, editors. *The Hollywood West: Lives of Film Legends Who Shaped It.* Golden, Colorado: Fulcrum Publishing, 2001.

Roberts, Randy, and James S. Olson. *John Wayne American.* New York: The Free Press, 1995.

Robinson, Charles III. *General Crook and the Western Frontier.* Norman: University of Oklahoma Press, 2001.

Rosenthal, Cindy Simon, editor. *Women Transforming Congress.* Norman: University of Oklahoma Press, 2002.

Schackel, Sandra. "Barbara Stanwyck: Uncommon Heroine," in Gary Yoggy, editor. *Back in the Saddle: Essays on Western Film and Television Actors.* Jefferson, North Carolina, and London: McFarland & Company, Inc., Publishers, 1998, pp. 113–128.

Schackel, Sandra Kay. "Women in Western Films: The Civilizer, the Saloon Singer, and Their Modern Sister," in Archie P. McDonald, editor. *Shooting Stars.* Bloomington and Indianapolis: Indiana University Press, 1987, pp. 196–217.

Schatz, Thomas, *Boom or Bust: American Cinema in the 1940s*. Berkeley Los Angeles London: University of California Press, 1997.

Schlesinger, Arthur M. *The Crisis of the Old Order*. Boston: Houghton Mifflin Company, 1957.

Schoenecke, Michael K. "James Stewart: An American Original," in Gary Yoggy, editor. *Back in the Saddle: Essays on Western Film and Television Actors*. Jefferson, North Carolina, and London: McFarland & Company, Inc., Publishers, 1998, pp. 97–112.

Seydor, Paul. *Peckinpah, the Western Films: A Reconsideration*. Urbana and Chicago: University of Illinois Press, 1997.

Shesol, Jeff. *Mutual Contempt: Lyndon Johnson, Robert Kennedy and the Feud that Defined a Decade*. New York and London: W.W. Norton & Company, 1997.

Sickels, Robert C. "A Politically Correct Ethan Edwards: Clint Eastwood's *The Outlaw Josey Wales*." *Journal of Popular Film and Television*, Volume 30 (Winter, 2003), pp. 220–227.

Simmon, Scott. *The Invention of the Western Film: A Cultural History of the Genre's First Half-Century*. Cambridge, United Kingdom: Cambridge University Press, 2003.

Slotkin, Richard. *Gunfighter Nation: The Myth of the Frontier in Twentieth Century America*. New York: Harper Perennial, 1993.

Smith, Robert Barr. *Daltons: The Raid on Coffeyville Kansas*. Norman: University of Oklahoma Press, 1996.

_____. *The Last Hurrah of the James-Younger Gang*. Norman: University of Oklahoma Press, 2001.

Sragow, Michael. "Ride the High Country," in *The Austin Chronicle Screens*. http://www.austinchronicle.com/isssues/dispatch/1999-10-22/screens features4.html

Stanfield, Peter. *Horse Opera: The Strange History of the 1930s Singing Cowboys*. Urbana and Chicago: University of Illinois Press, 2002.

Stevens, Brad. "Pat Garrett & Billy the Kid," in Ian Cameron and Douglas Pye, editors. *The Book of Westerns*. New York: Continuum, 1996, pp. 269–276.

Swinhart, Nick J. *Wyatt Earp Historical Homepage*. http//oldwesthistory.net

Tefertiller, Casey. *Wyatt Earp: The Life Behind the Legend*. New York: John Wiley & Sons, Inc., 1997.

Tompkins, Jane. *West of Everything: The Inner Life of Westerns*. New York and Oxford: Oxford University Press, 1992.

Tuska, Jon. *The American West in Film: Critical Approaches to the Western*. Westport, Connecticut: Greenwood Press, 1985.

_____. *The Filming of the West*. New York: Doubleday, 1976.

Utley, Robert. *Billy the Kid: A Short and Violent Life*. Lincoln and London: University of Nebraska Press, 1989.

Wills, Garry. *John Wayne's America: The Politics of Celebrity*. New York: Simon & Schuster, 1997.

Worland, Rick, and Edward Countryman. "The New Western American Historiography and the Emergence of the New American Western," in Edward Buscombe and Roberta E. Pearson, editors. *Back in the Saddle Again: New Essays on the Western*. London: British Film Institute, 1998, pp. 182–196.

Wright, Will. *The Wild West: The Mythical Cowboy & Social Theory*. London, Thousand Oaks, and New Delhi: Sage Publications, 2001.

Zmijewsky, Boris, and Lee Pfeiffer. *Films of Clint Eastwood*. New York: A Citadel Press Book, Revised and Updated Edition, 1990.

INDEX

311